D0041059

"David Limbaugh's *The True Jesus* is a worthy successor to his bestselling book *The Emmaus Code*. The latter exposed a generation to how the Old Testament reveals Christ. Now *The True Jesus* directs attention to the Jesus of the Gospels, in His full humanity and deity. Limbaugh's presentation is tactical, yet forthright. He carefully blends the four portraits of Jesus in Matthew, Mark, Luke, and John into a single streamlined, coherent narrative, free from academic distraction and jargon. The result is that the Gospels are allowed to speak for themselves. If you've wondered whether media portrayals of Jesus are dishonest, or found reading four seemingly disparate versions of the life of Jesus a little bewildering, or if you know nothing about Jesus at all, *The True Jesus* is precisely what you need."

> —DR. MICHAEL S. HEISER, Scholar-in-Residence, Faithlife / Logos Bible Software, author of *The Unseen Realm: Recovering the Supernatural Worldview of the Bible*, and host of the *Naked Bible Podcast*

"The question of the identity of Jesus is the most important question of all. In *The True Jesus*, David Limbaugh makes a case for the reliability of the Gospel tradition, but more importantly, invites readers to personally encounter Jesus through the Gospels. This is an easy-to-read, meticulously researched, and insightful book. If you are open to encountering the most influential person of all time, Who is also God in human flesh, this book is a helpful guide."

> —SEAN McDOWELL, Ph.D., Biola University Professor, Speaker, and Author

"In *The True Jesus*, the Son of God of the Gospels truly comes alive for readers. This is the Case for Christ from the life of Jesus Himself—and Limbaugh tells it in a way that will inspire you to read and study the Gospels like never before."

> —LEE STROBEL, bestselling author of *The Case for Christ* and *The Case for Faith*

"How could an ancient carpenter from the tiny town of Nazareth be the most influential human being to ever walk the earth? Who was Jesus and how does His life affect yours? Like a captivating tour guide, David Limbaugh leads you through the brilliant and sacrificial life of Jesus of Nazareth and inspires you to connect your life with the Savior—the true Jesus. There are few books better about life's most important topic!"
 —FRANK TUREK, founder and president of
 www.CrossExamined.org

"David Limbaugh strikes again. *The True Jesus* is a brilliant, must-read book on the real Jesus of Scripture destined to be another bestseller. If you have faith, it will deepen it; if you don't, you just might change your mind after reading it."
 —SEAN HANNITY, host of *The Sean Hannity Show* and Fox
 News Channel's *Hannity*

THE TRUE JESUS

THE TRUE JESUS

UNCOVERING THE **DIVINITY** OF **CHRIST**
IN THE **GOSPELS**

DAVID LIMBAUGH

REGNERY
PUBLISHING
A Division of Salem Media Group

Regnery® is a registered trademark of Salem Communications Holding Corporation

Scripture quotations are from the following sources: The ESV® Bible (The Holy Bible, English Standard Version®) copyright © 2001 by Crossway, a publishing ministry of Good News Publishers. ESV® Text Edition: 2011. The ESV® text has been reproduced in cooperation with and by permission of Good News Publishers. Unauthorized reproduction of this publication is prohibited. All rights reserved; and THE HOLY BIBLE, NEW INTERNATIONAL VERSION®, NIV® Copyright © 1973, 1978, 1984, 2011 by Biblica, Inc.® Used by permission. All rights reserved worldwide.

The map on page 112 is taken from Mark Allan Powell, *Introducing the New Testament: A Historical, Literary, and Theological Survey*, Baker Academic, a division of BakerPublishing Group, copyright © 2009. Used by permission. The map on page 113 is taken from *NIV Zondervan Study Bible* Copyright © 2015 by Zondervan. Used by permission of Zondervan. www.Zondervan.com

Hardcover ISBN 978-1-62157-637-2
Signed Hardcover Edition ISBN 978-1-62157-667-9
E-book ISBN 978-1-62157-648-8

Cataloging-in-Publication Data on file with the Library of Congress

Published in the United States by
Regnery Publishing
A Division of Salem Media Group
300 New Jersey Ave NW
Washington, DC 20001
www.Regnery.com

Manufactured in the United States of America

10 9 8 7 6 5 4 3 2 1

Books are available in quantity for promotional or premium use. For information on discounts and terms, please visit our website: www.Regnery.com.

Distributed to the trade by
Perseus Distribution
www.perseusdistribution.com

To my uncles and aunts, Stephen N. Limbaugh Sr., Anne Limbaugh, Manley O. Limbaugh, and Mary Limbaugh, who exemplify Christian living and familial love.

CONTENTS

INTRODUCTION

I n my last book, *The Emmaus Code*, I detailed how each of the Old
Testament books points to Jesus Christ. This assertion was surely
shocking to some, but it was hardly my idea. The title refers to Jesus'
encounter with two of His disciples on the Emmaus road, near Jerusalem, in one of His resurrection appearances. Joining the distraught pair
as they walk down the road, Jesus asks what they are discussing. As
"their eyes are kept from recognizing him," the disciples ask Jesus if He
is the only visitor to Jerusalem unaware of the things that recently
occurred there. He asks, "What things?" and they tell Him the religious
authorities crucified and buried a great prophet they had hoped was
Israel's redeemer. On the third day His tomb was found empty, and some
women said they had seen angels who had told them He was still alive.

The disciples prove themselves doubly blind—they fail to recognize
Jesus and fail to understand that He is the Messiah promised by the Old
Testament scriptures. So Jesus opens the scriptures to them and shows

how they all point to Him (Luke 24:27). Later, during a meal with Jesus, the disciples' eyes "are opened," and they finally recognize him (Luke 24:31). After Jesus vanishes as quickly as He'd appeared, they exclaim to each other, "Did not our hearts burn within us while he talked to us on the road, while he opened to us the Scriptures?" (Luke 24:32).

From this inspired New Testament account we know that the Old Testament prefigures Jesus Christ throughout, and that the two Testaments form a single, continuous chronicle whose focus is Jesus Christ. He is foreshadowed, typified, and prophesied in the Old Testament, and in the New Testament He brings God's redemptive plan to completion. The New Testament presents Jesus as God in the flesh—a human being Who fulfills the Old Testament prophecies, perfects the Old Testament offices of prophet, priest, and king, and becomes the perfect, once-and-for-all sacrifice and the culmination of God's salvation plan for mankind.

This book picks up where *The Emmaus Code* left off. Just as *The Emmaus Code* is both an Old Testament primer and a showcase for the pervasiveness of Christ in each book, *The True Jesus* is a primer on the Gospels that highlights the Christ-centeredness of Matthew, Mark, Luke, and John. It emphasizes Christ's dual nature as fully human and fully divine, examines His teachings and miracles, and celebrates Him as the promised Savior and long-awaited King who ushers in the kingdom of God.

The centrality of Christ to the Old Testament may be surprising to many, but everyone already believes the New Testament—especially the Gospels—is all about Christ, right? In a sense this is true, but we must dig deeper and train our eyes to see the real person of Christ and His works on our behalf. The New Testament isn't merely a manual on Jesus' ethical teachings or a handbook of abstract moral lessons. It is not a collection of embellished ancient tales of a mythical deity who upstaged the pantheon of Greek and Roman gods with his charisma and a kinder, gentler message.

Instead, it is a God-breathed account of the Son of God, Who lowered Himself to become a human being and directly intervene in human history, experienced all the indignities of human existence, walked among us, taught us, and lived a sinless life. He suffered, died, and was resurrected, thereby conquering Satan, sin, and death, and providing a means of salvation for all those who place their trust in Him. "The central message of the New Testament," declares Graeme Goldsworthy, "concerns God incarnate, Jesus of Nazareth, who did for us what we could not do for ourselves, in order to bring us, a lost people, back to God.... No New Testament document makes sense apart from the central affirmation that Jesus Christ has come among us as the bringer of salvation."[1]

"The first question that must be addressed concerning the New Testament," writes Mark Dever, "is, did the deliverer whom God promised in the *Old* Testament actually come? The New Testament answers that *Old* Testament question with a resounding yes! And he is not just an ordinary human deliverer, he is God come in the flesh. The one and only Son, Jesus perfectly displayed the Father, so that God's people might know him and be delivered from their sins. The New Testament squarely focuses on Christ. He is the heart of it all. He is the center of its message."[2]

We must, then, read the New Testament—just as we read the Old Testament—with awe. We should delve into it not just with our eyes, but also our hearts, trained on Jesus Christ. "Seeing and savoring Jesus Christ is the most important seeing and savoring you will ever do," affirms John Piper. "Eternity hangs on it. When I speak of *seeing* Jesus Christ, I don't mean seeing with the eyes of your head, but the eyes of your heart."[3] When we read, study, and meditate on the Good News, we must delight in the Savior and be grateful for the hope He provides us. As the Apostle Paul tells the Ephesians, "I do not cease to give thanks for you, remembering you in my prayers, that the God of our Lord Jesus Christ, the Father of glory, may give you the Spirit of wisdom and of revelation in the knowledge of him, having the eyes of your hearts enlightened, that you may know what is the hope to which he has called you, what are the riches of his glorious inheritance in the saints, and what is the immeasurable greatness of his power toward us who believe" (Eph. 1:16–19).

It may seem obvious that Christians should focus on Christ. In our modern culture, however, some believe they needn't dwell on Him but on a bland, undemanding message they wrongly presume He taught. They have swallowed the lie that Christianity is simply a feel-good religion that promises its faithful adherents health, wealth, and other temporal rewards. John MacArthur rejects this view as unbiblical. "In a word, what Christianity offers you," says MacArthur, "is Christ, Jesus Christ.... The surpassing theme of the Scripture, the surpassing theme of the New Testament, in particular, is Jesus Christ. And in not having Christ, you have nothing. And in having Christ, you have everything."[4] Christianity is about knowing Christ—and the New Testament, beginning with the Gospels, reveals who He is.

◇◇◇

My previous two Christian-themed books were in large part polemics. In *The Emmaus Code* I attempted to show that the Old Testament prefigures, prophesies, and promises Christ throughout, and that Jesus was the God-man the Old Testament promised. In *Jesus on Trial* I shared my own experience as a skeptic who came to faith in Christ, and I devoted much of the remainder of the book to apologetics—defending the Christian faith. In both books I started with a premise and marshaled evidence to support it, relying heavily on the research and insights of the giants in apologetics and theology.

This book is different.

The True Jesus is not a polemic in the same way the previous books were. In those books I debunked liberal critical scholars of Scripture who challenge the Bible and Christ from every imaginable angle. They dispute the divine inspiration of Scripture and the notion that Scripture is inerrant. They raise doubts about the authorship of many biblical books and about when they were written, arguing that some books such as Isaiah were compiled by multiple authors.

They further speculate that the Old Testament books were manmade constructs as opposed to God-inspired works, that they are more allegorical than historical, that the God of the Old Testament is different in character from the God of the New Testament, and that Jesus was a mere human being Who was not actually crucified and Whose resurrection is mythical. They argue that Jesus did not claim or believe He was the Messiah, that Jesus and the Apostle Paul presented conflicting views of Christianity, that there were initially many competing versions of the

Gospels, and that the four Gospels were canonized for reasons other than their authenticity and reliability.

In short, you can name almost any aspect of Christianity, from the integrity of the scriptures to the legitimacy of core Christian doctrine, and you can find a critic who has challenged it.

This criticism has taken its toll over the years. It seems that every other year some writer pops out of the woodwork to advance his "new" idea that not only was Jesus not divine, but that He in fact never existed. Moreover, a torrent of criticism from ostensibly Christian scholars, when coupled with the attacks by secular skeptics, has done a real number on the Gospel. Our universities and intellectual elites often treat Christianity as mythical and Christians as superstitious, science-denying, ignorant rubes. These challenges have also made their way into the Church itself and its seminaries, diluting the Gospel message and eroding the credibility of Scripture. This trend should concern all Christians because the more the Gospel is seemingly undermined, the fewer converts to Christ there will be. Thankfully, armies of Christian apologists and conservative scholars are fighting back for the integrity of the Christian message and the glory of Jesus Christ.

I addressed many of these issues in *Jesus on Trial*, in which I tried to show that the Bible truly is the inspired Word of God and that we can rely on it as historically and factually accurate. Some friends suggested that I take a similar approach in this book—that I explain the Gospels primarily by presenting and annihilating the major attacks being leveled at them.

But I have something else in mind.

While in this book I do address various historical and critical challenges to Scripture, this is not my main concern. My primary goal is to introduce you to the true Jesus of the Gospels, and the best way to do that is by helping you sink your teeth into the Gospels themselves. Yes, I contend that the Gospels are the inspired Word of God and that they reveal Jesus Christ as a human being and the Son of God, but I don't make a systematic argument to prove that or to disprove opposing arguments.

Rather, I let the Gospels speak for themselves. As I frequently argue, the Bible is its own apologetic. If people immerse themselves in

Scripture, they will come to see for themselves that it's the Word of God—and hopefully, they will accept Jesus Christ as their personal Lord and Savior. The Bible itself affirms this in passages such as Romans 10:17—"So faith comes from hearing, and hearing through the word of Christ"—and 2 Timothy 3:15—"From infancy, you have known the holy Scriptures, which are able to make you wise for salvation through faith in Christ Jesus."

Since I became a believer, I've been immensely excited about the Bible, including the Gospels. They change lives every day. They reassure believers and transform skeptics into Christians. As a former skeptic, however, I also understand that many people are intimidated by the Gospels and by the prospect of reading them for themselves and fully understanding their meaning. Even when they do make an effort, some quickly grow frustrated in trying to keep track of all the events, or in deciphering the seemingly obscure meanings of the messages, or in trying to comprehend all the elements of a story told in four separate accounts.

With this book I hope to help newer readers become more familiar with the Gospels so they can read the books for themselves and begin a lifetime of spiritual growth through the Word. I want to share what I have learned in my own studies and help ignite a passion in you to appreciate the Gospels—and the entire Bible—the way I've come to appreciate them. They never disappoint.

In short, I want to teach you—to share with you what I've learned, hoping that I can inspire you to learn more yourself. I want this book to serve as a layman's introduction to the Gospels. To achieve that goal, I begin with several chapters outlining the history of Israel between Old and New Testament times, and describing the cultural and religious climate at the time Christ intervened in human history. I also offer a brief overview of the New Testament and a deeper introduction to the Gospels, both collectively and individually.

In line with my belief that the Bible itself is an unrivaled apologetic, I devote the rest of the book—Chapters 5 through 12—to retelling the story related by the Gospels, combining information from all four books into a unified account. This format, I hope, will make the transformative story of Jesus Christ more accessible to readers who may be daunted, confused, or otherwise discouraged from reading the Gospels directly. But make no mistake—I aim to introduce you to the Gospels as a step toward convincing you to read them yourself. Only if you study the Gospels—and not what others, no matter how learned or convincing, say about them—will you truly be interacting with God.

The Gospels are not like reading some fascinating fictional account of the most wonderful human being the human mind ever conceived, for they aren't fiction and the human mind didn't conceive Jesus. He conceived us. No fiction writer could invent such a character. The perfection and sublimity of Jesus Christ is beyond the capacity of the human intellect and imagination to construct. To read the Gospels in earnest is to come face to face with the living Son of God, Who is the radiance of the glory of God and the exact imprint of His nature (Heb. 1:3). No mere human being could act like He acted, speak as authoritatively as He spoke, empathize like He empathized, serve people like He served them, instruct like He instructed, exhibit the wisdom He exhibited, live sinlessly like He lived, sacrifice like He sacrificed, and prove Himself to be God in the flesh and the Messiah, exuding divinity with every breath.

I used to prefer the epistles to the Gospels because they are so rich with theology. But now I realize nothing compares with reading the Gospels, which allow us to witness directly what Jesus actually said and did. We get to experience Him firsthand because the Gospel writers, under the inspiration and guidance of the Holy Spirit, recorded His words and deeds precisely. Jesus jumps off the pages and comes alive for us once we immerse ourselves in these writings. If we only read what others say instead of the Gospels themselves, or if we get too bogged down chasing alleged inconsistencies in the accounts—all of which can be satisfactorily explained—we'll be reading from a distance, far removed from the amazing account of God becoming one of us in the greatest conceivable act of love.

Sadly, atheists, agnostics, cynics, and skeptics will be denied this experience as long as pride darkens their hearts and clouds their vision. But if they ask God in prayer to reveal Himself to them, they will discover He is there, and He is there for them and has been all along. As for the rest of us, let's not trifle ourselves trying to reconcile every apparent difficulty in the text. Let's jump right in and get to know the real Jesus as He reveals Himself to us in Matthew, Mark, Luke, and John.

In my summation of the Gospels I paraphrase many of the events and speeches, but I include others verbatim, especially Jesus' long discourses. I strongly believe we shouldn't tinker with the Bible's message because I am convinced that every word is inspired by God. So in attempting to relate every substantive section of the Gospels in one digestible book, I have summarized and condensed some sections, but I have always tried to remain absolutely faithful to the source material. I hope the end result will be even a fraction as beneficial to you as writing it has been for me.

In some cases you will find repetition of events and ideas, but that's because there is repetition in and among the Gospels themselves, as the same ideas are explored in different contexts. Jesus Himself seems to believe repetition is useful for learning, for He often repeats themes and ideas in ways that help us remember and understand them. This repetition also highlights the striking consistency of His teachings.

Overall, I hope this book will enrich your understanding and stimulate you to begin or resume a lifetime of serious reading and meditation on the Gospels and all of God's Word.

<hr/>

As we survey the four Gospel accounts, it should become clear how they complement one another and show, each in its own unique way, how Jesus fulfills Old Testament promises and prophecies of the coming Messiah and Son of God, and completes God's salvation plan. We will see how they interweave Old Testament passages to illustrate the continuity and unity of the biblical message. And above all, we shall steady our gaze on Jesus Christ, who is the Alpha and the Omega, our Redeemer, and our King. We will discover the true Jesus, not the fictitious Jesus conceived by popular culture, which tries to make Him to be like us rather than the other way around.

Modern churches can take justifiable steps toward making services more inviting to unchurched people. But to be true to Christ, they must not dilute their message, whitewash difficult Bible passages, or present

Jesus as something He is not. It would be better to avoid church altogether than to attend one that teaches a false Gospel or a culturally pleasing but fraudulent picture of Jesus. He is the creator, and we are His created beings. We cannot remake Him, but He will remake us.

People have advanced many false messiahs and imposter Jesuses in their own image, but none has the power to save us or to transform us into new creations.[5] That is the sole prerogative of Jesus Christ, if we'll follow and surrender to Him. By staying true to the scriptures we will find the real Jesus and enhance our ability to recognize the pretenders. So we must read the Bible seeking to discover Christ and to accept what its inspired words tell us about Him. We dare not change one word of Scripture to make ourselves more comfortable (Rev. 22:18; Deut. 4:2; Prov. 30:5–6). As Paul proclaims, "All Scripture is breathed out by God and profitable for teaching, for reproof, for correction, and for training in righteousness, that the man of God may be complete, equipped for every good work" (2 Tim. 3:16–17). Scripture's purpose is not to make us more comfortable, but to show us how inadequate and lost we are apart from our Savior and to make us "wise for salvation through faith in Christ Jesus" (2 Tim. 3:15).

Now let's begin our journey by taking a look at the four-hundred-year period between the close of the Old Testament and the beginning of the New Testament—a timespan known as the intertestamental period—and examine the land of Israel and the wider world that Christ entered in His incarnation. We'll also take a bird's eye view of the New Testament, exploring its historical reliability, literary value, structure, and genres. Then, with that background established, we'll dive into the Gospels and explore what Jesus said and did to convince billions of people throughout history that He was, and remains, mankind's Lord and Savior.

PART I

BACKDROP TO THE GREATEST STORY EVER TOLD

CHAPTER 1

THE OVERLOOKED ERA
LIFE BETWEEN THE OLD AND NEW TESTAMENTS

[The intertestamental period] was a crucial era, for this is when God was preparing the world for the coming of His Son as Saviour and Lord (read Gal 4:4). With the help of outside sources, study the religious, political, social, and secular preparations which were involved. Such a study will enhance your appreciation and understanding of the two Testaments and of the connections between the two.

—I. L. JENSEN[1]

To study the history of Israel and the Jewish people in the centuries preceding Christ's birth is hardly a pointless or boring exercise. Summaries of this period in our favorite study Bibles aren't, as I once suspected, filler to add heft to those works. Familiarity with the historical, religious, and cultural background of the New Testament helps us to understand the world Jesus entered, the context and setting of the Gospels, and the development of the early Church. It gives us a fuller comprehension of the Gospel writings, enhancing our appreciation of the events they relate and of Jesus' teachings. We will see the reasons for the mercilessness of Herod the Great, the reluctance of Pontius Pilate, and the

Apostle Paul's confidence in demanding that his case be tried before Roman authorities.[2] The historical events of the intertestamental years providentially laid the foundation for the rise of Christianity. This turbulent period—a hinge that connects the Old and New Testaments[3]—particularly affected the Jews as their land was conquered by various empires.

The intertestamental period spans roughly four hundred years, from the end of the Old Testament times around 400 BC—the approximate date of the writing of Malachi, the last book of the Old Testament in the Protestant canon—to about 4 AD and the birth of Jesus. Most Christian writers use the term "intertestamental period" while others refer to it as the "Second Temple period," though this period is longer, stretching from 516 BC—the time of the building of the Second Temple—to about 70 AD, when the Romans sacked Jerusalem and destroyed the Temple.[4]

Some writers have called the intertestamental period the "dark period" or "silent period" of Israel's pre-Christian history because no prophets or inspired writers were active then, and also because the Jews remained dispersed among the nations.[5] The Jews in New Testament times believed that prophetic inspiration had ceased with Malachi.[6] Although no canonical books were written and no direct revelation came through prophets during this period,[7] there are sources that relate Israel's political history at this time.[8] The main ones are *Jewish Antiquities* by the Jewish historian Josephus; the apocryphal books including 1 and 2 Maccabees;[9] the pseudepigrapha (early non-canonical Jewish books written mostly before Jesus' birth);[10] and works by Greek and Latin historians such as Polybius, Tacitus, Livy, and Appian.[11]

During this period, the Jews who had returned to their land from captivity lived under the control of successive foreign kingdoms.[12] One writer contends that this bleak period was foreseen by the psalmist, who writes, "We do not see our signs; there is no longer any prophet, and there is none among us who knows how long" (Psalms 74:9).[13] Many Jews believed that after Malachi, prophecy would not resume until the coming of the Messiah and his kingdom.[14] Though no prophets of God spoke during this time, God was still sovereignly directing events, and history unfolded just as the prophet Daniel had predicted, with control of the land changing hands from Babylon to Medo-Persia, to Greece, and to

Rome—one of the Old Testament's most amazing prophecies (Daniel 2:39, 40; 7:5–7).[15]

Readers open the New Testament and find an entirely different world from that which existed at the close of the Old Testament, so let's review in broad strokes Israel's history leading up to the intertestamental years and then examine the important events that occurred during that period.

ISRAEL BEFORE THE INTERTESTAMENTAL PERIOD

Israel transitioned from a group of disorganized tribes under the leadership of various "judges" to a united kingdom in 1050 BC, then remained unified for some 120 years under the consecutive kingships of Saul, David, and Solomon. The Israelites had come out of Egypt almost five hundred years earlier, and now that they had conquered the Promised Land and all the tribes were settled, it was time to build the Temple to God and centralize their worship.[16] David wanted to construct the Temple, but God prohibited him because he had shed so much blood and waged so much war (1 Chr. 22:7–8). Instead, his son Solomon would build it, as he was "a man of rest" (1 Chr. 22:9). Around 964 BC, Solomon completed the historic project (1 Kings 6:37–38).[17]

Shortly after Solomon's death in 931 BC, Israel divided into two separate kingdoms, the Northern Kingdom (Israel) and the Southern Kingdom (Judah). In 722 BC the Assyrian Empire conquered the Northern Kingdom and took thousands of its people into captivity. The Assyrians partially repopulated Israel with Gentiles from other countries. Some married Jews who had remained in the land, and others married those who later returned.[18] These couples' interracial offspring, known as Samaritans, intermixed Judaism with pagan religions and earned the Jews' disdain for adulterating their ethnicity and religion. The Southern Kingdom remained intact for another century and a half. The Babylonian Empire conquered it and took its people captive beginning in 605 BC, and destroyed the Temple in Jerusalem in 586 BC.

Around 539–536 BC, the Persians conquered the Babylonians. In fulfillment of another astounding Old Testament prophecy, in which

Isaiah specifically mentioned "Cyrus" by name more than 150 years earlier (Isaiah 44:28; 45:1, 13), King Cyrus freed the Jews to return home and rebuild their Temple: "That the word of the Lord by the mouth of Jeremiah might be fulfilled, the Lord stirred up the spirit of Cyrus king of Persia, so that he made a proclamation throughout all his kingdom and also put it in writing: 'Thus says Cyrus king of Persia: The Lord, the God of heaven, has given me all the kingdoms of the earth, and he has charged me to build him a house at Jerusalem, which is in Judah. Whoever is among you of all his people, may his God be with him, and let him go up to Jerusalem, which is in Judah, and rebuild the house of the Lord, the God of Israel—he is the God who is in Jerusalem'" (Ezra 1:1–4).

By 516 BC, over fierce opposition from those who had remained in the land during the exile (Ezra 4:1–6),[19] the people had rebuilt the Temple. In 458 BC, the scribe Ezra returned to the land along with a few thousand Jews and their families, and reinstituted the Law and the religious rituals (Ezra 7:21–25). In 444 BC, Nehemiah returned to the land with another group of exiles and was appointed governor of Judah. By the authority of Persian King Artaxerxes (Neh. 2:6), Nehemiah organized the rebuilding of the city's walls, fulfilling Daniel's century-old prophecy (Daniel 9:25). He completed the project in fifty-two days despite persistent opposition from neighboring non-Jews (Neh. 2:10, 19–20; 6:15).

THE INTERTESTAMENTAL PERIOD

The first part of the intertestamental period (400 BC to 331 BC), when the Persians ruled Israel, was by most accounts uneventful for both the Persians and Jews.[20] Persia was quite tolerant of the Jewish people, leaving them largely undisturbed and allowing them to retain considerable autonomy over their own religious affairs under the authority of the Jewish high priest. But Israel had not suddenly become free—it remained under the direct authority of a Persian governor, who on one occasion partially destroyed Jerusalem due to a rivalry over the high priest's office.[21]

Persian rule over the Jewish state ended around 331 BC, when Alexander the Great defeated Persian King Darius III and gained control of the Persian Empire.[22] In some ways Alexander, like the Persians, was permissive toward the Jews, allowing them to observe their laws and rituals, and giving them a tax exemption during their sabbatical years.[23] As a result of Alexander's efforts to spread Greek culture throughout his empire, Koine Greek (common Greek as spoken by non-native Greeks) eventually became the main language of the eastern Mediterranean as well as the language of the New Testament.[24]

Alexander's precipitous death in 323 BC at age thirty-two resulted in a struggle for succession among his generals, as he left no heir to inherit his kingdom. At first the empire was divided into four parts, then three, and finally just two—the Seleucids and Ptolemies. The Seleucids were based in Syria and controlled the northern part of the empire, and the Ptolemies, in Egypt, controlled the southern part. Seleucid rulers were usually named Seleucus or Antiochus, and those of Egypt used the title Ptolemy. Located between the two powers, Israel was under constant threat of expansionism from both.[25]

Israel was ultimately absorbed into Ptolemy's Egyptian empire around 321 BC. The Jewish people lived peacefully in this period except during periodic conflicts between the Ptolemies and Seleucids, which diminished their quality of life and prosperity.[26] At this time, Alexandria, in Egypt, became an important center of Judaism.[27] Ptolemy Philadelphus (285–247 BC) had Jewish scholars begin translating the Old Testament into Greek for the benefit of Greek-speaking Jews in Egypt.[28] The Pentateuch (the first five books of the Old Testament) was translated into Greek around 250 BC and the remainder of the Old Testament by about 130 BC.[29] This version of the Old Testament, called the Septuagint because seventy-two scholars compiled it, was invaluable to Jews living outside Palestine, as the land of Israel was called during various historical times beginning with the ancient Greeks. The Septuagint also later became the Bible of the early Christian Church.[30]

The Seleucids gained control of Israel in 198 BC, when their ruler Antiochus III defeated Egypt.[31] At first, the Seleucids were tolerant of Jewish customs and religious practices, but tensions later mounted between Jews supportive of Hellenistic (Greek) culture and those hostile to it.[32] In 167 BC, Seleucid ruler Antiochus IV Epiphanes ordered the Hellenization of the land as a means to unite all the peoples of his

kingdom. A brief review of his persecution of the Jewish people gives us
a flavor of what this beleaguered people has endured through the ages.
He commanded the Jews to follow customs "strange to the land," pro-
hibiting them from observing their Sabbath, ancestral laws, festivals,
sacrifices, and circumcision rituals. He destroyed and burned copies of
the Torah, built altars, sacred precincts, and shrines for idols, and
ordered the Jews to offer unclean sacrifices and eat swine's flesh.[33] He
even dedicated the Temple to the Greek god, Zeus.[34]

Furthermore, the Jews were to make themselves abominable by everything unclean and profane, so that they would forget the Law and change
their ordinances. Anyone who disobeyed would die. Antiochus appointed
inspectors over all the people and ordered all the towns of Judah to offer
sacrifices. Anyone found in possession of the Torah, or who adhered to
the Law, was condemned to death by the king's decree. Women who had
their children circumcised were killed, and their infants were hung from
their mothers' necks. Many in Israel resisted and chose to die rather than
to profane their laws (1 Macc. 1:44, 48–51, 56–57, 60–63; 2 Macc. 6:2).

Mattathias, an elderly Jewish priest, refused to obey a Seleucid official's order to offer a pagan sacrifice. "Even if all the nations that live under
the rule of the king obey him, and have chosen to obey his commandments, everyone of them abandoning the religion of their ancestors, I and
my sons and my brothers will continue to live by the covenant of our
ancestors," Mattathias proclaimed. "Far be it from me to desert the law
and the ordinances. We will not obey the king's words by turning aside
from our religion to the right hand or to the left" (1 Macc. 2:19–22). When
a renegade Jewish bystander came forward to make the sacrifice, Mattathias, in a righteous rage, killed him and the king's official and tore down
the altar (1 Macc. 23–25).[35] Mattathias cried out, "Let everyone who is
zealous for the law and supports the covenant come out with me!" Then
he and his five sons fled to the hills with their followers, who joined them
in a rebellion known as the Maccabean revolt (1 Macc. 2:27–28).[36]

When Mattathias died, his son Judas took over the rebellion. He
came to be known as Judas Maccabeus or just Maccabeus (the "ham-
mer") because of the guerilla warfare tactics he employed.[37] In 165 BC,
an army led by Judas recaptured the Temple area and other parts of
Jerusalem, an event Jews commemorate in the festival of Hanukkah.[38]

Some twenty years later, in 142 BC, the Jews became independent and self-governing under the Hasmoneans, the descendants of Judas' older brother Simon.[39]

Though Mattathias and Judas Maccabeus were committed to following God's law, the Hasmonean kings were enticed by competing Hellenistic ideas and were compromised by the allure of their political power.[40] In 63 BC, Roman general Pompey intervened in Jewish civil strife and took control of the land,[41] annexing Judea to Rome.[42] Gary Burge writes, "No doubt the most important event for the average Jew was the conquest of Israel by Rome in 63 BC."[43] Pompey's large armies soon placed Israel under Roman administration. "The reality of this occupation—its tax burden, its Jewish collaborators, its Jewish resistors—shaped the world of Jesus and Paul," says Burge.

When Pompey seized control of Jerusalem he entered the Temple and even its most sacred area, the Most Holy Place. This was sacrilegious and insulting to the Jews, contributing to mutual distrust that lasted more than a century, up to 70 AD, when the Jews rebelled and the Romans destroyed the Jewish state and the Temple.[44] In 40 BC, the Romans appointed Herod the Great as king of Judea, a position also called king of the Jews. Though he didn't actually ascend to the throne until 37 BC, he ruled for more than thirty years, until 4 BC, and was king when Jesus was born (Matt. 2:1, 2). In the meantime, the Roman Senate made Julius Caesar's nephew, Octavian, imperator—supreme military leader—after he defeated Antony and Cleopatra at Actium in 31 BC, giving him the title Augustus ("exalted one") and placing him above the Senate in authority. This event signified the end of the Roman Republic and the beginning of the Roman Empire.[45]

As king of Judea, Herod quashed an insurrection in Galilee,[46] helping to bring order to Israel and advancing Augustus' plans to spread Greco-Roman civilization throughout the Roman Empire.[47] Though Herod refurbished and expanded the Temple, Jews largely viewed him as a usurper of the throne in Jerusalem (because he was partly Idumean, or Edomite)[48] and as an instrument of Roman oppression who had abolished Jewish self-rule.[49] He was a cruel ruler who put to death his own wife Mariamne, their two sons, his son by another wife, and the respected Jewish High Priest Hyrcanus II.[50] He also notoriously ordered the death of all baby boys in Bethlehem when he was trying to kill the infant Jesus (Matt. 2:16–18).[51]

After Herod's death, Archelaus became ruler of Judea, Samaria, and Idumea. He severely persecuted the Jews, slaughtering some three thousand in the Temple in 4–3 BC,[52] and was replaced for incompetence in 6 AD by various governors and prefects. The most consequential of these was Pontius Pilate. Serving from 26 to 36 AD, Pilate was prefect during Jesus' ministry and crucifixion, Pentecost, the early days of the Church, Stephen's speech and death, and the first Christian missions.[53]

THE RELIGIOUS BACKGROUND TO NEW TESTAMENT TIMES

At the dawn of the New Testament era, many religions and philosophies were coursing through the Roman Empire, largely due to the Hellenization of the Roman world. The Greek philosophical systems of Pythagoreanism, Stoicism, Cynicism, and Epicureanism, in their respective ways, attempted to explain the universe through human reason.[54] Many Greek philosophies featured a dualistic notion of reality, with the physical world being only a shadow of the spiritual world. The material world was temporal and evil, while the spiritual world was eternal, real, and good.[55] These philosophies influenced the worldview of the empire's inhabitants at the time of Christ's birth, though they were not particularly prominent.[56] The New Testament suggests, however, that people at the time were quite fascinated by philosophy and "new" ideas. As the Book of Acts relates, "Now all the Athenians and the foreigners who lived there would spend their time in nothing except telling or hearing something new" (17:21).

Epicureanism, founded by Epicurus in the late fourth century BC, promoted the values of pleasure and friendship, and encouraged withdrawal from civic activities.[57] Pleasure—meaning the absence of pain, as opposed to self-indulgence[58]—was the chief good in life.[59] Epicurus was not an atheist, as he believed in immortal and blessed gods. He did not believe in the afterlife, however, and he thought prayer was pointless because, in his view, the gods didn't exercise providence over human affairs.[60]

Stoicism was founded by Zeno of Citium (335–263 BC), who taught in the famed Stoa of Athens. Instructing people to achieve happiness through self-control, he stressed virtue as the only good worth pursuing. Zeno's philosophy was pantheistic ("everything is god")[61] and encouraged its adherents to align themselves with nature.[62] Along with Epicureans, Stoics are mentioned in Acts as accusing the Apostle Paul of babbling as he preaches the Gospel and asking him to clarify his "new teaching" (17:16–21).

Antisthenes (445–365 BC), a contemporary of Socrates, founded Cynicism, which lasted into the early fifth century AD. The Cynics flouted conventional wisdom and distrusted everything associated with it. They taught that ordinary standards of value are based on an illusion. Their extreme positions in combating society's supposed prejudices, such as their defense of incest and cannibalism as natural actions, led to the modern connotation of the word "cynic." They adopted the lifestyle of beggars, appearing unkempt with long beards and coarse cloaks.[63]

The Skeptics were the forerunners of today's moral relativists, teaching that relativizing all claims to knowledge was the way to a peaceful soul.[64]

As Greek influences spread through the Roman Empire, the Roman gods and goddesses became identified with those of the Greek pantheon. For example, the Roman god Mercury was identified with the Greek god Hermes[65] and the Roman god Jupiter with the Greek god Zeus.[66] Overall, as the New Testament era began, faith in the gods had declined because of their perceived immorality, their inability to help their worshippers, and the popularity of secular philosophies.[67] But worship of these gods did not altogether cease, as evidenced by several New Testament references. For example, in Acts 14 local priests call Paul "Hermes" and Barnabas "Zeus" when they heal a crippled man; and in Acts 19 Demetrius, a silversmith who makes shrines to the goddess Artemis, complains to his colleagues that Paul is hurting their business by turning many people away from Artemis.[68]

Deceased Roman emperors were also considered deities by order of the Roman Senate. Some, such as Nero, proclaimed their own deity. One reason the Roman authorities persecuted Christians was that they were considered disloyal because their monotheism precluded worshipping emperors.[69] In fact, the Romans viewed Christians as atheists because they rejected Roman gods.[70] This was not the only reason they were persecuted, as Jews were the original monotheists and rejected Roman gods, yet unlike Christians they were exempted from worshipping the emperor.[71] Rome's most intense periods of Christian persecution, however, did not occur with the immediate appearance of Christianity, but rather between the close of the New Testament period[72] (circa 100 AD)[73] and Constantine's rule (306–37 AD).[74]

RELIGION IN ISRAEL IN NEW TESTAMENT TIMES

Though many religions and philosophies in the Roman Empire impacted the culture into which Jesus was born, the dominant influence came from the various sects and institutions of Judaism.[75] The most important Jewish religious institutions were the priests, the Temple, the synagogues, and the Sanhedrin. The main Jewish sects were the Pharisees, the Sadducees, and the Essenes, although many scholars believe there were at least seven, and as many as twelve, Jewish sects at the time.[76] There were also groups better labeled political parties than religious sects, such as the Herodians and the Zealots.[77]

There were many priests—twenty thousand according to Josephus—who were supported by tithes from the community. Most did not live in Jerusalem but regularly went there to perform rituals. They functioned as teachers of the Law and as judges and mediators over legal and other disputes.[78] Among them was a much smaller group, the chief priests—aristocratic elites who answered to Rome for the people's actions.[79] Jesus had little quarrel with the village priests, reserving His admonitions mostly for the chief priests.[80] For example, after He cleanses the leper, Jesus instructs him, "See that you say nothing to anyone, but go, show yourself to the priest and offer for your cleansing what Moses commanded, for a proof to them" (Mark 1:44). Most of the chief priests, along with other aristocrats, were Sadducees.[81]

The Temple in Jerusalem, site of the Jews' religious sacrifices and feasts, was the crucial center of Jewish worship. King Solomon, as noted, built the original Temple in 964 BC and the Babylonians destroyed it in 586 BC. The Persians authorized its reconstruction, resulting in the

Second Temple, which was completed around 516 BC. It was plundered and defiled by Antiochus Epiphanes in 168 BC but was soon restored by Judas Maccabeus. As Herod the Great ordered the Temple's renovation and expansion (20–19 BC),[82] it was called the Herodian Temple in New Testament times. It was surrounded by a large outer court, which Gentiles were permitted to enter ("the court of the Gentiles"), though they were banned from the two inner courts.[83]

Scattered throughout the Roman Empire, synagogues were the hubs of Jewish life at the time of Christ (Mark 1:21; 6:2; Luke 4:16, 31; 6:6; 13:10; Acts 13:14, 27, 42, 44; 15:21; 16:13; 17:2; 18:4). The religious services held in the synagogues generally included the reading of a doctrinal creed, readings from the Law and the prophets, a sermon, and benedictions. Most religious instruction occurred at the synagogues.[84]

In Jerusalem, the community's lay leaders and the Temple priests formed a "high council" known as the Sanhedrin (Matt. 5:22; 26:59; Mark 15:1), which functioned as the Jews' main judicial and administrative body,[85] and also ran the city's affairs. One such lay leader was Joseph of Arimathea, who received Pilate's permission to bury Jesus in his tomb (Mark 15:43; John 19:38–42).[86] The Sanhedrin frequently clashed with Jesus, trying to have Him arrested (John 7:32) and even wanting to kill Him (Luke 22:2). It had seventy members (seventy-one, counting the high priest who led the body),[87] patterned on the seventy elders Moses had appointed (Num. 11:16). Significantly, Jesus sent about that many disciples—seventy-two—to prepare for his ministry in Galilee (Luke 10:1).[88]

The Pharisees were devout Jewish believers. The word Pharisee comes from the Hebrew and Aramaic words for "one who separates." They separated themselves from the impurities they observed in the priests, the common people, the Hellenists, and certain political groups.[89] Strict observers of the Law, they were vociferous critics of those who yielded to Hellenistic influences. Some believe their origin can be traced to efforts to purge the land of Hellenism during the time of the Maccabean revolt.[90] They are considered to be direct descendants of the Hasidim—a group of pious Jews who joined the Maccabean rebellion.[91] They anticipated a Messiah who would usher in a time of righteousness.

Concerned foremost with purity and kosher requirements,[92] Phar-isees emphasized tithing, observance of the Sabbath, and food purity laws.[93] They mainly operated in the synagogues, and they were intent on protecting the Torah.[94] Jewish historian Josephus was a self-described Pharisee who identified the group as "a certain sect of the Jews that appear more religious than others, and seem to interpret the laws more accurately."[95] The New Testament reveals that they believed in angels, spirits, and the resurrection of human beings (Acts 23:8). They were quite influential in Israel, though they were a relatively small group of some six thousand members.[96] The Pharisees are featured prominently in the Gospels, often as recipients of Jesus' sharp criticism. They strongly opposed Him, especially when He appeared to break their legalistic rules, as when He healed on the Sabbath (Luke 6:6–11). Pharisaism is considered the forerunner of modern Orthodox Juda-ism.[97] The Apostle Paul had been an ardent Pharisee before his conver-sion (Phil. 3:5).

The Sadducees, probably named for Zadok, who was appointed high priest by Solomon (1 Kings 2:35), were a smaller group than the Pharisees. They were educated and wealthy elites, often in positions of political authority, such as many of the priests (Acts 5:17). Prizing their social positions, they were closely connected with the Roman author-ities and accepted many aspects of Hellenism.[98] Unlike the Pharisees, they did not believe in angels or demons, resurrection, or the afterlife (Acts 23:8), but taught "that souls die with the bodies."[99] They did not anticipate a coming Messiah,[100] and they had their conflicts with Jesus, though not to the extent the Pharisees did. The Sadducees tried to trip up Jesus on theological questions such as the resurrection (Matt. 22:23–33), which Jesus parried by citing a passage from the Pentateuch instead of a more obvious text from Isaiah or Daniel, knowing the Sadducees didn't consider non-Pentateuch biblical books as sources of doctrine.[101] The Sadducees ceased to exist as a sect after the Romans sacked Jerusalem in 70 AD.[102]

The Essenes, who are not directly mentioned in the New Testa-ment,[103] left the cities and lived in isolated communities such as Qumran near the Dead Sea. The group, which included some four thousand members,[104] originated in the second century BC[105] and is widely associated with the Dead Sea Scrolls, which were discovered in eleven caves near Qumran. They are believed to be the writers of the non-biblical portion of the scrolls, which have provided much of our information on the culture and history of Judaic Israel a few centuries before and at the time of Christ.[106] Of the scrolls' nearly 900 manuscripts, about 210 are copies of biblical books.[107]

The Essenes lived frugally and held their property in common, though their theology was similar to that of the Pharisees.[108] They rejected the significance of the Temple, which they thought had been compromised, and were quietly waiting and praying for the arrival of the Messiah,[109] believing they were the true Israel to whom he would come.[110] Like the Sadducees, the Essenes virtually disappeared from history after the Romans suppressed the Jewish revolt in Jerusalem.

The Zealots were activists, believing they should do what they could, including waging war, to hasten the establishment of God's messianic kingdom. They had a zeal for the Law, which fueled their opposition to the Romans, and they led the ill-fated revolt against Rome. The Apostle "Simon the Zealot" likely broke from the Zealots to follow Christ (Acts 1:13).[111]

The Herodians were more a political coalition than a religious one, which supported King Herod and his family. Various Roman leaders who ruled Palestine at different times were among this group, which conspired with the Pharisees to entrap Jesus (Mark 3:6; 12:13).[112]

The scribes weren't a party or sect, but a class of well-educated Israelites who taught and interpreted the Law and prosecuted its violators. Most scribes were Pharisees and were probably the most elite members of that sect.[113]

N. T. Wright says that the great majority of Jews didn't belong to a particular sect or party, but were devoted to the basic tenets of Judaism.[114] Though a widely diverse people, they cared about their God, scriptures, and heritage, and therefore sought to observe biblical law. They prayed, fasted, attended synagogue, and traveled to Jerusalem for the celebrated feasts. They kept the Sabbath, eschewed pork, and obeyed their religious duty to circumcise their male children.[115] Most expected deliverance through the coming Messiah and the resultant kingdom of God.[116]

JEWISH RELIGIOUS STRUGGLES DURING THE INTERTESTAMENTAL PERIOD AND JEWISH MESSIANIC EXPECTATIONS

When the Persians permitted the Jews to return to their land and rebuild the Temple, most chose to remain in exile. Those who returned appreciated the new Temple, though at the time it was far less resplendent than its predecessor had been (Haggai 2:3). Those who stayed abroad, called the Diaspora (Greek for "the scattered"), were determined to retain their covenant identity with God, allegiance to the Torah, and religious observances. Diaspora Jews had varying success in these endeavors, but they retained their sense of national identity as God's chosen people and vested their hope in Him. The Jewish people in both Palestine and the Diaspora built synagogues for prayer, Scripture study, and Sabbath worship. These became the central institution of Jewish communities, though they were not a complete substitute for the Temple,[117] and many Jews made pilgrimages to Jerusalem for important festivals.[118]

Though the Jews had been freed, the impact of the Babylonian destruction of the Temple and the ensuing exile remained. They regarded Jerusalem and the Temple as the center of their homeland and their religion, and their removal from both challenged their faith in their covenantal God.[119] Where was the God Who had specially chosen them? They faced the jolting reality that His prophetic predictions of judgment were now historical facts.[120] They were still the chosen people, but that privilege came with responsibilities, which they hadn't honored.

As the intertestamental period began and exiled Jews flowed back to their homeland, they did not reestablish their kingship but longed for the day when this would occur. They became increasingly focused on studying and following the Law because they were convinced that their disobedience had led to their exile and that only through obedience could they regain their freedom.[121] They sought to please God by observing the sacrifices and ceremonies, and by remembering His roles as lawgiver and judge.[122] But obedience was difficult at a time when they were dominated by foreign powers and were pressured to adopt pagan Hellenistic ideas and practices.[123]

Still, their return from captivity was a powerful testimony to God's patience, faithfulness, forgiveness, and mercy—in short, He had not forsaken them. Thus, much of the intertestamental writings reflect the Jews' continued faith in God's loving-kindness and His sovereign care of the Jewish nation.[124]

MESSIANIC HOPES

Craig Bartholomew and Michael Goheen contend that five fundamental beliefs, developed over Israel's two-thousand-year communion with God since Abraham's time, molded the lives of the Jews—both in the homeland and outside it—during the intertestamental period:

1. Monotheism—Belief in one God, the Creator and sovereign Ruler.
2. Election—God had chosen Israel as His people, who would bless all nations through Abraham.
3. Torah—God would bless them for obedience to His Law.
4. The holiness of the land and the Temple—The land wasn't just holy because it was a choice piece of real estate, but because God promised it to Abraham as an everlasting possession (Gen. 17:8), and He dwelt with Israel there (Zech. 2:12). There was no other land on earth where the people could enjoy that level of communion with Him.
5. Redemption—Though God had punished them for their disobedience, He would remain faithful and redeem them as promised.[125] But their beliefs were constantly being tested as they suffered under the domination of foreign powers. When would God step in and save them?[126]

What did the Jews have in mind as they looked to God for redemption? The answer can largely be gleaned from intertestamental literature, which provides insight into the Jews' messianic expectations at the time of Christ's incarnation.[127]

Some Jews believed that someday the Gentile nations would acknowledge Israel's God and joyfully live under His rule. But more believed that Israel would come to rule over all the nations that had oppressed the Jews. "Israel's long years of humiliation," write Bartholomew and Goheen, "had bred such hatred for the pagan oppressors that the dominant note sounded in Israel was not that the nations would flock to Zion to learn the way of God (Isaiah 2:3). Instead, Israelites looked for the nations to be dashed into pieces like a Potter's vessel (Psalm 2:9).... In vengeance God would destroy the oppressors who had so long sought to keep Israel from serving him according to his covenant. And so God would deliver his people."[128] This act of deliverance would be led by the Messiah—an anointed king who would usher in God's renewed kingdom. "Israel looked to a day when there would be 'no king but God,'" Bartholomew and Goheen maintain.[129]

Thus, Israel expected a different kind of Messiah than Jesus—not one who would suffer, die, and be resurrected for them, but one who would deliver them from their political and military oppressors. The Jews' perspective was strongly influenced by the tyranny of foreign governments and by their own failures in self-governance. They longed for the coming Messiah to deliver justice.[130] Until then, they would hope, pray, study the scriptures, observe the feasts, remain obedient to the Law, and be prepared for military action.[131] When Jesus claimed to be the Messiah but didn't follow the pattern they anticipated, they were offended and appalled.

F. F. Bruce writes, "No single form of messianic expectation was cherished by Jesus' contemporaries, but the hope of a military Messiah predominated. The promises of a prince of the house of David who would break the oppressor's yoke from his people's neck seemed to many to be designed for such a time as theirs, whether the yoke was imposed by a Herodian ruler or by a Roman governor."[132]

Some modern Christians criticize the Old Testament Israelites' misunderstanding of the type of Messiah the scriptures promised and the first-century Jews' initial blindness to Jesus. But today we read the Old Testament with the benefit of the New Testament's clarifying revelations, and we cannot assume we would have had greater perception than they did before these revelations existed.

Biblical scholar Mike Heiser explains that many Old Testament passages that modern Christian readers see as clear references to the Messiah would not have been seen as such by Old Testament and first-century Jews. Heiser notes that even the disciples initially missed Jesus as the Messiah when He appeared to them in His resurrected body. "Do you realize," he asks, "that there isn't a single passage in the Old Testament that actually has the Messiah dying and rising again.... The disciples were not ignoramuses."

Even in Isaiah 53, the well-known passage we now see as containing numerous messianic prophecies involving a suffering servant, the Hebrew word for Messiah never appears. Heiser contends that God deliberately did not spell out the messianic plan all in one place in the Old Testament. "What you do see," he says, "is what I call a messianic profile. The full profile of who the Messiah was going to be and, more importantly, what He was supposed to do, is splintered and scattered in hundreds of places in the Old Testament so that you can only...see the mosaic after the fact." In fairness, it's not surprising that Jesus had to open His disciples' eyes to the passages in the Old Testament pointing to Him. But with the illumination He provided them, which the New Testament writers passed on to us, we can now read the Old Testament with much greater clarity.[133]

George Eldon Ladd takes essentially the same position as Dr. Heiser. "The Gospels," writes Ladd, "represent the disciples as hopeless after Jesus' death. When he appeared to them, they did not believe it was he. 'They were startled and frightened, and supposed that they had seen a spirit' (Luke 24:37).... Modern Christians...read Isaiah 53 with its vivid depiction of a suffering, dying servant and see Jesus' sufferings and death clearly foretold in the Old Testament."[134]

But we must put ourselves in the disciples' shoes to understand their expectations, which means reading the Old Testament messianic prophecies not through our Christian eyes but in the context and setting of first-century Jews. Then we discover that they expected the Messiah to be, in Ladd's words, "a Davidic king who would arise from among men but would be supernaturally endowed to destroy the national and political enemies of Israel to gather God's people—Israel—into the earthly kingdom of God with Jerusalem as its capital." But how "could a celestial glorious being become the helpless victim of lawless men and die the death of a criminal?"[135] Yes, the Old Testament predicts a suffering servant, but not in connection with the Messiah. Ladd quotes an expert in Jewish literature who argues, "In the whole Jewish Messianic literature of the Tannaitic period [before AD 200] there is no trace of the 'suffering Messiah.'"[136]

It's true, Ladd concedes, that the Old Testament didn't point to a resurrected Messiah absent the benefit of New Testament hindsight, and so it's understandable that His disciples didn't get it based on the Old Testament alone. But why didn't they understand it even after Jesus predicted His suffering, death, and resurrection to them? Could it be that Jesus' predictions of His death were fabrications of the early Church and not historically trustworthy? How else do you explain the disciples' blindness to what they were witnessing?[137]

Ladd denies that the scriptural passages were an invention of the early Church. He says the "explanation for the disciples' utter inability to grasp Jesus' predictions about suffering, death, and resurrection" is that they were "a flat contradiction of everything they believed about the Messiah and the Son of Man. He was to conquer and reign, not suffer and die. The two ideas seemed mutually exclusive. He was to destroy the wicked, not be destroyed by the wicked. He was to establish the Kingdom of God, not fall victim to the kingdoms of men."[138]

Yes, Jesus affirmed that He was the Son of Man who would descend from heaven and establish God's kingdom, as the prophet Daniel wrote (Daniel 7:13–14, 26–27), but that would happen eschatologically—in the future, at the end of the age. But before that day could come—whenever that might be—He had to suffer and die. It was this aspect that seemed so contradictory and unscriptural to His disciples. When Jesus began to instruct them that His mission was to suffer and die (Matt. 8:31), "the disciples were sure something was wrong."[139]

So it's not that Jesus failed to warn His disciples about His suffering, death, and resurrection, and it was not a myth propagated by the early Church. It's that this part of the message seemed so inconsistent with their firmly established scriptural beliefs that it didn't fully register with them.

Ladd therefore concludes that the Gospel story describing the disciples' initial blindness to Jesus' necessary suffering and death is completely credible—both psychologically and historically. Jesus was fulfilling none of the roles expected for the Messiah. In fact, when the people tried to force His hand, He withdrew, such as when they tried to make Him their king after He miraculously fed the five thousand (John 6:15).[140] Of course, He could have made Himself king, but it was not His time. In fact, when Jesus refused to accept their timetable and immediately assume the role they anticipated for the Messiah, "many of his disciples drew back and no longer went about with him" (John 6:66).

The Old Testament prophets didn't predict that the Messiah would suffer and die. Yes, Isaiah 53 and other passages foretold a suffering servant. However, writes Ladd, "it was completely hidden from the disciples that the Son of Man must fill the role of the Suffering Servant of Isaiah 53 before he comes in the power and glory of God's Kingdom."[141] In other words, the Old Testament predicted a Messiah and a suffering servant, but not that the Messiah *would be* the Suffering Servant.

This historical backdrop underscores the reliability of the Gospels. The disciples weren't unquestioning cult members salivating at the prospect of creating a new religion founded on a lie. Something dramatic had to occur before the scales were lifted from their eyes. That something was the resurrection of Jesus Christ after His crucifixion—and even then, they didn't fully grasp the full import of what had occurred until He opened their eyes on the Emmaus road and elsewhere. Only then did they begin to see the many passages of the Old Testament as a cohesive mosaic—one that distinctly shows the image of Jesus Christ.

PROVIDENTIAL CONFLUENCE OF EVENTS

The providential hand of God prepared the New Testament world and Palestine in particular for Christ's entrance into human history. The Middle East was situated in the center of an empire rich with Hellenistic influences. From the time of Alexander the Great's conquest of the region—about three hundred years before the birth of Christ—Greek was a common second language and culture, allowing for the spread of new ideas and information between the Roman Empire's various nations.[142]

Relative peace prevailed throughout the empire (Pax Romana) from the reign of Augustus (27 BC–14 AD) to the reign of Marcus Aurelius (161–180 AD), which was conducive to the spread of the Gospel.[143]

The Romans had established a sophisticated and comprehensive system of roads, facilitating travel, trade, and communications. The Apostle Paul and other early Christians utilized the Roman roads and waterways to spread the good news throughout the Mediterranean world.[144] The Romans' uniform system of justice helped to provide stability to the region. Furthermore, as Rome relied on Palestine and its neighbor Egypt for much of its corn supply, it was in Rome's economic and strategic interests to protect the Jewish homeland.[145] Palestine also served as a buffer against Rome's rival, the Parthian Empire, which lay beyond the Euphrates, the eastern border of the Roman Empire.[146]

The birth of Christianity occurred at an ideal time in the history of philosophical thought. Classical Greek philosophers such as Plato, Aristotle, and their successors raised profound questions but provided few soul-satisfying answers, which contributed to the development of the various philosophical schools we've discussed. "Into this intellectual situation," writes Mark Noll, "the Gospel came as a cleansing breeze. It was not that Christianity solved all philosophical problems easily; rather, it provided an intellectual confidence and a personal certainty resting not in the powers of human intelligence, but in the God revealed through Jesus Christ."[147]

Moreover, the state of Judaism in the time of Jesus readied the Mediterranean world for the spread of the Gospel. God-fearing Jews, steeped in the Law of Moses and the writings of the prophets, lived in small communities throughout the Mediterranean basin. They were among the first people the apostles approached and converted, preaching that Jesus Christ fulfilled the promises of their God, Yahweh.[148]

Many scholars believe Paul was referring to this combination of God-ordained events when he wrote, "But when the fullness of time had come, God sent forth his Son, born of woman, born under the law, to redeem those who were under the law, so that we might receive adoption as sons" (Gal. 4:4). Paul was particularly suited to preach when he strategically visited local synagogues, which the Jews had established inside and outside Palestine. Using his intimate knowledge of the Old Testament, he stressed Christ's fulfillment of Israel's messianic hopes.[149] Jesus taught in the synagogues as well, as He acknowledged in His trial before the high priest: "I have always taught in synagogues and in the temple, where all Jews come together" (John 18:20).

Undeniably, an extraordinary confluence of circumstances enabled the spread of the Gospel. There was the Jewish influence—the existence of unquenched messianic expectations; the Roman influence—the Pax Romana; and the Greek influence—the common language and culture.[150] This notion of God's hand at work is almost as old as Christianity itself. As the early Church father Origen writes,

> For righteousness has arisen in His days, and there is abundance of peace, which took its commencement at His birth, God preparing the nations for His teaching, that they might be under one prince, the king of the Romans, and that it might not, owing to the want of union among the nations, caused by the existence of many kingdoms, be more difficult for the apostles of Jesus to accomplish the task enjoined upon them by their Master, when He said, "Go and teach all nations." Moreover, it is certain that Jesus was born in the reign of Augustus, who, so to speak fused together into one monarchy the many populations of the earth. Now the existence of many kingdoms would have been a hindrance to the spread of the doctrine of Jesus throughout the entire world; not only for the reasons mentioned, but also on account of the necessity of men everywhere engaging in war, and fighting on behalf of their native country, which was the case before the times of Augustus, and in periods still more remote, when necessity arose as when the Peloponnesians and the Athenians warred against each other, and other nations in like manner. How, then, was it possible for the Gospel doctrine of peace...to prevail throughout the world, unless at the advent of Jesus a milder spirit had been everywhere introduced into the conduct of things?[151]

NEW TESTAMENT CULTURE AND BACKGROUND

Everett Ferguson, an expert in early Christian studies, likens the historical setting of the New Testament to a series of concentric circles. Beginning from the outside and moving inward toward the center of the circle, the Romans' governmental, legal, and economic systems represent the outer circle. Next are the Greek cultural, educational, and philosophical influences, followed by the Jewish world, which provided the immediate religious context for early Christianity. Further inward is the already Hellenized land of Palestine, which was the home of Jesus and His disciples and the setting of Jesus' ministry. At the center are the diaspora synagogues, which provided the most important entry points for early Christianity into the wider Greco-Roman world.[152]

The Roman military, which was the tip of the spear in expanding the empire, kept the peace, which facilitated social, cultural, and economic progress.[153]

Patronage—a reciprocal relationship between patron and client—was prevalent in the Roman world and aided the early spread of Christianity. Patrons and clients were of different social statuses, having entered into their relationship voluntarily. The clients assisted their patrons in their private, public, and political lives, and the patrons provided them with gifts or money, invited them to their homes for visits and meals, and extended them legal protection. The Book of Romans mentions that Phoebe, a Church servant, was a patron of many people (16:2).[154] Patrons of a religious group were usually affluent or prominent people who allowed its members to meet in their home.[155]

At the dawn of the New Testament era, only 10 percent of the Roman Empire's population lived in cities, yet that is where most Christian evangelism and worship occurred. Rome and Alexandria were the most populous cities, followed by Carthage and Antioch, then Corinth, Ephesus, and Pergamum.[156] Private houses played a crucial role in the spread of Christianity, as shown by Paul's references to people hosting meetings in their homes (Romans 16:3–5, 23; Phil. 2; Col. 4:15; 1 Cor. 16:19).[157] These meetings helped early Christians develop a sense of community, friendship, and mutual support.

This close-knit relationship is illustrated in Paul's frequent references to fellow believers, males and females, as "brothers." Paul naturally uses this term because Ananias called him "brother" shortly after Paul's conversion, when he laid his hands on Paul and returned Paul's sight lost after his encounter with the resurrected Jesus (Acts 9:17; 22:13). Throughout his letters we see that Paul considers his fellow believers as a family and "of the household of faith" (Gal. 6:10). His instructions on how Christians should treat each other reflect this: "Do not rebuke an older man but encourage him as you would a father, younger men as brothers, older women as mothers, younger women as sisters, in all purity" (1 Tim. 5:1–2). Paul was protective of those he brought to the faith and mentored, referring to them as "my beloved children" (1 Cor. 4:14), whose "father in Christ Jesus" he had become through the Gospel (1 Cor. 4:15).[158] He considers them his personal responsibility spiritually, calling them "my little children, for whom I am again in the anguish of childbirth until Christ is formed in you!" (Gal. 4:19).

CITY LIFE

The cities generally had theaters, amphitheaters, baths, temples, basilicas, ornamental fountains, and porticoes, but they were beset by narrow streets, sanitation problems, and overcrowding. People spent most of their time outside in public, whether at work or leisure, because the average house was small and unclean. The artisans, however, generally worked in their homes.[159]

Both natives and foreign immigrants often lived among neighbors of the same ethnicity, and within these ethnic areas, people of similar occupations lived on the same streets. People of the same trade weren't as competitive with each other as they are today.[160] This could explain why Barnabas has little problem finding Paul, who he knows would be among the tentmakers, when he goes to Tarsus to bring Paul back to Antioch to evangelize and minister there (Acts 11:25–26). Likewise, Paul easily locates Aquila and Priscilla, who have the same occupation, in Corinth (Acts 18:1–3).[161]

Roman houses were generally made of brick or concrete, but those in Palestine were made of stucco, sun-dried brick, or stone—either white limestone, which was abundant and cheap, or black basalt.[162] The roofs were commonly made with wooden beams covered with brush and topped off with mud or clay. Homeowners had to roll their roofs after every heavy rain, using an outside staircase or wooden ladder to access the rooftops, which were enclosed with parapets to keep people from falling. People did various activities on the roofs such as washing clothes and drying fruits and vegetables. The Book of Acts records Peter praying and having a vision on a housetop in Joppa (Acts 10:9–10). A more momentous event involving a housetop occurs when four men bring a paralytic to Jesus for healing and enter the home by climbing to the roof, making a hole, and lowering the man, on his bed, down to Jesus (Mark 2:1–12).[163]

Palestinians usually ate two meals a day, mostly of vegetables, fruit, and bread, with meat representing a less common luxury. In some areas they ate fish as a source of protein. Wealthy Romans, on the other hand, enjoyed richer foods and ate four times a day.[164]

Men and woman wore loose-fitting tunics throughout the year, donning cloaks over their garments in the cold. This explains Jesus' instructions to His disciples to give their cloaks to someone who had successfully sued them and taken their tunics (Matt. 5:40), after telling them to turn the other cheek to one who slaps them. All but the destitute, who went barefoot, wore open leather sandals.[165]

Having reviewed the historical and cultural backdrop to the New Testament, we will now examine the development of the New Testament canon and the historical reliability of the New Testament documents and writers.

CHAPTER 2

NEW TESTAMENT BASICS
BUILDING BLOCKS OF THE REVELATION

The evidence for our New Testament writings is ever so much greater than the evidence for many writings of classical authors, the authenticity of which no one dreams of questioning. And if the New Testament were a collection of secular writings, their authenticity would generally be regarded as beyond all doubt. It is a curious fact that historians have often been much readier to trust the New Testament records than many theologians.

—F. F. BRUCE[1]

T he Bible contains sixty-six books, thirty-nine in the Old Testament and twenty-seven in the New.[2] The Old Testament covers a far longer time period than the New Testament—from the creation of the world until some four hundred years before Christ arrived. In it, God promises He will redeem fallen man through the Messiah, and the New Testament records God's fulfillment of that promise and explains its significance.

The title "New Testament" derives from *novum testamentum*, the Latin translation of a Greek phrase meaning "new covenant."[3] We know this title was used at least as early as the fourth century AD because it's found in fourth-century manuscripts called the Codex Sinaiticus and

Codex Vaticanus. The Codex Sinaiticus (340 AD) includes the oldest complete copy of the New Testament and much of the Old Testament,[4] while the Codex Vaticanus (325–350 AD) contains most of the New Testament and almost all the Old Testament.[5]

THE NEW TESTAMENT CANON AND INSPIRATION

The twenty-seven books of the New Testament are called the New Testament "canon" to denote the books universally accepted by the Church as inspired by God. Bible scholar F. F. Bruce explains, "When we speak of the canon of scripture, the word 'canon' has a simple meaning. It means the list of books contained in scripture, the list of books recognized as worthy to be included in the sacred writings of a worshipping community. In a Christian context, we might define the word as 'the list of the writings acknowledged by the Church as documents of the divine revelation.'"[6]

The word "canon" is derived from the Greek "kanon," which refers to an architectural measuring rod. The term evolved to mean a criterion or standard used to measure an idea's authenticity.[7] The word's first known use to describe the complete canon accepted today occurred in 367 AD in a letter by Athanasius, Bishop of Alexandria.[8] As applied to the Old and New Testament books, it means those writings accepted as authoritative.

But who decided which writings would be accepted as canonical? What standard did they use? Jesus wrote no books, but taught orally and by example.[9] As shown throughout the New Testament, His followers and others recognized Him as divinely authoritative long before His words were written down, much less assimilated and officially canonized by the Church. For example, the officers who refused to arrest Jesus declare, "No one ever spoke like this man" (John 7:46). Similarly, Peter proclaims that Jesus spoke the words of eternal life (John 6:68).[10] F. W. Beare notes that the Church had the essence of the New Testament canon before any of the books had been penned. After they were written down and began circulating in the churches, they were considered authoritative not as holy books as such, but as writings that contained the holy words of Jesus. "The authority of the words was primary;" writes Arthur G. Patzia, "that of the books was secondary and derivative."[11]

Thus, to qualify as canonical, the books had to be closely associated with Christ's apostles or prophets—either written by them or having their stamp of approval.[12] Scripture affirms this by proclaiming the Church was "built on the foundation of the apostles and prophets, Christ Jesus himself being the cornerstone" (Eph. 2:20). Christ promised He would send the Holy Spirit, Who would teach them all things, bring to their remembrance all that He had said to them (John 14:26), and "guide" them "into all the truth" (John 16:13).

The early Church took those words to heart. While the prophets had been silent since the close of the Old Testament period, the early Christian community believed another age of prophecy, promised by the Old Testament prophets (Mal. 4:5–6; Joel 2:28–29; Ezek. 36:27; 37:14), had begun, first through John the Baptist and Jesus, and then in the Church's witness to the resurrected Lord (Acts 1:8).[13]

New Testament writers were aware their writings were inspired and guided by the Holy Spirit. Paul writes to the Corinthians, "And we impart this in words not taught by human wisdom but taught by the Spirit, interpreting spiritual truths to those who are spiritual" (1 Cor. 2:13). He also tells the Thessalonians, "And we also thank God constantly for this, that when you received the word of God, which you heard from us, you accepted it not as the word of men but as what it really is, the word of God, which is at work in you believers" (1 Thess. 2:13). Likewise, Peter informs his readers they have been "born again, not of perishable seed but of imperishable, through the living and abiding word of God" (1 Peter 1:23). As R. M. Raymer affirms, "This imperishable Word was the content of Peter's preaching. His hearers must be affected by its life-changing power."[14]

Divinely inspired, the New Testament writers confidently instructed the recipients of their missives to share them with other believers. Paul tells the Thessalonians, "I put you under oath before the Lord to have this letter read to all the brothers" (1 Thess. 5:27), and to the Colossians he says, "And when this letter has been read among you, have it also read in the church of the Laodiceans" (Col.

4:16). John alludes to the inspiration of his Gospel when he writes, "Now Jesus did many other signs in the presence of the disciples, which are not written in this book; but these are written so that you may believe that Jesus is the Christ, the Son of God, and that by believing you may have life in his name" (1 John 20:30–31). John revisits the theme in a more ominous form in the Book of Revelation: "I warn everyone who hears the words of the prophecy of this book: if anyone adds to them, God will add to him the plagues described in this book, and if anyone takes away from the words of the book of this prophecy, God will take away his share in the tree of life and in the holy city, which are described in this book" (22:18–19). This stern warning is reminiscent of those in the Old Testament books of Deuteronomy—"You shall not add to the word that I command you, nor take from it" (4:2)—and Proverbs—"Do not add to his words, lest he rebuke you and you be found a liar" (30:6).[15]

THE CHURCH DID NOT CREATE THE CANON

Some critics argue that the early Christian councils determined which books to include in the New Testament as essentially a top-down decision. However, as Josh McDowell observes, "The church did not create the canon; it did not determine which books would be called Scripture, the inspired Word of God. Instead, the church recognized, or discovered, which books had been inspired from their inception.... A book is not the Word of God because it is accepted by the people of God. Rather, it was accepted by the people of God because it is the Word of God."[16] F. F. Bruce states that the words of Jesus and His apostles were deemed to be equal in authority to the Old Testament scriptures. "Authority," writes Bruce, "precedes canonicity; had the words of the Lord and his apostles not been accorded supreme authority, the written record of their words would never have been canonized."[17]

The early Church had several incentives to formally canonize the inspired books. It had long used these books, which satisfied the Church's worship, teaching, and missionary requirements,[18] and since they were prophetic—spoken by God's prophets—they had to be preserved. The Church also needed a complete collection of authoritative books to fight heresies, a problem that arose early in the Church's history. Marcion, a notorious second-century heretic, rejected the entire New Testament except for the Gospel of Luke and ten of Paul's epistles. Montanus, in the latter half of the second century, taught that revelation was continuing during his time.[19]

Formalizing its canonical collection helped the Church combat these efforts to discredit the inspired works and enabled it to translate the Bible into different languages to spread the Word to other nations. Additionally, the persecutions of Christians by Roman Emperors Diocletian and Maximian in the early fourth century motivated the Church to settle on the canon because believers would not have risked severe punishment and even death to defend books they weren't sure were scriptural.[20]

Dr. Norman Geisler acknowledges that the Church did not officially recognize the canon prior to the late fourth century, but contends the books nevertheless were widely recognized as authoritative. "As with the Old Testament books," writes Geisler, "there is ample evidence available to confirm that the inspired books were received immediately as such, circulated, and even collected." The New Testament process was complicated, however, because it was written over a period of fifty years by eight or nine authors writing to various individuals or churches in different locations.[21]

Many critics of Christianity argue that the New Testament Gospel was just one of many competing gospels and only prevailed because its adherents were superior evangelists, not because it is based on historical fact. One of these allegedly competing philosophies was Gnosticism, which held that some people had a special knowledge of the truth, and that man's main spiritual problem was ignorance, not sin. Gnostics believed that the material world is evil and that Christ was not human so His crucifixion was illusory.[22] While the ideas leading to Gnosticism initially appeared in the first century, however, the philosophy didn't fully develop until the mid-to-late second century, so it couldn't have competed with the New Testament Gospel, which was already established.[23]

DEVELOPMENT OF THE CANON
AND THE ORAL TRADITION

The New Testament canon developed in stages. Before the New Testament books were written, the only written scriptures for Christians were the Old Testament books. But the apostles, teachers, missionaries, and others shared the apostles' teachings about Jesus orally.[24] Paul acknowledges as much when he says, "For what I received I passed on to you as of first importance: that Christ died for our sins according to the Scriptures, that he was buried, that he was raised on the third day according to the Scriptures, and that he appeared to Peter, and then to the Twelve" (1 Cor. 15:3–5). Even liberal scholars believe that Paul's testimony was part of an early Christian creed that developed between eighteen months and eight years after the resurrection.[25]

Paul's passage cited above—"When you received the word of God, which you heard from us, you accepted it not as the word of men, but as what it really is, the word of God" (1 Thess. 2:13)—shows the accepted authority of apostolic oral tradition and teaching by eyewitnesses to Christ's life.[26] "In fact, in the case of the gospels," writes William Lane Craig, "it would be more accurate to speak of 'oral history' rather then 'oral tradition,' since the living eyewitnesses and apostles were still around."[27]

Likewise, Paul tells the Corinthians, "Now I commend you because you remember me in everything and maintain the traditions even as I delivered them to you" (1 Cor. 11:2). Luke states that he had prepared an orderly account of the narrative that "those who from the beginning were eyewitnesses and ministers of the word have delivered...to us" (Luke 1:2). These facts had been delivered orally among Jesus' early followers.[28]

Obviously, the oral Gospel originated with Jesus, Who shocked the Jews with His level of scriptural understanding despite having no formal rabbinic training (John 7:15). Jesus taught through sayings and parables. These forms of communication were not introduced by Jesus but were rooted in Jewish and Greco-Roman culture, which readied His audience for these methods.[29]

Darrell Bock and Daniel Wallace maintain that Christian orthodox teachings and traditions—doctrinal summaries, hymns, and sacraments that emphasize the Church's core theology—were being passed on orally when the New Testament books were being written. They deny there were competing versions of the Gospel vying for prominence in the early churches. At the heart of these oral teachings was that Jesus was exalted—that He participated in creation and is the resurrected Redeemer, seated above all other spiritual forces, Who would return as Lord. Bock and Wallace conclude, "Our earliest Christian sources (from 49 through 95 or so) indicate that the picture of an exalted, enthroned Jesus was a given for the earliest church community in places as widespread as Jerusalem, Asia Minor, and Rome. Historically, there is no question that this emphasis on Jesus and his role in salvation is at the center of the texts that are our earliest sources of Christianity."[30]

What about the reliability of these oral traditions? Let's understand that Jesus' followers lived in an oral culture in which people routinely memorized large chunks of material. The early witnesses to Jesus' acts and sayings were skilled in conveying information verbally with great accuracy. But the New Testament writers didn't just pass on any information no matter the source. Many of them were eyewitnesses or were writing on behalf of "those who from the beginning were eyewitnesses and ministers of the word" (Luke 1:2).[31] Those who passed on the word were highly motivated to be precise because they were communicating matters of the utmost importance originating from the most important person who ever lived.

This oral transmission of the Gospel likely continued even after the first books were written down and circulated. In the second century, Church father Eusebius reported that Papias, the Bishop of Hierapolis in Phrygia (125 AD), admitted he preferred oral communications about Jesus to written ones, "for I do not think that I derived so much benefit from books as from the living voice of those that are still surviving."[32]

By this oral tradition, or oral history, the Christians of the first two centuries understood the Old Testament writings as bearing witness to Christ.[33] Also scholars have identified numerous creedal formulas, or teachings, the early Christians knew and shared about Jesus that predated the New Testament writings. Lee Strobel and Alex McFarland cite forty examples of such teachings:[34]

1. Jesus was really born in human flesh (Phil. 2:6; 1 Tim. 3:16; 1 John 4:2).
2. Family line descended from David (Acts 13:23; Rom. 1:3–4; 2 Tim. 2:8).
3. Implication of His baptism (Rom. 10:9).
4. His word was preached (1 Tim. 3:16).
5. People believed in His message (1 Tim. 3:16).
6. Came from the town of Nazareth (Acts 2:22; 4:10; 5:38).
7. John preceded Jesus' ministry (Acts 10:37; 13:24–25).
8. Jesus' ministry began in Galilee (Acts 10:37).
9. Jesus' ministry expanded to Judea (Acts 10:37).
10. Jesus performed miracles (Acts 2:22; 10:38).
11. Jesus fulfilled numerous Old Testament prophecies (Acts 2:25–31; 3:21–25; 4:11; 10:43; 13:27–37).
12. Jesus attended a dinner (1 Cor. 11:23).
13. This was on the evening of His betrayal (1 Cor. 11:23).
14. He gave thanks before this meal (1 Cor. 11:23).
15. Jesus shared bread and beverage (1 Cor. 11:23).
16. Jesus explained that the bread and drink represented His impending substitutionary death for sin (1 Cor. 11:23).
17. Jesus stood before Pilate (Acts 3:13; 13:28).
18. Jesus affirmed His identity as King of the Jews (1 Tim. 6:13).
19. Jesus was killed (Acts 3:13–15; 13:27–29).
20. Jesus died for humanity's sin (1 Pet. 3:18; Rom. 4:25; 1 Tim. 2:6).
21. This execution was carried out despite His righteous life (1 Pet. 3:18).
22. His crucifixion was specified as the mode of death (Acts 2:23, 36; 4:10; 5:30; 10:39).

23. His crucifixion was performed in the city of Jerusalem (Acts 10:39; 13:27).
24. His crucifixion was carried out by wicked men (Acts 2:23).
25. Jesus was buried (Acts 13:29).
26. After His death, Jesus resurrected (Acts 2:24, 31–32; 3:15, 26; 4:10; 5:30; 10:40; 13:30–37; 2 Tim. 2:8).
27. Jesus resurrected on the third day (Acts 10:40).
28. The risen Jesus appeared to His followers (Acts 13:31).
29. In His resurrected state, Jesus ate with His disciples (Acts 10:40–41).
30. His disciples were eyewitnesses of these events (Acts 2:32; 3:15; 5:32; 10:39, 41; 13:31).
31. After rising from the grave, Jesus ascended into heaven and was glorified and exalted (Acts 2:33; 3:21; 5:31; 1 Tim. 3:16; Phil. 2:6).
32. The risen Jesus instructed that salvation be preached in His name (Acts 2:38–39; 3:19–23; 4:11–12; 5:32; 10:42–43; 13:26, 38–41).
33. The resurrection and subsequent events showed God's approval of Jesus by validating His person and message (Acts 2:22–24, 36; 3:13–15; 10:42; 13:32–33; Rom. 1:3–4; 10:9–10).
34. Jesus is called "the Son of God" (Acts 13:33; Rom. 1:3–4).
35. Jesus is called "Lord" (Luke 24:34; Acts 2:36; 10:36; Rom. 1:4; 10:9; Phil. 2:11).
36. Jesus is called "Christ" or "Messiah" (Acts 2:36, 38; 3:18, 20; 4:10; 10:36; Rom. 1:4; Phil. 2:11; 2 Tim. 2:8).
37. Jesus is called "Savior" (Acts 5:31; 13:23).
38. Jesus is called "Prince" (Acts 5:31).
39. Jesus is called "the Holy and Righteous One" (Acts 2:27; 3:14; 13:35).
40. It is said that—regarding His essential nature—Jesus is God (see Phil. 2:6).[35]

The oral tradition, however, was not suitable for transmission of the Gospel message to the general public indefinitely in the same way a body of teaching was preserved in rabbinical schools, which trained students to learn and pass on their instruction "without losing a drop."[36] The Christian message was to be shared throughout the world, so it needed to be reduced to writing to be preserved and unchanged.[37] David deSilva explains how the formation of a written record was largely inevitable:

> Just as the Jewish Scriptures contained the texts that bore witness to the formation and living out of the first covenant at Sinai, so early Christians began to gather and collect the texts that bore witness to the new covenant in Christ, all the more as the living voice of the apostolic witnesses became less accessible. It was only natural that the books that preserved this apostolic witness and that spoke to the Christian community's central questions and concerns as it dedicated itself to the promises and obligations of this new covenant would rise to a position of authority and centrality in that community.[38]

FOUR GOSPELS, LIKE FOUR DIRECTIONS OF THE WIND

The New Testament reports that once the messages were written down they were read with scriptural authority and circulated among the churches. As noted, Paul instructs the Thessalonians to read his letter "to all the brothers" (1 Thess. 5:27), and John, in Revelation, commands believers to "read aloud the words of this prophecy" (1:3), relating that he has been directed to send his written prophecy to the seven churches (1:11). Likewise, Paul tells the Colossians to ensure his letter is read to the Laodicean Church (Col. 4:16). These passages indicate the apostles intended their writings to be read beyond their immediate addressees and to be accepted as authoritative.[39] Peter endorses Paul's letters as scriptural in warning that some seek to twist his difficult writings (2 Peter 3:15–16). Paul quotes from Luke's Gospel, treating it as equal in authority to the Old Testament (1 Tim. 5:8).[40] This evidence shows that several centuries before the Church officially canonized the New Testament books, many were acknowledged as Scripture and read in churches.

Before the end of the first century, all the New Testament books had been written.[41] The early Church fathers referred to all the books within a century of when they were written, and almost all of them were recognized as inspired and authorized by the Church by the end of the second century.[42] Indeed, "In letters written between 95 AD and 110 AD," note Norman Geisler and Frank Turek, "three early church fathers—Clement, Ignatius, and Polycarp—quoted passages out of 25 of the 27 books in the New Testament."[43] The four Gospels and all of Paul's thirteen epistles had been accepted in some parts of the Church as authoritative witnesses of apostolic teaching by 130 AD, and by the end of the second century these books were accepted as Scripture, equal in authority to the Old Testament. Church Father Irenaeus, around 180 AD, named twenty-one of the twenty-seven New Testament books as being used by the churches. He maintained there must be only four Gospels, just as there are four directions of the wind.[44]

Other New Testament books were accepted later,[45] and by 230 AD, based on the work of Origen,[46] there was general agreement about the great majority of New Testament writings, though doubt remained about certain books, some of which were later included and others excluded. The Book of Hebrews, for example, remained in question for a time largely because of uncertainty about its author.[47] Eusebius, Bishop of Caesarea, in his *Church History*, written in the early fourth century, mentioned all twenty-seven New Testament books, but acknowledged that some had been "spoken against": James, 2 Peter, 2 and 3 John, and Jude. Any such doubts disappeared by 367 AD, when Athanasius authoritatively listed the twenty-seven books as canonical.[48]

The Church officially recognized all the New Testament books in the councils of Hippo in 393 AD and Carthage in 397 AD.[49] But as we've seen, nearly all the New Testament books were widely copied, circulated, used, and authorized by the Church during the first four centuries and well before the final canonical list was formalized.[50]

HISTORICAL RELIABILITY OF
THE NEW TESTAMENT

As I wrote in *Jesus on Trial*, abundant evidence supports the reliability of the Bible. I want to briefly review this evidence to establish that the topic of this book—the New Testament's account of the words and deeds of Jesus Christ—is in fact true. The remarkable unity of the entire Bible, both within and between the Old and New Testaments, is a powerful apologetic, as are the hundreds of Old Testament prophecies that are fulfilled in the New Testament. The more we read the Bible, the more we discover its intrinsic inspiration.

The New Testament's historical reliability is shown in the authenticity of the New Testament documents, the credibility of its writers, non-Christian sources corroborating Jesus' existence, and archaeological evidence substantiating the Bible's historical record. No matter what measure is used, no other ancient document is nearly as reliable as the New Testament.

First, let's revisit the popular modern fiction, alluded to in Chapter 1, that many different versions of Christianity were circulating in the first century, and the New Testament Gospels just happened to prevail over other credible accounts. New Testament historian Craig Evans flatly rejects the claim, as do many other scholars. The early Christians had disagreements, but not over such fundamental questions as whether Jesus was the divine Messiah or whether He was crucified for our sins and resurrected. The bizarre ideas of the Gnostics and other heretical sects celebrated today by popular books and movies are mythical speculations unsupported by the evidence. The Gnostics engaged in most of their mischief in the second century, not the first. Evans notes that while liberal scholars are "trying to smuggle into the first century a mystical, Gnostic understanding of God and the Christian life...first century Christians had never heard of these things."[51] He observes simply, "That Jesus is the Messiah, he's God's Son, he fulfills the Scriptures, he died on the cross, and thereby saved humanity, he rose from the dead—these core issues were not open for discussion."[52]

There were a number of "apocryphal Gospels," many written in the second century. Some are attributed to particular apostles such as Peter,

Thomas, and even Judas. While many today are eager to embrace them—and anything else that purports to debunk the biblical Jesus—most are based mainly on the four canonical Gospels or were spawned by certain speculative and visionary theological schools of the second, third, and fourth centuries. Serious scholarship gives little credence to these books as containing any historical value, and the writings were never included in any authoritative lists of early Christian books.[53] Biblical scholar John P. Meier describes the whole lot of these non-canonical works as "a field of rubble, largely produced by the pious and wild imaginations of certain second-century Christians."[54]

The historicity of Jesus Christ and the historical reliability of the Gospels wasn't always disputed, but beginning in the late eighteenth century, liberal scholars began to construct alternative versions of Jesus' life—His identity, character, motivations, and nature—ideas Albert Schweitzer calls the "fictitious lives of Jesus."[55] Some argued that Jesus staged the miracles He appeared to perform. Others claimed He healed with medicines, not through supernatural powers. Some contended He didn't die on the cross but "swooned" and that the Essenes nursed Him back to health so He could visit His followers in the guise of resurrection appearances.[56] Grounded in raw supposition rather than evidence, these hypotheses gained little scholarly attention.[57]

In the nineteenth century, Protestant liberal critics concocted many more alternative biographies of Jesus that differed markedly from the Gospel accounts. In these, Jesus was portrayed as uniquely moral but not divine—he was a mere human who did not actually perform miracles.[58] Famed twentieth-century apologist C. S. Lewis ridicules the flagrant self-contradictions of these theories. Jesus, says Lewis, could not have been a great moral teacher and merely a human being, for He plainly asserted His own deity, which means that if He wasn't divine, He must have been either a liar or a lunatic. "Let us not," cautions Lewis, "come with any patronizing nonsense about His being a great human teacher. He has not left that open to us. He did not intend to."[59]

Indeed, too many people, especially in our post-modern era, overlook or reject the uniqueness of Christianity's truth claims. It reminds me of a short story nicely illustrating the point, attributed to R. J. Morgan, who writes:

> Auguste Comte, the French philosopher, and Thomas Carlyle, the Scottish essayist were deeply engaged in conversation. Comte said he was going to start a new religion that would supplant the religion of Christ. It was to have no mysteries and was to be as plain as the multiplication table; its name was to be positivism. "Very good, Mr. Comte," Carlyle replied, "very good. All you will need to do will be to speak as never a man spake, and live as never a man lived, and be crucified, and rise again the third day, and get the world to believe that you are still alive. Then your religion will have a chance to get on."[60]

FANTASTICAL QUESTS FOR THE HISTORICAL JESUS

Despite scholarship debunking these myths, so-called "quests for the historical Jesus" continue to proliferate, generating reappraisals of the accuracy of the biblical record as well as differing accounts of their reliability and of who Jesus actually was.[61] In our modern era, another such "quest" has surfaced in popular literature.

Novelist Dan Brown's *The Da Vinci Code* sparked renewed interest in this question and titillated skeptics' itching ears. It is remarkable how much credence is accorded to this account, which is counter to the evidence and relies on wild speculation—compared to the doubt skeptics voice about the Gospels, whose reliability is supported by copious evidence. Brown's work asserts that Christ's deity became Christian doctrine only because Church leaders, on a close vote, affirmed it in the Council of Nicea in 325 AD, where they also allegedly decided on the biblical canon.[62] Brown attempts to show that the true story of Jesus is not in the New Testament but in Gnostic writings, which depict Jesus as a mere human being who married Mary Magdalene and sired children.[63]

As we've seen, however, the early Church accepted Jesus' divinity from the start because that is what the apostles taught from the beginning and what the New Testament documents attest. Yes, Church leaders met at the Council of Nicea in 325 AD at the direction of Roman Emperor Constantine, in part to address the claims of Arius and his followers that the Father created the Son and thus the Son had not always existed and was inferior to the Father.[64] The Council overwhelmingly rejected this heresy and adopted the Nicene Creed, which affirmed Jesus' deity, His co-equality with the Father, and His being "one essence with the Father." The Council of Constantinople in 381 AD reaffirmed this conclusion.[65] It didn't even vote on the question of Christ's deity, and when more than three hundred Church leaders present were asked to sign off on the creed, only two refused. As Richard Howe observes, that "is far from the 'close vote' that *The Da Vinci Code* claims."[66] This heresy was not some long-standing controversy within the Church— Arius was the first to introduce it there. It may have existed outside the Church, though there is little information on the subject.[67]

As for Brown's claim that the Nicean Council created the biblical canon, we've already seen that the early Church accepted the mainstream doctrines about Jesus long before the Church officially recognized the canon. The four Gospels (and the great majority of the other New Testament books) were well established and accepted as authoritative long before the Council.[68] Similarly spurious are Brown's fantastic theories that the Gnostics told the true story of Jesus and that He was married, let alone to Mary Magdalene.[69]

We should also acknowledge the self-authenticating nature of the New Testament. Thomas Griffith observes that it is common knowledge that in the world's entire corpus of literature, past and present, "there is no trace of the picture of a perfect character. Poets, novelists, dramatists, philosophers, essayists, have given the world wonderful creations and yet no writer has ever attempted to portray a perfect man or woman.... And yet in the Gospels, written by ordinary men, not literary geniuses, we have a perfect character depicted. How did the Evangelists accomplish what no writer has ever attempted with success?"[70] In other words, is it more likely that these four men created a literary miracle or that their presentation of Christ is true?

THE AUTHENTICITY OF THE
NEW TESTAMENT DOCUMENTS

As discussed in *Jesus on Trial*, the authenticity of the New Testament documents is shown by dating the original writings—none of which still exist—and determining how much time passed between those writings and the events they record, assessing how many copies we have of those writings and examining them for accuracy, measuring the time gap between the original writings and the oldest copies we have, and then comparing our findings with those of manuscripts of ancient secular history.[71]

Most scholars—liberal and conservative—agree Christ died between 30 and 33 AD, and that all the Gospel accounts were written in the first century between twenty-five and fifty years after those dates.[72] This is a short period considering this was an oral culture in which people would have memorized these accounts before reducing them to writing.[73] Many scholars believe the Gospel writers may have referred to earlier written accounts for some of their material.[74] As noted, Christians agreed on and shared much creedal information about Jesus well before the New Testament writings, and many references to this "Jesus tradition" appear in Paul's epistles, some of which predate the writing of the Gospels.[75] In fact, Christianity was accepted by thousands of people before a single word of the New Testament had been written because Christianity is based on historical events—the life, death, resurrection, and ascension of Christ.

The original twenty-seven New Testament manuscripts probably perished within decades of their composition because the writers didn't write on bricks, rocks, or wooden tablets, but on paper—Egyptian papyrus (see John's reference to his writing tools in 2 John 12; 3 John 13; and Paul's similar reference in 2 Cor. 3:3).[76] What remains are handwritten copies (more accurately, copies of copies) called manuscripts, as there was no other means of producing copies for more than a thousand years after the originals were written.[77] Inevitably, mistakes occurred in the copying process, no matter how meticulous and skilled the scribes were. To evaluate the accuracy of manuscript copies for the New Testament writings or any other ancient books, textual critics study the differences in wording to determine the precise composition of the original manuscript. This is not practical if few manuscript copies exist, and the more the critics have, the more accurately they can pinpoint the original text. This is because the more copies that agree with each other—especially if they are from different locations—the more equipped they are to cross-check and identify the text of the original document.[78] New Testament manuscripts are so plentiful that, according to Professor Craig Blomberg, textual criticism enables us to reconstruct what the New Testament authors wrote with a high degree of accuracy.[79]

The New Testament was translated from early times into many languages, including Latin, Coptic, Syriac, Armenian, Georgian, Gothic, and Arabic. In total, there are more than 25,000 New Testament manuscripts in existence, some 5,800 of which are in Greek, which range from the early second century to the sixteenth century. Though we don't have a complete manuscript dated before the third century, many fragments exist that include a substantial amount of the New Testament.[80] Even if all these manuscripts were destroyed, almost half of the New Testament could be reconstructed just by using the million-plus New Testament quotations in the writings of the early Church fathers.[81] The number of extant New Testament manuscripts dwarfs those of ancient secular writings. There are one thousand times as many existing manuscripts of the New Testament (25,000) than of the average classical author's works (between ten and twenty).[82] Homer's *Iliad* and Demosthenes are exceptions, but there is still no comparison, as there are only about 1,800 manuscripts of the *Iliad*, less than 10 percent of the New Testament number.

Many ancient documents don't have enough manuscripts to allow us to compare their accuracy to that of the New Testament, but where sufficient manuscripts exist, critics have concluded the New Testament manuscripts are exceedingly more reliable—99.5 percent accuracy—compared to the *Iliad* at 95 percent or the ancient Indian work *Mahabharata* at 90 percent.[83]

Apart from the comparisons, what about the errors in the New Testament? Aren't they terribly problematic for those who maintain the Bible is inerrant? In a word, no. As Carl F. H. Henry explains, "Inerrancy pertains only to the oral or written proclamation of the originally inspired prophets and apostles. Not only was their communication of the Word of God efficacious in teaching the truth of revelation, but their transmission of that Word was error-free." "Inerrancy," writes Henry, "does not extend to copies, translations or versions, however."[84]

When I first heard this argument I was not persuaded, because I wondered what difference inerrancy makes to Bible readers through the ages if the copying process corrupts the originally pristine document. That's before I realized that while the copies contain errors, these are not on matters of doctrine. Dr. Geisler shows that the great majority of the errors are in spelling, style, and other grammatical trivialities, and that only about 1 percent of these "variants"—differences in wording—bear on the meaning of the text, with none affecting any major Christian doctrine.[85] (Note that this refers to 1 percent of the variants, not 1 percent of the entire text.) Richard Bentley, a classical English biblical critic, confirms that these minor errors do not pervert or set aside "one article of faith or moral precept."[86]

Even Bart Ehrman, the most famous manuscript scholar who is skeptical of orthodox Christianity, affirms that "the essential Christian beliefs are not affected by actual variants in the manuscript tradition of the New Testament." Evangelical scholars Ed Komoszewski, M. James Sawyer, and Daniel B. Wallace observe, "Any uncertainty over the wording of the original New Testament does not have an impact on major teachings of the New Testament. They certainly do not affect the deity of Christ. There is simply no room for uncertainty about what the New Testament originally taught."[87] What matters, says Carl Henry, is whether these variants corrupt the substantive content of the original and whether they "convey the truth of revelation in reliable verbal form, and infallibly lead the penitent reader to salvation."[88]

The gap between the earliest New Testament manuscript fragment—the John Rylands Fragment (117–138 AD), which contains five verses from John 18—and the original is less than fifty years. Another New Testament fragment, the Bodmer Papyri, which contains most of John's books and Luke, 1 Peter, 2 Peter, and Jude, is dated circa 200 AD, so there is a gap of between 100 and 140 years between the manuscript and the original. Even more impressive is the Chester Beatty Papyri (circa 250)—a gap of 150-plus years from the completion of the originals—which contains most of the New Testament. The Codex Vaticanus (325–350 AD) contains the great majority of the New Testament and the Greek Old Testament. The Codex Sinaiticus (340 AD), as noted, is the oldest existing manuscript of the entire New Testament and contains much of the Old Testament. These date some 250 years from the originals. Again, compared to existing manuscripts for ancient secular texts, the gap between the original and the copies is much smaller for the New Testament. The time gap between the original *Iliad* and the oldest existing manuscript of the work is between 350 and 400 years, but for most other secular works, the gap exceeds a thousand years.[89]

Dr. Geisler definitively summarizes the evidence: "The New Testament documents are copied accurately—the New Testament has more manuscripts, earlier manuscripts, and more accurately copied manuscripts than any other book from the ancient world."[90] As British paleographer and biblical and classical scholar Sir Fredric Kenyon puts it, "The interval between the dates of the original composition and the earliest extant evidence becomes so small as to be in fact negligible, and the last foundation for any doubt that the Scriptures have come down substantially as they were written has now been removed. Both the authenticity and the general integrity of the books of the New Testament may be regarded as finally established."[91]

THE RELIABILITY OF THE NEW TESTAMENT WRITERS

In assessing the reliability of the New Testament writers, Dr. Geisler notes that there were more writers, earlier writers, and more accurate writers than for any other book from the ancient world.[92] Contrary to the naysayers, the New Testament writers were eyewitnesses, their close associates, or were directly related to Jesus. Of the Gospel writers, Matthew and John were apostles, and Mark and Luke were closely associated with the apostles and also interviewed eyewitnesses. It's generally believed that Peter was Mark's main source for eyewitness stories about Jesus.[93] Paul and Peter were apostles, and the writer of Hebrews was evidently an associate of the apostles if not an apostle himself.

Meanwhile James and probably Jude were Jesus' half-brothers.[94] All the New Testament writers highly valued eyewitness testimony, says New Testament professor Mark Strauss (John 19:35; 21:24; Acts 1:21–22; 10:39, 41; 1 Cor. 15:6; 1 Peter 5:1; 2 Peter 1:16; 1 John 1:1–3; Romans 6:17; and 1 Cor. 7:10, 12).[95] "The earlier preachers of the gospel knew the value of… first-hand testimony," writes F. F. Bruce, "and appealed to it time and again. 'We are witnesses of these things,' was their constant and confident assertion."[96]

Repeatedly, the New Testament writers express their fervent commitment to truthful and accurate reporting. Luke begins his Gospel stressing the importance of writing "an orderly account for you, most excellent Theophilus, that you may have certainty concerning the things you have been taught" (Luke 1:3–4). In the Book of Acts he writes, "For we cannot but speak of what we have seen and heard" (Acts 4:20). Peter declares, "For we did not follow cleverly devised myths when we made known to you the power and coming of our Lord Jesus Christ, but we were eyewitnesses of his majesty" (2 Peter 1:16). Paul writes, "I want you to know, brothers, that the gospel I preached is not something that man made up. I did not receive it from any man, nor was I taught it; rather, I received it by revelation from Jesus Christ" (Gal. 1:11–12). John states, "That which was from the beginning, which we have heard, which we have seen with our eyes, which we looked upon and have touched with our hands, concerning the word of life" (1 John 1:1). John reports that Jesus said, "And you also will bear witness, because you have been with me from the beginning" (John 15:27). The writer of Hebrews proclaims, "How shall we escape if we neglect such a great salvation? It was declared at first by the Lord, and it was attested to us by those who heard, while God also bore witness by signs and wonders and various miracles and by gifts of the Holy Spirit distributed according to his will" (Heb. 2:3–4).

Of the New Testament writers, J. P. Moreland asserts, "There is no adequate motive for their labors other than a sincere desire to proclaim what they believed to be the truth."[97] The Gospel writers, the apostles, and the disciples still had doubts about Jesus before He appeared to them in His bodily resurrection. Those appearances transformed them from cowardly and fair-weather followers to bold declarants of Jesus Christ, His deity, His life, His death, His resurrection, and His unique saving power. These men had everything to lose and nothing to gain by proclaiming Christ and His Gospel. New Testament scholar Gary Habermas notes that the disciples had no incentive to concoct an elaborate hoax to start a new religion.[98]

If the New Testament writers were trying to construct an airtight case for their claims, would they have penned different Gospel accounts or coordinated every minute detail in unassailable uniformity? Would they have painted themselves in an embarrassing light, as they often did (such as Peter denying Jesus three times), or would they have depicted themselves as heroes? Would they have woven a story in which the promised Messiah was anything but what they expected, Who not only didn't defeat Israel's Roman oppressors, but allowed Himself to be crucified without lifting a finger in His own defense? As ardent Jewish believers, would they have preached what Jewish leaders considered blasphemy?[99]

Yes, adherents of cults and other religions through the years have been willing to die for their beliefs too. But in those cases all they had was their beliefs. The New Testament writers, by contrast, were reporting what they actually witnessed, heard, and experienced, much of which was witnessed by multiple sources. Why would they have subjected themselves to ridicule, hardship, persecution, and death for something they *knew* was a lie?[100]

Moreover, in reporting Christ's miracles and other acts, the New Testament writers were addressing an audience that could easily have contradicted them, but there is no record this ever happened.[101]

Finally, Jesus not only vouches for the inspiration of the Old Testament (Matt. 5:17–18), but also promises the New Testament writers would be inspired with the guidance of the Holy Spirit (John 14:26; 16:13). "Christ's authentication of the Old Testament," argues Robert Gromacki, "forms the basis of His preauthentication of the New Testament."[102] As Christ Himself declares, "Heaven and earth shall pass away, but my words shall not pass away" (Matt. 24:35). But how, asks Gromacki, would we come to know Jesus' words unless they were going to be written down? Jesus foretells the content of the writings, saying the Holy Spirit will "teach you all things and bring to your remembrance all that I have said to you" (John 14:26). Jesus insists the Holy Spirit will guide them into all truth, and "he will declare to you the things that are to come" (John 16:12–14). In promising the Holy Spirit will bring all things to their remembrance, notes Gromacki, Christ is hinting at the Gospel accounts. When He says the Spirit will teach them all things and guide them into all truth, He is pointing to the epistles. In saying the spirit will "declare to you the things that are to come," Jesus could be talking about prophetic sections, including the Book of Revelation.[103] In addition, the New Testament writers claim to be writing with the divine authority Jesus gave them (John 20:31; 1 John 1:1; 1 John 4:1, 5–6).[104]

The accuracy of the New Testament record is further supported by voluminous archaeological studies and discoveries, but it is beyond the scope of this book to review those as I did in *Jesus on Trial*. Moreover, Jesus' existence is corroborated by a large number of other non-biblical Christian writers and by many ancient non-Christian authors: Josephus, Julius Africanus, Thallus, Pliny the Younger, Tacitus, Suetonius, Mara bar Serapion, Lucian of Samosata, and Celsus, to name a few.[105]

Having established the reliability of the New Testament and reviewed the development of the canon, we will next turn to an overview of the New Testament, examining the arrangement and structure of the books and how the New Testament is in perfect harmony with the Old Testament and completes God's divine plan of salvation.

CHAPTER 3

MIRACULOUS
THE LITERARY WONDER OF THE NEW TESTAMENT

To read the New Testament as literature is to read the Bible in ways that literature in general is read. A literary reading does not diminish the understanding of Scripture, but rather enhances the meaning that is in the text.

—J. L. RESSEGUIE[1]

Recognizing the Bible's literary qualities will deepen our understanding and enhance our reading experience, as the writer of the Old Testament Book of Ecclesiastes—probably Solomon—attests: "Besides being wise, the Preacher also taught the people knowledge, weighing and studying and arranging many proverbs with great care. The Preacher sought to find words of delight, and uprightly he wrote words of truth" (12:9–10).

The Bible is not simply a glorified rulebook on ethical conduct. It certainly teaches how we should live and prioritize our lives, but it does so in various narrative and historical contexts. In fact, people encountering the Bible for the first time may be intimidated when they come across several different types of literature.[2] But Leland Ryken, a scholar on the Bible as literature, argues this is one of the things that makes the Bible unique.

Ryken identifies three main types of writing in the Bible, which are often intermingled:[3]

- **Theological writing** conveys propositional truths.
- **Historical writing** imparts information—facts about what actually occurred, though the writers often willingly share their moral interpretations of the events.
- **Literary writing** recreates the scenes or events in enough detail that we can experience them imaginatively. Whereas theological sections often express theological arguments directly, literary sections incorporate such messages in examples. Literary writing can be seen in the Bible's stories, poetry, proverbs, and visionary writing, including both prophetic and apocalyptic writing.[4]

These different types of writing, however, often overlap. In the story of Adam and Eve, for instance, we understand the serpent is subtle and deceitful because Moses explicitly says so, but he also illustrates it through the serpent's words and actions in the narrative. In this example, the story contains at least two of the three types of writing. It is a historical account of the events, and it is literary because it recreates the scene in sufficient detail to inspire our imaginary experience of what occurred. These three types of writing are seen throughout the Bible, and one usually dominates a passage, though one or both of the others are also often evident.[5]

The Old and New Testaments both have immense literary merit, but Australian pastor J. Sidlow Baxter argues that the latter is in a class of its own. "The New Testament is the most vital book in the world," he insists. "Its supreme *subject* is the Lord Jesus Christ. Its supreme *object* is the salvation of human beings.... He who figures in the Old as the Christ of *prophecy* now emerges in the New as the Christ of *history*. He who is the *super-hope* of the Old is the super-*fact* of the New. Expectancy in the Old has become *experience* in the New. *Pre*vision has become *pro*vision. That which was latent has now become patent. The long-predicted is the now-presented."[6]

THE ARRANGEMENT OF THE
NEW TESTAMENT BOOKS AND GENRE

The twenty-seven books of the New Testament aren't ordered chronologically but according to literary type, or genre. The books are divided into four main classifications: the Gospels; History (the Book of Acts); the Epistles (letters written by the Apostle Paul and others); and Apocalypse (the Book of Revelation).

Appearing in narrative form, the Gospels and Acts contain much historical information, with the former focusing on Christ's life and works, and the latter on the origins and early development of the Church. The twenty-one New Testament epistles interpret the person and work of Christ and apply His teachings. Paul wrote at least thirteen of these, while the others were written by Peter, John, Jesus' brother James, and His half-brother Jude. The exception is the Book of Hebrews, whose writer is unknown.

The Book of Revelation, as noted, is considered a prophetic and apocalyptic book. Apocalyptic literature, according to S. W. Crawford, is "a genre of revelatory literature with a narrative framework, in which a revelation is mediated by an other-worldly being to a human recipient, disclosing a transcendent reality which is both temporal...(and which) involves another, supernatural world."[7] Apocalyptic writing includes visions, symbolism, human seers, otherworldly mediators, an emphasis on cosmic events rather than those in the earthly, human realm, and often features angels and demons.[8]

Norman Geisler helpfully summarizes the Christ-centeredness of the various sections of the New Testament as follows: "The Gospels...record the historical *manifestation* of Christ, the Acts relate the propagation of Christ, the Epistles give the *interpretation* of Him, and in Revelation is found the *consummation* of all things in Christ."[9]

Some scholars see parallel structures in the two testaments. Old Testament professor Jason DeRouchie observes that each testament begins with a narrative section, is followed by commentary on the narrative, and closes with another narrative section.[10] "The Epistles are to the Gospels what the Prophets were to the Law," writes Dr. Norman

Geisler. "The latter in each case is the structure built on the foundation of the former."[11]

Another proposed parallel is that the New Testament begins with the four Gospels, which are somewhat biographical accounts of Jesus' life, just as the first five books of the Old Testament (the Law) revolve around Moses.[12] Others note that the Old Testament books of the Law provide the fundamental revelation of the Old Testament, and the Gospels provide the fundamental revelation of the New Testament.[13] Acts is a book of history that records the experiences of the early Church, which is comparable to the Old Testament historical books. The New Testament epistles are instructive and theological, generally interpreting the Gospel message, just as the Old Testament's prophetic books interpret the books of Moses and other Old Testament scriptures. Revelation is an apocalyptic book that some compare to the Book of Daniel in the Old Testament. No New Testament book is comparable to Psalms, though psalms and hymns are sprinkled throughout New Testament writings. Nor does the New Testament have any wisdom books resembling the Old Testament books of Proverbs, Job, etc., though some believe the Book of James constitutes wisdom literature.[14]

Let's explore the four main New Testament classifications we've identified: Gospels, Acts, Epistles, and Apocalypse.

THE GOSPELS

The Gospels represent a unique genre blending history, biography, and theology. The word "gospel" is derived from the Greek "evangelion," which means "good news." The Greeks and Romans used the term in announcing news such as the accession of a new emperor.[15] Paul uses the word throughout his letters to mean the coming, life, death, and resurrection of Jesus (e.g. Romans 1:1–4, 16; 1 Cor. 15:1; 2 Cor. 2:12).[16]

Old Testament writers used the concept of good news to announce the coming of Yahweh (God) to save His people.[17] Isaiah writes, "Go on up to a high mountain, O Zion, herald of good news; lift up your voice with strength, O Jerusalem, herald of good news; lift it up, fear not; say to the cities of Judah, Behold your God!" (Isaiah 40:9). He repeats the concept twelve chapters later: "How beautiful upon the mountains are the feet of him who brings good news, who publishes peace, who brings good news of happiness, who publishes salvation, who says to Zion, 'Your God reigns'" (Isaiah 52:7). Isaiah reiterates the idea in chapters 60 and 61, the latter of which Jesus quotes when he opens a scroll to preach in Nazareth. "The Spirit of the Lord is upon me, because he has anointed me to proclaim good news to the poor," declares Jesus. "He has sent me to proclaim liberty to the captives and recovering of sight to the blind, to set at liberty those who are oppressed, to proclaim the year of the Lord's favor" (Luke 4:18).

Though the Jews had different messianic expectations, they did anticipate the Messiah's coming would be "good news," and readers of the New Testament could later see the connection between those passages in Isaiah and the Gospel of Jesus Christ. When Jesus inaugurates His public ministry in Nazareth, He proclaims that the good news has arrived and is embodied in His person. Accordingly, the early Church comes to identify the message of good news with the messenger Himself—Jesus, the promised Messiah, *is* the good news.[18] Mark underscores this idea when he begins his Gospel, "The beginning of the good news about Jesus the Messiah, the Son of God" (Mark 1:1). It followed that all four written accounts of Jesus' life and salvation message would come to be called the Gospels of Matthew, Mark, Luke, and John, respectively.[19]

Recognizing the genre of the New Testament books clarifies their messages and helps us to imagine how their initial readers received these works. Scholars, however, wrestle with pinpointing the genre or combination of genres in the Gospels. Many have compared them with various types of ancient literature, most notably the works of Plutarch, Suetonius, Philostratus, and Diogenes.[20] The main one of these was Plutarch (46–120 AD), a Greek who wrote parallel biographies of famous Romans and Greeks. In his work on Alexander the Great, Plutarch proclaims,

It being my purpose to write the lives of Alexander the king, and of Cæsar, by whom Pompey was destroyed, the multitude of their great actions affords so large a field that I were to

blame if I should not by way of apology forewarn my reader
that I have chosen rather to epitomise the most celebrated
parts of their story, than to insist at large on every particular
circumstance of it. It must be borne in mind that my design
is not to write histories, but lives. And the most glorious
exploits do not always furnish us with the clearest discoveries
of virtue or vice in men; sometimes a matter of less moment,
an expression or a jest, informs us better of their characters
and inclinations, than the most famous sieges, the greatest
armaments, or the bloodiest battles whatsoever. Therefore,
as portrait-painters are more exact in the lines and features
of the face, in which the character is seen, than in the other
parts of the body, so I must be allowed to give my more particular attention to the marks and indications of the souls of
men, and while I endeavour by these to portray their lives,
may be free to leave more weighty matters and great battles
to be treated of by others.[21]

Evidently, Plutarch intended to write biographies focusing on the
lives of great people and not as much on events, which are the province
of historical writings. Steve Walton and David Wenham observe that
scholars used to argue that the Gospels are not biographies, mainly
because they were comparing them to today's biographies, which treat
the subject's life more comprehensively from birth to death.[22] But these
ancient biographies were different, and the Gospels resemble them in
being incomplete accounts. The Gospels barely cover Jesus' early years
and, apart from His birth and a short section on events occurring when
He was twelve years old, they focus almost exclusively on the three
years of His public ministry, especially His final week. The Gospel
writers, then, described Christ's life in a literary form familiar to a wide
readership in the Mediterranean basin.[23]

But significant differences exist between the Gospels and the ancient
biographies. Walton and Wenham explain that Jesus was not merely
remembered by the early Christians—they "experienced Him as alive
and present with them by the Spirit."[24] The Gospels, they argue, "are
the church's testimony about Jesus rather than biography."[25] The Gospels

are also unique because they emphasize Jesus' last days, His death, and His resurrection, especially in Mark, in which those subjects take up half the book. While these books bear some resemblance to ancient biographies and contain vital historical facts, they are like no other literature ever written because they uniformly proclaim the "good news" from God that is manifested in the life, death, resurrection, and ascension of Jesus Christ.[26]

The Gospels are also grounded in history. If the Gospel writers didn't believe the events they recorded actually occurred, they wouldn't have written their accounts, much less risked their lives to share the good news. If they hadn't lived with Jesus and either witnessed His miracles, death, resurrection, and ascension themselves or learned about these events directly from witnesses, they wouldn't have preserved and told their story. They were adamant about reporting exactly what happened and Jesus' precise words because His actions and teachings affect our eternal destiny. As we saw in Chapter 2, the New Testament writers paid strict attention to detail in the research, assimilation, and recording of their messages, and they believed it was crucial that we trust their sincerity and historical reliability. Luke, for example, wants us to "know the certainty of the things" he is writing (Luke 1:4).

The Gospels are theological as well. They would not have been written but for the authors' inspired determination to present Jesus Christ as the good news of God's salvation. They report the climax of God's salvation history—the culmination of Scripture's narrative of redemption. Despite the theological implications of the Gospels, however, the Gospel writers' theological restraint is also noteworthy. Rarely do they explain the theological significance of the historical events they record, though John does so more than the others. They faithfully report the historical events and mostly leave the implications of the history to the epistles. This lends historical credence to the writings because had they been forgers, they would have written advocacy pieces.[27]

Finally, the Gospels include apologetic elements, especially the Book of John, as evidenced by John's assertion, "Now Jesus did many other signs in the presence of the disciples, which are not written in this book; but these are written so that you may believe that Jesus is the Christ, the Son of God, and that by believing you may have life in his name" (20:30–31).

Though scholars lack consensus on the genre of the Gospels, most agree they combine various genres. Professor William Klein maintains we should consider them portraits of Jesus' life and ministry: "They are not pure history, though they do report what actually happened. They're not pure biography, but…a good news account of Jesus' life…written to demonstrate Jesus' authority and significance for the story of God's plan to redeem lost humanity. A Gospel is, therefore, theological biography."[28] Similarly, Robert Guelich writes, "Formally, a gospel is a narrative account concerning the public life and teaching of a significant person that is composed of discreet traditional units placed in the context of Scriptures…. Materially, the genre consists of the message that God was at work in Jesus' life, death, and resurrection effecting his promises found in the Scriptures."[29]

The Gospels are a unique genre not just because they contain elements of various major genres, but also because they record a unique event—the Son of God's entrance into human history.

THE BOOK OF ACTS

Luke wrote the Book of Acts, a history of the early Church following Christ's resurrection, which is part two of his two-volume work that begins with his Gospel. He begins Acts by testifying, "In the first book, O Theophilus, I have dealt with all that Jesus began to do and teach, until the day when he was taken up, after he had given commands through the Holy Spirit to the apostles whom he had chosen" (1:1–2). He implies he will proceed to the rest of the story, which he does.[30]

Acts covers a period of transition from Judaism under the Old Covenant to the Church age under the New Covenant.[31] It shows the new Christians struggling with how Christian religious practice should overlay onto Jewish practice and what parts of the latter should remain. While Acts is considered primarily a historical book, it is not merely a history. Ben Witherington maintains it is unlike other ancient historical books, which focus on political or military history. Instead, it relates "the social and religious history of a particular group or subculture within the Roman Empire."[32] Though it is a history of the early Church, it is not a complete history of the Church's growth, but documents only those events Luke was familiar with personally or through his investigation. Spiros Zodhiates and Warren Baker note, for example, that Luke "does not record how the gospel spread to the east and south of Palestine, or why there were already believers in Damascus before Paul arrived." But he includes enough information from the lives and ministries of prominent evangelists, and especially his hero Paul,[33] to "sufficiently demonstrate the shift of the evangelical concerns of Christianity from Jews to Gentiles."[34]

Acts' partial history ends abruptly, reporting that Paul continued to preach boldly and without hindrance as he remained under house arrest for two years (28:30–31).[35] Pastor Ray Stedman contends the book is intentionally unfinished because the Holy Spirit intended it to be. Why? Because it "is still being written.... Jesus isn't finished yet. He began His ministry in His human body, as recorded in the Gospels. He continued in His body, the church, through the book of Acts. He continues His ministry today through you and me and every other believer on the planet." But it will be completed someday, and we must ask ourselves what our part will be in that great story.[36]

Acts includes biographical information on Paul and others. But as much as Luke revered Paul and his work, he was more determined to trace the progress of the Church and its message than to complete a character study of Paul or relate the full story of his missions.[37] Even in the ending chapters of the book, Luke is more concerned with Paul's continuing proclamation of "the kingdom of God and teaching about the Lord Jesus Christ" than with Paul's ultimate fate. "Acts 28," writes David Peterson, "is a significant indicator of Luke's purpose in writing, and it suggests that his interest is historical and theological rather than strictly biographical."[38]

Like the Gospels, Acts is not strictly one genre but a hybrid. It relates history not for its own sake, says William Klein, but contains a profound theological message. Jesus began His work in person, as recorded in the Gospels, and Acts records His continued work through the Holy Spirit, mainly through Paul and Peter as human agents. Whereas the Gospels can be classified as theological biographies, Acts can be seen as theological history.[39] Luke also wrote the book as an apologetic—to convince people of the truthfulness of the Gospel message that they might respond in faith.

A logical progression flows from the Gospels to Acts. The Gospels show Christ in all His humiliation and suffering on our behalf, whereas Acts presents the work of the exalted Christ, Who has defeated death and begun, through the Holy Spirit, to build His Church and spread the good news.[40] In the Gospels Jesus comes to earth and takes a human body; in Acts, the Holy Spirit takes a different kind of human body, the Church.[41] Acts is the bridge between the Gospels and the epistles. It provides the historical background for most of Paul's epistles and the context in which he wrote them.

THE EPISTLES

Letters were a common method of communication in the Greco-Roman world. They ranged from eloquent missives intended for wide readership to short, mundane, personal notes. The New Testament letters comprised both literary and personal elements. They were a particularly useful form of communication for the New Testament writers because they could deliver their message long distances while retaining their intimacy. The epistles enabled the apostles to serve as long-distance pastors when necessary,[42] and also functioned as missionary letters to encourage the Church's growth.[43]

Whereas the Gospels deal with the life of Christ, Who dwelled among men, the epistles, like Acts, speak to the following period when the Spirit of God had been poured out and Christ dwelled in the hearts of believers. The epistles repeatedly emphasize that believers and the churches are "in Christ." Theologian Louis Berkhof declares that the epistles "clearly interpret the significance of Christ's work for believers out of every nation and tribe, and point out that his experiences are paralleled in the life of every believer.... The origin of that new life, its conditions, its nature, its progressive and communal nature, and its final perfection and glory, are all clearly described in the Epistles."[44]

Of the twenty-one epistles, the first thirteen (Romans through Philemon) are called Pauline epistles because most believe Paul wrote them.

The following eight (Hebrews through Jude) are called general epistles, or sometimes Catholic Epistles,[45] as they are written to a general or unspecified audience, as distinguished from Paul's letters to specific individuals and churches.[46] These are not strictly defined categories, as several of the general epistles, such as the second and third epistles of John, are addressed to individuals.[47] Further, not all of Paul's letters were intended only for the named addressee. Some were meant for the churches as well, such as the Book of Romans, but others were more personal, such as Paul's letter to Philemon. As we saw in Chapter 2, this is true of many of the other epistles as well—though initially addressed to specific people, they were also intended for circulation among the churches (James 1:1; 1 Peter 1:1; Col. 4:16; Rev. 1:4).[48] Perhaps this is why some scholars classify the epistles as either Pauline or non-Pauline. Regardless of the writers' intended addressees, however, God intended all the epistles to be read across the world and throughout the ages.

The epistles usually follow a certain structure that begins with a salutation, with the sender addressing and greeting the recipient and giving thanks or blessing. The main body follows and covers doctrinal issues or gives ethical instructions, and the epistles usually end with a farewell, a blessing to God, or a doxology.[49]

THE BOOK OF REVELATION

The Book of Revelation is classified by itself among the New Testament books. The Greek title is Apokalypsis, translated as "disclosure," "unveiling," or "revelation," implying that it reveals information that has been hidden.[50] The entire Bible is about God's redemptive plan for mankind, and Revelation relates, in big-picture terms, how God will bring about the consummation of man's salvation from his fall described in Genesis—this explains why it is the final book in the New Testament canon.[51] The book assures us our sovereign God will fulfill all His promises, and believers in Jesus Christ will live forever with Him in the new heaven and new earth.[52] The Old Testament Book of Daniel, which includes apocalyptic features, provides detailed prophecies concerning the period from Daniel's time until Christ's first coming (His incarnation), and touches on the tribulation, Christ's Second Coming, and His earthly rule. Revelation amplifies these prophecies, providing further details of endtime events and the completion of history.[53]

Revelation is a combination of at least three literary genres—apocalyptic, prophecy, and epistle[54]—though biblical scholars usually classify it as apocalyptic. Apocalyptic writings were familiar to readers of the New Testament era. Leland Rykin describes them as "visionary works that transport us to an alternate world from one in which we live."[55] They have numerous characteristics, all of which are present in Revelation: they have a dualistic perspective, seeing the world in terms of good and evil; they are eschatological, meaning concerned with future (mostly endtimes) events; and they are presented in an ecstatic vision of a supernatural world or one that is remote from us in time.[56]

Revelation focuses on the work of the Messiah, prominently features angels and demons, and utilizes animal symbolism. It includes fantastic imagery, which reminds readers that an invisible supernatural battle has continually raged between the forces of good and evil.[57] The Apostle Paul alludes to this spiritual battle when he commands the Ephesians to "put on the whole armor of God" to prepare them to resist "the schemes of the devil" because "we do not wrestle against flesh and blood, but against the rulers, against the authorities, against the cosmic powers over this present darkness, against the spiritual forces of evil in the heavenly places" (Eph. 6:10–12). Observing that Revelation describes itself as a prophecy (1:3; 22:6–7, 10), G. K. Beale describes apocalyptic writing as an *intensification* of prophecy because "it contains a heightening and more intense clustering of literary and thematic traits found in prophecy."[58] Notably, the book uses the term "apocalypse" or "revelation" in the very first verse: "The revelation of Jesus Christ, which God gave him to show his servants the things that must soon take place" (1:1).

Revelation, written from John to the seven churches in Asia (1:4), takes the form of an epistle and concludes with a benediction of God's grace (22:21). Like many of the New Testament epistles, Revelation addresses problems that had arisen in the churches. Describing the book's genre, Beale writes, "The most preferable view is that Revelation is 'a prophecy cast in an apocalyptic mold and written down in a letter form' in order to motivate the audience to change their behavior in the light of the transcendent reality of the book's message."⁵⁹ While acknowledging this combination of genres, Ramsey Michaels emphasizes the uniqueness of each within the book. "If a letter," writes Michaels, "it is like no other early Christian letter we possess. If an apocalypse, it is like no other apocalypse. If a prophecy, it is unique among prophecies."⁶⁰

The climax of biblical revelation, the Book of Revelation describes the final chapter of world history. It is a fitting ending to the story of mankind that began with the fall, was followed by God's promise of redemption, and finishes with his eternal salvation and presence with God in fulfillment of God's promise.

"A WONDERFULLY CONSTRUCTED ARCHWAY"

Some believe the order of the New Testament books is providentially arranged. I don't know if this is true, but it makes sense. William McDonald observes that the order of the books is ideally suited for the Church—it begins with Christ's life, proceeds to the development of the Church, continues to instructions for the Church, and finally, reveals the future of the Church and the world.⁶¹

Pastor J. Sidlow Baxter compares the New Testament's structure to a literary archway. Its twenty-seven books are "God's wonderfully constructed archway into saving truth, into the true knowledge of Himself, into eternal blessedness." And it makes perfect sense that as God supernaturally inspired the writing of the books and guarded them over millennia, He would also superintend their arrangement in the canon.⁶²

The first five books—the four Gospels and Acts—provide essential historical information that is foundational to the rest of the canon. These are followed by the epistles, which break down into three groups:

1) The nine Christian Church epistles Paul writes to particular churches, which are mainly doctrinal but also instructional: Romans, 1 and 2 Corinthians, Galatians, Ephesians, Philippians, Colossians, and 1 and 2 Thessalonians.

2) The four pastoral epistles Paul addresses to individuals: 1 and 2 Timothy, Titus, and Philemon.

3) The nine Hebrew Christian epistles: Hebrews, James, 1 and 2 Peter, 1, 2, and 3 John, Jude, and Revelation, which Baxter includes as an epistle. These books are unmistakably Christian but are also "distinctively Hebrew in their primary adaptation and application." They are not addressed to Christian churches though they deal with many doctrinal issues. Hebrews is obviously intended for the Hebrew nation, as is James, which begins, "James, a servant of God and of the Lord Jesus Christ, to the twelve tribes in the Dispersion" (1:1). Peter likewise addresses his first letter to "those who are elect exiles of the Dispersion" (1 Peter 1:1). John doesn't address his first epistle, but his second and third are each addressed to Jewish individuals, and in the text he discusses certain servants of the Lord as having gone forth "taking nothing of the gentiles," which he wouldn't have said had he been writing to Gentiles.[63]

In Baxter's archway, the Gospels and Acts are the foundation, the two nine-fold groups of epistles are the side-pillars, and the four pastoral epistles bridge the pillars from above, with its high vertex epitomized by the passage, "Great indeed, we confess, is the mystery of godliness: He was manifested in the flesh, vindicated by the Spirit, seen by angels, proclaimed among the nations, believed on in the world, taken up in glory" (1 Tim. 3:16).[64]

OTHER STRUCTURAL PARALLELS

Baxter sees many other parallels within the structure—designs among *and* within the groupings. Both groups of nine epistles begin with a doctrinal treatise—Romans for one and Hebrews for the other, and they both end with Christ's return and a revelation of the "things to come"—1 and 2 Thessalonians and Revelation, respectively. Romans teaches salvation through Christ as the *only* way, while Hebrews shows salvation as the *better* way, in the sense of a superior sacrifice. The Thessalonian epistles describe Christ's return relative to the Church, and Revelation shows it in relation to Israel and the nations.[65]

Baxter admits the archway analogy is limited because the New Testament structure is dynamic—"an orderly unfolding movement."

There is more than design; there is development, or a certain "progress of doctrine," that involves a course of progressive instruction. The four Gospels, for example, are not chronologically arranged in relationship to one another, either by the dates they were written or in their contents—there is no consecutive narrative flowing from Matthew through John, and they were surely not written in the order they appear. The same is true of the epistles. Though there is no adherence to chronology, both groups of books display a "consistent sequence of revelational truth."[66] The books are optimally arranged to facilitate the communication of doctrine.

The first three Gospels—the synoptics—introduce the *visible* aspects of Christ's person and ministry, preparing us for the "crowning presentation in John, where the *inward* mystery and majesty of it is interpreted to us." Baxter argues that Matthew must be the first book because it specifically links the testaments, showing the New Testament as the fulfillment of the Old. Additionally, Matthew's narrative is adapted to the Jews, from whom Christ came. Many agree that Matthew was first in order because it was the most Jewish of the Gospels and provided the clearest link to the Old Testament.[67] Edgar Goodspeed, in his book *The Formation of the New Testament*, suggests that the Gospels are arranged in order from the most Jewish to the most Greek.[68]

Mark and Luke follow with fewer connections to Jewish life and thought than Matthew. Mark presents Christ as "commanding the present"[69] rather than emphasizing His connection with the past. Luke goes further with an "[all-embracing] outlook, and a Savior so presented as to engage the Gentile mind at large."[70] He presents Christ as "the Son of Man" and dedicates his book to a Gentile convert.

The Gospels demonstrate the common humanity that the perfect Man shares with the entirety of mankind regardless of race or ethnicity. This progressive unfolding in the Gospels, "from Jewish Matthew, through Jew-Gentile Mark, to Gentile Luke," corresponds to the expansion of the Church recorded in Acts where the Gospel is first preached to Jews, then spreads out until the message is taken to the outer reaches of the Roman Empire and to the entire Gentile world.[71] The synoptics are the perfect buildup to the more theological Gospel of John,[72] for what they point to less directly, John plainly declares: Jesus is the eternal Son of God. "He who is Israel's Messiah is Himself Jehovah. He who is the world's Savior is the world's Maker. He not only teaches truth: He *is* the truth. He imparts life because He *is* the life."[73] Kenneth O. Gangel observes, "Following on the heels of the three synoptic Gospels in the arrangement of the New Testament books, John introduced a different way of looking at the life of Jesus with greater focus on Jesus' message than the events of his earthly life."[74]

Baxter maintains that God providentially kept John alive to write his Gospel after the synoptic Gospels had been well circulated and skeptics were beginning to hatch heresies about the person and deity of Christ. It was the perfect time to put these doubts to rest—the historical facts had been well established by Matthew, Mark, and Luke, yet not too much time had passed for John, himself an eyewitness and an apostle, to make "an authoritative endorsement and interpretation" of the first three Gospel accounts. John provided eyewitness affirmation in his Gospel of what he declared in his first epistle, "That which was from the beginning, which we have heard, which we have seen with our eyes, which we have looked upon and have touched with our hands concerning the word of life—the life was made manifest, and we have seen it, and testify to it and proclaim to you the eternal life, which was with the Father and was made manifest to us—that which we have seen and heard we proclaim also to you, so that you too may have fellowship with us; and indeed our fellowship is with the Father and with his Son Jesus Christ" (1 John 1:1–3). It's as if John had held back, allowing time for the Gospel message to circulate and sink in, then vouched for those historical accounts as a fellow apostle and providentially illuminated their transcendent meaning, establishing for the Church that Jesus is the Man Who is God.

THE NEW AND OLD COVENANTS

Bible Professor Paul Benware describes the structure of the New Testament in terms of the New Covenant. The Gospels relate Christ's sinless life, authoritative teaching, and authenticating miracles, all proving He is the Messiah and the Son of God. His sacrificial death on the cross inaugurated God's New Covenant, which provides a means of salvation for sinners. Acts describes the activities of the early Church in spreading the news of the New Covenant. The epistles provide Christians instructions on how to live as a New Covenant people, and Revelation "tells of the final, glorious application of the New Covenant," assuring us that God is sovereign and wholly fulfills His promises.[75]

What is the New Covenant? In *The Emmaus Code* I detailed God's major covenants, as they provide the framework for God's saving activities on behalf of mankind. Since we must grasp the Old Covenant to properly understand the New Covenant, it's worthwhile here to briefly review the Old Covenant.

God enters into a covenant with Israel when He gives His divine Law to Moses on Mount Sinai, promising to make Israel His treasured possession out of all nations, a kingdom of priests, and a holy nation, provided His people obey Him fully and keep His covenant (Exodus 19:4–6).[76] We refer to this as the "Old Covenant," also known as the "Mosaic Covenant" or "Sinaitic Covenant."[77] God lays down for Israel not just the Ten Commandments but moral, civil, and ceremonial laws. Rabbis identify a total of 613 specific laws in Moses' writings.[78] The Law, however, cannot bring salvation—as Pastor John MacArthur notes about the Old Covenant, "There's nothing in it that can save."[79] According to Paul, "If a law had been given that could give life, then righteousness would indeed be by the law" (Gal. 3:21), and Christ would have died in vain. But that is impossible. Righteousness can only come by faith (Gal. 2:21; Heb. 7:11); salvation is through faith alone (Eph. 2:8–9).

Blood sacrifice is a principal element of the Mosaic Law (Lev. 17:11). Sacrifices covered the people's sins and restored their fellowship with God,[80] but they didn't permanently remove sins, which is why they had to be repeated continually. The writer of Hebrews says, "For since the law has but a shadow of the good things to come instead of the true form of these realities, it can never, by the same sacrifices that are continually offered every year, make perfect those who draw near. Otherwise, would they not have ceased to be offered, since the worshipers, having once been cleansed, would no longer have any consciousness of sins? But these sacrifices are a reminder of sins every year. For it is impossible for the blood of bulls and goats to take away sins" (Heb. 10:1–4). In other words, the Old Testament sacrifices prefigure Christ's once-and-for-all perfect sacrifice. "Christ," writes Vern Poythress, "is the final offering to which all the animal sacrifices look forward."[81] As John the Baptist proclaimed, "Behold, the Lamb of God, who takes away the sin of the world!" (John 1:29). All the Old Testament sacrifices were imperfect symbols pointing to the true and perfect Lamb, Jesus Christ (Heb. 10:11–14).

The Old Covenant was never intended to be permanent, but was to last until the coming of the Messiah, at which time the New Covenant would replace it (Gal. 3:19).[82] God's prophets promised the coming of this New Covenant.[83] Jeremiah is first to announce it, declaring, "Behold, the days are coming, declares the Lord, when I will make a new covenant with the house of Israel and the house of Judah, not like the covenant I made with their fathers on the day when I took them by the hand to bring them out of the land of Egypt.... I will put my law within them, and I will write it on their hearts.... I will forgive their iniquity, and I will remember their sin no more" (Jer. 31:31–34). Ezekiel reiterates and expands the New Covenant, affirming, "I will sprinkle clean water on you, and you shall be clean from all your uncleannesses, and from all your idols. I will cleanse you. And I will give you a new heart, and a new spirit I will put within you" (Ezek. 36:25–26).

Paul explains, "The law was our guardian until Christ came, in order that we might be justified by faith" (Gal. 3:24). The blood of Christ alone has the power to permanently remove sin. "For by a single offering," declares the writer of Hebrews, "he has perfected for all time those who are being sanctified" (Heb. 10:14). Christ "is the mediator of a new covenant, so that those who are called may receive the promised eternal inheritance, since a death has occurred that redeems them from the transgressions committed under the first covenant" (Heb. 9:15). Jesus confirms that He fully satisfied the Law (Matt. 5:17–18).

The New Covenant is markedly different from the Old Covenant. It does not depend on Israel's obedience—rather, it is unconditional. With this covenant, God replaces the Old Covenant and its system of sacrifices with the one perfect and permanent sacrifice, the blood of Jesus Christ. The New Covenant promises full justification and forgiveness for believers, that their hearts will be regenerated, and that the Holy Spirit will indwell them. It guarantees that God will write the Law on the hearts of believers of Jesus Christ and give them immediate access to God's presence. Through faith in Christ, believers experience the New Covenant promise that they will receive eternal life in Him.

The Old Covenant must be understood in light of God's Old Testament covenants that preceded it, which make clear that mankind's salvation was never through his works, but through God's grace alone. No sooner than God pronounces punishment upon mankind for Adam and Eve's sin—man's physical and spiritual death (Gen. 3:14–19)—He promises a Redeemer who will bring salvation to mankind, a promise theologians call "the Adamic Covenant." God tells the Serpent (representing Satan), "I will put enmity between you and the woman, and between your offspring and hers; he will crush your head, and you will strike his heel" (Gen. 3:15, NIV).

The New Testament illuminates this scripture. Christ is the offspring, or seed, of the woman because He is the only person ever born to a woman alone (through the Holy Spirit), and He will crush Satan's head (kill him), while Satan will merely strike His heel—hardly a fatal blow. Paul confirms this in identifying Christ as the offspring of the woman. "But when the fullness of time had come," writes Paul, "God sent forth his Son, born of a woman, born under the law, so that we might receive adoption as sons" (Gal. 4:4). Yes, the devil inflicts suffering on Christ, but only because Christ allows it, and more important, by this very act of suffering, Christ destroys Satan, sin, and death. Through the temptations of Satan, sin enters the world, and God imposes His death penalty on man, but He immediately promises salvation through the sacrificial death of His Son Jesus Christ for all who believe in Him.

In his first epistle, John proclaims, "The reason the Son of God appeared was to destroy the works of the devil" (1 John 3:8). Theologians refer to God's promise of mankind's redemption in Genesis 3:15 as the protoevangel, the first announcement of the Gospel. M. S. Mills writes, "The protoevangel (3:15) is of the utmost importance (reminding us of God's eternal purpose of salvation through the death of Jesus Christ), manifest the very day that sin first infected the human race. Genesis clearly records the beginnings of God's redemptive process."[84]

God's eternal grace is seen in His first promise of salvation in the face of man's betrayal. It is this type of unmerited grace that prompts the prophet Micah to marvel, "Who is a God like you, pardoning iniquity and passing over transgression for the remnant of his inheritance? He does not retain his anger forever, because he delights in his steadfast love" (Micah 7:18).[85]

THE ABRAHAMIC COVENANT

Long before God initiates the Old Covenant with Moses, He calls Abram (later known as Abraham) out of his country and commands him to go to the land that God would show him. He promises to make his name great, make a nation out of him, and to bless those who bless him and curse those who dishonor him. God declares, "And in you all the families of the earth shall be blessed" (Gen. 12:1–3). This is a pivotal moment in salvation history—the call of Abraham—in which God initiates the redemptive work He promises in Genesis 3:15 of destroying Satan through the offspring of the woman (Jesus Christ).[86] In subsequent passages in Genesis (12:1–4; 13:14–17; 15:1–7; 17:1–8; 22:17–18), God formalizes the Abrahamic Covenant, reiterating the promises He makes in 12:1–3 and making additional ones—that He will give Abraham's nation the land as an everlasting possession and that His blessings to all nations through Abraham will be accomplished through Abraham's descendants.

God's promise to Abraham to bless all mankind through him means He will send His Son, the Messiah, to save all those who believe in Him. Thus God's promise in Genesis 3:15, coupled with His unconditional, eternal promises that constitute the Abrahamic Covenant, clarify for all time that God is a God of grace Who provides a means of salvation for undeserving man and that this salvation will be mediated by His Son. Just as the Abrahamic Covenant expands on the Adamic Covenant, later covenants develop and expand on the promises God makes to Abraham—His land promise, His promise of blessing, and His promise that He'll accomplish these blessings through Abraham's descendants.

Nothing is inconsistent between the Old Covenant and the Abrahamic Covenant. It's not as if God was going back and forth between grace and works salvation. It was never about works. The Old Covenant, which came long after the Abrahamic Covenant, neither contradicted it nor replaced it. God's promise of salvation, which preceded the Old Covenant, was based on His grace and not man's works. The Old Covenant did not change that—it *complemented* God's unconditional and eternal promise of salvation to mankind. The Old Covenant builds on the foundation of the Abrahamic Covenant in providing laws and guidelines to the Israelites on how to live their lives to serve as the nation of priests and mediators for the ultimate benefit of all nations. The Old Covenant was, says Paul Williamson, "the means by which the goal of the promise would be advanced in and through Abraham's national descendants (Gen. 12:2; cf. 18:18–19)."[87] Craig Blaising and Darrell Bock concur that the Old Covenant "set up an arrangement by which God would relate to the descendants of the patriarchs as a nation, distinguishing them from other nations on earth.... It provided the means for blessing an entire nation and, through them, all peoples on earth."[88]

The Abrahamic Covenant, then, contains the seeds of God's foundational promise that constitutes a unifying thread throughout the Bible—a promise of salvation grounded in God's grace that will eventually be consummated in the New Covenant. The New Covenant fulfills for all nations the spiritual promises made to Abraham and his descendants.[89] The New Covenant is an enlargement of the Abrahamic Covenant and specifically of God's promise to bless all mankind through Abraham.[90] That blessing would be the salvation of all believers in Jesus Christ. God's grace through the Adamic Covenant and the Abrahamic Covenant *preceded* the Law God gave Israel pursuant to the Old Covenant, continued *uninterrupted* during that period, was reinforced and expanded with the New Covenant, and *remains* in full force now and forever.

GOD'S PROMISE-PLAN AND PROMISE-DOCTRINE

As I wrote in *The Emmaus Code*, Walter Kaiser argues that God makes many promises and covenants with Israel, but most of these are part of the larger promise to redeem mankind through a coming

Messiah, which he calls God's promise-plan.[91] God makes the Old Covenant with Israel alone, but its ultimate purpose is to facilitate the Abrahamic Covenant, which is to benefit all nations. He gives the Law to Israel and makes it a kingdom of priests and a holy nation to serve as mediator between God and all the people of the earth.[92] Through Israel, God brings His promise of salvation to all mankind.

In his classic *The Prophets and the Promise*, American theologian Willis Judson Beecher makes essentially the same argument, but he calls it the promise-doctrine.[93] Beecher notes that Christianity's distinguishing feature from other religions is its doctrine of the Messiah. Christians are taught that the Old Testament prophets made many predictions of a coming "Deliverer," and that these were fulfilled in Jesus' life and mission, which proves the prophets were divinely inspired and Jesus' mission was divine.

Beecher notes that despite the diversity of God's promises, they all converge in Christ's fulfillment, as shown in the New Testament. Moreover, the prophecies themselves are all offshoots of a single, foundational promise, which Beecher describes as "one prediction, repeated and unfolded through successive centuries, with many specifications, and in many forms; always the same in essential character, no matter how it may vary in its outward presentation or in the illustrations through which it is presented."[94]

Beecher and Kaiser agree, then, that the Bible emphasizes one promise rather than many predictions. "This is the prevailing note in both Testaments," declares Beecher, "a multitude of specifications unfolding a single promise, the promise serving as a central religious doctrine." He continues,

> This biblical generalization of the matter may be formulated as: God gave a promise to Abraham, and through him to mankind; a promise eternally fulfilled and fulfilling in the history of Israel; and chiefly fulfilled in Jesus Christ, he being that which is principal in the history of Israel.
>
> The most prominent thing in the New Testament is its proclamation of the kingdom and its anointed king. But it is on the basis of the divine promise that its preachers proclaim the kingdom, and when they appeal to the Old Testament in

proof of Christian doctrine, they make the promise more prominent than the kingdom itself.[95]

As evidence that there is one central promise, Beecher cites Paul's defense to Agrippa during his trial for blasphemy and inciting riots: "And now I stand here on trial because of my hope in the promise made by God to our fathers, to which our twelve tribes hope to attain, as they earnestly worship night and day. And for this hope I am accused by Jews, O king!" (Acts 26:6–7). Beecher argues that Paul, facing such serious consequences, would have scrupulously chosen his words. Paul's precise words convey that he is basing his messianic hope on a single promise— and not just on any promise. Beecher explains:

> He founds his appeal to Agrippa not on a good many scattered predictions, but on the one promise; and he expects Agrippa to understand him. Speaking of his hope as a Christian, he describes it as "the hope of the promise made of God unto our fathers", and he speaks of the twelvetribe Jewish nation as hoping to attain to this promise. The thing he is speaking of he calls, not prediction, but promise; not promises, but promise; not a promise but the promise. The word he uses is singular and definite. The whole essential messianic truth, as he knows it, he sums up on this one formula, "the promise made of God unto our fathers."[96]

Beecher maintains that Paul not only speaks of the singular promise, but that some forty New Testament passages refer to the one promise. In addition, these passages "are the central, conspicuous passages of the New Testament. They affirm that all revelation concerning the Messiah is the unfolding of the one promise. Into this mold all the New Testament teaching on the subject may readily be cast."[97]

Beecher states that the New Testament writers uniformly identify the one promise that sustains the hope of Christians: God's promise to Abraham. "They identify it for us as the promise that was made to Abraham when God called him," argues Beecher, "the promise that in him all the nations of the earth should be blessed."[98]

The Book of Hebrews substantiates the point: "For when God made a promise to Abraham, since he had no one greater by whom to swear, he swore by himself, saying 'Surely I will bless you and multiply you.' And thus Abraham, having patiently waited, obtained the promise.... So when God desired to show more convincingly to the heirs of the promise the unchangeable character of his purpose, he guaranteed it with an oath...so that...we who have fled for refuge might have strong encouragement to hold fast to the hope set before us" (6:13–15, 17–18). A few chapters later, the writer of Hebrews states that Isaac and Jacob, along with Abraham, are heirs of the same promise (11:9).

Likewise, Paul writes, "For the promise to Abraham and his offspring that he would be heir of the world did not come through the law but through the righteousness of faith. For if it is the adherents of the law who are to be the heirs, faith is null and the promise is void" (Romans 4:13–14). A few verses later Paul adds about Abraham, "No unbelief made him waver concerning the promise of God, but he grew strong in his faith as he gave glory to God, fully convinced that God was able to do what he had promised" (4:20–21).

Beecher acknowledges that New Testament writers sometimes use the plural "promises." But it is almost always accompanied by the definite article "the," as in "the promises"—Romans 9:4 and 15:8–9 are examples. In these instances and others, the plural is only used to describe a specific group of promises—the group of promises made to Abraham. Beecher contends, "The one promise is capable of being thought of as divided into specifications, and when so thought of, the plural number is used."[99]

Beecher observes that the New Testament writers treat this one promise with its subparts, or specifications, as the central theme of the entire Old Testament. They trace it from Abraham and his descendants through King David and beyond, "and regard it as having been continually fulfilled, but likewise as always moving forward to larger fulfillment." We can see this in Stephen's speech defending himself in the Book of Acts (7:1–60). Finally, Beecher notes that the New Testament writers adopt Old Testament terminology in their writing, especially when expounding on the promise.[100]

THE PROMISE AND THE UNITY OF THE BIBLE

To summarize Beecher's argument, which is affirming for me: The Old Testament contains many messianic prophecies, but they are all subordinate to a single promise—that God would send His Son to redeem mankind—and that promise was first made to Abraham when God promised to bless him, make his name great, and bless all nations through him. The New Testament writers regard this one promise, with all its specifications, as the central theme of the Old Testament. They show this, among other ways, by adopting the terminology of the Old Testament writers. Even when they refer to "promises" in the plural, they are referring to a group of promises that together constitute one central promise.

I believe Beecher is emphasizing that there is one central promise, demonstrating the providential unity of the Bible from beginning to end. God's revelation, from Genesis to Revelation, is grounded in His promise—His guarantee to redeem mankind. Even if the various prophecies and promises He spoke through His prophets concerned many different subjects and weren't fully understood by those who first heard them, or sometimes even by the prophets themselves, we can see with the hindsight of the New Testament writings that they were all integrally tied together.

Almost all His promises are connected to or in service to God's central promise to redeem mankind through His Son, and this promise was first made to Abraham, the father of the nation God established to be His holy nation and kingdom of priests. The Israelites would be the sacred guardians and mediators of this redemptive message throughout history until "the fullness of time had arrived" when God's Son, the Messiah, would come and fulfill the promise. God reiterated, reinforced, and expanded the promise to the Jewish people throughout history, and the unfolding of the promise was delivered by God's prophets and memorialized in His Old Testament revelation, which was sovereignly written and preserved for all mankind.

Not only was this single promise *made* to Abraham and then to his successive heirs, it was also *fulfilled* in his heirs—in King David and ultimately in Christ. Jesus was a direct descendant of Abraham, Isaac, and Jacob, and was heir to David's throne—the Son of God who became a human being to die and be resurrected to conquer sin and death and offer life to all who believe in Him. He will come in glory in His Second Coming to consummate God's triumphant kingdom on earth.

Whether you prefer Kaiser's terminology ("God's promise-plan") or Beecher's (the "promise-doctrine"), it's clear that these two intellectual giants of their respective eras came to the same conclusion—that one central promise courses through the entire Bible. It is made, repeated, and expanded by God's many prophets in the Old Testament, and fulfilled by Jesus Christ as recorded in the New Testament. God knew before He created us that we would fall into sin and need a savior, and He planned then to send His only Son to provide a means of salvation for mankind. He first announced His plan, in shadowy form, at the same time He administered judgment on mankind for His sin, formalized it in His covenantal promise to Abraham, repeated and expanded it through His Old Testament prophets, and fulfilled it in His Son, as the New Testament writers show.

It is enormously comforting that the singular promise to which we've referred in this chapter doesn't apply only to God's chosen nation, but to all nations and to all people, including you and me. The Gospel is more than good news in the abstract. It is personal, as it applies to each of us, individually. But we must act on it. It can and will change your life, if you place your trust in Jesus Christ. It is "the power of God for salvation to everyone who believes" both Jew and Gentile (Romans 1:16). If you haven't done so before, I urge you to humble yourself with the innocence of a child (Matt. 18:3–4), place your saving faith in Jesus Christ and begin an everlasting relationship with Him.

Whereas in this chapter we looked at the New Testament as a whole, in the next we will provide an overview of the Gospels specifically before turning, in the remaining chapters, to an in-depth review and analysis of the Gospels themselves.

CHAPTER 4

THE GOSPELS
FOUR PERSPECTIVES, ONE MESSAGE

That God should be kindly disposed to a world that hates him so as to bring the gospel of good news to them all is gracious, and that he should go further and actually apply that gospel in such a way as to rescue men and transform them is marvellous.

—E. HULSE[1]

HARMONIZING THE GOSPELS?

J. Sidlow Baxter cautions against efforts to combine the four Gospels into one cohesive narrative. "It has been argued that thus to combine them would preserve us all the matter, yet provide one short memoir, and present it in strict order," says Baxter. "All such attempts, however, while they are valuable in further demonstrating the consistency of the four accounts, fail to produce the perfect '*one*.'"[2] Indeed, attempts to consolidate the Gospels into one unit destroy the features and emphases the Holy Spirit provided, through the human authors, in the four accounts. They were never intended to be perfect chronological accounts, and it's not feasible to organize them that way. Similarly, Rev. E. A. Thompson writes,

A harmony of the Gospels in strict chronological order is impracticable. We cannot possibly work it out, at least with anything like scientific certainty; for this plain and obvious reason... the evangelists do not write chronologically: each of them has his own distinct plan and system of arrangement; and this is so independent of chronological order that if we attempt to put them together in such an order we find ourselves at once entangled in inextricable difficulties, and expose ourselves to the caustic rebuke of a sagacious citizen respecting an old minister of the High Church of Edinburgh, who was engaged for many years in constructing a Harmony of the kind: "He is a minister...who spends his time and strength in trying to make four men agree [who] never quarreled."[3]

I agree. Nevertheless, beginning in the next chapter I present a narrative of the four Gospels in roughly chronological order, though without attempting to reconcile perfectly any differences among the accounts. My purpose is not to harmonize these unique divinely inspired works or to undertake the presumptuous task of improving on them. My foremost goal, as with all my Christian-themed books, is to stimulate people to read the Bible itself. After becoming a believer I discovered that good books about the Bible make it less intimidating and easier to understand. They inspire me to read it more, not less. I hope this book will do the same for you.

The Rev. George Whitefield, a leading evangelist in Britain and the American colonies during the Great Awakening, whose spellbinding sermons mesmerized thousands at a time including Benjamin Franklin,[4] stressed the immeasurable importance of Scripture reading. He notes that Jesus, though He is the eternal God, "made the scriptures his constant rule and guide" during his incarnation. In each of his encounters with Satan, He responds with Scripture. "But how few," asks Whitefield, "copy after the example of Christ? How many are there who do not regard the word of God at all, but throw the sacred oracles aside, as an antiquated book, fit only for illiterate men? Such do greatly err, not knowing what the scriptures are, or for what they are designed."[5]

Whitefield says it is every person's duty to read the Bible and always with Christ in view. Because of our fallen condition, we need Christ for our salvation. If we "search the scriptures as we ought," we'll discover that their purpose is to point us to Christ. Moreover, Whitefield's explanation for people's skepticism about "divine revelation" rings true. He writes,

> I appeal to the experience of the most learned disputer against divine revelation, whether he does not find in himself, that he is naturally proud, angry, revengeful, and full of other passions contrary to the purity, holiness, and long-suffering of God. And is this not a demonstration that some way or other he is fallen from God? And I appeal also, whether at the same time that he finds these hurtful lusts in his heart, he does not strive to seem amiable, courteous, kind and affable; and is not this a manifest proof, that he is [aware] he is miserable, and wants, he knows not how, to be redeemed or delivered from it?
>
> . . . What does God in his written word do more or less, than show thee, O man, how thou art fallen into that blindness, darkness, and misery, of which thou feelest and complainest? And, at the same time he points out the way to what thou desirest, even how thou mayest be redeemed out of it by believing in, and copying after the Son of his love.
>
> . . . [God gave us the Bible] for no other end, but to show us our misery, and our happiness; our fall and recovery; or, in one word, after what manner we died in Adam, and how in Christ we may again be made alive. Hence then arises the necessity of searching the scriptures: for since they are nothing else but the grand charter of our salvation, the revelation of a covenant made by God with men in Christ, and a light to guide us into the way of peace; it follows, that all are obliged to read and search them, because all are equally fallen from God, all equally stand in need of being informed how they must be restored to, and again united with him.

... Have Christ, then, always in view when you are reading the word of God, and this, like the star in the east, will
guide you to the Messiah, will serve as a key to every thing
that is obscure, and unlock to you the wisdom and riches of
all the mysteries of the kingdom of God.[6]

NEW TESTAMENT CHRONOLOGY

As I was poring over the four Gospels to organize a narrative timeline for this book, I became immersed in the glory of the writings. Using
numerous timelines and Gospel harmonies as checklists, I read and
reread every sentence of all four Gospels, along with scores of commen-
taries and other books that illuminate their message. While I understood
that a perfect chronological account was not possible, I wanted to present a comprehensive narrative of all the events recorded in the Gospels.

As I researched, I discovered that scholars differ on the chronological order of some of the events. Early on this troubled me, but as I got
deeper into the material I realized that chronological exactitude is far
less important than covering the events themselves, capturing the actions
and words of Christ, the disciples, and others, and sharing insightful
commentary to facilitate readers' understanding. I hope this approach
will help give new Gospel readers a jump-start on the material while
providing deeper understanding to more advanced students. But most
of all, I want to encourage readers to read the Gospels for themselves
from beginning to end—again and again. No other books compare to
the Gospels because all other books—including this one—can only help
us to learn *about* Jesus. The Gospels help us to *know* Him.

I want to stress this point before moving forward. When I say I
became immersed in the glory of the writings, I mean it literally. The
entire Bible is the living, breathing Word of God, and it can't help but
impact us like no other writing, for it comes directly from God. The
Gospels are particularly moving as they give us the words and actions
of Christ Himself. Carl F. H. Henry beautifully articulates the point.
"Divine revelation palpitates with human surprise," writes Henry. "Like
a fiery bolt of lightning that unexpectedly zooms toward us and scores

a direct hit, like an earthquake that suddenly shakes and engulfs us, it somersaults our private thoughts to abrupt awareness of ultimate destiny.... It drives us to ponder whether the Other World has finally pinned us to the ground for a life-and-death response. Even once-for-all revelation that has occurred in another time and place fills us with awe and wonder through its ongoing significance and bears the character almost of a fresh miracle."[7]

Before beginning the narrative section in the next chapter, I want to provide a short introduction to the Gospels collectively, and then individually, to examine the different emphases of each of the four writers.

"CONTRADICTIONS" IN THE GOSPELS

First, a word on the alleged inconsistencies in the Gospel accounts. Just as the entire Bible's unity is shown through its diversity, the same is true of the four Gospels. Each writer offers a different perspective on the life of Jesus Christ. Admittedly, the Gospels sometimes treat the same subject matter differently, as should be expected from different witnesses reporting on the same events. But these variations are not contradictions.[8] In fact, they add weight to the authenticity of the writings, since if the writers aimed to produce fully synchronized narratives they could have colluded to vet any discrepancies. "It's clear," write Norman Geisler and Frank Turek, "that the New Testament writers didn't get together to smooth out their testimonies. This means they certainly were not trying to pass off a lie as the truth. For if they were making up the New Testament story, they would have gotten together to make sure they were consistent in every detail. Such harmonization clearly didn't happen, and this confirms the genuine eyewitness nature of the New Testament and the independence of each writer."[9]

Some critics try to undermine the Gospels' authenticity by citing "apparently contradictory" accounts, but Geisler and Turek refute these attempts. Matthew, for example, mentions one angel at Jesus' tomb while John mentions two. This is not a contradiction, however; Matthew doesn't explicitly say there is only one angel there. Sometimes two reporters relating the same event emphasize different details, and this is no different. Perhaps Matthew includes only the angel who spoke (Matt. 28:5), while John relates the number of angels Mary saw (John 20:12). Such differences are common among eyewitnesses.[10] The accounts are complementary, as are the accounts of Jesus' resurrection appearances, in which each of the writers provides different details but all agree that Jesus rose from the dead. Homicide detective J. Warner Wallace observes that the Gospels reflect a fairly typical collection of accounts provided by multiple eyewitnesses to an event:

> If it was God's desire to provide us with an accurate and reliable account of the life of Jesus, an account we could trust and recognize as consistent with other forms of eyewitness testimony, God surely accomplished it with the four gospel accounts. Yes, the accounts are *messy*. They are filled with idiosyncrasies and personal perspectives along with common retellings of familiar stories. There are places where critics can argue that there appear to be contradictions, and there are places where each account focuses on something important to the author, while ignoring details of importance to other writers. But would we expect anything less from true, reliable eyewitness accounts? I certainly would not, based on what I've seen over the years.[11]

Another way to approach this question is to consider the works of Plutarch, who wrote around the same time as the Gospel writers, used the same language (Greek), and provided much of the information we have about the classical world. Of Plutarch's fifty surviving biographies, nine of them involve subjects who lived at the same time, knew one another, and participated in the same events. In his books, Plutarch thus tells the same stories multiple times. Dr. Michael Licona identifies thirty-six stories that appear in Plutarch's *Lives* two or more times. Thirty of these contain differences, and the same kind of differences appear repeatedly, forming a pattern suggesting they are deliberate compositional devices—the same type of devices Plutarch's contemporary historians were using. Licona notes that we find the same stories told in the Gospels multiple times in different ways, and that we might likewise account for these differences as compositional devices rather than contradictions.[12]

The fourfold Gospel accounts troubled some in the Church's early days. Marcion (75–155 AD) advocated that the Church accept only one Gospel, while Tatian (120–190 AD), in his *Diatessaron*, written in the latter part of the second century,[13] urged that the four Gospels be combined into one harmonious account to eliminate all discrepancies.[14] The Church rejected those heretical efforts and retained all four. In his *Against Heresies*, Bishop Irenaeus of Lyons (140–202 AD), as noted earlier, writes, "It is not possible that the Gospels can be either more or fewer in number than they are. For, since there are four zones of the world in which we live, and four principal winds, while the Church is scattered throughout all the world, and the 'pillar and ground' of the Church is the Gospel and the spirit of life; it is fitting that she should have four pillars, breathing out immortality on every side, and vivifying men afresh. From which fact, it is evident that the Word, the Artificer of all, He that sitteth upon the cherubim, and contains all things, He who was manifested to men, has given us the Gospel under four aspects, but bound together by one Spirit."[15]

Bible scholars have long observed that each Gospel emphasizes particular aspects of Jesus, His life, and His work. Matthew presents Jesus primarily as the King, Mark as the Suffering Servant, Luke as a human being, and John as God. When first hearing this years ago, I thought these were artificial classifications developed by well-meaning but over-eager believers with creative imaginations. After studying the writings more, I changed my mind.

These four aspects of Christ are foreshadowed in the Old Testament. The prophets Isaiah, Jeremiah, and Zechariah, among others, describe Christ (the Messiah) as the coming King of Israel. This led to the Jews' expectation, as described earlier, that the Messiah would be an earthly king who would conquer their oppressors, contributing to their rejection of Jesus as the Messiah when He took on the entirely different mission of dying for our sins. The Old Testament, however, also foretold a suffering servant in Isaiah 53, the Genesis account of Joseph, and elsewhere. Other Old Testament prophecies alternatively portray the Messiah as a man or as God.[16]

Ray Stedman insists that all the Old Testament prophecies and pictures of Jesus can be placed under the four Gospel depictions of Christ: king, servant, human being, and God. In four places in the Old Testament the word "behold" appears in connection with these four pictures. The use of this word is significant because it's intended to direct the reader's attention to the connected passage in a striking manner.[17] "Behold" calls attention to the new and unexpected, often to rivet biblical attention upon God's awesome intervention.[18]

1. Zechariah writes, "Rejoice greatly, O daughter of Zion! Shout aloud, O daughter of Jerusalem! Behold, your *king* is coming to you; righteous and having salvation is he, humble and mounted on a donkey, on a colt, the foal of a donkey" (Zech. 9:9). Jesus fulfills this prophecy in His triumphal entry into Jerusalem (Matt. 21:7–11; Mark 11:7–10; Luke 19:35–40; John 12:12–19).

2. Isaiah writes, "Behold my *servant*, whom I uphold, my chosen, in whom my soul delights; I have put my Spirit upon him; he will bring forth justice to the nations" (Isaiah 42:1).

3. Zechariah writes, "And say to him, 'Thus says the Lord of hosts, "Behold, the *man* whose name is the Branch: for he shall branch out from his place, and he shall build the temple of the Lord"'" (Zech. 6:12).

4. Isaiah writes, "Go on up to a high mountain, O Zion, herald of good news; lift up your voice with strength, O Jerusalem, herald of good news; lift it up, fear not; say to the cities of Judah, 'Behold your *God*'" (Isaiah 40:9).[19]

These four depictions are not a fanciful construct of zealous Bible students; they have been recognized almost from the beginning. Before the third century, an identification was made between the Gospel accounts and the four living creatures of Revelation 4:7,[20] which was largely based on the prophet Ezekiel's vision of a four-faced cherubim.[21] According to Ezekiel, from the midst of a stormy wind out of the north, came the likeness of four living creatures. And this was their appearance: they had a human likeness, but each had four faces, and each of them had four wings. Their legs were straight, and the soles of their feet were like the sole of a calf's foot. And they sparkled like burnished bronze. Under their wings on their four sides they had human hands. And the four had their faces and their wings thus: their wings touched one another. Each one of them went straight forward, without turning as they went. As for the likeness of their faces, each had a human face. The four had the face of a lion on the right side, the four had the face of an ox on the left side, and the four had the face of an eagle (Ezek. 1:5–10).

Similarly, in Revelation John describes four living creatures as "full of eyes, in front and behind: the first living creature like a lion, the second living creature like an ox, the third living creature with the face of a man, and the fourth living creature like an eagle in flight" (4:6–7).

Although writers differed as to which Gospel should be identified with each living creature, the Church fathers and popular artists saw a connection.[22] J. Sidlow Baxter's interpretation rings true: "In Matthew," he writes, "we see the Messiah-King (the lion). In Mark we see Jehovah's Servant (the ox). In Luke we see the Son of Man (the man). In John we see the Son of God (the eagle)." Baxter explains that lions frequently symbolize kings; the ox represents lowly service; the man illustrates Christ's humanity; and the eagle is the "greatest of all creatures in the natural heavens, solitary, transcendent, mysterious."[23]

Ray Stedman observes that Matthew includes abundant evidence of Christ's kingship. The book begins with His genealogy, tracing His royal line through King David back to Abraham. In Matthew, Christ speaks authoritatively in forms such as, "Moses said this to you, but I say this." He frequently passes judgment on the Pharisees and scribes as hypocrites and repeatedly employs the phrase "the kingdom of heaven," as we'll see in later chapters. Moreover, Matthew depicts Christ being born as King of the Jews and crucified as "King of the Jews." English Bible scholar Arthur Pink thinks it's no coincidence that Matthew is the only Gospel writer who presents Christ in an *official* relationship—as the Messiah and King of Israel—while "Matthew himself was the only one of the four who filled an official position [tax collector]."[24]

Depicting Jesus as a servant, Mark provides no genealogy for Christ. This should be expected, as no one traces the lineage of a servant. While Matthew and Luke contain many parables, Mark has only four, each relating to servanthood. In Mark, Jesus isn't called "Lord" until after His resurrection.

Luke shows in Christ the perfection of manhood—"the glory, beauty, strength, and dignity of His humanity." He includes a genealogy of Christ, tracing the line back to Adam, the first human being. Christ is often seen in prayer in Luke's Gospel, as "prayer is a picture of humanity's proper relationship to God—total dependence upon the sovereign, omnipotent God."[25] Luke poignantly illustrates Christ's human sympathy, as when He weeps over the city of Jerusalem.

John, from the first verse, presents Christ as God. Stedman notes that John includes a different kind of genealogy: "In the beginning was the Word, and the Word was with God, and the Word was God" (John 1:1). Just two beings are mentioned—the Father and the Son. In John's Gospel, Christ makes seven "I am" declarations, which echo God's assertion of deity to Moses from the burning bush: "I am who I am" (Exodus 3:14).[26]

The four Gospels fittingly emphasize different aspects of Christ, as they are written primarily for different audiences: Matthew writes mostly to the Jews, Mark to those living in and around the city of Rome, Luke to the Gentiles, and John to the Church and potential believers.[27] I should note again that while the Gospel writers were addressing certain audiences primarily, God certainly intended their writings to be universally read.

THE SYNOPTIC GOSPELS

Despite their varying emphases, Matthew, Mark, and Luke are called the synoptic Gospels, or synoptics, because overall they present a similar approach to the life of Christ and provide comparable pictures of Jesus' ministry and teaching.[28] The term "synoptic" comes from the Greek word "synopsis," which means "seeing together" or "viewing together."[29] It suggests seeing something from the same vantage point. These three accounts contain much common material, while John includes some of it but presents it from a different viewpoint and adds a significant amount of original material. Professor Darrell Bock argues that the synoptics tell the story from an "earth up" perspective—as the story unfolds, it dawns on the people who Jesus is. John, however, beginning with the first verse, emphasizes a "heaven-down" approach, "telling you right at the start that Jesus is God who became incarnate."[30]

THE SYNOPTIC PROBLEM

Scholars refer to "the synoptic problem," which questions how these three accounts contain such strikingly similar material. Did they borrow from each other or did they rely on other unidentified sources? Researchers on the synoptic problem examine these similarities, study the Gospels' composition, and devise theories to explain the literary interrelationship between them. The majority view among scholars is the Markan Hypothesis, which holds that Mark was a source for Matthew and Luke.[31] Matthew and Luke, however, contain similar material not found in Mark, so the Markan view speculates that a hypothetical document called "Q" was also a common source for Matthew and Luke.[32] Another theory, the Griesbach Hypothesis, posits that Matthew was written first and was followed by Luke, which used material from Matthew. Mark was written third, according to this view, and borrowed from both Matthew and Luke.[33]

While the similarities and differences among the Gospel accounts and speculation about their sources fascinate some, such questions have never troubled me. As discussed earlier, since the Gospels are based on eyewitness observations, we should expect the types of variations that exist among the different accounts unless there was conspiratorial collaboration among the writers. It strikes me as presumptuous to assert with any degree of confidence that certain writers borrowed from others. They presumably had access to the same or similar information, and we can never know precisely what it was—but in the end it doesn't matter. God can use any process He wants to disseminate His story, and He did so through four separate people who reported the most marvelous story ever told, so that we may believe.

WHAT IS THE GOSPEL?

The Gospels tell the story of the Son of God Who became a human being, lived a sinless life, died a sacrificial death, was resurrected from the dead, and ascended back to the Father, offering salvation for all who believe (trust) in Him. The "good news" of the Gospel is the availability of God's salvation to everyone who believes (Romans 1:16). Not everyone is open to the message, of course, and to some it sounds absurd. As Paul observes, "For the word of the cross is folly to those who are perishing, but to us who are being saved it is the power of God" (1 Cor. 1:18). He summarizes the Gospel message in his first letter to the Corinthians: "Now I would remind you, brothers, of the gospel I preached to you, which you received, in which you stand, and by which you are being saved, if you hold fast to the word I preached to you—unless you believed in vain. For I delivered to you as of first importance what I also received: that Christ died for our sins in accordance with the Scriptures, that he was buried, that he was raised on the third day in accordance with the Scriptures" (1 Cor. 15:1–4).

Pastor Cliff McManis posits that the Gospel comprises five main themes:

a. Who Jesus is.
b. The meaning of His death.
c. The reality of His resurrection.
d. A call to repent.
e. A call to believe.[34]

Let's briefly explore each of these in turn.

a) *Who is Jesus?* This is the most important question a person could ever ask. We must know Who He is, and the Gospels provide the answer.

Herod, the tyrannical tetrarch who had John the Baptist beheaded, is perplexed by Jesus and by reports of His works because some said He was John the Baptist raised from the dead, others that He was Elijah, and others that He was some other Old Testament prophet who had risen. Herod declares, "John I beheaded, but who is this about whom I hear such things?" (Luke 9:7–9). Even Jesus' mortal enemies ask the question, "Who is Jesus?" After reporting Herod's perplexity, Luke—as if to answer the question by showing Jesus' supernatural power—tells the story of Jesus miraculously feeding five thousand people with just five loaves of bread and two fish, with an abundance of food left over (Luke 9:10–17).

Luke immediately returns to the question, but this time Christ Himself is the questioner. Christ asks His disciples, "Who do the crowds say that I am?" They respond with the same options that puzzled Herod: John the Baptist, Elijah, and other risen Old Testament prophets. Jesus asks Peter pointedly "But who do you say that I am?" Peter answers, "The Christ of God" (Luke 9:18–20).

The disciples have been slow to grasp fully Who Jesus is, and His earthly ministry is coming to a close. He is about to head to Jerusalem where He will suffer and die.[35] Jesus must drill into them Who He is because, as His allies, they'll need strength to face the coming challenges and attacks. Peter's confession seems sincere, but he obviously isn't yet wholly committed to Christ, as he would soon betray Jesus three times. But Peter would later remember this conversation, among many others, and it would strengthen him. Note that Jesus isn't addressing this question only to Peter. He died for all of us, and we have to treat the question as if directed to each of us individually—because it is. Who do I say Jesus is? Who do you say He is?

b) *What is the meaning of His death*? Jesus' death served many purposes, some of which are interrelated. It was *substitutionary*—He died for our sins so that we will be freed from death, which is the penalty of sin. It is an *atonement* for our sins—though we were separated from God through sin, we are now *reconciled* to Him (Romans 5:10; 2 Cor. 5:18–20; Eph. 2:16; Col. 1:20, 21), thereby reuniting God and man in a personal relationship; thus the term "at-one-ment."[36] It is a *propitiation*—it appeases God's wrath[37] (Romans 3:25; 1 John 2:2; 4:10) and *expiates* our guilt.[38] It *redeems* us. We are *ransomed* "with the precious blood of Christ, like that of a lamb without a blemish or spot" (1 Peter 1:18–19; Mark 10:45; Matt. 20:28), and are *forgiven* (Col. 1:14) and redeemed or delivered from the curse of sin (Eph. 1:7). Through His death we are *adopted* as children of God, having been born again through faith in Christ (John 1:12), and we are *justified*, as we are declared righteous legally (Romans 3:21–26).[39] Charles Spurgeon argues that when God sees saved sinners, He no longer sees sin in them but instead sees His dear Son Jesus Christ covering us as a veil. "God will never strike a soul through the veil of His Son's sacrifice," says Spurgeon. "He accepts us because He cannot but accept His Son, who has become our covering."[40]

c) *The reality of His resurrection.* Paul writes, "If you confess with your mouth that Jesus is Lord and believe in your heart that God raised him from the dead, you will be saved" (Romans 10:9). The Christian message that Jesus conquered Satan, sin, and death is not allegorical. As previously mentioned, Jesus allowed Satan to "strike His heel" by voluntarily dying on the cross, but in the very process of dying (and being resurrected), Jesus "crushed [Satan's] head" (Gen. 3:15 NIV), thereby defeating Satan, sin, and death. "Death stung himself to death when he stung Christ," notes William Romaine.[41] William Plummer adds, "The death of Christ was the most dreadful blow ever given to the empire of darkness."[42] Christ's resurrection consummates God's salvation plan for mankind. The historical fact of Jesus' resurrection is pivotal to Christianity. Paul writes, "And if Christ has not been raised, then our preaching is in vain and your faith is in vain.... And if Christ has not been raised, your faith is futile and you are still in your sins. Then those also who have fallen asleep in Christ have perished. If in Christ we have hope in this life only, we are of all people most to be pitied" (1 Cor. 15:14, 17–19).

d) *A call to repent.* Repentance is not a separate requirement for salvation. We are saved through faith alone, but repentance goes hand in hand with believing. "Repentance and faith are Siamese twins,"[43] writes Walter J. Chantry. Sinclair Ferguson comments, "Faith and repentance must be seen as marriage partners and never separated."[44] Repentance is a change of attitude and action from sin toward obedience to God. The Greek word for repentance is derived from a word meaning "to radically change one's thinking." It signifies a person attaining a divinely provided new understanding of his behavior and feeling compelled to change and begin a new relationship with God (Heb. 6:1; Acts 20:21).[45] Walter Elwell declares that it is "literally a change of mind, not about individual plans, intentions, or beliefs, but rather a change in the whole personality from a sinful course of action to God."[46]

e) *A call to believe.* To believe in Jesus Christ requires more than mere intellectual assent that He is the Son of God. Saving faith is not merely accepting certain propositions as true ("even the demons believe— and shudder!" James 2:19), but trusting a person—the Person of Jesus Christ[47]—for the remission of your sins. It involves an act of the will. We can think of it as a faith-union with Christ, in which the believer cleaves to his Savior. We need only to believe in Christ for our eternal salvation. Nothing else is required. The Bible is clear on this. When the Philippian jailor asks Paul and Silas what he must do to be saved, they respond, "Believe in the Lord Jesus and you will be saved" (Acts 16:30–31). We cannot earn our way to salvation. It is solely a gift from God. "For by grace you have been saved through faith," Paul proclaims in Ephesians. "And this is not your own doing; it is the gift of God, not a result of works, so that no one may boast" (2:8–9).

Now, let's take a brief look at each of the Gospels individually.

THE GOSPEL OF MATTHEW

The Apostle Matthew is believed to have written the Gospel that bears his name, possibly as early as 50 AD and almost certainly prior to the destruction of the Temple in 70 AD, since Matthew makes no mention of this catastrophic event.[48] The book was written mainly to convince non-Christian Jews of the truth of the Gospel[49] and to reinforce the faith of Jewish Christians.[50] Matthew emphasizes fulfillment of the Old Testament prophecies in Jesus, presenting Him as Israel's long-promised Messiah and King, and depicting His ministry as the beginning of the messianic age. Matthew states five times that Old Testament Scripture has been fulfilled, and his demonstration of fulfillment permeates the entire Gospel.[51] Matthew reports Jesus saying He came not to abolish the Old Testament Law but to fulfill it (5:17–19).[52] Only Matthew uses the phrase "kingdom of heaven" instead of "kingdom of God," probably to avoid alienating his Jewish audience by using the name of God, which they shunned out of reverence for Him.[53]

Emphasizing Jesus' ministry, Matthew's Gospel contains the largest sections of His teachings. It includes the Sermon on the Mount (5–7), in which Jesus lays down the most sublime moral standards ever contemplated by man and explains life in the kingdom of heaven; the Lord's Prayer (6:9–13); the Golden Rule (7:12); and the Olivet Discourse (24–25), which addresses the future of Jerusalem and Israel. It relates Jesus' calling of His disciples and His warnings and instructions as He sends them out to minister (10). It contains Jesus' parables of the kingdom of heaven (13) and His stern condemnations of the religious leaders (23).[54] It concludes with the Great Commission (28:19–20). Matthew strongly stresses righteousness, likely because Torah-observant Jews sought righteousness in God's eyes. While Jesus presents a different pathway to righteousness (faith, not works), this nevertheless addresses their concerns.

Much of the material in Matthew is arranged thematically instead of chronologically. One of the book's main purposes is to demonstrate that Jesus has the authority to command His disciples to spread the Gospel throughout the world and to embolden them to do it. Matthew closes with the resurrected Jesus meeting with His disciples on a hill in Galilee and declaring His divine authority: "All authority in heaven and on earth has been given to me. Go therefore and make disciples of all nations" (18:18–19).[55]

Many believe the early Church placed Matthew as the first book in the New Testament because it was thought to have been written first. Though most scholars no longer believe this, its placement is logical, as Matthew provides a bridge between the Old and New Testaments. It begins with a genealogy tracing Jesus back to Abraham and David, two towering figures of the Old Testament, and prominently features the role of the Mosaic Law as well as numerous Old Testament citations.[56]

Scholars divide the book into three main sections: the events leading up to Jesus' public ministry, including His ancestry, infancy (1:1–2:23), baptism, and temptations (3:1–4:16); His public ministry, including His teachings, works, and clashes with religious leaders (4:17–16:12); and His rejection and suffering, culminating in His crucifixion and followed by His resurrection (16:13–28:20). As Matthew presumably relies heavily on Mark's Gospel, He traces Jesus' ministry in the same geographical sequence, beginning with His Galilean ministry, then Jesus' journey to Jerusalem, and finally His trial, death, and resurrection in Jerusalem.[57]

THE GOSPEL OF MARK

The early Church fathers unanimously identified Mark as the author of this Gospel, believing he was the interpreter of the Apostle Peter, who was an eyewitness to many of the events related by Mark. Papias (ca. 110 AD) quotes John the elder (probably the Apostle John) saying Mark was not an eyewitness follower of Christ but that he accompanied Peter, heard Peter's preaching, and recorded all of Peter's recollections about Jesus' words and works, but not necessarily in order. Many other Church fathers corroborated this information.[58]

Most evangelical scholars, as noted, believe Mark's Gospel was written first, between 50 and 70 AD.[59] Geisler and Turek argue that it could have been written in the mid-to-late 50s because it probably preceded Luke, which was likely written around 60 AD.[60] The book was targeted primarily to a Gentile audience and was written in Rome, mainly to Roman Christians but for the wider Church as well.[61]

Mark portrays Jesus' life in simple, action-packed vignettes,[62] repeatedly using the words "immediately" and "then."[63] As the shortest Gospel, the book includes few long discourses.[64] Jesus is presented as a suffering servant (8:31; 10:45; 14:21, 36) Who came to die for mankind's sins. He exhorts His followers to emulate Him in humble service and denial of self (8:34–38; 9:35–37; 10:35–45). Mark introduces Jesus' universal call to discipleship.[65] He stresses fellowship with Jesus (discipleship implies a personal relationship with Jesus), trusting Him, following His teachings, and preparing for the inevitable rejection Christians will face.[66] This Gospel presents two indispensable requirements for discipleship—self-denial and taking up one's cross to follow Jesus (8:34).[67]

Mark emphasizes the coming of God's kingdom in Jesus (1:15), urging people to repent and believe in Him and the Gospel. But in this Gospel, it becomes clear that the Jews had different expectations for the Messiah and the kingdom of God He would bring—as noted, they were expecting a military leader to vanquish their oppressors and establish a dominant earthly kingdom. Jesus gradually lets His disciples in on His "messianic secret" but forbids them and others to speak openly about His identity and His great works.[68] When he addresses the crowds, He usually speaks in parables. During His trial, Jesus publically discloses His identity as the Messiah (14:61–62). His frequent preaching on the advancement of God's kingdom alienates the religious leaders who thoroughly misapprehend His message. As we'll develop more fully later in this book, the kingdom of God has both a present and future component. Jesus inaugurates the kingdom at His first coming, but His initial reign is mostly spiritual. His future kingdom will arrive with His Second Coming when He will reign over all creation.

Mark has two main sections, the first dealing with Jesus's Galilean ministry (1:1–8:26) and the second relating His crucifixion, resurrection, and the preceding events in Jerusalem (8:27–16:8).[69]

THE GOSPEL OF LUKE

The consensus is that Luke, the physician and companion of the Apostle Paul, wrote this book with the Book of Acts as a two-part report. Luke's authorship is supported by Church tradition and references in the book itself.[70] Geisler and Turek contend the book was probably written in or before 60 AD because there are several reasons for dating Acts no later than 62 AD, and Luke was written before Acts. Furthermore, Paul, writing between 62 and 65 AD, quotes Luke 10:7 as Scripture (1 Tim. 5:18). Obviously, Luke's Gospel had to have been written and established for some time for Paul to put it on the same level as the revered Old Testament.[71]

The text of Luke supports scholars' view that the book was written mostly to a Gentile audience. Craig Evans notes that unlike Matthew and Mark, Luke is determined to show that the Jewish story about the

Jewish Messiah fulfilling Old Testament prophecies is relevant to Gentiles as well, as they are also part of God's salvation plan for mankind. Jesus takes the Gospel message to the Gentiles and includes them in His ministry and healings. In Luke, we see Jesus' love for the poor and downtrodden.[72]

As previously shown, Luke has been validated as a meticulously accurate historian. He states in his prologue that he went to great lengths to investigate and present a historically accurate account (1:1–4). He portrays Jesus as the Son of Man who came to seek and save lost sinners (9:56; 19:10) but was rejected by Israel.[73] As noted, Luke emphasizes Jesus' full humanity.[74]

Luke shows that the Church has unified, having settled most of its internal disputes. As Matthew focuses on Jesus' fulfillment of Old Testament prophecies, Luke presents Jesus' Old Testament fulfillment in His passion and resurrection (24).[75] The book shows Jesus twice in His resurrection appearances demonstrating to His disciples that He is foreshadowed and predicted throughout the Old Testament.[76] Luke showcases the sovereignty of God, the saving work of Jesus, and the empowerment of the Holy Spirit. He includes several passages that reference all three persons of the Holy Trinity—the birth announcement (1:26–38), the baptism (3:21–22), the temptation (4:1–13), and Jesus' final words to His disciples (24:46–49).[77] Scholars say Luke is not easily outlined in discrete sections and is more of an itinerary of Jesus' unfolding ministry.[78]

Other recurring themes in Luke's Gospel are forgiveness, joy, wonder at the mysteries of divine truth, and Jesus' practice of praying, especially before undertaking important events in His ministry.[79]

THE GOSPEL OF JOHN

The Gospel of John has long been one of my favorite books of the Bible because shortly after I became a believer, friends recommended it to me as the most theological of the Gospels, powerfully picturing Christ's deity. Both internal evidence and Church tradition strongly indicate that the Apostle John, the disciple whom Jesus loved (20:2), is the author.[80]

Most scholars ascribe a later date to John than the other Gospels because the Church fathers say John wrote in his elderly years, between 80–95 AD,[81] although some assign an earlier date before 70 AD.[82] John wrote the book for new Christians and seeking non-Christians.[83]

This Gospel is distinct from the synoptics in its content, order, wording, and themes. Right off the bat, it identifies Jesus as the Word of God—the pre-existent One who became a human being. In every section of the book, John stresses Christ's deity (1:1–18; 2:1–11; 4:46–54; 5:1–15; 6:5–14; 6:16–21; 8:24, 58; 9:1–12; 11:1–44; 19:1–20:30). The first main section (1:19–12:50) relates Jesus' public ministry, showing His activities during the Jewish feasts, including Passover (2, 6, 11–12), Tabernacles (7–9), and Dedication (10). The second section (13–17) involves Jesus' final meal before His crucifixion (13) and includes a powerful, substantive discourse (14–17), which we examine in depth later in this book. The final section (18–21) records Jesus' arrest, trial, death, and resurrection appearances.[84]

We needn't speculate on John's purpose in writing this Gospel because he tells it to us: "Now Jesus did many other signs in the presence of the disciples, which are not written in this book; but these are written so that you may believe that Jesus is the Christ, the Son of God, and that by believing you may have life in his name" (20:30–31).

John constructs his Gospel around Jesus' use of signs, how they reveal His identity, and His great discourses in which He proclaims their significance and substantiates His deity, to lead us to saving faith in Him.[85]

Throughout this Gospel, Jesus uses "I am" statements, which equate Him with the God of the Jewish people—the Old Testament God Yahweh (6:35; 8:24, 58; 10:11, 14: 13:19; 15:1; 18:5–9, cf. Exodus 3:14–16).[86]

The Gospel of John is a counterweight to the synoptics, showing that Jesus is not only fully human but also fully divine. "Taken together, the four gospels weave a complete portrait of the God-Man, Jesus of Nazareth," Bruce Barton contends. "In Him were blended perfect humanity and deity, making Him the only sacrifice for the sins of the world, and the worthy Lord of those who believe."[87]

THE LIFE AND MINISTRY OF CHRIST

Before we begin the more detailed narrative of the Gospel accounts in the next chapter, let's look at a short sketch of Christ's life and ministry, which will provide an overview before we dig deeper.

Jesus was the only person who came into the world to die. "Death," writes Bishop Fulton Sheen, "was the goal and fulfillment of His life, the gold that He was seeking. Few of His words or actions are intelligible without reference to His Cross.... The story of every human life begins with birth and ends with death. In the Person of Christ, however, it was His death that was first and His life that was last.... It was not so much that His birth cast a shadow on His life and thus led to His death; it was rather that the Cross was first, and cast its shadow back to His birth. His has been the only life in the world that was ever lived backward."[88]

Though He was born to die and He intended from the beginning to do just that, His death would be in God's time. Before He (and the Father) would allow Himself to be captured, He had to complete His ministry. He came to preach a message of redemption, salvation, and life. But it wasn't as if He said to Himself, "I am going to say the most controversial things I can to antagonize the religious authorities into killing Me." No, His message was what it was—and is—and some would accept it and others would reject it, because the Truth causes division (Luke 12:51). Yet His message is precisely why they wanted to kill Him. He challenged their authority, traditions, and interpretations of their sacred Law, including the right to heal on the Sabbath. He "blasphemously" claimed to be the Messiah and the King, and made a triumphal entry into the Holy City. He claimed to be the Son of God who had the authority to forgive sins, and He had the audacity to cleanse *their* Temple.[89]

In his sermon to the Gentiles recorded in the Book of Acts, Peter provides a summary of Jesus' ministry and His substitutionary death. In this brief, inspired account we see an apostle on fire for Christ and evangelizing to the Gentiles:

So Peter opened his mouth and said: "Truly I understand that God shows no partiality, but in every nation anyone who fears him and does what is right is acceptable to him. As for the word that he sent to Israel, preaching good news of peace through Jesus Christ (he is Lord of all), you yourselves know what happened throughout all Judea, beginning from Galilee after the baptism that John proclaimed: how God anointed Jesus of Nazareth with the Holy Spirit and with power. He went about doing good and healing all who were oppressed by the devil, for God was with him. And we are witnesses of all that he did both in the country of the Jews and in Jerusalem. They put him to death by hanging him on a tree, but God raised him on the third day and made him to appear, not to all the people but to us who had been chosen by God as witnesses, who ate and drank with him after he rose from the dead. And he commanded us to preach to the people and to testify that he is the one appointed by God to be judge of the living and the dead. To him all the prophets bear witness that everyone who believes in him receives forgiveness of sins through his name" (10:34–43).

Let's not pass over Peter's declaration lightly. *Everyone* who believes in Jesus receives forgiveness. "There are no incurable cases under the gospel," writes J. C. Ryle. "Any sinner may be healed if he will only come to Christ."

Because the Gospels don't provide complete biographical data and sometimes present material thematically rather than chronologically, the precise order of some events is uncertain. Matthew (1–2) and Luke (1–2) both provide information on Jesus' birth and early life. Both report that Jesus' birth is pre-announced and that Mary gave birth to Him as a virgin. Both include genealogies tracing Jesus' human ancestry, whereas John opens his Gospel declaring that the Word—the second person of the Triune God—is eternal and an agent in the creation. In Luke the shepherds visit the baby in Bethlehem after an angel of the Lord appears to them. In Matthew, the wise men visit to worship Him after seeing His star, and Herod, after trying unsuccessfully to find the baby, orders the murder of innocent children in Bethlehem in an attempt to kill Jesus (2:1–18). Herod fails because Joseph obeys an angel of the Lord who appears to him in a dream and tells him to take Mary and Jesus to Egypt until it's safe to return (Matt. 2:13–15). When Herod dies, the angel tells Joseph to return to Israel with Jesus and Mary (Matt. 2:19–21). Other than Luke's brief reference to Jesus at the Temple when He is twelve years old, we have no other information about Jesus' life until shortly before He begins His ministry.

In preparation for Jesus' public ministry, John the Baptist announces His coming and calls all to repentance (Matt. 3:1–12; Luke 3:1–17). John baptizes Jesus (Matt. 3:13–17; Luke 3:21–22), who undergoes the temptations of Satan, each time invoking Scripture as a defense against Satan's wiles and demonstrating His obedience as the Son of God (Matt. 4:1–11; Luke 4:1–13).

Jesus begins His ministry when He is about thirty years old (Luke 3:23). He ministers in Judea following His baptism and makes contacts there with some of His future disciples (John 1:35–42). He next goes into Galilee (John 1:43) and performs His first miracle, or sign, by turning water into wine (John 2:1–11). He generally ministers in Galilee at this point because the Jews in Judea are seeking to kill Him (John 7:1). But He makes periodic trips into Judea, such as when He goes to Jerusalem for the Passover, where he drives the money-changers from the Temple (John 2:14), and meets the Pharisee Nicodemus (John 3:1).

Jesus calls His disciples (Mark 3:13–19) and does extensive teaching. He delivers the Sermon on the Mount (Matt. 5–7), calls for repentance and belief in the Gospel (Mark 1:15), and announces the arrival of the kingdom of God (Luke 11:20). He performs miracles of healing (Mark 1:40–3:12; Matt. 8:1–9:34), exorcisms (Matt. 8:28–34), and miracles involving nature, such as quieting a storm (Mark 4:35–41). He is well received by many people (Matt. 4:23–25) who are impressed by His miracles, though they don't fully understand His mission. But the religious authorities oppose Him (Mark 2:5–12), and their antagonism intensifies as the news spreads about His works and ministry (Matt. 12:24).

While Jesus is busy with His own ministry, He appoints His twelve disciples and trains them before sending them out to preach repentance, cast out demons, and perform healings (Matt. 10:1–42; Mark 6:7–13). During this period, He often instructs in parables (Matt. 13:1–53; Mark 4:1–34). He is rejected in His hometown of Nazareth (Matt. 13:53–58), feeds the five thousand (Matt. 14:13–21), and is further challenged by Pharisees from Jerusalem (Matt. 15:1–20; Mark 7:1–23), leading Him to shift His ministry into the Gentile areas close to Tyre and Sidon (Mark 7:24–31).

Some believe Jesus' ministry reaches a turning point at Caesarea Philippi (Matt. 16:13–20; Mark 8:27–38; Luke 9:18–27), when He fully acknowledges to Peter that He is the Messiah. Shortly thereafter He proves His assertion when He is transfigured before Peter, James, and John (Matt. 17:1–8).

Jesus tells His disciples many times over an extensive period that He is the Messiah and that He must die, and even predicts His own death, but they don't fully grasp His message until after He dies and is resurrected. He doesn't broadcast publicly that He is the Messiah, however, because He isn't yet ready to be captured. But He does tell some people, such as the Samaritan woman at the well, because they are outside the region where His life could be threatened. He must complete His ministry before He allows the authorities to capture Him, which is why we see Him narrowly escaping capture numerous times long before His final week.

Jesus heads from Galilee back toward Jerusalem (Luke 9:51; John 7:10) and continues His ministry with His disciples. Luke devotes a large portion of his Gospel to this period, when Jesus goes to the home of Mary and Martha, teaches about prayer, tells many parables including the Good Samaritan, clashes again with the Pharisees, and lectures His disciples on the great costs of discipleship and servanthood. He casts out a demon from a mute man, which so threatens the Pharisees that they accuse Him of doing it through the power of Satan, to which Jesus responds that Satan wouldn't cast himself out. He announces that blasphemy against the Son of God is forgivable but blasphemy against the Holy Spirit is not—for Jesus cast out demons through the power of the Holy Spirit. He rebukes the Pharisees for their obsession with external observances of righteousness while neglecting their souls. They care about the trappings of power but do not serve the poor or otherwise do God's work.

Jesus makes His triumphal entry into Jerusalem as was prophesied in the Old Testament and pursues His controversial ministry, further challenges the Pharisees, and teaches His disciples about the future, the End Times, and the coming of the Son of Man—His Second Coming (Mark 13). During this week He and His disciples eat the last supper (Matt. 26:17–30).

Jesus predicts His betrayal, and that night He is arrested in the Garden of Gethsemane at the behest of His traitorous disciple, Judas Iscariot. He is tried before Annas, the Sanhedrin (the Jewish tribunal), Herod Antipas, and Pontius Pilate. The Jewish authorities charge Him with blasphemy, but since they have no power under Roman law to crucify Him, they pressure Pilate to convict Him of treason against Rome for claiming He is the King of the Jews. Pilate finds no guilt in Him and tries to avoid administering punishment by offering the Jews the opportunity to call for the release of one prisoner, which is a Passover tradition. Pilate is hoping he can pacify them by punishing but not crucifying Jesus. The Jews, however, want Him dead and call for the release of Barabbas, a criminal prisoner, instead of Jesus.

Knowing Jesus is innocent, Pilate could have released both Him and Barabbas, but he finally acquiesces and orders Jesus' crucifixion. Jesus is mocked, spit on, flogged, and crucified with two common thieves on the eve of the Sabbath at Golgotha (Mark 15:22). He is buried in the tomb of Joseph of Arimathea (John 19:38), a member of the Sanhedrin and follower of Jesus, who requests permission to bury Him. Though Roman guards are posted at the tomb because of the Jews' fear that His disciples will steal His body, Jesus' body disappears from the tomb, and He rises on the third day just as He had predicted (Luke 24:1–7). For the next forty days He makes many appearances to His followers and others, then ascends into heaven (Acts 1:1–11), promising to send His disciples the Holy Spirit, Who would empower them to carry on His ministry.[90]

GEOGRAPHY OF PALESTINE IN THE TIME OF JESUS

Some knowledge of the geographical area of Palestine is helpful when tracing Christ's early work. Most of Jesus' teaching ministry takes place in the fields and small towns of Galilee and Judea. Yet the focus of at least the last third of each Gospel is on Jerusalem, the Holy City. There, Christ drives the money-changers from the Temple, challenges the religious authorities, and is illegally tried and condemned. Just outside the city Jesus is crucified, buried, and resurrected.[91]

At the end of the Old Testament period, Palestine is a Persian province. But by the time Christ comes, it is divided into three provinces: Galilee in the north, Samaria in the center, and Judea in the south.[92] Judea is mostly the same area as that occupied by the Southern Kingdom of Judah after Solomon's United Kingdom was divided, though its boundaries were never firmly set. Judea is directly under Roman control until 37 AD, when Herod Agrippa I becomes its king, although Agrippa and subsequent rulers still serve at the pleasure of the emperor, and the land ultimately remains under Roman authority.[93] Galilee and Samaria together comprise the land of the former Northern Kingdom of Israel. When the Assyrians conquered the Northern Kingdom in 722 BC and took its people captive, they brought in pagan immigrants to settle the area, which is why the Bible refers to it as "Galilee of the Gentiles" (Isaiah 9:1; Matt. 4:15). The Judeans considered the Galileans inferior, as two references in John's Gospel make clear: "Can anything good come out of Nazareth?" (1:46), and "Are you from Galilee too? Search and see that no prophet arises from Galilee" (7:52).

The Samaritans live in Samaria, which is between Judea in the south and Galilee, where Jesus often ministers, in the north. The Jews look down on the Samaritans as mixed racial descendants of the foreign colonists the Assyrians brought into the land after conquering the Northern Kingdom and the Israelites who remained there during the captivity. Both Jews and Samaritans forbid having any contact with or intermarrying one another, though these marriages occur anyway. The Samaritans' worship practices offend the Israelites because they have corrupted the Jewish religion by introducing pagan practices and by building a temple on Mount Gerizim.[94]

Perea is a small territory on the east side of the Jordan River, across from Samaria and Judea, mainly populated by Jews. The Gospels refer to it as the land "beyond the Jordan" (Matt. 4:15, 25; 19:1; Mark 3:7–8). Jesus does much of His teaching there and makes His final trip to Jerusalem from there (John 10:40; 11:54). The Decapolis is also on the east

side of the Jordan and consists of ten cities the Greeks established following Alexander the Great's conquest of the region. Jesus allows
demons to enter swine near Gadara, one of the ten cities (Mark 5:1–20),
and He becomes popular throughout the Decapolis (Matt. 4:24–25;
Mark 7:31–37).[95]

◇◇

Now that we've explored the historical, cultural, and religious backdrop to Jesus' arrival and undertaken a broad overview of New Testament writings, in the next chapter we'll turn to a more detailed historical
narrative of the life, ministry, death, and resurrection of Jesus Christ as
told in the Gospels. As we begin these chapters I want to reiterate that
we should let the Gospel message speak for itself. "The power," writes
Bruce Barton, "lies in the message itself."[96] The message, of course, is
that Jesus Christ was crucified for our sins so that we can live.

As we read the Gospels we must also be mindful of what Mark
Dever calls the Christian's ultimate inquiry. "Do you believe," asks
Dever, "that Jesus is the Christ, the Son of God? If you do not, or if you
are not certain, you may wish to consider further why the identity of
Jesus is absolutely central to Christianity. Not only that, you may wish
to consider why two thousand years' worth of Christians would tell you
this is the most important question you could ever ask. Who is Jesus?"[97]

Bruce Gordon underscores the same question, but with Jesus as the
questioner. Gordon writes, "'Who do you say I am?' This is the question
Jesus asked His disciples over 2000 years ago and is asking us the same
question today. 'Who do you say I am?' This is the most important question we will ever face. Our answer to this question will affect literally
everything concerning our life, death, and our life after death."[98]

Indeed, Jesus' question distills the Gospel to its essence. Jesus asks it
of His disciples because He knows they aren't quite getting it. They aren't
quite getting *Him*. Contemplate this exchange one more time: Jesus says,
"Who do people say that the Son of Man is? And they reply, 'Some say
John the Baptist; others say, Elijah; and others, Jeremiah or one of the
prophets.'" (Matt. 16:13–14). He then presses his disciples for *their* opinion. "He said to them, 'But who do you say that I am?'" (Matt. 16:15).

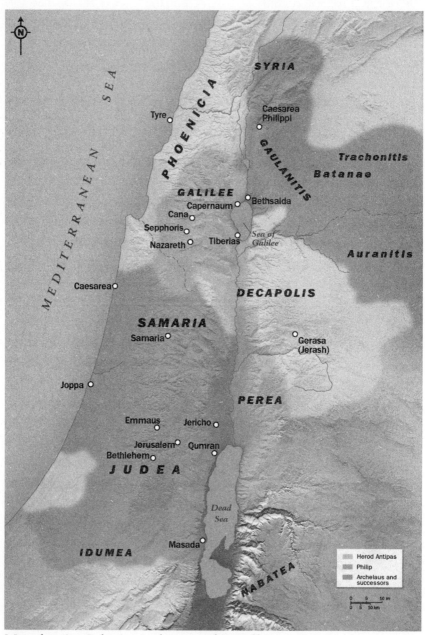

Map showing Palestine in the time of Jesus.[99]

Mark Allan Powell, Introducing the New Testament: A Historical, Literary, and Theologi-cal Survey, *Baker Academic, a division of BakerPublishing Group, copyright © 2009. Used by permission.*

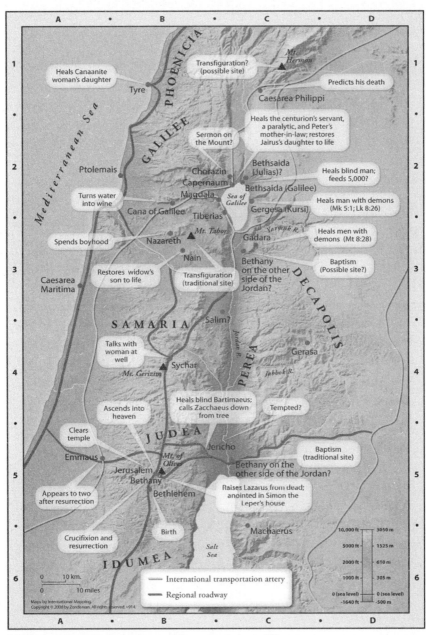

Map showing the locations of Jesus' ministry.[100]

Taken from NIV Zondervan Study Bible *Copyright © 2015 by Zondervan. Used by permission of Zondervan. www.Zondervan.com*

Peter answers, "You are the Christ, the Son of the living God" (Matt. 16:16).

So as you read the following chapters and the Gospels themselves, please keep at the forefront of your mind this question: "Who do you say I am?"

PART II

A VISIT FROM GOD

CHAPTER 5

FROM JESUS' BIRTH TO HIS INITIAL TEACHINGS

Religion is the story of what a sinful man tries to do for a holy God; the gospel is the story of what a holy God has done for sinful men.

—R. GUSTAFSON[1]

JESUS' GENEALOGIES (MATT. 1:1–17; LUKE 3:23–38)

The Gospel of Matthew begins the New Testament, appropriately, with Jesus' line of descent from Abraham, the father of the Jewish nation, through King David, which remarkably connects the New Testament with the Old. In His covenant with Abraham, God promised He would bless all families and nations through him and his descendants. God reiterated and expanded on His promises to Abraham in subsequent covenants, including the Davidic Covenant, whereby God promised King David that his descendants would rule in Israel forever. This kingdom, David's throne, and the Davidic line of kings would continue eternally (2 Samuel 7:5–16; 1 Chron. 17:10–14, 23–27; 2 Chron. 6:10, 15–17, 42; 7:17–18; 13:8; 23:3).[2] With this genealogy, Matthew confirms that God is fulfilling His promise to bless mankind through Abraham's descendant—Jesus Christ—and that Jesus is in King David's line of succession.

The Gospel of Luke includes a genealogy of Jesus that differs from Matthew's, as Luke begins with Jesus and works back to God, whereas Matthew begins with Abraham and comes forward. Some theologians believe Luke traces Mary's line to show Jesus descended through David legally via Joseph and by blood via Mary, removing any question as to His legitimacy as the Messiah in David's line pursuant to God's promise. Others believe Luke traces the actual line of Joseph.[3] J. A. Martin says that irrespective of which view, if either, is correct, it's significant that Luke traces Jesus' descent all the way back to Adam, the first human being. It "is an indication of the universal offer of salvation, which is common to his Gospel—that Jesus came to save all people—Gentiles as well as the nation of Israel (cf. Luke 2:32)."[4] Pastor Donald Fortner observes that though the Jewish leaders attacked Christ's divinity and His messianic claims from every angle, they didn't challenge His genealogy because it was a matter of public and biblical record.[5]

JESUS' BIRTH AND CHILDHOOD
(MATT. 1:18–2:23; LUKE 1:26–35; 2:1–52)

The angel Gabriel goes to Mary in Nazareth and informs her of her upcoming virgin birth of Jesus through the Holy Spirit, relating that her son will be great and will be called holy—the Son of God. Gabriel tells Mary, "And the Lord God will give to him the throne of his father David, and he will reign over the house of Jacob forever, and of his kingdom there will be no end."

When Joseph learns of Mary's pregnancy he plans to divorce her, assuming she has committed adultery. But as a righteous man, he plans to do it quietly to avoid shaming her. He changes his mind when an angel of the Lord appears to him in a dream and tells him the baby has been conceived by the Holy Spirit. They should call Him Jesus, the angel says, because He will save His people from their sins. This would fulfill Isaiah's prophecy about the virgin birth (Isaiah 7:14).

The Roman emperor Caesar Augustus issues a decree requiring everyone in the empire to be registered for tax purposes. To comply with the census decree, Joseph and Mary travel from Nazareth to

Bethlehem—some seventy miles[6]—because Joseph is of the house and line of David. While they're in Bethlehem Jesus is born, fulfilling the prophecy that the Messiah would be born there (Micah 5:2). An angel of the Lord appears to shepherds in the field and announces the birth of Christ, the Savior. The shepherds go to Bethlehem to witness the baby lying in a manger, and they praise God.

Mark Moore notes that as shepherding was a lowly occupation, the shepherds' involvement in the birth story shows, from the beginning, that God's mercy extends to all people. The shepherd symbolizes those who care for God's people, from David the shepherd boy to Jesus the Great Shepherd.[7] "Shepherding," writes Thomas Golding, "is one of the most frequent and powerful images in the Bible.... The primary roles of a shepherd with his sheep were guiding, providing food and water, protecting and delivering, gathering scattered or lost sheep, and giving health and security."[8]

After eight days, the baby is circumcised and is called "Jesus" as the angel had commanded. When Jesus is still a baby, Joseph and Mary take Him to the Temple in Jerusalem for presentation to the Lord and for purification according to God's law concerning the firstborn (Exodus 13:2, 12). While there, they meet a righteous and devout man named Simeon and a prophetess called Anna. Having been told by the Holy Spirit that he will not die before seeing the Messiah, Simeon sees Jesus, takes Him in his arms, and blesses God for fulfilling His promise of salvation for the Gentiles as well as the Jews. Joseph and Mary marvel at Simeon's words—while the angel Gabriel had already told them their Son would be great, Simeon is presenting a new revelation about Jesus' significance. Simeon also prophetically tells Mary that Jesus will cause many to rise and fall, probably referring to His coming judgment and His salvation. Simeon then warns Mary that a sword would pierce her soul—widely interpreted as a prediction of Mary's future suffering when Jesus is rejected and crucified.[9] Anna praises God and testifies about Jesus to those in Jerusalem waiting for Israel's redemption.

Three wise men from the east (Babylon or Persia) come to Jerusalem to see the newly born King of the Jews after seeing His star rise. The trio may have known about Jewish messianic hopes,[10] perhaps through the Old Testament prophecy of Balaam that a world ruler would arise out of Israel (Num. 24:17). When Herod, King of Judea, learns about the wise men, he and all of Jerusalem are troubled. Herod asks Jewish leaders where Christ is to be born and is told He will be born in Bethlehem as Micah had prophesied (Micah 5:2; Matt. 2:3–6). Fearing competition for his throne, Herod sends the wise men to Bethlehem to search for the child on the pretense that he wants to go to Him and worship Him. They go to the child, worship Him, give Him gifts, and then return to their country without talking to Herod, having been warned in a dream to avoid him.

An angel of the Lord appears to Joseph in a dream, telling him Herod will try to kill Jesus so he should take Jesus and Mary to Egypt. Joseph obeys, which Matthew says fulfills Hosea's prophecy, "Out of Egypt I called my son" (Hosea 11:1). Realizing the wise men have tricked him, Herod seeks to kill Jesus by ordering the murder of all boys two years old and younger in and around Bethlehem. Matthew says this cruel act fulfills Jeremiah's prophecy (Jer. 31:15; Matt. 2:17–18). After Herod dies, an angel tells Joseph in a dream to return to Israel with Jesus and Mary. But Joseph, to avoid Herod's son and successor Archelaus, who is reigning over Judea, takes his family to live in Nazareth.

Of the four Gospel writers, only Luke provides information about Jesus' life between the time of his family's arrival in Nazareth and the beginning of His public ministry. When He is twelve years old, Jesus goes with His parents to Jerusalem for their annual visit for the Passover feast. On their way home, Mary and Joseph notice Jesus is missing and return to Jerusalem to search for Him. They find Him in the Temple conversing with teachers. Because Jesus is so young and lacks formal rabbinical training (John 7:15), "all who heard him were amazed at his understanding and his answers."[11] These extraordinary displays of wisdom would continue into His adult ministry, when He would astonish crowds with His authoritative teaching (Matt. 7:28–29).

When Mary rebukes Him for disappearing, Jesus tells them He had to be in His "Father's house." Thus, at this early age, Jesus already shows awareness that He is God's Son.[12] He is not being disobedient to His parents but showing His love for the Temple, the house of His Father.[13] Nevertheless, He leaves with His parents and obeys them, and He grows in wisdom, stature, and in favor with God and man.

JOHN THE BAPTIST (MATT. 3:1–12; MARK 1:2—8; LUKE 1:5–25, 36–80; 3:1–20)

The Gospels depict John the Baptist as the conscious forerunner of Christ who was preannounced by the prophet Isaiah (Isaiah 40:3; cf. Mal. 3:1) as the "voice of one crying in the wilderness: Prepare the way of the Lord." John preaches repentance in preparation for Christ's coming. He contrasts his baptism of water with Christ's baptism of the Holy Spirit. Jesus isn't the only one who will confront the Sadducees and Pharisees, as John rebukes them as a "brood of vipers" and tells them to repent and prove their sincerity through their actions—"Bear fruit in keeping with repentance." John's boldness is reminiscent of the Old Testament prophets.[14]

The Gospels and Acts convey that John's ministry is profoundly relevant to Christianity, and his preparatory teachings are included in all four Gospel accounts. He is the first recognized prophet in Israel for hundreds of years, since the close of the Old Testament, and thereby constitutes the prophetic bridge from the Old Testament prophets to the New.[15] Other prophets also appear in the Gospels, such as Zechariah, Elizabeth, Simeon, and Anna,[16] who accompany Christ's coming and, as God's messengers, proclaim what God has done in sending His Son into the world.[17]

Paul mentions John in his brief explanation of the Gospel to the "brothers" in Antioch in Pisidia. Before Jesus' coming, Paul says, "John had proclaimed a baptism of repentance" and assured the people he was not Christ and was unworthy of Christ, Who was to follow him (Acts 13:24–25). Paul reiterates this to the Ephesian Christians (Acts 19:4). Peter also tells Gentiles in Caesarea about John (Acts 10:37). Further, Luke describes John's parents as "righteous before God, walking blamelessly in all the commandments and statutes of the Lord." Jesus Himself regards John's role as indispensable, declaring, "Truly, I say to you, among those born of women there has arisen no one greater than John the Baptist" (Matt. 11:11).

John's importance is evident even before his birth, when the angel Gabriel announces in the Temple to Zechariah the priest that his wife Elizabeth will bear him a son whom he shall call John. Gabriel assures

Zechariah many will rejoice at John's birth, "for he will be great before the Lord." John will "be filled with the Holy Spirit" from the time he is in his mother's womb, and he will "make ready for the Lord a people prepared." Because Zechariah expresses doubts to Gabriel that these things will happen, Gabriel tells him that he will be unable to speak until John's birth. When Zechariah comes out of the Temple he is mute and makes signs to the people.

John's special bond with Jesus is seen when Mary visits her cousin Elizabeth immediately after Jesus is conceived in Mary's womb, at which point Elizabeth is six months pregnant with John. When Mary enters Elizabeth's house and greets her, the baby John leaps for joy in her womb and Mary praises God for His goodness in choosing her as the mother of the Messiah, and for His faithfulness in fulfilling His promises to Israel.[18]

When John is born, instead of naming him after his father Zechariah, Elizabeth calls him John. Zechariah, still mute, writes on a tablet, "His name is John." Immediately Zechariah's mouth is opened, his tongue loosed, and he blesses God out loud. Overcome by fear, the people talk about these things throughout Judea, saying, "What then will this child be?" Once Zechariah can speak again, He is filled with the Holy Spirit and begins prophesying, predicting that the Messiah will deliver Israel, that God will honor His holy covenant with Abraham, and that his son John will be "the prophet of the Most High" (Jesus) who would go before Him and prepare the way for Him.

When John is preaching in the Jordan Valley, many Jews come to hear him and regard his preaching as authoritative and prophetic.[19] During His ministry Jesus would ask the chief priests, the scribes, and the elders whether John's baptism is "from heaven or from man" (Mark 11:30), they don't dare say from heaven because they had rejected him, but they are afraid to tell the people he is merely from man because "they were afraid of the people, for they all held that John really was a prophet" (Mark 11:32).

When the Jews send representatives to find out John's identity and role, he plainly denies he is the Christ (John 1:20). He says he is the one who has come before Christ to prepare people for His ministry. Why, then, does he baptize, they ask. He replies, "I baptize with water, but among you stands one you do not know, even he who comes after me, the strap of whose sandal I am not worthy to untie" (John 1:26–27).

F. F. Bruce says John's baptism had some antecedents in Israel, but it "was distinctive in that he administered it to others, and in its eschatological significance [its relevance to End Times and the coming of the Messiah]."[20] The Old Testament prophet Ezekiel, continues Bruce, "promised that at the dawn of the new age God would purify his people from their defilement with clean water and give them a new heart and a new spirit—his own spirit."[21] Ezekiel, like Jeremiah, was announcing the New Covenant, as discussed in the previous chapter.

John's ministry is essential to ready people for Christ and His message. When John instructs his disciples to repent, he does so in the context of the coming kingdom of heaven. Matthew repeatedly quotes Jesus using the phrase "kingdom of heaven" rather than "kingdom of God." Mark generally uses "kingdom of God." Most scholars regard the terms as interchangeable,[22] so we should consider them synonymous.[23] As previously mentioned, Matthew may have avoided using "kingdom of God" because his Jewish audience would have been offended at the use of the divine name.[24]

John proclaims, "Repent, for the kingdom of heaven is at hand." Jesus reiterates this theme when He begins His public ministry, demonstrating its providential continuity. The Old Testament contains a rising expectation of God coming to establish justice, crush His opposition, and renew the universe.[25] Accordingly, the phrase "kingdom of heaven" originated with the late-Jewish expectation of God's decisive future intervention to restore His people's fortunes and liberate them from the power of their enemies[26] by sending His Messiah, who would pave the way for His kingdom.[27] As noted, however, Jewish messianic expectations were markedly different from Jesus' true messianic mission.

JOHN BAPTIZES JESUS (MATT. 3:13–17; MARK 1:9–11; LUKE 3:21–23; JOHN 1:32)

Jesus asks John to baptize Him, but John is initially reluctant, believing Jesus doesn't need repentance. However, John performs the ceremony anyway, and this baptism, in fact, is the high point of John's ministry and the inauguration of Christ's ministry,[28] which begins when Jesus is about thirty years old. Once Jesus has been baptized and is praying, the Holy Spirit descends on Him in the form of a dove. A heavenly voice says, "You are my beloved Son, with you I am well pleased." The Father makes the same declaration during Jesus' transfiguration (Matt. 17:5), which tells us, writes Donald Fortner, "that Christ, our ascended, exalted Savior, is that One in whom alone we find acceptance with God. As the Holy Lord God is well pleased with his Son, so he is well pleased with his elect in his Son, our Substitute."[29] When John the Baptist proclaims that Jesus is the Son of God (John 1:29–34), it's a glorious manifestation of the three persons of the Holy Trinity and of their mutual love and unity of purpose.[30] The Father blesses Jesus and anoints Him with the Holy Spirit, Who will be with Jesus throughout His earthly ministry.

Some wonder why the Son of God, a sinless man, should undergo baptism, which is associated with repentance. That this troubles some readers lends credence to the historicity of the account.[31] The Gospel writers would not invent a story that would cause further skepticism when their purpose was to win converts, not stir unbelief. One possible reason is that His baptism symbolizes His formal acceptance of the work of redemption, which He would now begin and would culminate in His suffering, death, and resurrection.[32] So His symbolic gesture of repentance should not give us pause. God's salvation scheme involved God the Son becoming a man, taking on Himself the people's guilt, and vicariously enduring their punishment.[33] In being baptized, He fulfills all righteousness, validates John's ministry, identifies with human sin and sinners, and provides an example for Christians to follow.[34]

THE TEMPTATION OF CHRIST
(MATT. 4:1–11; MARK 1:12–13; LUKE 4:1–13)

The Holy Spirit leads Jesus into the wilderness to endure the devil's temptation. This is not to be understood as a symbolic battle—Satan is a created being, an archangel who has fallen because of his pride.[35] Jesus is hungry, having fasted for forty days and forty nights. The devil subjects Him to three temptations, and in each case He responds with the armor of Scripture. Satan tells Him if He is the Son of God He should command the stones to become loaves of bread. Jesus answers that man doesn't live by bread alone but also by God's words. The devil takes Him to Jerusalem, sets Him atop the Temple, and taunts Him to throw Himself off because God's angels would save Him. Satan is twisting Scripture to suit his evil purposes, so Jesus invokes the passage from Isaiah that forbids putting God to the test (Deut. 6:16; Isaiah 7:12). Finally, Satan promises to give Jesus control of the world immediately if He will worship him. Jesus responds, "You shall worship the Lord your God and him only shall you serve."

Commentators have categorized these temptations as the "lust of the flesh," "pride of life," and "lust of the eyes." In his first epistle, John asserts that these temptations are "not from the Father but...from the world" (1 John 2:16–17). "If anyone loves the world," writes John, "the love of the Father is not in him" (1 John 2:15). James endorses the same principle: "Do you not know that friendship with the world is enmity with God? Therefore whoever wishes to be a friend of the world makes himself an enemy of God" (James 4:4). This does not contradict God's pronouncement that His entire creation is good (Gen. 1:4, 10, 12, 18, 21, 31; 1 Tim. 4:1–4; Romans 14:14). The epistle writers use the term "the world" to denote the system of evil controlled by Satan (1 John 5:19)[36]—that portion of human society that is under the influence of evil and at war with God.[37] The cravings and lusts of sinful man are antithetical to God,[38] so Christians should avoid them.[39] Paul instructs us to "put to death therefore what is earthly in you: sexual immorality, impurity, passion, evil desire, and covetousness, which is idolatry" (Col. 3:5).

Some also don't understand why Christ would allow Himself to be tempted or how it's possible for the Son of God to experience temptation at all. But was Jesus tempted in the sense human beings are? Temptation usually means we actually consider, however briefly, committing the sin, which is itself sinful. Surely Jesus isn't tempted in that way because Hebrews 4:15 says He is without sin—yet the same verse says Jesus is actually tempted. I think it means that the devil subjected Jesus to temptations, but He didn't let them take root for a microsecond. "Jesus did not let the sinful suggestions of Satan come into his heart," argues Werner Franzmann. "At their very approach he rejected and repulsed them."[40]

But the question remains: why would Jesus subject Himself to this ordeal? One reason is that to be fully man, Christ must endure the experiences common to all men (see Heb. 2:17–18; 4:14–15).[41] Human beings grow through adversity, and our faith grows and is purified through our trials (1 Peter 1:6–7). Alfred Edersheim, in his classic *The Life and Times of Jesus the Messiah*, explains that Jesus had to experience temptation to be fully human:

> That at His consecration to the Kingship of the Kingdom, Jesus should have become clearly conscious of all that it implied in a world of sin; that the Divine method by which that Kingdom should be established, should have been clearly brought out, and its reality tested; and that the King, as Representative and Founder of the Kingdom, should have encountered and defeated the representative, founder, and holder of the opposite power,[42] "the prince of this world"—these are thoughts which must arise in everyone who believes in any Mission of the Christ.[43]

Edersheim explains that we will understand how the life and work of Christ would begin with "the temptation" if we understand His mission. Edersheim, a Christian convert from Judaism, says that such a concept was never conceived in Judaism "because it never conceived a Messiah like Jesus."[44] As noted, Jesus came not to deliver Israel from its political oppressors, but to save sinners—and this involved Him condescending to human form, suffering the indignities of human existence, and dying on the cross (Phil. 2:1–11). Edersheim contends that the story of the temptation, like Jesus' baptism, lends credence to the Bible because "it cannot have been derived from Jewish legend."[45] The event was so contrary to the Jewish concept of the Messiah that the Gospel writers wouldn't have dared include it if they were concocting a fable to persuade Jews.

While the concept would have been foreign to them, however, it's perfectly consistent with God's salvation scheme and squares with God's acknowledgment in Genesis 3:15 that Satan would strike Christ's heel. If Christ can die on our behalf, He can certainly be subjected to Satan's series of impotent temptations, and His triumph over them brings further glory to the Father and to the Son, Who God promised would crush Satan's head. It is fitting that Jesus takes on Satan directly before His ministry begins, draws the battle lines, and sends a message to His adversary, whose challenges He will overcome now and whom He will defeat permanently in the future. We can have a personal relationship with our Savior because He experienced the types of trials (and far worse) we experience. He is not an unapproachable, indifferent deity—He is a personal, compassionate God Who has given everything for us so that we can live. Above all else, this is what makes our own suffering endurable.

Jesus' temptation reflects His triumph over the human struggles that challenge every man and shows His pure motives and His other-directedness. "It is the open window of his soul," Charles Foster Kent writes, "through which it is possible to study the simple yet divine principles that found expression in all that he taught and did. It shows that Jesus regarded life and humanity with eyes that had looked into the very heart of the Father, and that he recognized that he was therefore in a unique sense called to reveal God to his fellow men."[46] Jesus' character is revealed in these temptation accounts, which illustrate that in the process of perfectly fulfilling His mission, He disappoints the hopes of those who had anticipated a different kind of Messiah.[47] He eschews power and glory over men (e.g., He washes their feet), refusing to satisfy their desire that He present Himself as their political and military savior. But in this restraint, He satisfies our desire for salvation. As Bruce Shelley observes, "Christianity is the only major religion to have as its central event the humiliation of its God."[48]

THE "LAMB OF GOD" CALLS HIS DISCIPLES (JOHN 1:29–51)

The day after the Jews ask John the Baptist if he is Christ, John sees Jesus walking toward him and says, "Behold, the Lamb of God, who takes away the sin of the world! This is he of whom I said, 'After me comes a man who ranks before me, because he was before me.'" John is not being gratuitously self-deprecating. Rather, he is matter-of-factly asserting that Christ's superiority inheres in His pre-existence—the same pre-existence the Apostle John affirms in the introduction to his Gospel: "In the beginning was the Word, and the Word was with God, and the Word was God. He was in the beginning with God. All things were made through him, and without him was not any thing made that was made" (1:1–3).

The following day, when standing with two of his disciples, John again identifies Jesus as the Lamb of God as He walks by. This prompts the disciples to begin following Christ, further evidencing John's handing of the baton to Jesus. One of the two disciples, Andrew, tells his brother Simon Peter they have found the Messiah and brings him to Jesus, and the two follow Him. Andrew is thus the first person to proclaim Jesus as the Messiah.[49] The other disciple is believed to be John the Apostle who, along with his brother James, also begins to follow Jesus (Mark 1:18–20; Luke 5:1–11).[50] Next, Jesus calls Philip and Nathanael in Galilee.

JESUS TURNS WATER INTO WINE AND CLEANSES THE TEMPLE (JOHN 2:1–22)

Jesus performs His first miracle, or "sign," at a wedding at Cana in Galilee by turning water into wine, "which manifested his glory and his disciples believed in him." New Testament Professor Gerald Borchert notes that the term "sign" means more than just a wonder—it is a powerful act that demonstrates the reality of Who Christ is.[51]

Some people are unsettled by Jesus' reaction when His mother informs Him the wine has run out. "Woman, what does this have to do with me?" He asks. "My hour has not yet come." Addressing her as "woman," says Borchert, is not impersonal or disrespectful, as it might seem in Western culture. Nor is Jesus' question impolite. He is beginning His mission and establishing parameters, especially His principal duty to His Father—He greatly respects His mother, but He is focused on His

Father's business. "He came," writes Borchert, "to fulfill the Father's purpose for him; namely he came to make the Father known (John 1:18). To act on the Father's authority and to do his will was the work of the Son (John 5:19–20, 30, 36).... In this Gospel the ultimate focus of 'the hour' is on the glorification of Jesus—his death and resurrection (John 7:30; 8:20; 12:23, 27; 13:1; 17:1). Jesus is on His Father's timetable. What may seem to be harsh words, therefore, must be understood in the full context of Jesus' destiny and his obedience to the Father."[52]

Indeed, four times in the Gospel of John we see Jesus either delaying certain action or evading His enemies because "His hour" has "not yet come." But we shall see that when His hour does come—His time to die on the cross—He uses the same terminology to announce it: "Father, the hour has come; glorify your Son that the Son may glorify you."[53]

Nevertheless, Jesus performs the miracle, which is the first of seven miracles John records.[54] After the wedding Jesus, His disciples, His mother, and His brothers go to Capernaum, a village on the northwest shore of the Sea of Galilee—a city Gospel writers call Jesus' "own city" (Matt. 9:1) because He lives there for a while after He leaves Nazareth (Matt. 4:13).[55]

Following a few days' stay in Capernaum (John 2:12), Jesus goes to Jerusalem for the Passover and finds men selling oxen, sheep, and pigeons in the Temple courts while others exchange money. He pours out the coins of the money-changers, overturns their tables, and drives them out with a whip of cords, chastising them for making His "Father's house a house of trade." When the Jews defiantly demand He demonstrate His authority with a sign, He says, "Destroy this temple, and in three days I will raise it up." John reveals that Jesus is referring to His body. His disciples later remember this when He is raised from the dead, which causes them to believe "the Scripture and the word that Jesus had spoken."

John's Gospel has the Temple cleansing occurring at the beginning of Jesus' ministry, but the synoptics place it at the end (Matt. 21:12–13; Mark 11:15–17; Luke 19:45–46). Some commentators infer that Jesus must have cleansed the Temple twice,[56] while others contend that John wrote his Gospel later with more of a theological emphasis, and so he organized his material for maximum evangelical impact.[57] He didn't distort the facts or alter the story, but simply placed it at the beginning to capture the readers' attention and summon their focus on the dramatic struggle in which Jesus was engaged. That the disciples later remembered Jesus referring to His body as the Temple and then believed in the Scripture vindicates this approach.

John MacArthur, however, sees too much difference in the historical circumstances and literary contexts of the two accounts to equate them. He believes it's likely Jesus repeatedly cleansed the Temple because the Jewish nation as a whole never recognized His authority as Messiah (Matt. 23:37–39).[58] Leon Morris falls somewhere in between these two views, observing that if only one Temple cleansing occurred, we can reasonably assume John placed it early to maximize the theological impact. As the first five chapters of John contain material not in the synoptics, however, Morris believes it's more likely there were two cleansings.[59]

JESUS MEETS NICODEMUS (JOHN 2:23–3:21)

While in Jerusalem at the Passover Feast Jesus performs more "signs," causing many to believe in Him, but the scriptures indicate Jesus believes their faith is either inauthentic or tentative.[60] Jesus is aware of the fickleness of human nature and that people sometimes get caught up in a short-lived emotional experience. This still happens today, which is why we need to base our faith on more than a subjective, emotional encounter. Many would not understand the significance of His signs until His death and resurrection. Until then they might have believed in Him as a miracle worker, but not as the Messiah and Son of God.[61]

This passage is significant because one of John's main purposes is to prove Jesus is the Messiah and the Son of God. He makes that clear in the next section, when he relates Jesus' encounter with the Pharisee Nicodemus, who is a "ruler of the Jews"—one of the seventy-one members of the Sanhedrin, the highest Jewish council. "Rabbi, we know that you are a teacher come from God," exclaims Nicodemus, "for no one can do these signs that you do unless God is with him." Nicodemus respects Jesus as a teacher from God because of His performance of signs, but he doesn't understand He is more than God's messenger. His statement triggers a profound response from Jesus, including His now well-known revelations that one must be born again to see the kingdom of God, and that to be born again one must believe in Jesus.

Nicodemus asks, "How can a man be born when he is old? Can he enter a second time into his mother's womb and be born?" Jesus clarifies that He is referring not to a physical rebirth but a spiritual one, which a person can only have if he believes in Jesus. When one becomes a believer in Christ, he experiences regeneration—a spiritual rebirth—and becomes a new creature in Christ. This involves an inner cleansing and renewal of human nature by the Holy Spirit whereby man's spiritual condition is transformed from a disposition of sin to a new relationship with God (Titus 3:5). This does not occur because of human merit but through God's grace.[62] When one is born again, however, he is not immune to sin, but is no longer a slave to sin (Romans 6:6). He will still struggle with the "desires of the flesh (Gal. 5:17)," but is now empowered by the indwelling of the Holy Spirit to resist sin, which will involve a daily struggle where "sin remains, but no longer reigns."[63]

The point is explained simply and beautifully in John 4:17: "For God so loved the world that he gave his only Son, that whoever believes in him should not perish but have eternal life." This verse is described as a summary of the whole Gospel.[64] "Is there a verse anywhere in the Bible more well-known and loved than this one?" asks Kenneth Gangel. "How poignantly it states that eternal life comes not because of anything we do."[65] God gave His only Son, Jesus Christ, and Christ's deity is essential Christian doctrine. Those who say otherwise are not Christian. As previously noted, to "believe" does not mean mere intellectual acknowledgment that Christ is God. It is putting our trust and confidence in Him that He can save us—entrusting our eternal destiny to Him and Him alone.[66]

We must acknowledge not merely that Christ died for the sins of the world. "Saving faith," declares Gangel, "requires a recognition that he died for each of us individually."[67] We should pause and reflect on this. God loves each of us individually and offers salvation to each of us personally. This is not an abstract theological concept—we must grasp it and appropriate it for ourselves. Moreover, saving faith is not accomplished through human efforts but is a gift of God and His grace. "For by grace you have been saved through faith. And this is not your own doing; it is the gift of God, not as a result of works, so that no one may boast" (Eph. 2:8–9). Paul further notes, "If you confess with your mouth that Jesus is Lord and believe in your heart that God raised him from the dead, you will be saved" (Romans 10:9).

The revelation that God gave His only Son to die for our sins underscores the magnitude of God's sacrifice and love for us. God's love through Christ is reinforced by Jesus' assuring Nicodemus that the Father did not send Him to condemn the world but to save us—because as sinners we are already condemned. While the Bible depicts Jesus as the ultimate judge, sin is what leads to our condemnation. But Jesus, through His sacrifice, offers us the gift of life through belief in Him.

Jesus tells Nicodemus, "The light has come into the world, and people loved the darkness rather than the light because their works were evil. For everyone who does wicked things hates the light and does not come to the light, lest his works should be exposed. But whoever does what is true comes to the light, so that it may be clearly seen that his works have been carried out by God." John also contrasts light and darkness in the prologue to his Gospel (1:5), identifying Jesus Christ as the true light Who came into the world. Though He created the world, the world did not know Him, and His own did not receive him (1:9–11).

As always the Bible is consistent, for the Old Testament utilizes the image of darkness as well, especially in the poetic books in which darkness represents—appropriately—destruction, death, and the underworld (Isaiah 5:30; 47:5; Psalms 143:3; Job 17:13).[68] We know from observation and sometimes personal experience that many avoid or reject the Gospel because to accept it means having to come to terms with one's own sinful nature. While many resist the Gospel ostensibly on intellectual grounds or because they think they have no need of a savior, Jesus is telling us here that many simply refuse the light because it exposes the darkness in their own lives.

This is tragically ironic for we remain lost, and ultimately unhappy, if we are dishonest with ourselves by refusing to face up to our sin. We may enjoy temporary pleasure, but our addiction to sin keeps us from turning away from it. Jesus affirms, "Truly, truly, I say to you, everyone who practices sin is a slave to sin" (John 8:34). But this is not discouraging because "if we confess our sins, he is faithful and just to forgive us our sins and to cleanse us from all unrighteousness" (1 John 1:8–9). The darkness is no competition for the Light. "The light shines in the darkness, and the darkness has not overcome it" (John 1:5). As E. A. Blum puts it, "Light's nature is to shine and dispel darkness.... darkness is unable to overpower light."[69]

For now, Satan is in constant spiritual warfare against Christ and believers, but Jesus is the victor. Jesus promises us, "I am the light of the world. Whoever follows me will not walk in the darkness, but will have the light of life" (John 8:12). He adds, "I have come into the world as light, so that whoever believes in me may not remain in darkness" (John 12:46). God's marvelous Word, from beginning to end, is consistent in showing the superiority of light over darkness, of life over death. In the Old Testament, light is associated with life. To see light means to live (Job 33:28; 3:16). "For with you is the fountain of life," writes David. "In your light do we see light" (Psalms 36:9). In another psalm he exclaims, "For you have delivered my soul from death, yes, my feet from falling, that I may walk before God in the light of life" (Psalms 56:13). Similarly John writes, "In him was life, and the life was the light of men" (John 1:4).

JOHN THE BAPTIST CONTINUES TO PREACH AND IS ARRESTED (MATT. 14:3–5; MARK 6:17–20; LUKE 3:19–20; JOHN 3:23–36)

Meanwhile, John the Baptist is still preaching and baptizing, though he fully understands his ministry is purely preparatory for Christ's, which has now begun. In his Gospel, the Apostle John says John the Baptist has not yet been imprisoned, indicating he assumes his readers are already aware of John's later arrest. This shows John was adding further information to the synoptic Gospels to aid our understanding of these ministries.[70]

John the Baptist's disciples are worried Jesus' ministry is drawing more people than John's. When they voice their concerns, John responds by winsomely reiterating his deference to Christ, for whom he is merely the forerunner. John depicts Christ as the bridegroom, his followers as the bride, and himself as the friend of the bridegroom. He cautions his disciples that Christ's ministry must increase while his must decrease, as Christ is from heaven while he "is of the earth…and speaks in an earthly way" (John 3:31). John attests that the Father loves the Son and has given Him all things, and whoever believes in the Son has eternal life (John 3:35). Some commentators believe that John 3:31–36 are the words of the Apostle John, the author of this Gospel, and that John the Baptist's words end with his statement that his ministry must recede while Christ's must grow (John 3:30).[71] Others believe John the Baptist uttered those words.[72] Regardless, the Spirit-inspired message is powerful: Christ is the all in all, and John the Baptist came to announce Him.

Herod arrests and imprisons John the Baptist because John had rebuked him for unlawfully marrying Herodias, wife of his brother Philip. Though Herod wants to execute John, he refrains because he fears the people, who believe John is a prophet.

JESUS AND THE SAMARITAN WOMAN (JOHN 4:4–42)

When Jesus learns of John's arrest he heads toward Galilee (Matt. 4:12; Mark 1:14; Luke 4:14), going through Samaria on His way. This is the shortest route from Judea but most Jews go through Perea, which is east of the Jordan River, to avoid Samaria and the despised Samaritans, a racially mixed people whose religious practices were anathema to the Jews. What likely compels Jesus to take the disfavored route, however, is His heart for the lost (Luke 19:10), which results in His meeting with a Samaritan woman at Jacob's well in Sychar, a village about thirty miles north of Jerusalem.[73]

His disciples having gone into the city to buy food, Jesus is alone at the well when a woman comes to draw water. Jesus asks her for a drink, surprising her that a Jew would interact with her. Jesus tells her that if she knew who He was she would have asked Him for a drink and He would have given her "living water." The woman misinterprets

His meaning and asks whether He is too good to drink from this well when the Jewish patriarch Jacob had drank from it. Jesus replies, "Everyone who drinks of this water will be thirsty again, but whoever drinks of the water that I will give him will never be thirsty again. The water that I will give him will become in him a spring of water welling up to eternal life."

It would be hard to imagine a more vivid contrast between temporal and eternal things, and between the earthly life and life eternal, for water is hardly a human luxury—it's an absolute necessity. But as vital as it is to our earthly life, it's nothing compared to the gift of life Jesus gives us when we place our faith in Him. Again, the woman misunderstands Him, for she asks to have some of this water that has the power to permanently quench one's thirst so she wouldn't have to keep coming back to the well for more. Jesus tells her to get her husband, knowing it will prompt her to say she isn't married. When she does, He tells her she has had five husbands, and the woman realizes He's a prophet.

She questions Him about the conflicting religious practices of the Samaritans and Jews, with the former worshipping "on this mountain" (Mount Gerizim—the site of the Samaritans' temple,[74] which had been destroyed more than a hundred years earlier by John Hyrcanus, a Jew from Jerusalem),[75] and the latter worshipping in Jerusalem. Jesus informs her that the physical location of worship isn't nearly as important as the nature of her beliefs. He tells her she worships what she does not know and that she has a misperception about the true God. "Salvation," Jesus declares, "is from the Jews," meaning that the Messiah, who will bring salvation, is Jewish. Scripture is replete with God's assurances that Israel is God's chosen nation—His nation of Holy Priests, to which He has entrusted His Law and through whom salvation will come (Acts 13:23; Romans 11:26; 3:1–2; 9:3–5, 18; Psalms 147:19–20; Isaiah 2:3; Amos 3:2; Micah 4:1–2).

Still unaware of Jesus' identity, she says the Messiah is coming and will clear it all up for them, to which Jesus responds, "I who speak to you am he." Jesus usually avoids proclaiming He is the Messiah when He ministers in Galilee and Judea because the political fallout might interfere with His ministry in these areas.[76] But He's willing to reveal Himself here, probably because it poses no risk to His ministry.[77] That

Jesus' approach made an impact on the woman is shown in her enthusiastic retelling of the encounter to fellow Samaritans in town: "Come, see a man who told me all that I ever did. Can this be the Christ?"

When the disciples return they urge Jesus to eat, and He uses the occasion to teach them about His priorities. Just as He told the woman that the water of life is infinitely more important than drinking water, He informs them that His food is to do the Father's will and complete His work, showing His obedience to the Father.

Convinced by the woman's testimony, many Samaritans ask Him to stay. When He stays a few more days, many more come to believe: "They said to the woman, 'It is no longer because of what you said that we believe, for we have heard for ourselves, and we know that this is indeed the Savior of the World.'"

JESUS HEALS AN OFFICIAL'S SON (JOHN 4:43–54)

After Jesus leaves Samaria He goes to Galilee and begins His ministry in villages close to the Sea of Galilee (Matt. 4:12–17; Mark 1:14–15; Luke 4:14–15; John 4:43–45).[78] The people welcome Him because they have witnessed His activities in Jerusalem at the Passover Feast. In Capernaum an official asks Jesus to heal his deathly-ill son. Jesus mildly cautions the man for believing in Him only because of His miraculous signs. In his persistence, however, the man demonstrates his faith in Jesus' power to heal. Jesus tells him, "Go; your son will live," and before the man reaches his home his servants meet him and tell him his son had begun to heal—at the precise time Jesus had assured him. The man and his entire household believe.

JESUS IS REJECTED IN HIS HOMETOWN (LUKE 4:16–30)

Jesus goes to His hometown of Nazareth, enters the synagogue, and participates in the Sabbath service, as was customary for visiting rabbis.[78][9]He stands up to read from Scripture and is given the scroll of

Isaiah, which He unrolls to a specific point and begins to read. His choice of Scripture is no accident. He reads to them, "The Spirit of the Lord is upon me because he has anointed me to proclaim good news to the poor. He has sent me to proclaim liberty to the captives and recovering of sight to the blind, to set at liberty those who are oppressed, to proclaim the year of the Lord's favor" (Isaiah 61:1–2).

Jesus has already begun His ministry, and word is circulating about His healings and His teachings. Now in His hometown, he reads a passage that suggests He is the promised Messiah Who is "anointed" to proclaim the "good news."[80] He drives the point home by declaring, "Today this Scripture has been fulfilled in your hearing." J. A. Martin explains that with this statement, "the implication was clear. Jesus was claiming to be the Messiah who could bring the kingdom of God which had been promised for so long."[81]

The congregants marvel at His words but are incredulous that they are coming from the mouth of "Joseph's son." Jesus responds, "No prophet is acceptable in his hometown." He cites to them two examples of God's prophets ministering to Gentiles because Israel lacked belief— one involving Elijah (1 Kings 17:8–16) and the other, Elisha (2 Kings 5:1–19). This infuriates His listeners, who are intimately familiar with the scriptures and understand His point: that the unbelieving people of Nazareth are unreachable though even Syrian lepers and Phoenician widows are receptive to the message.[82] They drive Him out of town and try to throw Him off a cliff, but Jesus escapes. This is not the only time Jesus, against all odds, avoids being killed, proving that God is sovereign and will unfold events in His time. It was not yet Jesus' time to go.

Jesus' words and the people's reaction to them is a microcosm of the larger picture of Jewish rejection of Jesus' ministry and His messiahship. In reading from Isaiah He affirms His identity, and in citing the Old Testament prophets ministering to Gentiles, He describes His practice of preaching to unlikely people—such as the woman at the well—and taking His message to the Gentiles when the Jews reject Him. This is a model of the development of the Christian Church and its outreach to Gentiles. The book of Acts reports that in the same way, the apostles first take Jesus' message to the Jews and then turn to the Gentiles when they are rejected.[83] "The visit to Nazareth was in many respects decisive," Alfred Edersheim writes. "It presented by anticipation an epitome of the history of the Christ. He came to His own, and His own received Him not."[84]

In view of this remarkable story of Jesus reading from the scroll of Isaiah and applying the passage to Himself (as well as mountains of other examples), it baffles me that some critical scholars dispute that Jesus was aware or "self-conscious" that He is the promised Messiah of the Old Testament.[85] You see, if Jesus was unaware, then Paul and the other apostles must have originated the idea, which could mean that the Christian religion was founded on a lie, a construct designed to deify a man—an extraordinary man, perhaps, but not a God-man.

Conservative scholars believe that Jesus, in becoming a man, surrendered use of some of His divine attributes, including omniscience, but a fair reading of the Gospels shows He is well aware of His messiahship at least by the time He begins His public ministry, even if He sometimes seeks to keep His identity a secret (Mark 8:29–30).[86] James Edwards notes, "The messianic consciousness of Jesus is deeply imbedded in Jesus' speech, actions, and bearing, especially as expressed in...his divine authority that commenced at his baptism.[87] New Testament professor Sigurd Grindheim adds, "Jesus' words and deeds do not make him the outstanding divine representative. Jesus did what none of God's representatives had done or could do. Only God himself could say and do what Jesus said and did.... Jesus claimed to be God's equal."[88]

Jesus consciously acts in a role reserved in the Jewish tradition exclusively for God. He demonstrates His self-understanding in the extraordinary demands He makes of His disciples. He claims the authority to forgive sins and to heal.[89] He cleanses the holy Temple, assumes lordship over the Sabbath, and exercises the divine prerogative of reinterpreting divine Scripture.

Jesus repeatedly depicts Himself as the Son of Man, the Christ, and the One in Whom the hopes and prophecies of the Old Testament are being fulfilled. He mentions various Old Testament passages as being fulfilled in Him[90] such as Psalms 110:1, which we'll explore in Chapter 10. "Jesus places himself in the center of the world's salvation," writes Richard France. "It is in him that the prophecies are fulfilled, and in his coming that the new order is inaugurated."[91] Yes, and if Jesus were not proclaiming Himself as the Messiah and as God incarnate, the Jews would not pick up stones to throw at Him for blasphemy (John 8:59; 10:31). Those who deny Jesus is aware of His messianic role ignore His actions and words as well as the furious response they elicited.

JESUS PREACHES ON THE KINGDOM OF GOD (MATT. 4:12–17; MARK 1:14–15; LUKE 4:14–15)

From Nazareth, Jesus withdraws to Capernaum by the sea, in the regions of Zebulun and Naphtali, where He preaches that the people must repent because the kingdom of heaven is at hand. Matthew says that Jesus' move is a fulfillment of Isaiah's prophecy (Isaiah 9:1, 2) that the people "dwelling in the darkness" there "have seen a great light." We've already noted that Jesus *is* the light. Mark Moore observes, "Into a culture of darkness comes Jesus, the light of the world" (John 1:4–5, 9; 3:19; 7:52).[92]

In preaching repentance in anticipation of the kingdom of heaven, Jesus is echoing the message John the Baptist preached (Matt. 4:3). Their ministries begin on the same note and with the same vision.[93] But while Jesus' pronouncement of the kingdom mirrors John's in calling for repentance in view of God's coming judgment, it adds the component of salvation. "It is the saving significance of the kingdom that stands in the foreground," write K. A. Mitchell and T. C. Mitchell. "[Jesus] announced the kingdom not just as a reality which was at hand, something which would appear in the immediate future, but as a reality which was already present, manifested in his own person and ministry.... In him the great future has already become 'present time.'"[94] Paul, in his letters, uses "kingdom of God" frequently in terms of inheriting the kingdom of God in the future (1 Cor. 6:9; Gal. 5:21), and also suggesting it might already be present in the lives of Christians (Romans 14:17; 1 Cor. 4:20).[95]

As we've observed, the idea of the kingdom of God is central to Jesus' ministry.[96] Jesus expands the Old Testament concept of the kingdom of God not only to mean future expectations, but also that the kingdom has already come in an entirely unexpected way. Jesus still preaches that the kingdom of God will come in the future—in His Second Coming when He will establish His earthly rule. But it is also present now, in His incarnation. "The messianic promises of the prophets were not only about to be fulfilled," Walter Elwell argues, "they were actually in the process of fulfillment in his mission. In Jesus, God was visiting his people. The hope of the prophets in some real sense was being realized."[97] Elwell continues:

> John the Baptist had announced an apocalyptic visitation of God that would mean the fulfillment of the eschatological hope and the consummation of the messianic age. Jesus proclaimed that the messianic promise was actually being fulfilled in his person. This is no apocalyptic kingdom but a present salvation. In these words Jesus did not proclaim the imminence of the apocalyptic kingdom. Rather, he boldly announced that the kingdom of God had come. The presence of the kingdom was a happening, an event, the gracious action of God. This was no new theology or new idea or new promise; it was a new event in history.[98]

Douglas Moo explains that in one sense the kingdom of God has always existed, as the Old Testament describes God as the eternal king: "Your Kingdom is an everlasting kingdom, and your dominion endures throughout all generations" (Psalms 145:13). God has always been and will always be sovereign over the entire universe, but "His kingship, His ruling power, is not always seen in our world that is marred by evil and sin."[99] Thus, the Old Testament scriptures predict a future time when "a special form of God's kingdom would come into being." The prophet Daniel, for example, sees a vision of the "son of man" being granted everlasting authority and glory over all people and nations. Jesus' teaching clearly affirms the future aspect of the kingdom, when He will come and rule sovereignly forever. But He also teaches that the kingdom has already been inaugurated in His first coming, but will not reach its climax until His Second Coming.[100]

The Dictionary of Jesus and the Gospels explains how Jesus' teaching on the kingdom of God is consistent with Old Testament teachings, but is also more expansive:

The term "kingdom of God" or "kingdom of Heaven" signifies God's sovereign, dynamic and eschatological [future] rule.
The kingdom of God lay at the heart of Jesus' teaching. As
proclaimed by Jesus the kingdom of God had continuity with
the OT promise as well as with Jewish apocalyptic thinking,
but differed from them in important respects. For example,
it denoted God's eternal rule rather than an earthly kingdom,
its scope was universal rather than limited to the Jewish
nation, and it was imminent and potentially present in him
rather than a vague future hope, being inextricably connected
with his own person and mission.[101]

The kingdom of God is a time of God's rule anticipated in the Old
Testament, which God brings about through Christ but in a way the
Jews don't expect—because they believe the Messiah will establish God's
rule completely when He first appears. When Jesus fails to establish His
earthly rule and dies on the cross instead, His followers are initially
devastated, not only because they have lost their leader, but also because
their entire understanding of God's kingdom has been shattered. But
after His ascension and resurrection and the arrival of the Holy Spirit at
Pentecost, the disciples begin to comprehend God's greater plan.[102]

Jesus inaugurates the kingdom while on earth, and the Church continues to preach the existing kingdom that is now underway while speaking of a future time when Christ will return and consummate His
kingdom rule, which will be on earth and in Heaven.[103] Again, the
kingdom of God has a present and a future dimension. It involves the
"already-not yet" concept, meaning it is here now, but it is also coming
in the future in a different way that is tied to the original and will complete it. Craig Keener confirms the kingdom "is inaugurated through the
life, death, and resurrection of Jesus, but it is not yet consummated....
Jesus' announcement of the kingdom is an invitation to join in God's
movement of taking back His creation, reestablishing God's relationship
with His people."[104]

Jesus ushers the kingdom of God into the world at His first coming.
He invades the sinful world and dies for us. Following His resurrection
and ascension, He sends the Holy Spirit to us, to empower believers to

resist sin and evil. Paul says God "has delivered us from the domain of darkness and transferred us to the kingdom of his beloved Son, in whom we have redemption, the forgiveness of sins" (Col. 1:13). "Believers are new people living in an old world," J. Daniel Hays contends. "God has started his kingdom project, but he has not completely finished it. The kingdom of God has *already* arrived, but it has *not yet* come in all its fullness. The grand project has been launched, but it has not been finished."[105] "Believers," Hays continues, "are living in enemy-occupied territory between God's initial invasion (Jesus' first coming) and his total defeat of evil (Jesus' second coming). Believers live in the overlap between this age and the age to come."[106]

Believers in the current age are already enjoying some of the benefits of the kingdom because, through their faith in Christ, they have joined Christ's eternal kingdom today. They are now eternally safe and secure, and after their physical death they will be reunited with Christ—and they shall also join Him in His future reign over the new heaven and the new earth (Rev. 21).

JESUS CALLS DISCIPLES
(MATT. 4:18–22; MARK 1:16–20; LUKE 5:10–11)

John describes Jesus' calling of the first disciples as recounted above, and each of the synoptics record that Jesus calls the same disciples: Simon Peter, Andrew, James, and John. Jesus instructs Simon Peter and Andrew, "Follow me, and I will make you fishers of men." In Luke, Jesus says, "Do not be afraid; from now on you will be catching men." Many commentators surmise there were two different callings.[107] H. I. Hester maintains that Jesus called the first six disciples—these four plus Philip and Nathanael—when he found them with John the Baptist (reported in the Gospel of John), and sometime later they returned to their homes before Jesus traveled to Nazareth. That's probably why, when he called them again, they didn't hesitate to follow Him.[108] *The ESV Study Bible* adds that these men had been followers of Jesus for about a year but had returned home to their normal work before He called them again.[109]

By this calling, Jesus makes them full-time disciples. Jesus, as the first evangelist, shows God works through human beings. He knows the importance of building His ministry around a small group of men with whom He will work closely and mentor as leaders.[110] Leon Morris observes that Jesus calls the disciples He wants, whereas in Judaism the disciple chooses the rabbi.[111]

JESUS PREACHES IN CAPERNAUM
(MATT. 8:14–17; MARK 1:21–38; LUKE 4:31–43)

Jesus then goes into Capernaum and teaches in the synagogue on the Sabbath. He "astonishes" His hearers with His teaching, "for he taught them as one who had authority, and not as the scribes." This was also the initial reaction of those who heard His sermon in the synagogue at Nazareth (Matt. 13:54) before they turned on Him. His words, His manner, and His confidence demonstrate that He speaks not as any other prophet of God, but as God Himself. Jesus' teachings aren't just authoritative; they are uniquely attractive,[112] which is one reason so many readers have become believers just by reading the Gospels.

Jesus' words don't just sound authoritative. They convert His will into power. He needs no magical potions, formulas, or incantations. He heals a demon-possessed man simply by demanding it come out of him, just as on an infinitely grander level, He spoke the world into existence (Gen. 1:1–31; Psalms 33:6; John 1:3; 1 Cor. 8:6; Col. 1:16; Heb. 1:2).[113] Amazing people with His demonstration of authority and power, "his fame spread everywhere throughout all the surrounding region of Galilee."

After this, Jesus immediately leaves the synagogue and goes with James and John to Peter and Andrew's house, where Peter's mother-in-law is very ill. After Jesus touches her, she is instantly healed and begins to serve them. The Gospel writers say that the woman "begins to serve them" to show that Jesus' healing thoroughly restores her. As a result of this healing, the locals bring all their sick and possessed people to the house that evening and Jesus heals them and casts out the demons, in fulfillment of Isaiah's prophecy (Isaiah 53:4).

The next morning Jesus rises early, goes to a deserted place, and prays. Before undertaking important activities, Jesus often prays to gain strength. He prays when He is baptized (Luke 3:21), before choosing His disciples (Luke 6:12), concerning the feeding of the five thousand (Mark 6:41, 46; Matt. 14:19, 23), when He is about to question His disciples on an important matter (Luke 9:18), on the mountain of His transfiguration (Luke 9:28), before He says, "Come to me all who are weary" (Matt. 11:25–30; Luke 10:21), before He teaches His disciples the Lord's prayer (Luke 11:1), at Lazarus' tomb (John 11:41–42), on Peter's behalf before he is to deny Him (Luke 22:32), with the high priestly prayer (John 17), in the Garden of Gethsemane (Mark 14:32, 35, 36, 39; Matt. 26:39, 42, 44; Luke 22:42), on the cross (Luke 23:34; Mark 15:34; Matt. 27:46; Luke 23:46), and after He is resurrected (Luke 24:30), among other times.[114] If the God-man Jesus Christ needed prayer, how much more do we need it?

CHAPTER 6

FROM "CATCHING MEN" TO THE GOLDEN RULE

The key to the history of the world is the kingdom of God.... From the very beginning...God has been at work establishing a new kingdom in the world. It is His own kingdom, and He is calling people out of the world into that kingdom: and everything that happens in the world has relevance to it.... Other events are of importance as they have a bearing upon that event. The problems of today are to be understood only in its light.

—D. M. LLOYD-JONES[1]

JESUS PREACHES THROUGHOUT GALILEE (MATT. 4:23–25; MARK 1:37–39; LUKE 4:42–5:9)

Though His disciples tell Him everyone in Capernaum wants to see Him, Jesus must proceed to other towns to preach the good news. This shows that Jesus' main emphasis is preaching rather than healing. Though boundlessly compassionate, He doesn't intend to be seen as a miracle worker, but as the Savior.[2] His healing ministry mainly authenticates His preaching,[3] which has eternal implications, so he preaches in synagogues throughout Galilee. Jesus' fame spreads rapidly, as He is "healing every disease and every affliction among the people," including demonic possession and epilepsy.

In one instance, with the crowd pressing Him to preach, Jesus gets into Peter's empty boat in the lake of Gennesaret (also known as the Sea of Galilee), moves slightly offshore, and begins speaking. He instructs Peter to go into the deep water and put down his nets. Despite his skepticism after coming up empty all night, Peter lets down the nets. He then catches so many fish that the nets start breaking, and both boats become so full they begin to sink. Humbled and ashamed, Peter tells Jesus, "Depart from me, for I am a sinful man, O Lord." Jesus tells the amazed men, "Do not be afraid; from now on you will be catching men" (Luke 5:1–9).

JESUS HEALS A LEPER (MATT. 8:1–4; MARK 1:40–45; LUKE 5:12–16)

In one city a leper begs Jesus to heal him. Social norms discourage interaction with lepers, who are considered spiritually unclean.[4] Moreover, lepers offend every human sense—they look terrible and smell bad, leading people nearby to imagine a peculiar taste in their mouths. They are mutilated, their fingers and toes sometimes drop off, they lose their sense of touch, and they can become hoarse.[5] Nevertheless, moved by the leper's humility and childlike faith (Luke 5:12), Jesus heals him immediately merely by touching him. He then instructs the man not to tell anyone about it, but to show himself to the priest as a "proof to them" of His powers and authority. The man's rejuvenation is remarkable because leprosy is considered incurable (2 Kings 5:7). In fact, there is no record of any Israelite, other than Moses' sister Miriam (Num. 12:10–15), being healed of the disease.[6]

JESUS HEALS A PARALYZED MAN (MATT. 9:1–8; MARK 2:1–12; LUKE 5:17–26)

Jesus returns to Capernaum, and people gather at His home to listen to Him preach. A group with a paralytic can't get to Jesus due to the large crowd. (The average Capernaum home could fit about fifty people standing.)[7] So they make an opening in the roof and lower the man on his mat into the house. Moved by their faith, Jesus says, "Man, your sins are forgiven you." The scribes and Pharisees there believe Jesus has committed blasphemy because only God can forgive sins. Perceiving their thoughts, Jesus asks them whether it's easier to tell a person his sins are forgiven or to tell him to "rise and walk." But to show them "that the Son of Man has authority on earth to forgive sins," Jesus tells the paralytic, "I say to you, rise, pick up your bed and go home." The man immediately rises, picks up his bed, and goes home glorifying God, filling all the witnesses with awe.

As reported in the Bible and elsewhere, various people throughout history have performed miraculous healings.[8] But only God can forgive sins—and Jesus heals the paralytic precisely by doing that.[9] The strong implication is that Jesus *is* God.[10]

This account makes a clear connection between faith and healing, as the faith of the paralytic and his friends in Jesus' ability to heal is based, in part, on their faith in *Him*. This connection is highlighted repeatedly by the Gospel writers, especially Luke (Mark 5:34; 10:52; Luke 7:50; 8:48; 17:19; 18:42; Acts 3:16; 4:9–10; 14:9; 15:9, 11; 16:31).[11] The Greek word *sozo*, which is translated as "make well," means "save." The same word is used for "save" in a spiritual sense,[12] which is interesting considering Jesus' teaching that we are saved through faith—just as people's faith sometimes leads to their healing.

Later Jesus heals a group of ten lepers. Luke equates the healing with salvation and attributes it to faith in God, as Jesus declares to the group, "Rise and go your way; your faith has made you well" (Luke 17:19).[13] Similarly, Paul heals a cripple at Lystra based on the man's faith, which Paul recognizes when "looking intently at him" (Acts 14:9).[14] Though the connection between healing and faith is profound, it's important to note that these depictions do not mean everyone who has faith will be healed or that everyone who is healed will come to faith and salvation—only one of the ten healed lepers, for example, praises God (Luke 17:18–19).[15]

THE CALL OF MATTHEW (MATT. 9:9–13; MARK 2:13–17; LUKE 5:27–32)

Near Capernaum Jesus encounters Matthew, a tax collector, sitting at his booth. He tells Matthew, "Follow me," and Matthew obeys. Viewed as rich accomplices of the Roman authorities,[16] tax collectors are abhorred by the Jewish people, considered a disgrace to their families, and excommunicated from synagogues.[17] For Jesus to select such a man as His disciple is unusual—the fishermen He chooses aren't high society, but at least they aren't disreputable sinners.[18]

Matthew immediately surrenders his lucrative office to follow Jesus, recognizing He isn't merely inviting him but is calling him.[19] David Turner observes, "The radical character of Matthew's obedience is not lessened by the plausibility that he has already heard of John the Baptist's ministry and Jesus's words and deeds."[20] "Matthew," Douglas O'Donnell explains further, "was called by God's irresistible grace (cf. Gal. 1:15). What happened to Matthew is what happened to James, John, Peter, Andrew, you, me and every Christian who has ever come to follow Christ…. As Matthew looked into the face of Jesus Christ and heard Christ's command, he experienced the powerful call of God, a God who 'saved us and called us to a holy calling, not because of our works, but because of his own purpose and grace, which he gave us in Christ Jesus before the ages began' (2 Tim. 1:9)."[21]

When Jesus eats with Matthew and many other "tax collectors and sinners," the Pharisees are appalled, as eating together signifies acceptance of one another.[22] "Those who are well have no need of a physician, but those who are sick," Jesus counsels. "Go and learn what this means, 'I desire mercy, and not sacrifice.' For I came not to call the righteous, but sinners." Jesus here is paraphrasing an Old Testament passage in Hosea, "For I desire steadfast love and not sacrifice, the knowledge of God rather than burnt offerings" (6:6). Simply stated, God values internal commitment and transformation more than external ritual observances.[23]

It's not that God's Old Testament system of sacrifices was meaningless—far from it. But without a loving heart oriented toward God, the offerings were hollow.[24] Only people who recognize their need for Jesus will seek and receive His help. With this statement, Jesus is also explaining that God extols mercy, which Jesus displays by associating with sinners.[25] The self-righteous Pharisees, however, are oblivious to their own spiritual sickness[26]—they don't believe they need a savior since they always follow the Law, and they are uncompassionate toward sinners. "When mercy is lacking," writes L. A. Barbieri, "then religious formalities are meaningless."[27]

A DISPUTE OVER FASTING (MATT. 9:14–17; MARK 2:18–22; LUKE 5:33–39)

Though John the Baptist shows no jealousy when Jesus' ministry supersedes his, John's disciples aren't always so gracious.[28] When they ask Jesus why His disciples don't fast like they and the Pharisees do, He answers with several illustrations. He asks them whether wedding guests mourn when they are still with the bridegroom. When the bridegroom is taken away from them, He explains, they will fast. He is speaking to John's disciples in terms they will understand, since John had earlier used the wedding metaphor in identifying himself as the friend of the groom and Jesus as the groom (John 3:29).[29] Old Testament prophets applied the bridegroom metaphor to God, and Jews used it to analogize the coming of the Messiah or the messianic banquet.[30] Jesus is relating to John's disciples while signaling that the messianic age has begun and identifying Himself as the bridegroom.[31] By saying He will be "taken away" from them, He reveals He isn't the kind of Messiah they are expecting—He will be crucified.[32] In the meantime, they shouldn't fast and mourn as if some calamity has befallen them when in fact His coming is cause for rejoicing.

Jesus explains that no one puts a piece of unshrunk cloth on an old garment because it creates a worse tear, and no one puts new wine into old wineskins because they will burst. In other words, He has not come to abolish the Law but to fulfill it (Matt. 5:17), as a New Covenant is in place. He has come not to patch up the Law but to inaugurate a new system that the Old Testament prophets promised. The old system of sacrifices and rituals never had the power to save and were only "a shadow of the things to come" with the New Covenant (Col. 2:17). Jesus offers us growth in righteousness[33] based on our faith in Him, and through the power of the Holy Spirit. As evidence of the dawning of the New Covenant, He has performed healings, exorcisms, and cleansings of lepers. He has provided food for the hungry and made possible salvation for believers—hardly reasons to mourn.

HEALING A LAME MAN AT THE POOL ON THE SABBATH (JOHN 5:1–47)

◇◇

In Jerusalem for a Jewish feast, Jesus sees an invalid lying by the pool of Bethesda and asks him if he wants to be healed. "Get up, take your bed, and walk," He commands. The man, instantly healed after being impaired for thirty-eight years, takes up his bed and walks away. When some nearby Jews scold the man for taking up his bed on the Sabbath, he explains that the healer told him to do so, though he doesn't know who the healer is. Afterward Jesus finds the man in the Temple and tells him to sin no more.

The Jews denounce Jesus after learning He is the healer. Jesus replies, "My Father is working until now, and I am working." Infuriated, the Jews become determined to kill Him—for breaking the Sabbath, blasphemously calling God His own Father, and grounding His own Sabbath work in that of God's, thereby making Himself God's equal. This is particularly galling because Jesus is implying that, like the Father, He is above the Sabbath.[34]

British pastor Charles Spurgeon observes that while the Sabbath is a day of rest, Christ doesn't break His rest by performing miracles—because He is God. "He was refreshed by what, to others, might have been wearisome," Spurgeon notes, "and assuredly, whenever the Lord Jesus wrought a deed of mercy, it was rest to his heart. And, moreover, it was giving rest to others. To those who had been afflicted so long, what rest his miracles wrought!"[35] Besides, nothing in the Old Testament specifically prohibited such minor activities as lifting a mat on the Sabbath (Exodus 20:8–11). Jesus had not broken the Law, but only their tradition—a man-made rule that defined such trivial actions as work.[36]

In admonishing the man to quit sinning, Jesus isn't attributing the man's disability to his prior sins.[37] When Jesus healed a blind man earlier, he denied the man was born blind because of his or his parents' sin, explaining that His healing was to display God's glory in the man (John 9:1–5). In this case, in contrast with other healings we've discussed, the man exhibited no faith before Jesus healed him. So perhaps Jesus is telling him he should henceforth attend more to his spirituality than his physical condition.

By this point, the Jews there assume Jesus is challenging their foundational belief in monotheism,[38] which of course He is not. In a long passage, Jesus explains to them His perfect devotion to the Father and His complete harmony of mind, action, and love with Him. Though they are already convinced Jesus is asserting His own deity, He dispels all doubt with these words: "For as the Father raises the dead and gives them life, so also the Son gives life to whom he will. The Father judges no one, but has given all judgment to the Son, that all may honor the Son just as they honor the Father. Whoever does not honor the Son does not honor the Father, who sent him. Truly, truly, I say to you, whoever hears my word and believes him who sent me has eternal life. He does not come into judgment but has passed from death to life."

Jesus further tells the Jews that in the future the dead who hear His voice will live because the Father has given Him, as the Son of Man, authority to grant eternal life to believers and eternal judgment to others. He reminds them that John the Baptist vouched for Him, but that His real authority comes from the Father, and that the works He is doing on the Father's behalf prove the Father sent Him. "The Father who sent me has himself borne witness about me," He proclaims. "His voice you have never heard, his form you have never seen, and you do not have his word abiding in you, for you do not believe the one whom he has sent."

The concept of witnessing is integral to John's Gospel.[39] He describes many different types of witnesses that testify to Jesus' identity as the Messiah.[40] These include John the Baptist, Jesus' works that lead many to faith, the scriptures, Jesus Himself, the Holy Spirit, and Jesus' disciples.[41] They also include God the Father, Who testifies to Jesus at His baptism (Matt. 3:17), at the transfiguration (Matt. 17:5), at the

Triumphal Entry (John 12:28), in empowering His works (John 3:2), and in people's hearts and minds (John 6:45).

Jesus then drops a bombshell on them, telling them, just as He would later tell the disciples on the Emmaus road, that their own scriptures (the Old Testament) bear witness to Him. They search in vain for eternal life in their scriptures, Jesus says, because they refuse to come to Him that they "may have life." Because they reject Him, they don't have the love of God within them. Instead of seeking glory from God, they receive it from each other. He assures them He is not their accuser but Moses is—the one "on whom you have set your hope. For if you believed Moses, you would believe me; for he wrote of me. But if you do not believe his writings, how will you believe my words?"

Just imagine the shockwaves this sent. It is not that their scriptures are wrong, but that the Jews don't understand how their own sacred writings point to Him. They claim to follow Moses and even cite Moses' writings to reject Him, but if they actually believed Moses they would believe Him. This is a direct affront to them, for Jesus is claiming that He, a man with no formal rabbinic training, has superior understanding of their scriptures. In their minds He is coopting their role, and His condemnation incenses them. He's turning their world upside down—not only do they misunderstand their own scriptures, but they don't comprehend God Himself and certainly not His triune nature.

JESUS IS LORD OF THE SABBATH (MATT. 12:1–14; MARK 2:23–36; LUKE 6:1–11)

Jesus expands on His Sabbath teachings when the Pharisees confront Him for allowing His disciples to pick wheat on the Sabbath. He points out that when David was hungry, he entered the tabernacle and ate the priests' bread (Lev. 24:9), yet Scripture does not condemn him since he was trying to escape from Saul. The Law is supposed to benefit people, not harm them. Jesus also notes that the priests arguably violate the Sabbath tradition by the hard work they do butchering sacrificial animals.[42] Jesus tells the Pharisees, "The Sabbath was made for man, not man for the Sabbath.... I tell you, something greater than the temple is here. And if you had known what this means, 'I desire mercy, and not sacrifice,' you would not have condemned the guiltless. For the Son of Man is lord of the Sabbath." Jesus here is asserting that He represents something even greater than the Temple, for He is God incarnate. This grabs the priests' attention because they serve in the Temple, which is God's dwelling place.[43]

This exchange reinforces Jesus' earlier teachings about the Sabbath. He is not challenging the Sabbath law but the Pharisees' interpretation of its purpose.[44] Mired in legalisms, they lack compassion for man's basic needs such as food, which must take precedence over the general rule. Again, He invokes the law of sacrifice to show He is more interested in their spiritual condition than in appearances.[45]

Identifying as Lord of the Sabbath, Jesus establishes His sovereignty over the Law and His divine authority to interpret it, which is another proclamation of His deity. This especially offends the Pharisees because Jesus is not only asserting His authority, He's directly challenging theirs. He, not they, is the Lord of the Sabbath. He will interpret the rules and the exemptions.[46] They don't even have standing to criticize Him. This jars the Pharisees because they nearly deify the Law and can't imagine God contradicting their teachings on it. "The Creator is always greater than the creation," Bruce Barton writes, "thus Jesus had the authority to overrule their traditions and regulations."[47]

Jesus adds insult to injury by entering the synagogue on the Sabbath and healing a man with a withered hand. The Pharisees challenge Him again, and He reiterates the purpose of the Sabbath and asks if they would rescue a sheep if it fell into a pit on the Sabbath. Noting man has more value than sheep, He asserts that "it is lawful to do good on the Sabbath." This enrages them, and they again conspire to kill him.

New Testament scholar Lynn Cohick observes that Jesus often quotes Scripture to explain His actions. "Let's not forget," says Dr. Cohick, "that His teaching and His action go hand in glove. They're two sides of the same coin.... So...as we look more closely at parables and how Jesus teaches, never forget that this teaching is in the context of His healings, of His works of ministry and mercy, because this is how His first-century audience experienced it—what He said and what He did. They had to line up."[48] It's not just that Jesus' teachings and actions are consistent; He ties His lessons to His actions, rather than just teaching abstract concepts of theology.

Charles Spurgeon sums it up: "He was preaching sermons while he was healing the sick, and the best sort of sermons too, sermons that must strike and be remembered, for men could see them with their eyes as well as hear them with their ears. His cures are acted discourses. Whenever we try to interpret any of the miracles, I am sure you feel that we do not put truth into them, but that the truth is there already."[49]

JESUS CHOOSES HIS TWELVE APOSTLES (MATT. 12:15–21; MARK 3:7–19; LUKE 6:12–19)

Aware of the plot to kill Him, Jesus leaves toward the Sea of Galilee to continue His ministry. He doesn't leave out of fear, but because His time to be crucified has not yet come, and He still has essential work to accomplish. Many people from different areas follow Him, and the afflicted press around Him to touch Him and be healed. He heals them all and casts out demons, again ordering people not to talk about it. News of His miracles is a two-edged sword, for while it helps to spread the Gospel, it stirs up His opponents.

His command not to publicize His works fulfills Isaiah's prophecy about the Messiah quietly doing his work on behalf of the people: "He will not quarrel or cry aloud, nor will anyone hear his voice in the streets; a bruised reed he will not break" (Isaiah 42:1–4). He is not the type of Messiah they expected. In His first coming, He would not destroy armies, but would minister peacefully and with little fanfare.[50] This period of secrecy will eventually be replaced by a time of broad publicity, when the Church will fulfill its mission to the Gentiles "and in his name the Gentiles will hope." The Jews also didn't anticipate this coming global ministry.[51]

Strikingly, in quoting Isaiah's prophecy (42:1), Matthew alludes to all three persons of the Trinity: the Father speaks of Christ as His Servant, and He puts His Spirit on Him.[52] Evidence of the Trinity, as noted, is sprinkled throughout the New Testament.[53]

After performing these healings, Jesus goes up on a mountain and formally chooses His twelve apostles, who will be with Him and preach and cast out demons on His behalf: Peter, James the son of Zebedee, John, Andrew, Philip, Bartholomew, Matthew, Thomas, James the son of Alphaeus, Thaddeus, Simon the Zealot, and Judas Iscariot.

THE SERMON ON THE MOUNT
(MATT. 5:1–7:29; LUKE 6:20–49)

Jesus then delivers the greatest sermon ever preached, known as the Sermon on the Mount (or the Plain). Scholars differ on whether the Sermon on the Mount and Sermon on the Plain are different accounts of the same sermon or two similar sermons. Regardless, the message is what matters. Jesus lays down a virtually unattainable moral standard: "You therefore must be perfect, as your heavenly Father is perfect" (Matt. 5:48). Some conclude the exacting standard applies only to a future kingdom following Christ's Second Coming. Others believe it is to demonstrate man's incapability of living a sinless life on his own power, and will motivate him to turn to Christ in faith. Another view is that Jesus actually expects His followers to meet this standard.[54]

Perhaps it's a combination of all these things. Of course Christians should aspire to perfection, trust Christ, and lean on the Holy Spirit for empowerment to live this way. Though we surely won't measure up, this doesn't mean we should dismiss the standard as impractical. It reminds us of our inadequacy apart from Christ and motivates us to practice the spiritual disciplines—prayer, Bible reading, fasting, and others. Craig Keener argues that "to be faithful to the text, we must let Jesus' radical demands confront us with all the unnerving force with which they would have struck their first hearers."[55]

While the standard is rigorous, the rest of the Gospel narrative seasons these strict demands with grace, for it shows that Jesus rarely repudiates His disciples for their failings if they repent (Matt. 26:31–32), and so His grace always shines through.[56] He came to die for us precisely because we are sinners—none of us is righteous (Romans 3:10). As Isaiah declares, "All our righteous acts are like filthy rags" (Isaiah 64:6). Though we are not righteous, however, Scripture is clear that by practicing the spiritual disciplines, we become more Christ-like and more empowered to resist sin. The power of the Holy Spirit helps us to fight sin, but it will remain a daily struggle this side of eternity. As Pastor Timothy Keller surmises,

> See, the Christian ethic is unattainable, and the punishment for failing the Christian ethic is inescapable. Yet Jesus Christ, the Bible says, came and both fulfilled the requirements of the Christian ethic and took the penalty. If you look to him as your moral example, you're lost. If you look to him as a friend or a helper, you're lost. But if instead you look to him as your substitute, as your stand-in, if you trust in him as your Savior, if you trust in him as your mediator, the one who has fulfilled it all for you so once you rest and trust in him in that way, God gives you all Jesus deserves, all Jesus has earned, all the love and blessing and honor.[57]

We will ultimately be judged according to the highest possible standard, a standard of moral perfection: complete sinlessness. Though we can't be perfect, Christ models and teaches the standard of moral perfection in His incarnation. This turns us toward the cross because only through faith in Him are we justified. Being justified does not mean we actually become righteous, but that we are declared righteous and sinless in God's sight through faith in our sinless Savior, whose perfect righteousness is imputed to us. Once we are justified through our faith, we are freed from the penalty of sin and the power of sin. At the moment we are justified the Holy Spirit indwells us and empowers us to resist sin. Our subsequent walk toward holiness through the power of the indwelling Holy Spirit is called "sanctification." So while justification declares us righteous before God, it doesn't mean we are actually righteous. "To be justified is to be legally declared righteous," Samuel Hoyt explains, "not to be made experientially righteous by God."[58] But it begins the process of sanctification whereby we can become more righteous by leaning on God.[59]

Entire books have been written on the Sermon on the Mount, but I can only touch briefly on its basic principles and teachings. In His sermon, Jesus describes how a believer should live in the kingdom of heaven[60] or kingdom of God. We've already discussed the kingdom and its present and future components. In one sense the kingdom of God includes all creation because God is sovereign over all He made. But Jesus, in His teachings, uses the term to describe a subset of the concept. He equates entering the kingdom of God with entering into life (Matt. 7:13; 9:14, 16).[61] "All who are in the kingdom," writes Carson, "have life; all who are not in the kingdom do not have life."[62] Carson affirms that the kingdom has a present and future aspect. The kingdom has already arrived—Christ has come and died for our sins, so we can enter into the kingdom now and receive life now in full (John 10:10). But the kingdom is also to come in the future upon Christ's return. "Eternal life," says Carson, "though experienced now, is consummated then, in conjunction with such a renovation of the universe that the only adequate description is 'a new heaven and a new earth'" (Isaiah 65:17; 66:22; 2 Peter 3:13; Rev. 21:1; cf. Romans 8:21).[63]

But the kingdom of God means more than just entering life. It involves our whole-hearted allegiance to God mediated through Christ. This is why Christ stresses obedience: "Not everyone who says to me, 'Lord, Lord,' will enter the kingdom of heaven, but the one who does the will of my Father who is in heaven" (Matt. 7:21). You can't just glibly mouth intellectual belief in Christ, but must place your faith in Him—your trust in Him for eternal life. Genuine faith produces fruit (Matt. 7:15–20). Paul confirms that faith is more than lip service: "If you confess with your mouth that Jesus is Lord and believe in your heart that God raised him from the dead, you will be saved. For with the heart one believes and is justified, and with the mouth one confesses and is saved" (Romans 10:9–10). "This is not salvation by works," insists Leon Morris. "The contrast is not between merit and grace, but between profession and way of life.... Jesus is not saying that those saved will have earned their salvation, but that the reality of their faith will be made clear by their fruitful lives."[64]

THE BEATITUDES; SALT AND LIGHT; CHRIST CAME TO FULFILL THE LAW (MATT. 5:2–20)

Jesus begins His sermon with a series of beatitudes, which are the essence of the sermon.[65] A beatitude is a pronouncement of blessing phrased in a formula that begins with "blessed is" or "blessed are."[66]

Blessed means more than just happiness; it is a state of well-being for those who respond to Jesus' ministry.[67] It indicates being in God's favor.[68] "It speaks of more than a surface emotion," writes John MacArthur. "Jesus was describing the divinely-bestowed well-being that belongs only to the faithful. The Beatitudes demonstrate that the way to heavenly blessedness is antithetical to the worldly path normally followed in pursuit of happiness.... The Beatitudes give Jesus' description of the character of true faith."[69] They express internal qualities produced by faith, not external products of Pharisaic righteousness.[70]

The beatitudes are:

> Blessed are the poor in spirit, for theirs is the kingdom of heaven. Blessed are those who mourn, for they shall be comforted. Blessed are the meek, for they shall inherit the earth. Blessed are those who hunger and thirst for righteousness, for they shall be satisfied. Blessed are the merciful, for they shall receive mercy. Blessed are the pure in heart, for they shall see God. Blessed are the peacemakers, for they shall be called sons of God. Blessed are those who are persecuted for righteousness' sake, for theirs is the kingdom of heaven. Blessed are you when others revile you and persecute you and utter all kinds of evil against you falsely on my account. Rejoice and be glad, for your reward is great in heaven, for so they persecuted the prophets who were before you (Matt. 5:3–11).

The beatitudes promise a blessing from God specific to the character they describe. The blessings flow naturally from the character—they are not arbitrary approvals unconnected to the character described. Looking at these in order, a person who is poor in spirit is humble, he acknowledges his spiritual bankruptcy and unworthiness apart from God, and he understands he must rely on God.[71] It follows then that the kingdom of heaven belongs to the poor in spirit—those with a repentant, humble spirit.[72] Likewise, the mournful will be comforted. The mournful are not those wallowing in self-pity or the chronically unhappy, but those who genuinely grieve over their sinful state.[73]

The meek shall inherit the earth because they are humble and don't lord over others to achieve their agenda. They do not seek personal gain, but they place hope in the Lord.[74] Although meekness and poorness of spirit both involve humility, meekness concerns one's relationship with God and men while poorness in spirit involves one's self-assessment.[75] The person who thirsts for righteousness shall be filled with it, as those who thirst for righteousness long to conform to God's will.[76] God will show mercy to those who are merciful to others.[77]

Who are the pure in heart and why will they see God? Purity of heart means pursuing purity and righteousness in every area of life, as distinguished from outward displays of righteousness.[78] The pure in heart are morally pure, full of integrity, and have a single-minded commitment to God.[79] Because they sincerely pursue godly righteousness and purity, they will see God, meaning experience God's presence in this life and know Him intimately in the life to come.[80]

The peacemakers shall be called sons of God. These are not people who merely yearn for peace, but those who engage in action. "This is not appeasement," writes Bruce Barton, "but dealing with and solving problems to maintain peace."[81] Christ is the premier peacemaker—the Prince of Peace. As the good news of Jesus Christ is the ultimate peacemaking message, one who shares the Gospel is a peacemaker.[82] By demonstrating how to have inner peace with God, peacemakers are instruments of peace in the world.[83]

Those persecuted for righteousness' sake will inherit the kingdom of heaven. This group includes those who are severely persecuted, such as victims of totalitarian regimes, as well as those who are ridiculed or ostracized for their faith. This beatitude, writes D. A. Carson, "serves as a test for all the beatitudes. Just as a person must be poor in spirit to enter the kingdom (5:3), so will he be persecuted because of righteousness if he is to enter the kingdom of heaven."[84] It is self-defining: one will not be persecuted for righteousness sake, by definition, unless he seeks to act in conformity with God's will, and unless he seeks that, he will not enter the kingdom.

The final beatitude—"blessed are you when others revile and persecute you...on my account.... Rejoice and be glad, for your reward is great in heaven"—amplifies and personalizes this idea, switching from the third-person form ("they") of the previous beatitudes to the second-person form ("you"). Jesus is blessing the persecution that comes from allegiance and obedience to Him. "Rejoice and be glad" doesn't mean we should revel in our own pain. More an attitude than an emotion, this should be understood with the long view in mind—the persecution we endure in our earthly lives is infinitely outweighed by the joys eternity will bring.[85]

The beatitudes describe the Christian's character, and if Jesus stopped there one might infer that Christians are supposed to be passive, secluded monastics. But He encourages us to have a positive impact on others. We are the salt and light of the world—we must influence it for good and serve as living examples of Christ to draw people to faith. Jesus is the Light (John 1:12; 9:5), and if we are in Him we will reflect the light.

Christ emphasizes He came not to abolish the Law but to fulfill it. He neither eradicated nor invalidated the Old Testament, but reaffirmed it as the inspired Word of God (Matt. 15:3, 6) that is unbreakable (John 10:35). As earlier noted, Christ ushered in a New Covenant that supersedes the Old Covenant. It is a new contract between God and His people mediated by Jesus Christ, but the New Testament does not supersede the Old Testament—they are both part of the same inspired, inerrant Bible. The Old Testament is God's Word, just as the New Testament is, but the New Testament tells of Christ's New Covenant with His people. This replaces the Old *Covenant*, but the Old *Testament* remains. Christ represents the comprehensive fulfillment of the Law, not its destruction.

ANGER, LUST, AND OTHER SINS; LOVE YOUR ENEMIES (MATT. 5:21–48)

Jesus next expounds Old Testament teachings in what scholars call contrasts or antitheses. He interprets and expands on them but doesn't negate them.[86] For example, He proclaims, "You have heard that it was said to those of old, 'You shall not murder; and whoever murders will be liable to judgment.' But I say to you that everyone who is angry with his brother will be liable to judgment." We instinctively know this is true.

What is important is what is in our hearts. Of course it's better to refrain from acting on our evil thoughts, but such thoughts originate in our hearts, and it's sinful to harbor them. Similarly, the Law forbids adultery, but if we lust in our heart, we are also sinning.

Jesus counsels that if one part of our body causes us to sin, we must tear it out and throw it away. This is not to be taken literally, however, for Jesus uses hyperbole to stress obedience and faithfulness.[87] I think He means we shouldn't subject ourselves to temptation—we must look away if looking might lead to sinful action.[88] This is why the Lord's Prayer includes the petition, "Lead us not into temptation and deliver us from evil." Jesus continues in this vein in His treatment of divorce, oaths, retaliation, and loving one's enemies, showing in each instance that He demands greater righteousness than the Law requires. The command to love one's enemies, for example, is not in the Old Testament. But Jesus is saying that to love only your friends, family, and those who love you is nothing remarkable; even pagans meet that standard. If we are called to God's moral standards then we must also love those who don't love us—because God is love.

To better understand Jesus' message in this sermon let's set aside, for a moment, the issue of our own righteousness and whether we could ever live up to these standards—of course no human being could or ever has, apart from God's help, but that doesn't mean we should dilute the standard to conform to our sinfulness. God has written the Law on our hearts, and unless we are too calloused to recognize it or so selfish that we actually suppress it, we will see He is accurately defining perfect moral behavior. Jesus validates what we already know: possessing evil thoughts is sinful even if we don't act on them. So we shouldn't get puffed up with pride just because we behave better than the next sinner. God does not grade on a curve. But, by God's grace, He does something better: He gives us the gift of life through no merit at all on our part. By His grace, we all get an A when we place our faith in Him.

In addition to setting a higher moral standard, Jesus establishes Himself as the sovereign interpreter of the Law even as He fulfills it. With this, He is unequivocally asserting His deity, just as He did with the Pharisees in His discussion of the Sabbath. None of this, of course, goes unnoticed by the Jewish religious authorities.

GIVING TO THE NEEDY; THE LORD'S PRAYER; FASTING; STORING UP TREASURES IN HEAVEN (MATT. 6:1–34)

Jesus next turns to religious and moral hypocrisy in their many manifestations. He forbids us from making a public display of our righteousness to invite praise from others. So when you give to the needy you shouldn't broadcast your good works to earn accolades—your motive should be to do good, not to receive praise. Similarly, while there's nothing inherently wrong with praying publicly, you shouldn't make a spectacle of your piety.

Jesus provides an example of how we should pray, which we call "the Lord's Prayer." It's a model, not an exclusive method. The prayer contains these components: adoration, submission, confession, and supplication.[89] Some refer to them as "A-C-T-S" (adoration, confession, thanksgiving, and supplication),[90] though the element of thanksgiving, which is found in other Bible prayers, is not explicitly in this one.[91]

Similar principles apply to fasting. We must not fast to make ourselves look righteous to others, but do it inconspicuously as a matter between God and ourselves. This is not a blanket prohibition on fasting with others, but a general caution against improper motivation. Fasting is not a requirement for New Testament believers (see Acts 15:19–29), but it can be spiritually enriching in helping us to draw closer to God.[92]

Jesus instructs us not to store up treasures on earth but to turn ourselves toward God, to lay up treasures for ourselves in heaven, and to put our faith and hope in Him for spiritual fulfillment rather than obsessing over material fulfillment. It is not money but the *love* of money that is the root of all kinds of evil (1 Tim. 6:10). Preoccupation with material acquisitions is idolatry (Matt. 16:19–24). Jesus also admonishes us against needless worry and anxiety, urging us to rely on Him for our true needs—our spiritual needs. "Illicit worries," writes D. A. Carson, "indicate an acute shortage of confidence in God."[93] Jesus isn't saying we should be carefree or irresponsible,[94] but is instructing us on our proper priorities.

JUDGE NOT; ASK AND IT WILL BE GIVEN; ABBA—FATHER (MATT. 7:1-11)

Jesus' command, "Judge not, that you be judged," has been variously interpreted and often misunderstood.[95] Some claim Christ forbids us to exercise our God-given ability and God-imposed duty to discriminate between right and wrong, and between good and evil. Indeed, people in today's culture seem to think this Scripture warrants a suspension of all value judgments. But when they tell us not to judge, are they not judging us? I don't believe Jesus is telling us not to judge in that sense. As Frank Turek notes, we "make hundreds, if not thousands, of judgments every day—judgments between good and evil, between right and wrong, between danger and safety. [We'd] be dead already if [we] didn't make judgments."[96] Jesus does not forbid us from making these types of judgments. Rather, He is telling us not to be hypocritical, and to judge rightly—to get our own house in order before we judge others for the same behavior in which we ourselves engage.[97]

John Stott makes another important observation. "Our Lord's injunction to 'judge not,'" writes Stott, "cannot be understood as a command to suspend our critical faculties in relation to other people, to turn a blind eye to their faults (pretending not to notice them), to eschew all criticism and to refuse to discern between truth and error, goodness and evil."[98] To the contrary, Christ teaches us to distinguish between good and evil, integrity and hypocrisy. As we were made in God's image, we are able to make value judgments.

Note the two commands that follow the direction not to judge others: we must avoid giving what is holy to dogs or pearls to pigs, and we must recognize false prophets. "It would be impossible," says Stott, to obey these moral commands "without using our critical judgment. For in order to determine our behavior toward 'dogs,' 'pigs' and 'false prophets' we must first be able to recognize them, and in order to do that we must exercise some critical discernment."[99] Stott says that by "judge not" Jesus means we shouldn't be censorious (meaning hypercritical and disparaging). We can assess people critically without judging them harshly. One who is censorious destructively finds fault in people and enjoys criticizing them.[100] The command is not to be blind, but to be generous. We must be men—and continue to use our God-given critical faculties but "renounce the presumptuous ambition to be God (by setting ourselves up as judges)."[101]

Though He makes difficult moral demands in this Sermon, Jesus adds a note of encouragement on prayer. Who isn't uplifted when he reads, "Ask, and it will be given to you; seek and you will find; knock, and it will be opened to you. For everyone who asks receives, and the one who seeks finds, and to the one who knocks it will be opened." Jesus follows with a parable reinforcing the point: a father would never deny a request from his child for something he truly needed if he had the power to grant it. "How much more will our heavenly Father provide good things for those who ask Him!"

Prayer petitions are important. We know parents will provide their children's necessities whether or not they ask for them, and how much more will God do so! So we must ask God for help, though this doesn't mean He will grant all our wishes like He's a genie in a bottle. That's crucial because if He granted all our requests He would be delegating enormous power to imperfect human beings, who would inevitably make a mess of things. "It would impose an intolerable burden on frail human wisdom if by his prayer-promises God was pledged to give whatever we ask, when we ask it, and in exactly the terms we asks," writes John Stott. "How could we bear the burden?"[102] Rather, we must read and meditate on God's Word and learn to understand His will. Before we petition the Father, says Stott, "we must know what to ask for and whether it accords with God's will; we must believe God can grant it; and we must genuinely want to receive."[103]

Remarkably, Jesus describes God the Father as *our* Father ("Abba"), a term conveying a personal intimacy at the core of Christianity that is absent from other religions. After studying the prayers of ancient Judah, Joachim Jeremias found that "in no place in this immense literature is the invocation of God as *Abba* to be found...*Abba* was an everyday word a...family word. No Jew would have dared to address God in this manner. Jesus did it always...and authorizes his disciples to repeat the word *Abba* after him."[104] Jesus' invitation for us to accept *His* Father as *our* Father shows prayer in a completely different light. "What could be simpler than this concept of prayer?" asks John Stott. "If we belong to Christ, God is our Father, we are his children, and prayer is coming to him with our requests."[105] Scott continues, "There is no doubt that our prayers are transformed when we remember that the God we are coming to is 'Abba, Father', and infinitely good and kind."[106]

The idea that God is our Father is revolutionary because many people view God as unapproachable and incessantly disapproving. Brennan Manning, in his book *Abba's Child: The Cry of the Heart for Intimate Belonging*, maintains we unintentionally project onto God our feelings about ourselves. Manning quotes my favorite philosopher, Blaise Pascal, who writes, "God made man in his own image and man returned the compliment." Manning explains, "If we feel hateful toward ourselves, we assume that God feels hateful toward us."[107] But that's a terrible mistake because Jesus revealed to us, in human form, what God is like: "I and the Father are one" (John 10:30); "Whoever has seen me has seen the Father" (John 14:9); "The Father is in me and I am in the Father" (John 10:38); and "Holy Father, keep them in your name, which you have given me, that they may be one, even as we are one" (John 17:11; cf John 17:22; 5:19).

Manning argues that it was radical for Christ to encourage us to embrace His Father as *our* Father. Jewish children in Jesus' day reserved the term for addressing their human fathers affectionately. But applying it to God was blasphemous. "Abba, as a way of addressing God, is *ipsissima vox*, an authentic original utterance of Jesus," writes Jeremias. "We are confronted with something new and astounding. Herein lies the great novelty of the gospel."[108] But Manning explains what's truly remarkable and, to some, scandalous: "Jesus, the beloved Son does not hoard this experience for Himself. He invites and calls us to share the same intimate and liberating relationship.... The greatest gift I have ever received from Jesus Christ has been the Abba experience.... My identity as Abba's child is not an abstraction or a tap dance into religiosity. It is the core truth of my existence."[109]

Manning concedes that accepting this gift is easier said than done. "In my experience," he writes, "self-hatred is the dominant malaise crippling Christians and stifling their growth in the Holy Spirit."[110] Similarly Henri Nouwen notes, "Over the years, I have come to realize that the greatest trap in our life is not success, popularity or power, but self-rejection.... Self-rejection is the greatest enemy of the spiritual life because it contradicts the sacred voice that calls us the 'Beloved.'"[111]

The key to learning to trust God is to come to terms with our own self-disapproval. "We learn to be gentle with ourselves," writes Manning, "by experiencing the intimate, heartfelt compassion of Jesus.... Christ wants us to alter our attitude toward ourselves and take sides with Him against our own self-evaluation.... My own journey has taught me that only when I feel safe with God do I feel safe with myself. To trust the Abba who *ran* to His wayward son and never asked any questions enables us to trust ourselves at the core."[112] Manning shares Georges Bernanos's final entry into his *Diary of a Country Priest*, in which he reveals, "The strange mistrust I had of myself, of my own being, has flown, I believe forever.... The conflict is done.... I am reconciled to myself, to the poor, poor shell of me. How easy it is to hate oneself! True grace is to forget. Yet if pride could die in us, the supreme grace would be to love oneself in all simplicity—as one would love any of those who *themselves* have suffered and loved in Christ."[113]

I find this enormously insightful, for I have discovered that self-condemnation can be a formidable obstacle to faith. Part of trusting Christ is to give our sinfulness to Him and accept His word that He truly forgives us. We rest in His work; we are liberated because of what He's done for us. We may still have character and behavioral flaws that are sinful and should be avoided, but Christ has redeemed us completely despite our sinful nature and its consequences. If we continue beating ourselves up, we are rejecting the spiritual liberation He offers and keeping ourselves in bondage.

Once again, Manning—this time in another book, *Ruthless Trust*—explains it best. "Wallowing in shame, remorse, self-hatred, and guilt over real or imagined failings in our past lives betrays a distrust in the love of God," writes Manning. "It shows that we have not accepted the acceptance of Jesus Christ and thus have rejected the total sufficiency of his redeeming work. Preoccupation with our past sins, present weaknesses, and character defects gets our emotions churning in self-destructive ways, closes us within the mighty citadel of self, and preempts the presence of a compassionate God."[114]

Manning offers profound insight into our relationship to the Father, which is foundational to the prayer life Jesus encourages us to experience. We aren't just put on earth to occupy space and live rudderless lives. Rather, "We are sons and daughters of the Most High."[115] We can have a relationship with the Son *and* the Father, and we are cheating ourselves of life's fullness if we fail to do that.

Skeptics are dismissive of prayer, wondering why anyone would pray to an omniscient, sovereign God Who knows our requests before we even think them. Isn't it absurd to believe an omniscient God will respond to our entreaties? Scripture teaches otherwise (Exodus 32:9–14). But while we focus on using prayer to change God's mind, what we don't realize is that prayer often helps to change *our* mind and *our* perspective.[116] Indeed, the main reason we should pray is that Scripture tells us we should—unceasingly (1 Thess. 5:17; Col. 4:2). In fact, we'll fail to receive certain things if we simply don't ask for them (James 4:2).

Rest assured, God listens to our prayers (1 Kings 8:52). How exciting that the God of the universe hears us talking to Him! Though we don't always recognize answered prayer, Scripture attests, "The prayer of a righteous person has great power as it is working" (James 5:16; John 14:13–14). We must also broaden our selfish perspective to realize prayer isn't just about us and our needs and desires. As with the Lord's Prayer, we pray to express adoration to God (Rev. 5:13), confess our sins (1 John 1:9), seek His guidance (1 Samuel 14:36–41), praise Him (Psalms 18:3; 103:1), and give Him thanks (Philip. 4:6–7). But most of all, praying draws us closer to God.

THE GOLDEN RULE; FALSE PROPHETS; A TREE AND ITS FRUIT; BUILD YOUR HOUSE ON THE ROCK; THE AUTHORITY OF JESUS (MATT. 7:12–29)

Jesus exhorts us to treat others as we wish they would treat us (the Golden Rule)—this is the "Law and the Prophets" (the Old Testament) in a nutshell. Christ further teaches, "You shall love the Lord your God with all your heart and with all your soul and with all your mind. This is the great and first commandment. And a second is like it: You shall love your neighbor as yourself. On these two commandments depend all the Law and the Prophets" (Matt. 22:37–40). The key to acquiring the requisite righteousness to honor this command does not lie in the Law or in our own works. It is in "the narrow gate" of saving faith in Jesus Christ, through which we will demonstrate true righteousness toward others. The goal is *internal* transformation, not adherence to external rules.[117]

Jesus warns us of false prophets whom we can recognize by their "fruits." Beware of those who pretend to be godly to prey on vulnerable people for money or power. Eventually they will reveal their true character. A special place is reserved for such people. Jesus closes with a sobering warning. We have a choice: we can build our spiritual foundation on the Rock of Jesus Christ, on the shifting sands of phony gods and false promises, or on the lie that we can save ourselves through our good deeds rather than relying on His finished work on the cross.

When Jesus has finished speaking, the crowds are blown away by His teaching. "For he was teaching them as one who had authority, and not as their scribes." People listening to Christ at the time manifestly know, by the content of His teaching and His uniquely authoritative bearing, that He is the Son of the Living God—and we know that too, if we read His words with an open heart and a humble spirit.

CHAPTER 7

FROM HEALING A CENTURION'S SERVANT TO CONFRONTATIONS WITH PHARISEES

In essentials the synoptic gospels agree remarkably well, and form a consistent portrait of Christ. No one reading these scenes can doubt the reality of the figure behind them. That a few simple men should in one generation have invented so powerful and appealing a personality, so lofty an ethic and so inspiring a vision of human brotherhood, would be a miracle far more incredible than any recorded in the Gospels. After two centuries of Higher Criticism the outlines of the life, character, and teachings of Christ remain reasonably clear, and constitute the most fascinating feature in the history of Western man.

—W. DURANT[1]

JESUS HEALS A CENTURION'S SERVANT (MATT. 8:5–13; LUKE 7:1–10)

E ntering Capernaum after His Sermon, Jesus is implored by a Roman centurion (military officer) to heal his paralytic servant. When Jesus agrees to do it, the centurion protests that he isn't worthy of having Jesus come into his home, instead urging Jesus to heal the servant just by speaking. The centurion assures Jesus he understands the significance of authority because his soldiers follow his orders unquestioningly, but he also demonstrates humility before Christ and compassion for his subordinates. Far from treating his servant as inferior, he recognizes his human dignity and pleads with Christ to heal him. Jesus lavishes praise on the centurion for demonstrating faith like He hasn't seen before in Israel. "Go; let it be done for you as you have believed," Jesus declares, and the servant is instantly healed.

This story illustrates the importance of authentic faith and the sheer power of Jesus' words—even more than His healing power, which is already established. It emphasizes that Jesus' message is for everyone, Jew and Gentile alike.[2] We don't gain access to the kingdom by having Christian parents, but through our personal decision to trust Christ.

JESUS RAISES A WIDOW'S SON (LUKE 7:11–17)

Jesus leaves for the small town of Nain followed by His disciples and a great crowd. When He reaches the town gate, people are carrying out a widow's son who has died. Jesus, filled with compassion, tells her not to cry. He touches the bier (which is more like an open stretcher than a coffin)[3] and says, "Young man, I say to you, arise"—and the man sits up and starts to speak.

Again, Jesus appears to be breaking the rules, as the Jews consider it defilement to touch a dead body (Num. 19:11, 16), and touching the bier holding it would have made Him unclean.[4] The people declare Jesus a great prophet and proclaim that God has visited His people, meaning that through His prophet Jesus, God had visited His people. Their observation is correct as far as it goes—Jesus is a prophet. But He is also the Son of God. If Jesus can be resurrected, He can resurrect others. He has already performed striking miracles, but here He shows His power over death itself. In this incident, Jesus provides a foretaste of our own resurrection. He doesn't wait to be asked—He takes the initiative in restoring the man to life. Likewise, He beckons us to accept His offer of salvation, and we must only respond.

This is yet another miracle Jesus performs before many witnesses, including the crowds that accompany Him and those with the widow. Church Father Eusebius quotes from a speech by Bishop Quadratus of Athens in which he defends Christian truths against early critics: "'The deeds of our Savior,' says [Quadratus], 'were always before you, for they were true miracles; those that were healed, those that were raised from the dead, who were seen, not only when healed, and when raised, but were always present. They remained living a long time, not only whilst our Lord was on earth, but likewise when he had left the earth: so that some of them have also lived to our times.'"[5] Quadratus states that some of the witnesses to the event are still alive and could testify before the emperor.[6]

R. Kent Hughes movingly describes the wrenching situation in which Jesus intervened: "The death of a child is certainly one of the greatest agonies possible in this life—a burying of a part of oneself, a period before the end of a sentence, the death of a future. It is a burden that all parents fear. Such untimely pain was the emotional context of Jesus'…ministry event."[7] Indeed, this healing poignantly reveals Jesus' human side. He intimately feels the widow's agony over the loss of her only son. Unlike fallen human beings, Jesus' unique compassion stems from His infinite love and sinless perfection. Uncluttered with His own personal concerns, His empathy is wholly directed toward others. No matter the enormity of our pain, Jesus feels it, and we can always lean on Him for comfort.

JESUS AND JOHN THE BAPTIST
(MATT. 11:2–19; LUKE 7:18–35)

In prison for almost a year, John the Baptist apparently begins to have doubts. He sends his disciples to ask Jesus, "Are you the one who is to come, or shall we look for another?" Jesus tells them to inform John He has been healing, exorcising, raising the dead, and preaching the good news to the poor. Jesus adds, "And blessed is the one who is not offended by me."

It may seem odd that the very man who announced Jesus' arrival is having second thoughts, but John's imprisonment has probably left him feeling dispirited and abandoned. Additionally, even as Jesus' forerunner, John may not understand the full scope of Jesus' upcoming ministry, the nature of His messianic role, or some of His unorthodox actions. In announcing Christ's coming, John promised a Judge Who would baptize with the Holy Spirit and fire. He may have expected the Messiah to render His judgment on mankind—separating the wheat from the chaff (Matt. 3:11–12)—and bring in His full kingdom rule right then and there.[8] "Why would one who had promised to free the prisoners (Luke 4:18) not get John out of Jail," asks Craig Blomberg. "Most likely John also wondered why there were no signs of imminent judgment of the wicked that he had predicted (Matt. 3:10). In fact, Jesus' 'messiahship' little resembled the political and military program of liberation many Jews anticipated."[9]

This is a fitting lesson for us: John, while a great prophet, is still only human. He utters the question every person must ask of himself about Jesus: Is He the Messiah, the Son of God? Many Christians experience doubt, and it's better to explore and resolve that doubt than to ignore it. Jesus softly scolds John, saying those who don't question Him are blessed, but He never suggests it's wrong to have questions. Nor does He abandon John—compassionately, Jesus reassures him.

As John's disciples depart, Jesus praises John to the crowds, asking them if they think John is a "reed shaken by the wind" or "a man dressed in soft clothing." Far from it, Jesus assures them. He extols John as His messenger, as the greatest human being, and as Elijah—the prophesied messenger of Christ. This praise is well deserved. John's unique character is exhibited by his humility in the face of his disciples' adulation. While they sought to worship him, he dutifully retired to the background to emphasize Christ's incomparable greatness. "When," asks John Peter Lange, "has a more elevated character been seen?"[10]

But as great as John is, even the least of those in the kingdom of heaven is greater than he—meaning nothing is like the experience that awaits Christians in the kingdom. Jesus warns that people are resisting His kingdom which, He says, has been under attack "from the days of John the Baptist until now." But in the end "wisdom is justified by her deeds"—the coming triumph of the kingdom is inevitable, and even though John would die before seeing the risen Jesus inaugurate it, Jesus' life and ministry would vindicate God's wisdom.[11]

A SINFUL WOMAN ANOINTS JESUS' FEET
(LUKE 7:36–50; MARK 15:41; LUKE 8:1–3)

Jesus accepts an invitation to eat at the house of a Pharisee named Simon. A sinful woman comes to wash Jesus' feet with her tears, dry them with her hair, and anoint them with ointment. Simon doubts Jesus' legitimacy as a prophet because He interacts with a known sinner. Jesus responds with a parable, asking which man would be more appreciative if his debts were forgiven: one who owes five hundred denarii or one who owes fifty. Simon admits it would be the one who owes more. The point is that one who is in greater need of forgiveness is more likely to be grateful and an energetic evangelist and ambassador for the kingdom.

Jesus says that unlike Simon, the sinful woman has kissed and anointed Jesus, and so He forgives her many sins because "she loved much." Simon not only lacks love but humility, for in his haste to shun the woman he displays his unawareness of his own sinful nature. In this sense, this story is analogous to the parable of the Pharisee and the tax collector (which we'll discuss in Chapter 9), the former proudly beating his chest over his righteousness and the latter acknowledging his sinfulness and praying for forgiveness (Luke 18:9–14).

The people marvel at Jesus' authority to forgive sins. Jesus tells the woman her faith has saved her. Note that it's not her love, but her faith that leads to her forgiveness, as we cannot earn our salvation—though we must acknowledge that faith is usually accompanied by love, and she does respond in love when He forgives her. Again, Jesus ministers to the poor and lost, exercising His divine prerogative of forgiving sins.

Jesus continues to preach the good news of the kingdom of God throughout the cities and villages, with the twelve disciples accompanying Him along with some women (including Mary Magdalene) whom He'd healed and freed of demons. Seeing as Jesus lived in a patriarchal culture in which women were undervalued and mistreated, the Gospel writers probably mention the women's presence to emphasize Jesus' unorthodox, unexpected practices and that His love and ministry are not reserved for any special classes of people.[12]

JESUS' TRUE FAMILY (MATT 12:46–50; MARK 3:20–21; LUKE 8:19–21)

Speaking to people in a house as His mother and brothers stand outside, Jesus describes His family. He holds His hand toward His disciples and says, "Here are my mother and my brothers! For whoever does the will of my Father in heaven is my brother and sister and mother." As much as He loves His own mother and brothers, His messianic mission is even more important. He is not diminishing familial love—see Matthew 15:3–9, where He repeats and expands on the commandment to honor one's father and mother. But He's emphasizing the importance of our spiritual family and of one's faith and allegiance to Him.[13] Jesus does not disown His family or Israel, argues David Turner. "Rather, he challenges any notion that ethnic descent or family loyalty defines the people of God."[14] He reminds us that as Christians, we are a family, a community of believers who strengthen one another.

PARABLES (MATT. 13:3–52; MARK 4:2–34; LUKE 8:4–21)

Parables, a common form of Judaic teaching in Jesus' day, are instructive stories that have symbolic significance.[15] C.H. Dodd says a parable is "a metaphor or simile drawn from nature or common life, arresting the hearer by its vividness or strangeness, and leaving the mind in sufficient doubt about its application to tease it into active thought."[16] Parables come in various forms, including narrative stories, proverbs, and riddles. They even take the form of one-liners, such as Jesus' warning against throwing pearls before swine (Matt. 7:6). Some parables impart just one lesson while others contain several,[17] typically a main lesson alongside ancillary ones.[18] Sometimes Jesus uses parables to hide the truth from unbelievers while revealing it to His disciples and other devotees. He says He is fulfilling Isaiah's prophecy about unbelievers, who "will indeed hear but never understand" and "see but never perceive" (Isaiah 6:9, 10). As for believers, He declares, "Blessed are your eyes, for they see, and your ears, for they hear."

THE PARABLE OF THE SOWER (MATT. 13:3–9, 18–23; MARK 4:2–9, 13–20; LUKE 8:4–8, 11–15)

Jesus tells numerous parables to the crowds gathered off the shore of Galilee to hear His teaching. In those days, farmers used broadcast sowing, in which they took a bag of seed in their hands, scattered it across the ground, and plowed it into the dirt. Growth would vary depending on the kind of soil in which each seed landed.[19] In the parable of the sower, a farmer plants his seeds, and some fall along the path, some on rocky ground, some on thorns, and some on good soil. The seeds along the path are devoured by birds, which represents those who hear the word of the kingdom and don't understand it, so Satan comes and snatches the word away. The seeds in the rocky ground quickly spring up, but the plants are scorched by the sun and wither away because they have no roots. This symbolizes those who initially hear the word with joy but, because it doesn't fully take root, fall away when facing tribulation or persecution. The seeds that fall among the thorns are choked by the thorns, which typifies the person who hears the word but is lured away from it by the enticement of riches. The seeds sown on good soil are emblematic of one who hears and understands the word and bears fruit abundantly.

Jesus' parables are not just for His immediate audience, but all future readers of the Gospel. We should examine ourselves and see how they might apply to us. D. A. Carson says the parable of the soils, for example, "implicitly challenges hearers to ask themselves what kinds of soil they are."[20] Where are we on this continuum? Do we read the Bible with reverence, as the word of God? Do we meditate on it? Do we apply its lessons to our lives? Or are we just fair weather readers who are enthusiastic on Sunday but neglect the Bible and prayer the rest of the week?

DISCIPLES ASK JESUS ABOUT PARABLES
(MATT. 13:10–17; MARK 4:10–12; LUKE 8:9–10)

The disciples ask Jesus why He teaches in parables instead of speaking plainly. Jesus says He intends to reveal the secrets of the kingdom of heaven to certain people but not to others. "This is why I speak to them in parables, because seeing they do not see, and hearing they do not hear, nor do they understand."

Though Jesus may harden certain people's hearts, He only does so after they show their unbelief. Man, by himself, cannot unlock the secrets of the kingdom; they must be revealed to him.[21] "The secret things belong to the Lord our God, but the things that are revealed belong to us and to our children forever, that we may do all the words of his law" (Deut. 29:29). But once an unbeliever's heart is hardened against His message, Jesus withholds revelation from him, thus further hardening his heart. Jesus will reward believers—the humble and repentant—with greater insight but further confuse the unrepentant and rebellious. This doesn't mean He punishes doubters, but there's a difference between those who doubt yet earnestly seek the Truth, and those who shake their fists at Him in defiance. There must be a point at which God says, "Enough. If you want to continue in your prideful and defiant state and reject me, then I'll accommodate you."

There is precedent for this in the Old Testament. God says that the time is coming when He will send a famine on the land, but it will not be a famine of bread, nor a thirst for water, but of hearing the words of the Lord (Amos 8:11). "Since Israel had rejected all His words (Amos 2:11–12; 7:10–13, 16)," explains D. R. Sunukjian, "they would hear His words no more."[22] Yet God is a long-suffering God. He tells us to knock and He will open, to seek and we shall find, to pray unceasingly and He will answer us.

This is a lesson on God's superior wisdom and His grace. In this age, some secular-minded people believe science and unaided reason are the exclusive avenues to solving all man's problems. But even our minds and our ability to reason are gifts from God, and certain spiritual truths will be incomprehensible without God revealing the mysteries to us. As the Book of Romans exclaims, "Oh, the depth of the riches and wisdom and knowledge of God! How unsearchable are his judgments and how inscrutable his ways!" (11:33).

By teaching in parables Jesus also buys Himself more time to preach, as His indirect messages are less likely to antagonize the religious authorities and hasten His arrest.[23]

THE PARABLE OF THE WEEDS (MATT. 13:24–30, 36–43; MARK 4:26–34; LUKE 13:18–21)

Jesus compares the kingdom of heaven to a man who sows good seed in his field, after which the enemy sneaks in and sows weeds among the wheat so that when the plants come up weeds surround them. The man's servants offer to remove the weeds but the master protests that gathering the weeds will endanger the wheat. So he allows them to grow together until the harvest, when he will put the wheat in the barn and burn the bundles of weeds.

Jesus explains that the man who sows the good seed is the Son of Man (Jesus Himself). The field represents the world, the good seed signifies the sons of the kingdom, and the weeds are the sons of the evil one—the devil, who is the one who sows them. The harvest symbolizes the end of the age when the angels will serve as reapers, gathering out of His kingdom all causes of sin and all law-breakers, and throwing them into the fiery furnace where there will be weeping and gnashing of teeth. The righteous will shine like the sun in the Father's kingdom. The enemies of the kingdom will coexist with the kingdom in this age until the day of judgment.[24]

British evangelist G. Campbell Morgan emphasizes "three outstanding things" about this parable. First, the sower sows the field on his own property—he's at work in his own field. Second, two distinct sowings are involved: the owner sows the good seed and someone else attempts to sabotage the seed with weeds. The weeds described in Scripture are darnel, which initially resembles wheat so closely that they're indistinguishable—"yet they are absolutely different." Third, the man who sows the weeds is a trespasser who has no right to the field. "He was a trespasser, full of subtlety, animated by malice." The enemy gains nothing from his actions except to advance evil. "The absolute meanness of the action appalls."[25] Indeed the devil, says Morgan, has been likened to a squatter, and as believers we must tell the devil, "Hands off in the name of the Proprietor: to declare at every point that the whole field belongs to the Son of Man."[26]

Moreover, in His life and teaching, Jesus does what the owner did. He drags Satan from his hiding places into clear daylight. "It is as remarkable and valuable a fact that Jesus came to show up the work of the devil as that He came to reveal God," observes Morgan. "It is when a man submits himself to Jesus Christ that he sees clearly, not God only, not himself only, but his enemy also."[27] This concept is particularly meaningful to me. As I described in *Jesus on Trial*, the pervasiveness of evil in the world used to fan my skepticism, but now it reinforces my faith because no worldview besides Christianity so accurately describes the true state of the world and the fallen human condition.

Morgan notes that it's perfectly natural for the owner to wait until the harvest to separate the weeds from the wheat because at that point they'll be easily distinguishable from each other. "If these sowings are allowed to work themselves out to consummation," writes Morgan, "discrimination will be possible upon the basis of manifestation, and in that manifestation there will be vindication of the destinies of the darnel (weeds) and of the wheat. The darnel will be bound in bundles for burning. The wheat will be gathered into the garner of the owner."[28] God will allow each person to demonstrate, in time, whether he'll be part of the wheat or the weeds, and nothing could be fairer.

THE MUSTARD SEED AND THE LEAVEN
(MATT. 13:31–33)

Jesus says the kingdom of heaven is like a grain of mustard seed that a man sows in his field. It's the smallest of all seeds, but it grows larger than all the garden plants and becomes a tree, so that the birds come and make nests in its branches. Many commentators believe Jesus is not emphasizing the greatness of the kingdom in full flower because other parables make that point. Rather, he's calling our attention to how small the kingdom appears in its initial stages while noting that it will grow large and glorious.[29] This could represent the present and future aspects of the kingdom, as we've discussed, or it could symbolize the growth of Christendom, which began small and expanded worldwide.[30] God's work sometimes begins in small forms such as churches and student ministries, and often encounters roadblocks, but it can grow into something great.[31]

Jesus follows up with a short parable comparing the kingdom of heaven to "leaven that a woman took and hid in three measures of flour, till it was all leavened." The lesson is similar to that of the mustard seed parable in that they each describe positive growth in the kingdom. But here we don't notice the positive influences as they happen like we see the seed growing into a large plant or bush. The yeast is hidden in the flour and has a pervasive impact. "The leaven depicts," writes Arthur Robertson, "the silent, unobserved, yet permeating power of the gospel, which ultimately effects change in men and their culture."[32] Some interpret the parable differently, as yeast sometimes represents evil in the Bible, but that's not always the case. It's unlikely the case here, says L. A. Barbieri, because it would be redundant, as the evil has already been represented by the weeds.[33]

THE PARABLES OF THE HIDDEN TREASURE, THE PEARL OF GREAT VALUE, THE NET, AND NEW AND OLD TREASURES (MATT. 13:44–52)

Jesus teaches His disciples with several more parables. "The kingdom of heaven is like a treasure hidden in a field," He says, "which a man found and covered up. Then in his joy he goes and sells all that he has and buys the field." At first blush, it seems Jesus is solely stressing the kingdom's value—it's worth giving everything else up to acquire it. But there's something more. Professor Daniel Doriani observes that people sometimes stumble into Christ and bump into the kingdom after encountering someone who shares with them the Word of God. "And when that happens, be glad. It's worth all you have, and even at that price it's a bargain."[34] Others believe Jesus is referring to Israel as God's treasured possession, which several Old Testament passages affirm (Exodus 19:5; Psalms 135:4). One reason Jesus came into the world was to redeem

Israel, and He sold everything He had (His glory in sitting at the side of the Father in Heaven) to purchase (redeem) Israel.[35]

Jesus also likens the kingdom of heaven to "a merchant in search of fine pearls, who on finding one pearl of great value, went and sold all that he had and bought it." This is similar to the parable of the hidden treasure in emphasizing the kingdom's incomparable value. But it's different because the merchant, unlike the man in the field, is deliberately searching for something of great value. In comparing the two parables Professor Doriani observes, "When we discover the kingdom, it may be a delightful surprise, or it may be because we've been searching for a long time. Maybe someone has looked at all the religions of the world, all the philosophies of life, and after appraising them all and hearing the claims of Christ, he says, or she says, 'That's the truth. That's for me. I'm going to follow Jesus.'"[36] Some commentators see this parable applying to Jesus' redeeming the Church (believers) through His sacrificial death.[37]

Jesus next compares the kingdom to a net thrown into the sea that captures all kinds of fish. Once full, the men separate the good from the bad and discard the latter. This is what will happen at the end of the age. Angels will separate the righteous from the evil and will throw the evil into the fiery furnace where there will be weeping and gnashing of teeth. God will judge all people, gather the righteous (believers) to Himself, and reject the others.[38] This confirms that if the separation will occur at the end of the age, then evil will not be totally removed until then.[39]

Jesus asks if they've understood "all these things." When the disciples answer "yes," He says, "Therefore every scribe who has been trained for the kingdom of heaven is like a master of the house, who brings out of his treasure what is new and what is old." Jesus is training His disciples so they will grow to understand how God's revelation fits together and how He and His teachings fulfill the Old Testament promises.[40]

"O YOU OF LITTLE FAITH" (MATT. 8:23–27; MARK 4:35–41; LUKE 8:22–25)

The disciples follow Jesus into a boat and a storm ensues, imperiling the boat while Jesus is sleeping. In fear, the disciples wake Him and ask

Him to save them. He responds, "Why are you afraid, O you of little faith?" He rises and rebukes the wind, creating a great calm. The amazed disciples declare, "What sort of man is that, that even winds and sea obey him." Through His divine voice alone, Jesus exercises sovereign control over nature, causing awe and wonderment among His disciples. With this revelation, those of "little faith" acquire devotion and a greater sense of Christ's divinity. "In the boat with Jesus is a happy place," says Charles Spurgeon, "but storms may come when we are there."[41] Like the disciples, however, we must trust the power of Jesus in the storms of our lives.[42]

JESUS HEALS POSSESSED MEN
(MATT. 8:28–34; MARK 5:1–20; LUKE 8:26–39)

When Jesus reaches the country of the Gadarenes (a town about six miles southeast of the Sea of Galilee),[43] two fierce, demon-possessed men meet Him and cry out, "What have you to do with us, O Son of God? Have you come here to torment us before the time?" The demons beg Him to send them into a herd of pigs. Jesus obliges, and the entire herd rushes into the sea and drowns. Nearby herdsmen flee into the city to tell what has happened. The entire city comes out and, in fear, begs Jesus to leave.

Luke's Gospel sheds light on the demons' unexpected request. Here, just one man is possessed by many demons who implore Jesus to send them into the pigs because they don't want Him to cast them into the abyss—the underworld—where they will be tormented. They know that Jesus is God and their judge, but they hope to defer the unbearable judgment of torment as long as they can.[44] After being exorcised, the man begs to remain with Jesus. But Jesus tells him to go home to his friends and report how much the Lord has done for him, so he returns home and preaches it to the whole city.

It's noteworthy that Jesus does not command secrecy in this case as he has in several others (Mark 1:44; 5:43; 9:9). This is probably because the people in the Decapolis—a group of ten Hellenistic cities mostly located on the eastern side of the Sea of Galilee and the Jordan River,[45] where this event occurred—don't pose the same risk to Jesus as those in Galilee do.[46] This is the same reason He was willing to identify Himself as the Messiah to the Samaritan woman at the well and allow her to testify about Him (John 4:39–42). Jesus identifies Himself to the exorcised man as the Lord and as God, just as He had revealed Himself as the Messiah to the Samaritan woman.

JESUS HEALS AND RAISES THE SYNAGOGUE RULER'S DAUGHTER (MATT. 9:18–26; MARK 5:21–43; LUKE 8:40–56)

When Jesus crosses back to the other side of the Sea of Galilee, a crowd meets Him. Jairus, a synagogue ruler, falls at His feet and begs Him to heal his dying daughter. As Jesus goes with the man, a great crowd follows and gathers about Him. A woman who has discharged blood for twelve years approaches Jesus from behind and touches His garment, saying, "If I touch even His garment I will be made well." When she touches Him, her bleeding immediately stops. Feeling power leaving His body, Jesus asks who touched His garments. The woman falls down before Him and admits it was her. Jesus tells her, "Daughter, your faith has made you well; go in peace."

The woman accesses His healing power simply through her faith and by touching His garment, which is why He feels power leaving His body (though in Matthew's account she doesn't heal until after He speaks to her).[47] Mark gives other examples of Jesus healing by touching someone (Mark 1:31, 40–45; 7:31–37; 8:22–26) or someone touching Him (3:10; 6:56). We also see healings from indirect contact with Peter and Paul in Acts (5:15; 19:11–12). Concerning the relationship of faith, healing, and Jesus' powers, it's significant that when He's rejected as a prophet without honor in His hometown of Nazareth, Jesus can't perform many miracles or other works there (Mark 6:1–6; Matt. 13:53–58).

While Jesus is still speaking, someone from Jairus' house reports that his daughter has died and says not to trouble Jesus further. Hearing them, Jesus says to Jairus, "Do not fear, only believe." He proceeds to Jairus' house, allowing no one to follow except Peter, James, and John.

When they arrive, flutists are playing and people are weeping. Jesus asks, "Why are you making a commotion and weeping? The child is not dead but sleeping." After they laugh at Him, He sends them all outside and takes Jairus, his wife, and His disciples inside. He grasps the child's hand and tells her to rise, and she immediately gets up and begins walking. He tells them to feed her, which shows she has been restored to health.[48]

They are amazed, but He strictly commands those present to tell no one about this, though news of the event spreads throughout the area. Jesus realizes He can't completely suppress news of this event given the crowds present, but He's probably hoping to delay the reports until after He leaves the area because He's in Galilee, where His many Jewish opponents may seek to kill Him and prematurely end His ministry.[49]

JESUS HEALS TWO BLIND MEN AND A MUTE DEMONIAC (MATT 9:27–35)

When Jesus leaves, two blind men follow Him and say, "Have mercy on us, Son of David." He asks them whether they believe He can heal them, and they answer "yes." He then touches their eyes and pronounces, "According to your faith be it done to you." The men are instantly healed. Jesus sternly warns them to keep quiet about it, but they tell everyone in the area anyway. Here again we see the relationship between faith and healing, though as we've noted, Jesus' healings aren't always performed on those with faith. Before Jesus heals them, He invites them to profess their faith in His ability to do it, which is tantamount to their faith in Him as the Messiah. They show their faith not just in responding affirmatively, but also by persisting and following Him inside the house to plead for His healing.

When Jesus and His followers are leaving, a mute, demon-possessed man is brought to Him. Jesus casts out the demon, and the man speaks. The astonished crowds proclaim, "Never was anything like this seen in Israel." The Pharisees contend, however, that His power to exorcise comes from the devil. They have no other explanation for His supernatural healings, since they stubbornly refuse to accept Him as the Messiah. The Pharisees are increasingly furious at Jesus for challenging their authority and beliefs, weakening their influence, and exposing their hypocrisy and errors.[50] Jesus will later rebuke them for their blasphemy against the Holy Spirit as well (Matt. 12:22–32).

THE HARVEST IS PLENTIFUL, THE LABORERS FEW (MATT. 9:35–38; LUKE 10:2–3)

Throughout the cities and villages, Jesus continues His threefold ministry of teaching in the synagogues, preaching the Gospel, and healing the sick (cf. Matt. 4:23). He teaches to inform people of His identity, purpose, and work; He preaches to inspire their commitment; and He heals out of compassion and to authenticate His deity.[51] When He sees the crowds, He is moved because they're beleaguered and helpless like sheep without a shepherd. Jesus, in His humanity and as the Son of God, fully empathizes with their suffering, realizing the people are drifting aimlessly without a spiritual leader. The religious leaders are resisting the Gospel and leading the people astray, so Jesus enters the scene as a Shepherd to lead His people, as the prophet Micah prophesied (Micah 5:4). He tells His disciples, "The harvest is plentiful, but the laborers are few; therefore pray earnestly to the Lord of the harvest to send out laborers into his harvest."

They need additional workers—evangelists—to spread the good news of the kingdom. When we pray for God's help, He will sometimes answer by commissioning us for the project.[52] Jesus sends out His disciples "as lambs in the midst of wolves" (Luke 10:3), warning them they will be persecuted. He implies they are not to spread the Gospel by force, but to share the message and invite hearers to voluntarily accept it.[53]

JESUS SENDS OUT HIS TWELVE APOSTLES (MATT. 10:1–42; MARK 6:7–13; LUKE 9:1–6)

Ramping up His ministry, Jesus sends His twelve disciples in pairs on their first apostolic mission, investing them with authority over unclean spirits and commissioning them to heal every affliction. As vital as Christ's work is, He entrusts much of it to His disciples, which is a lesson for us on delegation. Notably there were twelve tribes of Israel, and Jesus later says the twelve disciples will "sit on twelve thrones, judging the twelve tribes" (Matt. 19:28). In one verse Matthew calls them disciples, which emphasizes learning and following, and in the next he calls them apostles, probably to indicate they're now vested with Jesus' delegated authority.[54] Similarly, in his first letter to the Thessalonians Paul claims apostolic authority, saying he and his colleagues did not seek glory for themselves, though they could have made demands as Christ's apostles (2:6).

Jesus tells them not to go among the Gentiles or Samaritans but to the "lost sheep of Israel." He focuses His earthly ministry on the Jews (though not exclusively, as we've seen), but when resurrected He will instruct His disciples to spread the Gospel throughout the world. Paul also first preaches to the Jews and then to the Gentiles (Romans 1:16).[55] Their first mission is to go to Israel because they are God's chosen people, who are to mediate the New Covenant to all nations.[56]

Jesus commands the disciples to preach that the kingdom is near and to heal the sick, raise the dead, and cleanse the lepers. As they "received without paying," they must "give without pay," meaning they received the Gospel freely so they must share it freely. He tells them to determine who is worthy (receptive to the Gospel) in the villages they enter, but if people are not receptive, "shake off the dust from your feet when you leave that house or town," signifying that even their dust is unworthy of His disciples. They are sheep in the midst of wolves, and they should be as wise as serpents and innocent as doves. They must be shrewd because they will face formidable obstacles, but must retain their Christian integrity. The disciples, writes G. F. Hasel, "need all the wisdom proverbially attributed to serpents, but deceitful cunning and treacherous guile are to be replaced by the harmless and gentle innocence attributed to doves."[57] They must be "streetwise peacemakers, compassionate confronters, and above all, patient disciples who understand that God can redeem even the worst situation for his glory," writes Marshall Shelley.[58]

When they are persecuted on His behalf and brought before the authorities, Jesus instructs, they should not worry about what to say in their own defense because the Holy Spirit will provide the words to them, just as He has guided and empowered Jesus (John 15:26; Matt. 4:1; 1:18, 20; 3:1).[59] He warns that brothers will betray brothers, and parents and children will be at odds. They will face hostility from all kinds of authorities and people, including friends and family. On His account they will be hated, but if they endure they'll be saved. If they're persecuted in one town they must flee to the next. They should be bold, but not foolishly sabotage their mission.[60]

Jesus avers, "A disciple is not above his teacher, nor a servant above his master. It is enough for the disciple to be like his teacher, and the servant like his master. If they have called the master of the house Beelzebul, how much more will they malign those of his household." If people are brazen enough to oppose and persecute Him—the Messiah—how much more will they abuse His followers? However, they shouldn't fear those who can only kill the body but not the soul. While persecution from mortals will be difficult and painful, only God can administer final judgment and give eternal life. Jesus assures them the Father loves them and knows everything about them—even the number of hairs on their heads.

Whoever acknowledges Him to men, He will commend to the Father, Jesus tells His apostles, but whoever denies Him, He will deny to the Father. "Do not think that I have come to bring peace to the earth," he warns. "I have not come to bring peace, but a sword. For I have come to set a man against his father, and a daughter against her mother, and a daughter-in-law against her mother-in-law." Unless they love Him more than their own father, mother, son, or daughter—unless they take their cross and follow Him—they are not worthy of Him. "Whoever finds his life for my sake," He says, "will find it. Whoever receives you receives me, and whoever receives me receives him who sent me."

Although He's ultimately the Prince of Peace, Jesus' first coming brings conflict and division, contrary to popular misconceptions about Christianity. This strife will remain between believers and unbelievers until He returns and fully establishes His kingdom.[61] Believers shouldn't love their family members any less, but remember that their commitment to God is paramount. As they face persecution for His sake, they must take up His cross and persevere on His behalf despite their suffering.

THE DEATH OF JOHN THE BAPTIST
(MATT. 14:6–12; MARK 6:21–29; LUKE 9:9)

Herodias' daughter dances at a birthday banquet for King Herod Antipas—a son of King Herod who inherited part of his father's kingdom. Pleased with her performance, Herod promises to grant her any request. Her mother tells her to demand the head of John the Baptist on a platter. Herod regrets his oath but dares not break it, so he sends an executioner to behead John in prison and return with his head. When John's disciples learn of this, they take John's body and bury him. Later, when Herod hears about Jesus' ministry and miraculous deeds, He wonders whether Jesus is actually John the Baptist resurrected (Matt. 14:1–2; Mark 6:14–16; Luke 9:7–9).

Jewish historian Josephus conveys the impact of John's ministry on Palestine's Jews at the dawn of the Christian era.[62] Describing a defeat of Herod Antipas' army, which some Jews believed God had inflicted as punishment for Antipas' execution of John, Josephus writes:

> For Herod slew him, who was a good man, and commanded the Jews to exercise virtue, both as to righteousness towards one another, and piety towards God, and so to come to baptism; for that the washing [with water] would be acceptable to him, if they made use of it, not in order to the putting away [or the remission] of some sins [only], but for the purification of the body; supposing still that the soul was thoroughly purified beforehand by righteousness. Now, when [many] others came in crowds about him, for they were greatly moved [or pleased] by hearing his words, Herod, who feared lest the great influence John had over the people might put it into his power and inclination to raise a rebellion (for they seemed ready to do anything he should advise), thought it best, by putting him to death, to prevent any mischief he might cause, and not bring himself into difficulties, by sparing a man who might make him repent of it when it should be too late.[63]

JESUS FEEDS THE 5,000, WALKS ON WATER, AND HEALS AT THE PLAIN OF GENNESARET (MATT. 14:13–36; MARK 6:30–56; LUKE 9:10–17; JOHN 6:1–21)

When Jesus hears of John's execution, He withdraws in a boat by Himself and the crowds follow Him on foot along the shore of the Sea of Galilee. When He goes ashore, He's moved with compassion and heals the sick. In the evening His disciples urge Him to send the crowds into the villages to get food for themselves, but Jesus insists that the disciples feed them. The disciples protest that they only have five loaves of bread and two fish. "Bring them here to me," says Jesus, and orders the people to sit on the grass. He looks up to heaven, says a blessing, breaks the loaves and gives them to His disciples to distribute to the people. All five thousand men and their women and children eat until they're full, and they even have twelve baskets of broken pieces left over.

The feeding of the five thousand is the only miracle reported in all four Gospels other than the resurrection.[64] It's reminiscent of God's provision of manna for the Israelites in their wilderness wanderings (Exodus 16; Psalms 78:18–30; 81:16; 105:40). Jewish tradition held that the Messiah would repeat that miracle on a larger scale.[65] But we shouldn't infer from this that God will always meet all our *physical* needs. Rather, Jesus is depicting, for His disciples, the kind of ministry they will pursue when He's gone. They will feed people, but with spiritual nourishment,[66] and like the crowds here, they will be satisfied.[67] "Christ," writes Warren Wiersbe, "through His Word, is the Bread of Life on whom we feed. It is the privilege—and responsibility—of His servants to give this bread to the hungry multitudes. The servants receive this bread personally from Christ, then pass it on to the others."[68] Ray Stedman adds, "You cannot read the story of the feeding of the five thousand without seeing that it is a marvelous demonstration of the Lord's desire to meet the deepest need of the human heart, the hunger for God."[69] It makes perfect sense that the physical feeding symbolizes spiritual feeding, as Christ has already declared, "Man shall not live by bread alone, but by every word that comes from the mouth of God" (Matt. 4:4).

While there is spiritual symbolism in this story, we must not overlook the fact that the feeding was an historical event that shows Jesus is the Messiah. Indeed, upon witnessing this miracle the people recognize Jesus as the promised Messiah, but they still misapprehend the type of Messiah He is, for they seek to make Him king. He withdraws again to the mountain alone. At night, the disciples leave on their boat toward Capernaum. It has grown dark and Jesus has not met them yet. With strong winds disturbing the water, they row three or four miles and then become terrified when they see Jesus walking toward them on the surface of the sea. He identifies Himself and tells them not to be afraid. They take Him into the boat and are amazed because, in spite of all the miracles He's performed, they still don't recognize Him, indicating they still aren't fully convinced of His messianic identity.[70] Even now they can say, "Truly you are the Son of God," as if that needs to be uttered anymore.

J. C. Ryle declares that this miracle should hearten all Christians because it shows nothing in creation is outside Christ's control. "All things serve him (see Mark 4:41)," writes Ryle. "He may allow his people to be tried for a period, and to be tossed to and fro by storms of trouble; he may be later than they wish in coming to their aid, and not draw near till the 'fourth watch of the night' (verse 25), but never let them forget that winds, and waves and storms are all Christ's servants. They cannot move without Christ's permission. 'Mightier than the thunder of many waters, mightier than the waves of the sea, the Lord on high is mighty!' (Psalm 93:4)."[71]

They land in Gennesaret, a densely populated and fertile plain southwest of Capernaum.[72] The people recognize Jesus, bring their sick to Him, and beg Him to allow them merely to touch the fringe of His garment. All who touch it become well, showing again the nexus between faith and healing. "What was involved," posits William Lane, "was not simply material contact with Jesus' clothing, but the touch of faith." We noted that Jesus' work is often associated with His teaching. But Lane says that in this case there is a notable "absence of any reference to preaching or teaching activity." This is because the people are not fully prepared for His teaching. "They understand only that power is channeled through his person. Jesus patiently bears with their limited insight and graciously heals those who reach out to him from the bed of affliction."[73]

JESUS IS THE BREAD OF LIFE (JOHN 6:22–59)

Those whom Jesus feeds with the loaves find Him on the other side of the sea and ask when He had arrived. He says they aren't seeking Him because they saw signs but because He fed them. He admonishes them, "Do not work for the food that perishes, but for the food that endures to eternal life, which the Son of Man will give to you. For on him God the Father has set his seal." Though they have seen His miracles, they're focused only on filling their stomachs and miss the significance of the miracle.

They ask how they can do the works of God. Jesus explains that they cannot attain eternal life through their works, but only through faith in Him. "This is the work of God, that you believe in him whom he has sent," He preaches. They ask what sign He would do for them so that they may believe in Him. They are asking for a sign greater than what Moses did in giving them manna in the wilderness. William Hendriksen says the people thought Moses' giving them bread out of heaven was a more impressive miracle than Jesus multiplying the loaves from already existing bread.[74] Jesus replies, "Truly, truly, I say to you, it was not Moses who gave you the bread from heaven, but my Father gives you the true bread from heaven. For the bread of God is he who comes down from heaven and gives life to the world."

When they ask Him to give them this bread, Jesus responds, "I am the bread of life; whoever comes to me shall not hunger, and whoever believes in me shall never thirst. But I said to you that you have seen me and yet do not believe. All that the Father gives me will come to me, and whoever comes to me I will never cast out. For I have come down from Heaven, not to do my own will but the will of him who sent me. And this is the will of him who sent me, that I should lose nothing of all that he has given me, but raise it up on the last day. For this is the will of my Father, that everyone who looks on the Son and believes in him should have eternal life, and I will raise him up on the last day." Just as He told the woman at the well (John 4:14), their focus must not be on tangible food, but on spiritual food that only He can provide.

Appalled, the Jews scoff that Jesus, the son of Joseph, has come down from heaven. He tells them not to grumble, explaining that no one can come to Him unless the Father draws him, and no one has seen the Father except He Who is from God. "Truly, truly, I say to you," declares Jesus, "whoever believes has eternal life. I am the bread of life. Your fathers ate the manna in the wilderness, and they died. This is the bread that comes down from heaven, so that one may eat of it and not die. I am the living bread that came down from heaven. If anyone eats of this bread, he will live forever. And the bread that I will give for the life of the world is my flesh." When they continue complaining Jesus says, "Truly, truly, I say to you, unless you eat the flesh of the Son of Man and drink his blood, you have no life in you. Whoever feeds on my flesh and drinks my blood has eternal life, and I will raise him up on the last day. For my flesh is true food, and my blood is true drink. Whoever feeds on my flesh and drinks my blood abides in me, and I in him."

Bruce Barton observes that the person who feeds on Jesus' flesh and drinks His blood "is one who accepts by faith Jesus' sacrificial death and thereby receives eternal life."[75] Those who "abide' in Jesus are not just those who have taken the Lord's Supper, says Gerald Borchert, "but those who have the life of Jesus in them…. Believing in Jesus' life poured out for the world is the genuine or authentic foundation for our lives as Christians."[76]

Many of Jesus' disciples are disillusioned by His discourse, so He asks them, "Do you take offense at this? Then what if you were to see the Son of Man ascending to where he was before?" If they are troubled that Jesus claims to have come from heaven, how will they react if He returns there?[77] What will they think when He is killed on the cross instead of conquering their political oppressors? The Spirit gives life, He tells them. "The flesh is no help at all" (John 6:63). Matthew Henry notes, "Without the soul of man the flesh is of no value, so without the quickening Spirit of God all forms of religion are dead and worthless."[78]

Jesus also says, "The words that I have spoken to you are spirit and life. But there are some of you who do not believe." This upsets many of the disciples and they leave, which is a remarkable example of unbelief by those who had the privilege of living and walking with the Son of God. They don't wait until they are persecuted to deny Him, but reject Him after witnessing Him and His ministry. Perhaps they're unwilling to adjust their misconceptions to accept that the Messiah isn't acting like they anticipated. Or maybe they refuse to digest His difficult teachings or His insistence on faith rather than works. He asks the twelve apostles whether they want to leave too. Peter assures Him they want to stay, for He has the words of eternal life, and they believe He is the Holy One of God. Jesus responds, "Did I not choose you, the twelve? And yet one of you is a devil" (John 6:70), referring to Judas, who will later betray Him.

PHARISEES CHALLENGE JESUS (MATT. 15:1–20; MARK 7:1–23; JOHN 7:1)

Pharisees and scribes come from Jerusalem and notice Jesus' disciples eating without washing their hands. When they ask Him why they break the tradition of the elders, Jesus gives no ground, demanding to know why they follow man-made traditions that break God's commandment to "honor your father and your mother." He says Isaiah had them in mind when he prophesied, "This people honors me with their lips, but their heart is far from me; in vain do they worship me, teaching as doctrines the commandments of men" (Isaiah 29:13).

Jesus is referring to a scribal tradition that allowed sons to declare resources set aside to care for their aging parents as "Corban," which legally excluded their parents from any claim on the property and exempted the sons from the commandment to honor their parents.[79] Jesus argues that Corban nullifies the scriptures because it allows sons to withhold gifts from their father and mother by designating them as holy and "retaining" them in their possession as if they're for God. He then addresses their hand washing tradition, insisting, "There is nothing outside a person that by going into him can defile him, but the things that come out of a person are what defile him."

What people consume can't defile them because it passes through their stomachs, not their hearts. It's what comes out of a person from within that defiles him—evil thoughts, sexual immorality, theft, murder, adultery, coveting, wickedness, deceit, sensuality, envy, slander, pride, and foolishness. Evil that comes out of a person's heart or mind makes the person morally unclean, which is far worse than ceremonial impurity from unclean hands. Scripture repeatedly uses "the heart" to refer to the center of a person's being, including his mind, emotions, and will.[80]

JESUS HEALS MORE PEOPLE AND PERFORMS OTHER MIRACLES (MATT. 15:21–38; MARK 7:24–8:9)

Jesus goes to the region of Tyre and Sidon (on the Mediterranean Sea, northwest of Galilee),[81] where a Gentile woman begs Him, as "Lord, Son of David," to cast out a demon from her daughter. When His disciples implore Him to send her away, He replies, "I was sent only to the lost sheep of Israel." She says, "Lord, help me," and He responds, "It is not right to take the children's bread and throw it to the dogs." She answers Him, "Yes, Lord, yet even the dogs eat the crumbs that fall from their masters' table." Jesus then declares, "O woman, great is your faith! Be it done for you as you desire"—and the child is healed instantly.

Jesus isn't being rude to the woman. He might mean that His first priority is to teach His disciples, who can go out and spread the Gospel there. Or He might mean that He ministers first to the Jews and then to the Gentiles. Regardless, He is not rejecting the woman, but may be testing her faith or demonstrating that the Gospel is for everyone.[82] Alfred Edersheim explains that in addressing Jesus as "Lord, Son of David," she is using the most distinctively Jewish designation of the Messiah, yet the text identifies her as a heathen. "It was," writes Edersheim, "an address by a stranger to a Jewish Messiah, Whose works were only miracles, and not also and primarily signs."

If Jesus had immediately healed her daughter without her first understanding His ministry, His healing would have been merely a work of His power. "And so He first taught her," explains Edersheim, "in such manner as she could understand—that which she needed to know, before she could approach Him in such manner—the relation of the heathen to the Jewish world, and of both to the Messiah, and then He gave her what she asked."[83] He made her understand what she was praying for, and as a result of her faith she became "a daughter of Abraham," entitled to the blessings God promised all people through him.

The Apostle Paul teaches that Gentiles, through their faith, are the spiritual sons of Abraham, entitled to God's promised blessings under the Abrahamic Covenant. Paul writes, "Know then that it is those of faith who are the sons of Abraham. And the Scripture, foreseeing that God would justify the Gentiles by faith, preached the gospel beforehand to Abraham, saying, 'In you shall all the nations be blessed.' So then, those who are of faith are blessed along with Abraham, the man of faith" (Gal. 3:7–9). Notice that Paul describes God's promise to Abraham that He shall bless all nations through him as "the gospel." This further validates our discussion in Chapter 3 of God's promise plan and promise-doctrine.

The original promise God made to Abraham to bless all nations through Him is indeed the Gospel. God would establish His chosen nation of Israel with Abraham's descendants, and it would serve as a nation of priests to mediate the Gospel to all nations. Through Abraham's line of descent would come King David and his descendant Jesus Christ, Who would die for our sins, be resurrected, then rule forever on His Davidic throne. Through faith in Him, both Jews and Gentiles alike will receive the gift of eternal life.

Jesus returns from Tyre and Sidon to the Decapolis region, on the eastern side of the Sea of Galilee and the Jordan River, another area inhabited by Gentiles. People bring to Him a deaf man with a speech impediment and plead that He lay His hand on the man. Jesus takes the man aside privately, puts His fingers into his ears, spits, and touches his tongue. He then sighs, looks up to heaven, and commands, "Be opened"—and instantly the man can hear and speak plainly. Jesus orders those assembled not to tell anyone what they've seen, but the more He utters this demand, the more the astonished people proclaim His works of healing.

Mark intentionally reports that Jesus sighs, which may signify Jesus' compassion for the man, or it could be His heartache over the condition of fallen man and Satan's powers operating in the world. Donald English argues Jesus' sigh is an indication of the spiritual battle taking place. "The battle against evil," writes English, "is joined in this man's healing."[84]

From there, Jesus walks beside the Sea of Galilee and goes up on a mountain, where crowds gather to Him and bring Him their lame, blind, crippled, and mute. The people are in awe of His healings, and "they glorified the God of Israel." Another Gentile praises the God of Israel, but many Jews remain blind to their Messiah.[85] Jesus continues to show that Gentiles will share the Messiah's blessings. These events recall Isaiah's words, "Then the eyes of the blind shall be opened, and the ears of the deaf unstopped; then shall the lame leap like a deer, and the tongue of the mute sing for joy" (Isaiah 35:5–6).[86]

Jesus tells His disciples He has compassion for the crowd because they have been with Him three days and have nothing to eat. His disciples ask how they can feed all these people with just seven loaves of bread and a few small fish. Jesus tells the people to sit on the ground, gives thanks to God, breaks the loaves, and gives them to His disciples to distribute to the crowd. All four thousand of them eat and are satisfied, and they have seven baskets full of pieces left. Some scholars believe this is the same event as the feeding of the five thousand,[87] but others surmise it's a separate event, as all four Gospels record the five thousand but only Matthew and Mark report the four thousand.[88] Jesus Himself, in Matthew, refers to both events (Matthew 16:9–10). So why would the disciples be skeptical about Jesus' feeding this crowd when they had recently seen Him feed the five thousand? It could be they assume He would not include Gentiles in such a blessing[89]—but as we know, Jesus is also the living bread for the Gentiles.[90]

THE PHARISEES AND SADDUCEES DEMAND SIGNS; JESUS HEALS AND TEACHES (MATT. 15:39–16:28; MARK 8:13–9:1; LUKE 9:18–27)

Jesus sends away the crowds and leaves in the boat for Magadan, a region located on the Sea of Galilee,[91] probably in Jewish territory.[92] The Pharisees and Sadducees, to test Jesus, ask Him for a sign from heaven.

This is unusual because these two groups are typically at odds, but in Jesus they face a common opponent. The Sadducees don't even believe in signs and supernatural events, much less the resurrection of the dead.[93] Jesus, however, refuses to take their bait, telling them they know how to interpret the appearance of the sky and determine the weather, but they cannot interpret the sign of the times. He will not perform miracles on demand, especially not for scoffers. The only sign He's willing to give them is the sign of Jonah (Matt. 16:4), which mirrors what He tells the Pharisees and scribes when they ask for a sign (Matt. 12:38–42). Jesus explains that Jonah was in the belly of the great fish for three days and three nights, just as the Son of Man would be three days and three nights in the heart of the earth—thereby validating the story of Jonah as actual history. "He promised them the sign of Jonah," says Blaise Pascal, "the great and wonderful miracle of the resurrection."[94]

When the disciples reach the other side, they're anxious because they only have one loaf of bread. Jesus asks them why they're worried about the bread, reminding them of the feedings of the five thousand and four thousand. "How is it that you fail to understand that I did not speak about bread?" he asks. "Beware of the leaven of the Pharisees and Sadducees." Then they realize He's not warning them about bread but about the teaching of the Pharisees and Sadducees. Just as it would take only a small amount of leaven, or yeast, to make a batch of bread rise, the evil teachings of the religious leaders could infect all of society and turn the nation away from the truth of the Gospel.[95]

Jesus and His disciples arrive at Bethsaida, a fishing village on the northern shore of Galilee and the hometown of Peter, Philip, and Andrew.[96] People bring a blind man to Jesus and beg Him to touch him. He takes the man by the hand and leads him out of the village, spits on his eyes, and lays His hands on him. The man says he can now see people, but they look like walking trees. Jesus again lays His hands on the man's eyes and he now sees everything clearly. Jesus tells him to go home and "do not even enter the village."

Some commentators suggest the man's initially blurred vision could be analogous to the disciples' limited understanding of Jesus—they see Him vaguely as the blind man sees the people as trees. That Mark 8:22–26 contains some nine terms related to "seeing" supports this interpretation. While the disciples begin to understand Jesus is the Messiah, they still can't see the whole picture—that He must be a suffering Messiah—until He explains it to Peter and the other disciples.[97] "If the immediately preceding context is the blindness of the disciples," notes Lamar Williamson, "the context immediately following depicts Peter who finally sees, but sees imperfectly. He will need a second, harsh touch from Jesus to rectify his hazy view of who Christ is and what he, and therefore his disciples, must do."[98] Geoffrey Grogan writes, "The two-stage healing prepares us for [Jesus' upcoming encounter with Peter], and may well show us how aware Jesus was of the limited nature of Peter's faith at this time."[99]

As Jesus and His disciples approach Caesarea Philippi, a town twenty miles north of the Sea of Galilee and 120 miles north of Jerusalem, at the "upper source" of the Jordan River,[100] He asks them about His identity: "Who do people say that I am?" They reply that some say John the Baptist, others Elijah, and others, one of the prophets. He presses, "But who do you say that I am?" Peter says, "You are the Christ, the Son of the living God." Jesus responds, "Blessed are you, Simon Bar-Jonah! For flesh and blood has not revealed this to you, but my Father who is in heaven. And I tell you, you are Peter, and on this rock I will build my church, and the gates of hell shall not prevail against it. I will give you the keys of the kingdom of heaven, and whatever you bind on earth shall be bound in heaven, and whatever you loose on earth, shall be loosed in heaven." He strictly commands them to tell no one He is the Messiah.

The verse, "you are Peter and on this rock I will build my church" is a much-debated passage. Roman Catholics believe it shows that Peter was the first pope. Protestants interpret it otherwise, arguing if Jesus had wanted to designate Peter as pope He probably would've said, "and on you I will build my church."[101] "Peter" in Greek is Petros ("stone"), which is related to petra ("rock"). Peter's other New Testament name is "Cephas," which is Aramaic for "rock." Many Protestants believe that even if "this rock" refers to Peter, Jesus was speaking of Peter's role in confessing Jesus as the Messiah and indicating that the other disciples would share in that role when they make the same confession.[102] Indeed, Paul says the Church is built on the foundation of all the apostles and prophets (Eph. 2:20). If Peter were to have more authority than the other apostles, why would Paul have publicly corrected him (Gal. 2:11–14)? The evidence and arguments on both sides are complex, and I don't intend to address them here, but I do want to draw your attention to this long-standing disagreement.

In saying the gates of hell shall not prevail against the Church, Jesus is promising victory for His Church over death and the forces of evil.[103] The next promise—"I will give you the keys of the kingdom of heaven, and whatever you bind on earth shall be bound in heaven, and whatever you loose on earth, shall be loosed in heaven"—probably means He will give Peter and the other apostles authoritative roles to spread the Word, to carry out God's will, and to oppose the powers of evil (cf. Matt. 18:18).[104]

Jesus is beginning to give His disciples a fuller picture of His role as the Messiah. He must go to Jerusalem and suffer and be killed, then be raised on the third day. Peter still firmly resists the message, telling Jesus, "Far be it from you, Lord! This shall never happen to you." Jesus replies, "Get behind me, Satan! You are a hindrance to me. For you are not setting your mind on the things of God, but on the things of man."

There is a reason Jesus is adamant. His purpose in becoming a man is to die for man's sins. Of all people, His disciples should understand this. It's one thing for the Pharisees to oppose Him and His mission, but it's wholly unacceptable for His disciples to be stumbling blocks to Him. He was not about to sabotage His messianic mission just to meet their distorted messianic expectations, for if He had delivered a temporal military victory over Israel's oppressors, people would still die in their sins. As Bishop Fulton Sheen writes, "Every other person who ever came into this world came into it to live. He came into it to die. Death was a stumbling block to Socrates—it interrupted his teaching. But to Christ, death was the goal and fulfillment of His life, the gold that He was seeking."[105] Likewise Charles Spurgeon declares, "You know how he had to say to Peter, well-beloved disciple though he was, 'Get behind me, Satan; thou savourest not the things that be of God.' Poor ignorant human friendship, would have kept him back from the cross, would have made him miss his great object in being fashioned as a man, and so have despoiled him of all the honor which only shame and death could win him."[106]

What an illustration of man's inability to fathom the mind and purpose of God! What a reminder of our duty to obey Him, even when we do not fully grasp His infinite wisdom. As Paul says,

> For the word of the cross is folly to those who are perishing, but to us who are being saved it is the power of God. For it is written, "I will destroy the wisdom of the wise, and the discernment of the discerning I will thwart." Where is the one who is wise? Where is the scribe? Where is the debater of this age? Has not God made foolish the wisdom of the world? For since, in the wisdom of God, the world did not know God through wisdom, it pleased God through the folly of what we preach to save those who believe. For Jews demand signs and Greeks seek wisdom, but we preach Christ crucified, a stumbling block to Jews and folly to Gentiles, but to those who are called, both Jews and Greeks, Christ the power of God and the wisdom of God. For the foolishness of God is wiser than men, and the weakness of God is stronger than men (1 Cor. 1:18–25).

The cross was a stumbling block to the Jews because Scripture asserted that a man hanged on a tree is cursed by God (Deut. 21:23). God's Messiah, therefore, could not be crucified and thereby be cursed by God (Acts 5:30; 10:39).

If man would have had his way, Christ would not have died for our sins and given us life, which profoundly validates this proverb: "There is a way that seems right to a man, but its end is the way to death" (Proverbs 14:12; 16:25).

CHAPTER 8

FROM THE TRANSFIGURATION TO AN ARGUMENT OVER ABRAHAM

A catalog of virtues and graces, however complete, would merely give us a mechanical view. It's the spotless purity and the sinlessness of Jesus as acknowledged by friend and foe that raises His character high above the reach of all others. In Him we see the even harmony and symmetry of all graces: His love for God and man, His dignity and humility, His strength and tenderness, His greatness and simplicity, and His self-control and submission. It's the absolute perfection of Christ's character that makes Him a moral miracle in History. It's futile to compare Him with saints and sages, ancient or modern. Even the skeptic Jean Jacques Rousseau was compelled to remark, "If Socrates lived and died like a sage, Jesus lived and died like a God."

—P. SCHAFF[1]

THE TRANSFIGURATION (MATT. 17:1–13; MARK 9:2–13; LUKE 9:28–36)

J esus takes Peter, John, and James up the mountain to pray. While praying, His face shines like the sun and His clothing is radiantly white. Moses and Elijah appear and begin talking with Jesus about what He is to accomplish in Jerusalem. Terrified, Peter offers to make a tent for each of the three. A voice emits from a bright cloud overshadowing them and says, "This is my beloved Son; listen to him." The disciples fall on their faces and Jesus touches them, telling them to rise and not to be afraid. When they look up, Jesus is alone. As they come down the mountain, Jesus tells them not to say anything about this until He is raised from the dead. The disciples ask Him why the scribes say Elijah must come first. Jesus says Elijah (meaning John the Baptist) has already come, and that Jesus will suffer just as Elijah did (Matt. 17:1–13; Mark 9:2–13; Luke 9:28–36).

Peter describes this event in his second epistle, testifying that he witnessed it firsthand and that it confirms Old Testament prophecies. Peter explains,

> For we did not follow cleverly devised myths when we made known to you the power and coming of our Lord Jesus Christ, but we were eyewitnesses of his majesty. For when he received honor and glory from God the Father, and the voice was borne to him by the Majestic Glory, "This is my beloved Son, with whom I am well pleased," we ourselves heard this voice borne from heaven, we were with him on the holy mountain. And we have the prophetic word more fully confirmed, to which you will do well to pay attention as to a lamp shining in a dark place, until the day dawns and the morning star rises in your hearts, knowing this first of all, that no prophecy of Scripture comes from someone's own interpretation. For no prophecy was ever produced by the will of man, but men spoke from God as they were carried along by the Holy Spirit (16–20).

Some believe the transfiguration was the apex of Jesus' early ministry.[2] It's worth noting that Jesus was possibly illuminated from the inside, not the outside.[3] The word translated as "transfiguration" supports this view, as it's also the origin of our English word "metamorphosis," which involves a comprehensive change, not just an external one.[4] The transfiguration gives us a hint of the splendor Christ will bring at His Second Coming when He returns in a cloud of glory (Luke 9:26–27).[5]

The transfiguration event is unique to the Gospels. Nothing like it is recorded in the Old Testament or any other ancient literature.[6] Walter Elwell observes that the voice at Jesus' baptism says directly to Jesus, "You are my beloved son," whereas at the transfiguration it speaks to the disciples, saying, "This is my beloved Son." From this Elwell infers that the incident is directed not so much at Jesus as at His disciples. It follows closely after Peter confesses Jesus as the Christ, the Son of God, at Caesarea Philippi, and God confirms his confession in the transfiguration.[7]

Note, however, that the voice doesn't stop there. It also commands, "Listen to him," and this is immediately followed by the narrative, "And suddenly, looking around, they no longer saw anyone with them but Jesus only." Rev. H. J. R. Marston surmises that "Christ must be all in all to each one of us. That is the lesson of the Transfiguration. Our Lord Jesus Christ must be the chief among the ten thousand.... Jesus Christ must take first place before everything else. We must remember that Jesus Christ alone can save us."[8]

Peter manifestly receives the message. In one of his glorious speeches recorded in the Book of Acts, Peter, filled with the Holy Spirit, boldly proclaims to the religious authorities, "This Jesus is the stone that was rejected by you, the builders, which has become the cornerstone. And there is salvation in no one else, for there is no other name under heaven given among men by which we must be saved" (4:11–12).

Lutheran clergyman John G. Butler portrays the transfiguration as "a momentary change in the appearance of Christ in which the manifestation of His humanity gave way to the manifestation of His Deity. This transfiguration emphasized that though Christ walked on this earth as a man, He was, in fact, still very God."[9] God's redemption plan comes into full view, as two towering Old Testament figures appear to Jesus the Messiah, and God divinely blesses the event which, of course, He orchestrated. The Father puts an exclamation point on His plan as He praises Jesus in the presence of Moses and Elijah for the suffering He is soon to endure for mankind's salvation. What a wonderful picture of the Old Covenant giving way to the New!

JESUS EXORCISES A BOY, PREDICTS HIS DEATH AGAIN, AND FINDS A COIN IN A FISH (MATT. 17:14–27; MARK 9:14–32; LUKE 9:37–45)

When they come down from the mountain the next day, Jesus and His disciples are met by a great crowd. A man steps forward and tells Jesus about his only son, who is possessed by an evil spirit and foaming at the mouth. He begs Jesus to help the boy, saying His disciples were unable to cast out the spirit. "O faithless and twisted generation," Jesus declares, "how long am I to be with you and bear with you? Bring your son here." The demon throws the boy down but Jesus rebukes the spirit and heals the boy, then returns him to his father. All are astonished at the majesty of God, which shows they recognize that Jesus is doing divine work whether or not they fully realize He is God. When the disciples ask Him why they can't drive out the spirit themselves, He says it's because they have insufficient faith: "For truly, I say to you, if you have faith like a grain of mustard seed, you will say to this mountain, 'Move from here to there,' and it will move, and nothing will be impossible for you."

Jesus is echoing the Song of Moses (Deut. 32:1–43), in which Moses describes those who have betrayed a perfectly faithful and just God as "a crooked and twisted generation" (Deut. 32:4–5). Paul uses the same term: "Do all things without grumbling or disputing, that you may be blameless and innocent, children of God without blemish in the midst of a crooked and twisted generation, among whom you shine as lights in the world" (Philip. 2:14–15). With "crooked and twisted generation," Jesus describes the insufficiency of the disciples' faith and probably the faithlessness of most people in general.

Here again we see the interrelationship between genuine faith and healing. Jesus invokes the mustard seed as an analogy for the power of faith because it's a tiny seed that grows into a ten-foot-high shrub or tree.[10] The point is that just a little faith can instigate powerful action—Jewish literature often expressed the same idea through the metaphor of moving a mountain.[11] Though some may dismiss this as hyperbole, know that God is omnipotent, and faith in this instance is tapping into God's power. Jesus would later say, when explaining the difficulty of entering into the kingdom of God, "With man this is impossible, but with God all things are possible" (Matt. 19:26).

While in Galilee, Jesus distresses His disciples by relating that He will be delivered to the authorities and killed, then he'll be raised on the third day. They don't understand Him because "it was concealed from them, so that they might not perceive it"—which will also be the case when Jesus predicts His death the third time (Luke 18:34). One might ask why Jesus would stress a point—"Let these words sink into your ears" (Luke 9:44)—and yet conceal its meaning. A simple explanation is that God is sovereignly choosing to conceal the truth from them until it's time for them to understand it, and then they would remember His words.

As the group arrives at Capernaum, the tax collectors meet them and ask Peter whether Jesus pays taxes (referring to the Temple tax). Jesus asks Peter, "From whom do kings of the earth take toll or tax? From their sons or from others?" Peter replies, "From others," and Jesus responds, "Then the sons are free." He instructs Peter to go to the sea, get a fish, and take a shekel from its mouth to give the collectors. Jesus is not obligated to pay a tax to support His Father's house, which is also His own house. Jesus is teaching Peter that He has inaugurated a New Covenant, and that He and His followers are not subject to the laws of the Old Covenant. Nevertheless, to avoid needless conflict in His ministry, He miraculously produces the necessary coinage to satisfy the tax bill.

This is consistent with Paul telling the Corinthian believers, "We aim at what is honorable not only in the Lord's sight but also in the sight of man" (2 Cor. 8:21). Paul explains that spreading the Word and winning converts is so important that he conforms to potential converts' traditions to minimize conflict and resistance. "For though I am free from all," Paul writes, "I have made myself a servant to all, that I might win more of them. To the Jews I became as a Jew, in order to win Jews. To those under the law I became as one under the law (though not being myself under the law) that I might win those under the law. To those outside the law I became as one outside the law (not being outside the law of God but under the law of Christ) that I might win those outside the law. To the weak I became weak, that I might win the weak. I have become all things to all people, that by all means I might save some. I do it all for the sake of the gospel, that I may share with them in its blessings" (1 Cor. 9:19–23). Similarly, Peter instructs his Christian brothers, "Keep your conduct among the Gentiles honorable, so that when they speak against you as evildoers, they may see your good deeds and glorify God on the day of visitation" (1 Peter 2:12). Jesus repeatedly demonstrates that winning souls for Christ is paramount and that compromising one's practices, though not one's principles, is warranted if it furthers that purpose.

JESUS TEACHES ABOUT GREATNESS, TEMPTATION, THE LOST SHEEP, AND CHURCH DISCIPLINE (MATT. 18:1–20; MARK 9:33–41, 42–50; LUKE 9:46–50)

The disciples begin to argue over which of them is the greatest in the kingdom. When they put the question to Jesus, He replies, "If anyone would be first, he must be last of all and servant of all." Jesus is emphasizing the importance of Christian service, which He exemplifies. He is the greatest, yet He lays down His life for us. He would tell them later, "For even the Son of Man came not to be served but to serve, and to give his life as a ransom for many" (Mark 10:45). To be Christ-like, we must display a servant's heart and put others before ourselves, not as their slaves but as cheerful Christians helping our fellow man. In the kingdom, greatness is not determined by status, but service.

Jesus places a child by His side and explains that unless people humble themselves like children they will never enter the kingdom. Saving faith requires humility—a childlike trust in Jesus Christ to save you.[12] "Whoever receives one such child in my name receives me," utters Jesus, "and whoever receives me, receives not me but him who sent me." To show kindness to those in need is to welcome both Jesus and the Father.

Jesus says that whoever causes one child who believes in Him to stumble would be better off with a millstone around his neck and thrown into the sea. While temptations will surely come, woe to the one from whom they come. If one's body part causes him to sin, it would be better to cut it off than be thrown into eternal fire.

I think Jesus means we will inevitably be tempted to sin, but we should do our best to avoid it and one way is to remove ourselves from tempting situations. Remember, in telling us how to pray, Jesus suggests we say, "And lead us not into temptation, but deliver us from evil" (Matt. 6:18). So, for example, if you have an addictive personality, then avoid addictive behaviors altogether. One might say Jesus is exaggerating and speaking metaphorically in telling us to cut off our hands or feet if they cause us to sin. Granted, but is there a better way to illustrate the gravity of sin that leads to death? Would it be hyperbole to advise someone to sacrifice everything he has in this life if it would preclude him from receiving eternal life?

Jesus is issuing a stern warning to those who lure people into temptation and away from Him. In this parable, children represent innocent people who might avoid temptation or unbelief but for the malicious influence of those enticing them to sin—those who drag others down into the pit with themselves. Such behavior is egregious because luring people from belief to disbelief is to lead them from life to death.

Jesus says not to despise children because their angels see the Father's face. This implies God cares so much for children that He uses guardian angels to watch over them (and perhaps all believers), and these angels have a direct line of communication with the Father. Jesus explains that if just one of a man's hundred sheep were lost he would leave the ninety-nine to search for the one, and if he finds it he'd rejoice over it more than the ninety-nine. "So it is not the will of my Father who is in heaven that one of these little ones should perish."

He then teaches His disciples how to handle a sinning brother. First you confront him directly. If he doesn't listen, you take one or two with you and confront him. If he still resists, take it to the Church, and if he still refuses to listen, "Let him be to you as a Gentile and a tax collector"—that is, treat him as an outsider. Jesus continues, "Whatever you bind on earth shall be bound in heaven, and whatever you loose on earth shall be loosed in heaven," meaning the Church will have authority over such disciplinary matters. "Again I say to you," Jesus adds, "if two of you agree on earth about anything they ask, it will be done for them by my Father in heaven. For where two or three are gathered in my name, there am I among them."

Some take this to mean God will grant any prayer requests when two or more pray together. Most commentators, however, believe this promise is limited by the preceding context and applies only to joint prayers concerning Church disciplinary matters, where two or three witnesses are required to render a decision.[13] Even so, Christians rightly believe that prayer strengthens the Christian community and that with prayer there is power in numbers. Few things exhibit the spirit of Christ like congregations of believers lovingly praying for one another.

John informs Jesus that the disciples tried to prevent someone from casting out demons in His name because the man isn't a follower. Jesus commands, "Do not stop him, for the one who is not against you is for you." The man apparently did not misuse Jesus' name. He's a believer, just not one of the apostles, and this upsets the apostles, who are more concerned with defending their own turf than with Jesus' work being accomplished.[14]

FORGIVENESS AND MERCY
(MATT. 18:21–35; LUKE 17:3–4)

Peter asks Jesus, "Lord, how often will my brother sin against me, and I forgive him? As many as seven times?" Jesus replies, "I do not say to you seven times, but seventy-seven times." Jesus compares the kingdom of heaven to a king who wants his servants to settle their debts to him. He threatens to sell one servant who cannot pay his debt of ten thousand talents, along with his wife and children and all his property. The servant begs for mercy and more time to pay. Out of pity, the king forgives his debt. But the servant later refuses to show similar compassion for a fellow servant who owes him a hundred denarii, even when he begs. Instead he puts him in prison, and other servants report the matter to the king, who severely chastises and imprisons him for failing to extend to the other servant the same sympathy the king had shown him. Jesus warns, "So also my heavenly Father will do to every one of you, if you do not forgive your brother from your heart."

Jesus forgives terrible sins of those who trust in Him, and He expects us to reflect His behavior in our dealings with others. "This is not because God is unwilling to forgive," Larry Richards observes. "It is because forgiveness is like a coin: it has two sides. We cannot have 'heads' (receive forgiveness) without having 'tails' (extend forgiveness) too."[15] Those who are unforgiving can't expect God to forgive them. "Blessed are the merciful," Jesus says, "for they shall receive mercy" (Matt. 5:7). He also includes forgiveness in the Lord's Prayer: "forgive us our debts, as we also have forgiven our debtors" (Matt. 6:12). James expresses the same sentiment, writing, "For judgment is without mercy to one who has shown no mercy. Mercy triumphs over judgment" (James 2:13).

In this parable, just as with the Sermon on the Mount, Jesus presents a higher ethic than the world would ever see. Rabbinic teaching held that a person must forgive another three times—not seven times, much less seventy-seven times.[16] But we should be heartened that in the parable, the servant holds the key to his jail cell. He will only be imprisoned until he pays his debt, which is a testament to Jesus' forgiving spirit and gracious mercy.

A larger point in this parable is that God forgives us infinitely more than seventy-seven times—more than we could ever repay. Based on our thoughts and behavior none of us deserve salvation on our own and yet, by appropriating the blood of Christ, we are forgiven. Indeed, our sinful nature even resists our efforts to nurture a forgiving spirit, but Christlikeness demands that we adopt that attitude, and so does our spiritual and mental balance. Robert Treat Paine, a signer of the Declaration of Independence, puts it well: "I am constrained to express my adoration of the Author of my existence for His forgiving mercy revealed to the world through Jesus Christ, through whom I hope for never ending happiness in a future state."[17]

WOE TO UNREPENTANT CITIES; THE SEVENTY-TWO MESSENGERS; JESUS REJOICES IN THE FATHER'S WILL (MATT. 11:20–24; LUKE 10:1–24)

Jesus denounces the cities where most of His works have been done because they don't repent despite seeing Him and witnessing His works in the flesh. "But I tell you," Jesus warns, "that it will be more tolerable on the day of judgment for the land of Sodom than for you."

Jesus appoints seventy-two disciples and sends them ahead of him, two by two, into every town where He is to go, saying, "The harvest is plentiful, but the laborers are few. Therefore pray earnestly to the Lord of the harvest to send out laborers into his harvest." Many need to hear the Gospel, but precious few evangelists are available to take the message to them.[18] Reiterating that they'll be lambs in the midst of wolves, He instructs them to go house to house, heal the sick, and tell them that "the kingdom of God has come near to you." But as for those who won't receive them, have nothing further to do with them.

The seventy-two return joyfully, saying, "Lord, even the demons are subject to us in your name," and Jesus confirms He has given them such authority. He cautions them, however, not to rejoice about this delegated authority, but that their names are written in heaven—in other words, don't gloat over your power, but cherish that you have been given the gift of eternal life. Jesus rejoices in the Holy Spirit and thanks the Father for hiding things from the wise and revealing them to little children: "All things have been handed over to me by my Father, and no one knows the Son except the Father, and no one knows the Father except the Son and anyone to whom the Son chooses to reveal him." Jesus is directly proclaiming His divinity and asserting that the Father has given Him total authority to do His work.

"God the Son and God the Father know each other perfectly in the intimacy of the Trinity," writes L. A. Barbieri.[19] There are no secrets between them.[20] That the Father gives the Son authority does not mean Jesus is inferior to the Father, but that within the Trinity the Father has authority over such things.[21] "The Son was willing to be the suffering servant of the Father," declares Kenneth Daughters. "He was willing to submit to the Father and carry out the Father's will. This kind of subordination is a function of order, office, and operation, not of essence or being. Difference in function does not imply inferiority of nature. Roles distinguish service and function, not value or worth."[22] R. C. Sproul expounds, "When we speak of the subordination of Christ, we must do so with great care. Our culture equates subordination with inequality. But in the Trinity all members are equal in nature, in honor, and in glory.

All three members are eternal, self-existent; they partake of all aspects of deity. In God's plan of redemption...the Son *voluntarily* takes on a subordinate role to the Father."[23]

Jesus turns to His disciples and privately tells them, "Blessed are the eyes that see what you see! For I tell you that many prophets and kings desired to see what you see, and did not see it, and to hear what you hear, and did not hear it." They are privileged to be living at this time—the coming of the Son, Who is inaugurating a new era in redemptive history. The prophets only distantly wrote and dreamed about this era, but they always earnestly longed for it.[24]

"COME TO ME...AND I WILL GIVE YOU REST" (MATT. 11:25–30)

Jesus says, "Come to me, all who labor and are heavy laden, and I will give you rest. Take my yoke upon you, and learn from me, for I am gentle and lowly in heart, and you will find rest for your souls. For my yoke is easy, and my burden is light." He is offering relief to those burdened by the weight of strict religious requirements and encumbered by their own sinfulness. He's inviting the weary to come to Him for solace. Jesus doesn't require less from believers than the Law requires. "In some ways," explains Michael Green, His standard is "more demanding. But it is the yoke of love, not of duty. It is the response of the liberated, not the duty of the obligated. And that makes all the difference."[25] Paul writes, "There is therefore now no condemnation for those who are in Christ Jesus. For the law of the Spirit of life has set you free in Christ Jesus from the law of sin and death" (Romans 8:1–2). Through His sacrificial death on the cross Jesus has fulfilled the requirements of the Law on our behalf (Romans 8:4).

Note that Jesus imposes no conditions, but simply tells us to come to Him as we are, with all our sins and problems, and He will give us rest and peace. Few passages are more comforting, for we know we can lay all our problems, no matter how great or small, at the foot of Jesus. He in turn will give us a peace that surpasses all understanding (Philip. 4:6–7)—though we may not understand how this peace comes about because it's a supernatural occurrence. Referencing Paul's ministering to other prisoners rather than dwelling on his own plight while in prison, Charles Stanley notes, "The one foundational truth he knew was that God's peace, though mysterious and impossible to comprehend rationally, is able to see anyone through the journey of life—on a routine day or in the midst of any trial."[26]

THE GOOD SAMARITAN (LUKE 10:25–37)

When a lawyer asks Jesus what he must do to inherit eternal life, Jesus asks him what is written in the Law. The lawyer responds, "You shall love the Lord your God with all your heart and with all your soul and with all your strength and with all your mind, and your neighbor as yourself." Jesus says his answer is correct. The lawyer asks who his neighbor is, and Jesus relates the story of a priest and a Levite who both refuse to stop and help a man robbed, beaten, and left half dead on the road. But a Samaritan comes along and treats the man's wounds, takes him to an inn, and pays the expenses. Jesus asks which of the three—the priest, the Levite, or the Samaritan—was a neighbor to the injured man, and the man answers that it's the one who had shown mercy. Jesus says, "You go, and do likewise."

This summarizes the Law's requirements as contained in the first two commandments. However, Jesus isn't upholding salvation by works. As Paul writes, "For in Christ Jesus neither circumcision nor uncircumcision counts for anything, but only faith working through love" (Gal. 5:6). Only through the love of Christ can we exhibit the kind of love the Law requires, and we can only achieve the love of Christ through faith in Him. "The answer given in Luke 10:27 involves a faith consisting of love for God and one's neighbor," writes Robert Stein, "for it is inconceivable to love God apart from faith. Furthermore, a faith that does not produce love of one's neighbor is dead (James 2:17). It is no faith; it never was faith."[27]

"The law," says Paul, "was our guardian until Christ came. But now that faith has come, we are no longer under a guardian, for in Christ Jesus you are all sons of God, through faith" (Gal. 3:24–25). John

MacArthur explains, "Since no sinner can obey perfectly, the impossible demands of the law are meant to drive us to seek divine mercy."[28]

The Good Samaritan, notes John Butler, resembles the reviled Jesus in many ways—he is scorned (like all Samaritans), seeking, sympathetic, steadfast, saving, sacrificing, sheltering, and sagacious.[29] He not only has compassion for the traveler but acts on it. He persists despite obstacles and inconvenience, and he sacrifices his time and money in the process. He saves the man's life, dresses his wounds, and provides him shelter. He also demonstrates wisdom in the use of his own resources by leaving some money with the innkeeper and promising to pay any related charges later. Christ is "the power of God and the wisdom of God" (1 Cor. 1:24), and in Him "are hidden all the treasures of wisdom and knowledge" (Col. 2:2).

MARY AND MARTHA; THE LORD'S PRAYER (LUKE 10:38–11:13; MATT. 6:9–13)

A woman named Martha invites Jesus to her home. Her sister Mary sits at Jesus' feet enraptured by His teaching while Martha busies herself serving Him. Martha asks Jesus to have Mary help her "serve." Jesus says, "Martha, Martha, you are anxious and troubled about many things, but one thing is necessary. Mary has chosen the good portion, which will not be taken away from her." Jesus is teaching Martha about priorities. Household chores are important, but we must focus our hearts and minds on Him. The word "portion" has scriptural significance, for many Old Testament passages teach that our greatest possession is fellowship with God—that is our portion in life (Psalms 16:5; 27:4; 73:26; 119:57; 142:5; Joshua 18:7).[30] Mary is safeguarding her portion, and Martha is neglecting hers. "When Jesus expects us to follow him all the way," writes Michael Wilcock, "he means not a frenzy of religious activity undertaken in our own strength, but the total abandonment of ourselves to him, for him to work in us both to will and to work for his good pleasure."[31] As Paul declares, "For it is God who works in you, both to will and to work for his good pleasure" (Philip. 2:13).

At the request of one of His disciples Jesus shows them how to pray, teaching them the Lord's Prayer. He next relates the story about a man who goes to his friend's house at midnight and asks for bread. The friend refuses at that hour, but when the visitor persists, the friend gives him whatever he needs. "I tell you," teaches Jesus, "ask and it will be given to you; seek, and you will find; knock, and it will be opened to you.... What father among you, if his son asks for a fish, will instead of a fish give him a serpent; or if he asks for an egg, will give him a scorpion? If you then, who are evil, know how to give good gifts to your children, how much more will the heavenly Father give the Holy Spirit to those who ask him!" (Matt. 6:9–13; Luke 11:1–13).

God is infinitely more merciful and loving than we are, even to our own children, but we should still ceaselessly go to Him in prayer and petition Him. This doesn't mean God will give us anything we request. As noted earlier, it often wouldn't be in our best interests if He did, for we lack His wisdom. Further, can you imagine the chaos that would ensue if the inevitably conflicting and sometimes destructive prayer requests of every believer were granted? Paul writes, "And we know that for those who love God all things work together for good, for those who are called according to his purpose" (Romans 8:28; cf. 1 Cor. 2:9). Jesus promises that God will give a far more important gift to His children—the Holy Spirit, Who will indwell believers, give them joy (Acts 13:52; Romans 14:17; 1 Thess. 1:6),[32] and empower them to resist and defeat sin (Romans 6:6).

JESUS AND THE PHARISEES (MATT. 12:22–45; MARK 3:22–30; LUKE 11:14–16; 17–54; 12:1–12)

When Jesus heals a blind and mute demon-possessed man, the amazed people ask if He is "the Son of David"—the expected Messiah. The Pharisees defiantly claim that Jesus is not working through God's power but Satan's. Jesus points out the absurdity of Satan casting out demons—it would be dividing his house against itself. Jesus castigates the Pharisees for blaspheming the Holy Spirit, which He decries as an unforgivable sin.

Some commentators say this sin can't be reproduced today because it presupposes that Jesus is on earth performing miracles through the Holy Spirit's power.[33] *The ESV Study Bible*, however, advises, "If a person persistently attributes to Satan what is accomplished by the power of God—that is, if one makes a flagrant, willful, decisive judgment that the Spirit's testimony about Jesus is satanic—then such a person never has forgiveness."[34] This describes someone who persists in hardening his own heart against God and puts himself outside the reach of God's provision for forgiveness and salvation. Christians worried about this, by definition, do not fall into this category, for they have not hardened their hearts to that extent.[35] Michael Wilcock explains that just as it's impossible for God to lie, "It is impossible...for God to forgive one who says, 'I will not listen to the Spirit when he brings me the message of forgiveness.'...'I will not follow the Spirit when he points me to the Savior.' The man who is determined to go to hell will certainly get there."[36]

The Pharisees and scribes ask Jesus for a sign, as the Pharisees and Sadducees did elsewhere (Matt. 16:1–4). Once again, He refuses to perform a gratuitous miracle on demand and says they shall only get the sign of the prophet Jonah. Just as Jonah was in the fish's belly three days and three nights, Jesus would be in the heart of the earth.

Jesus teaches that when an unclean spirit exits a person, it returns with seven more evil spirits, comparing that with this evil generation. If this generation continues to deny Jesus after witnessing His works and ministry, their condition might be worse than if they'd never seen Him.[37] Alternately, He could be inferring that Israel benefitted from the moral reformation John the Baptist and Jesus ushered in—but if the nation backslides into unbelief and hardness of heart after such a privilege, it could be left worse than it was before those ministries.[38] Bruce Barton observes, "God's people, this evil generation, privileged with prophecy and promises, would be faced with horrible judgment for rejecting their Messiah."[39] John Butler states that when a person is tempted, he must not just resist but seek positive reformation, otherwise the temptation will return with a vengeance. "Therefore, when turning from evil, do not stop there, but fill your life with the Word of God, with holy things so you do not have room for the return of evil."[40] As Paul implores, "Put on the whole armor of God, that you may be able to stand against the schemes of the devil" (Eph. 6:11).

Jesus accepts an invitation to eat with a Pharisee, who is aghast that Jesus does not wash before eating. Jesus says the Pharisees cleanse the outside of the cup and dish but are full of greed and wickedness on the inside. God made both the inside and the outside. "But woe to you Pharisees," says Jesus, "for you tithe mint and rue and every herb, and neglect justice and the love of God.... For you love the best seat in the synagogues and greetings in the marketplaces.... For you are like unmarked graves, and people walk over them without knowing it."

When one of the lawyers complains of being insulted, Jesus responds, "Woe to you lawyers also! For you load people with burdens hard to bear, and you yourselves do not touch the burdens with one of your fingers.... For you build the tombs of the prophets whom your fathers killed." He warns them that the blood of the prophets may be charged against this generation, from Abel to Zechariah. "Woe to the lawyers," He says, "for you have taken away the key of knowledge. You did not enter yourselves, and you hindered those who were entering." Unlike the milquetoast Jesus often portrayed in our culture, Jesus made bold judgments and called people to account for their sins, especially—as we've seen—those who led people away from a true relationship with God.

As Jesus leaves, the scribes and Pharisees try to provoke Him to speak of many things, hoping to catch Him in blasphemy. The Pharisees are filled with pride in wanting the best seats in the synagogues. Once again, their outward piousness masks internal impurity. They are preoccupied with rules but neglect the transformation of their hearts and the true spirit of the laws, which require justice and love for God. In comparing them to hidden graves, Jesus is condemning them as phony paragons of purity.[41] His message to the lawyers—who are experts in the Torah (the Law of Moses)[42]—is that they, too, are placing a heavy burden on the people but are not helping them get closer to God. While they had built and maintained the tombs of the prophets, they had dishonored their message and would be judged for doing so. By distorting the true teachings of the Old Testament, they are keeping people from true knowledge and entering the kingdom.

When a crowd of thousands gathers, Jesus warns His disciples to beware of the leaven of the Pharisees, meaning their hypocrisy. He says nothing is covered up that will not be revealed and nothing hidden that will not be known. Everything and everyone will be exposed in time, either in this life or on the day of judgment.[43] No one can hide his misdeeds from God, Who will ultimately judge everyone. They shouldn't worry about people, who can merely kill their body, but only about God, Who has authority over their soul. God even cares about sparrows; how much more does He care about people! Jesus declares that whoever acknowledges Him before men, He will acknowledge before the angels of God, and He will deny those who deny Him.

To acknowledge Him means to accept Him as the Messiah and place faith in Him. If we vouch for Him, He will vouch for us. "This is," says Leon Morris, "warm encouragement for judgment day."[44] Indeed, for as Warren Wiersbe observes, "How can we fear men when we know Jesus Christ is confessing us before the Father in heaven?"[45] Jesus repeats His warning against blaspheming the Holy Spirit and His assurance that in the future the Holy Spirit would provide them words to defend themselves against their accusers and persecutors.

THE PARABLE OF THE RICH FOOL AND LESSONS ON PRIORITIES AND WORRY (LUKE 12:13–34)

When a man asks Jesus to tell his brother to share his inheritance with him, Jesus warns him against covetousness, advising that material possessions are not the only things that matter. Covetousness is a strong desire to possess material things (Col. 3:5; Eph. 5:5; Heb. 13:5; 1 Tim. 6:9, 10; Matt. 6:20). It's an aggravated form of avarice involving a cold-hearted worldliness.[46] The Greek word translated in the New Testament as covetousness means, literally, an "inordinate desire to have more."[47]

To illustrate the point, Jesus shares the story of a rich man's abundant grain produce. The man says he will build larger barns to store his grain and goods, and he will relax, eat, drink, and be merry. God tells him he's a fool because he would lose his soul that night and his possessions won't help him. Jesus tells His disciples not to worry about their possessions, food, and clothing because life involves more than these things. They must consider the ravens, which have much less value than human beings and have no barns or storehouses, yet God feeds them. No one can add an hour to his life by worrying. God's lilies are more beautiful than Solomon in his glorious clothing. "But if God so clothes the grass, which is alive in the field today, and tomorrow is thrown into the oven," Jesus proclaims, "how much more will he clothe you, O you of little faith!"

The disciples shouldn't worry about these things because the Father knows what they need. "Instead, seek his kingdom and these things will be added to you." The Father wants to give them the kingdom, so they should sell their possessions, give to the needy, and pursue the "treasure in the heavens that does not fail, where no thief approaches and no moth destroys. For where your treasure is, there will your heart be also."

Worrying is destructive and keeps us preoccupied with worldly things, keeping us from our true purpose—glorifying God and having a relationship with Him. Corrie ten Boom writes, "Worry does not empty tomorrow of its sorrow. It empties today of its strength."[48] To be anxious demonstrates insufficient trust in God, Who promises He will provide for "all these things" (Matt. 6:33).[49] God wants us to keep our eyes on spiritual things because they're steady, dependable, and secure. Our circumstances can shift on a moment's notice, but if we are grounded in faith we'll be anchored and fulfilled. We cannot achieve true security through material possessions—only God can provide it. "Those who know God as Father," writes Joel Green, "will know God as the one capable of and committed to providing for his people. Knowing this, they are liberated from the consuming concerns of self-security."[50]

Promising the disciples "these things will be added to you" if they seek God's kingdom does not mean believers are guaranteed an abundance of riches. But they will receive a wealth of spiritual blessings and usually enjoy the basic necessities.[51] That said, it cannot be denied that some Christians starve and face terrible hardships. What God ultimately guarantees here is that from an eternal perspective, everything will be made right for those who believe in Christ. To believe that God knows our needs is a comfort for all believers. Secure in that knowledge, we can turn our attention to His kingdom.[52] Our ultimate destiny, eternal life with God, is what matters most.

YOU MUST BE READY FOR THE SON OF MAN'S RETURN (LUKE 12:35–48)

Jesus tells His disciples they must be spiritually prepared and always ready for His return, like servants waiting for their master to return from a wedding feast. "Blessed are those servants whom the master finds awake when he comes," says Jesus. "But know this, that if the master of the house had known at what hour the thief was coming, he would not have left his house to be broken into. You also must be ready, for the Son of Man is coming at an hour you do not expect."

The servant who wisely manages his master's household is blessed, and the master will put him in charge of all his possessions. But the one who abuses his fellow servants while his master is away and neglects the household will be surprised by the unexpected return of his master, who will cut him in pieces and put him with the unfaithful. The servant who intentionally disobeys his master will be punished more severely than one who disobeys him while ignorant of his will. "Everyone to whom much was given, of him much will be required," teaches Jesus, "and from him to whom they entrusted much, they will demand the more."

Christ will return but no one knows when (Matt. 24:36; Mark 13:32), so we must always be ready. I don't think this just applies to Christ's Second Coming, but also to our spiritual condition now. None of us knows how much time we have on this planet and our life could end at any moment, so we mustn't delay in accepting God's offer of salvation through trust in Jesus Christ. In the meantime, we must keep a heavenly focus[53] and work for the kingdom of God as if today is our last day.

Just as with the parable of the talents, we must be good stewards of God's gifts to us, and the greater the gifts, the more stewardship is required. "Those placed in positions where they will guide, influence and care for others have been entrusted with much," writes Bruce

Barton, "and therefore God has high expectations for their moral, spiritual, and ethical lives."[54] Arthur Pink extends the principle to compare our obligations, as believers, to those of the Old Testament saints. Our duties are much greater because our privileges and blessings are greater.[55]

NOT PEACE, BUT DIVISION (LUKE 12:49–53)

Jesus announces, "I came to cast fire on the earth, and would that it were already kindled! I have a baptism to be baptized with, and how great is my distress until it is accomplished! Do you think that I have come to give peace on earth? No, I tell you, but rather division. For from now on in one house there will be five divided, three against two and two against three. They will be divided, father against son and son against father, mother against daughter and daughter against mother, mother-in-law against her daughter-in-law and daughter-in-law against mother-in-law."

Jesus has come to bring judgment. But first He must be baptized by being crucified. He will bring peace, but not until His Second Coming when He will permanently destroy evil and reign forever. Until then conflict, not peace, will abound. He preaches Truth, He *is* Truth, and in the end, no one can avoid making a decision about Him. Some will accept and receive Him, and others will reject Him, which will cause bitter conflict, even among family members, as we noted in Chapter 7.

INTERPRETING THE TIME (LUKE 12:54–56)

Jesus admonishes, "You hypocrites! You know how to interpret the appearance of the earth and sky, but why do you not know how to interpret the present time?" At the time, people are closely watching the weather because it affects farming, their primary livelihood. But they ignore spiritual matters, which are far more important. They are ignoring the present aspects of God's kingdom—that Christ had come to fulfill the Old Testament prophecies and provide salvation for all who place their faith in Him. He is now with them, offering them the kingdom of God, but they are too preoccupied to grasp His message and accept His offer. Surely we can all agree on the timelessness of this message and its applicability to us today.

SETTLE WITH YOUR ACCUSER (LUKE 12:57–59)

Jesus rebukes the people for turning to judges rather than settling disputes among themselves. They must exercise their own good judgment. Through another parable, Jesus teaches they mustn't vacillate too long in making peace with Christ because judgment will come, as noted above. J. C. Ryle writes, "This passage teaches us...*the immense importance of seeking reconciliation* with God before it [is] too late.... Peace with God is by far the first thing in religion."[56]

REPENT OR PERISH (LUKE 13:1–5)

Informing Jesus about certain Galileans whom Pilate had killed while they were making sacrifices, some people ask Jesus whether the Galileans' unusual suffering meant they were particularly egregious sinners. Jesus clarifies that their physical suffering is not necessarily related to their spiritual state. All people are sinners and will die, so what's most important is that all repent and come to Jesus in faith to receive the gift of eternal life.

THE PARABLE OF THE BARREN FIG TREE (LUKE 13:6–9)

Jesus relates a parable involving a man whose fig tree hasn't produced fruit for three years, so he instructs his vinedresser to cut it down. The vinedresser orders him to leave it for another year while he digs around it and spreads manure. It will hopefully bear fruit the next year, but if not, he may cut it down then. The vinedresser is Jesus, our great Intercessor,[57] who appeals to the Father to give people, or the nation of Israel, another chance. God is patient and merciful, and gives people chance after chance while withholding His judgment. But they must repent before judgment comes upon them, and their faith must be genuine so as to produce fruit in their lives (James 2:14–26). What is this fruit? Paul answers the question: "The fruit of the Spirit is love, joy, peace, patience, kindness, goodness, faithfulness, gentleness, self-control; against such things there is no law. And those who belong to Christ Jesus have crucified the flesh with its passions and desires" (Gal. 5:22–24).

JESUS HEALS A DISABLED WOMAN (LUKE 13:10–17)

When Jesus is teaching in a synagogue on the Sabbath He notices a woman who is doubled over from an eighteen-year disability. Jesus calls her and says, "Woman, you are freed from your disability." When He lays His hands on her she is immediately healed and glorifies God. The ruler of the synagogue furiously scolds the people for this Sabbath healing—even though the people had nothing to do with it—because he isn't brave enough to confront Jesus. Jesus calls the ruler and his supporters hypocrites—they lead their oxen and donkeys to water on the Sabbath, so why can't this woman, a daughter of Abraham, be shown compassion and be healed on the holy day? The ruler is shamed but the people rejoice.

Earlier Jesus had established that He is Lord of the Sabbath, but now He demonstrates the meaning of the Sabbath.[58] The ruler is interested only in the rules of the Sabbath and misunderstands that God provided the Sabbath for man's benefit, not to further burden him. The ruler is actually in worse bondage than the woman was, for his self-enslavement is spiritual—a matter of the heart and mind.[59] Though Satan possesses her, he only enslaves her body, not her spirit, as evidenced by her attendance at this service. Her affliction is caused by demonic possession, and the Sabbath, of all days, should not be a day when Satan gets a pass.

THE UNBELIEF OF JESUS' BROTHERS (JOHN 7:1–9)

Jesus is in Galilee and will not go to the Jews' Feast of Booths (Tabernacles) in Judea, knowing they're seeking to kill Him. This is one of the most important Jewish feasts, in which Jews thank God for His past and present provision, and contemplate their wilderness wanderings when He protected them.[60] Jesus' brothers (his actual brothers, who are still not believers) chide Him for not going, claiming no one works in secret if he seeks to be known publicly and that He should show Himself to the world. They're arguing that Jesus could gain more converts by going where the crowds are—in Judea. They don't understand that He *is* preparing to show Himself to the world, though not in the way they anticipate—not strictly through more miraculous signs, but through His humiliation and death on the cross.

Jesus says His time has not yet come. A recurring theme in John (2:4; 7:6, 8, 30; 8:20) is that Jesus cannot allow Himself to be captured and crucified until He completes His earthly ministry, and His brothers obviously don't yet recognize this danger. The world hates Him because He exposes man's evil. Jesus is the light of the world Who shines brightly on man's evil deeds, and evildoers hate the light (John 3:19–21; 5:37–38, 41–45).[61] But the world cannot hate the brothers because, as unbelievers, they are part of the world that rejects Jesus, so they should go on to the feast. Jesus' brothers show they are of the world by second-guessing Him and presuming to know how to run His ministry better than He does.

JESUS REJECTED AT A SAMARITAN VILLAGE; THE COST OF DISCIPLESHIP (LUKE 9:51–62)

Jesus' ministry is at a turning point. He is ready to go to Jerusalem toward the cross, the resurrection, and the ascension.[62] As He is preparing to go, He sends messengers ahead of Him, and they enter a Samaritan village on the way to Jerusalem to make preparations for Him. The people, however, will not receive Him there because He is set on going to Jerusalem—Samaritans despise the city and view His traveling there as a rejection of Samaritan worship, which is centered on Mount Gerizim, not in the Temple in Jerusalem. James and John ask if He wants them to summon fire from heaven to consume those rejecting Him. He rebukes them for the suggestion, and they go on to another village. The Samaritans' rejection of Jesus is wrong, but He wants His disciples to focus on the mission—Jerusalem.[63]

When back on the road, someone promises Jesus, "I will follow you wherever you go." Jesus replies, "Foxes have holes, and birds of the air have nests, but the Son of Man has nowhere to lay his head." He has no time for a home or creature comforts because He's on His way to die for mankind's redemption. "This is an incidental glimpse of the cost of the incarnation," writes Leon Morris. "And it shows that the disciples must not reckon on luxurious living."[64] If they want to put their words into action and truly follow Christ, they must be homeless like He is and give up the shelter and security of a home.[65]

Jesus commands another person to "follow me," but the person says, "Lord, let me first go and bury my father." Jesus replies, "Leave the dead to bury their own dead. But as for you, go and proclaim the kingdom of God." Another person asks Jesus permission to first say goodbye to his family, and Jesus replies, "No one who puts his hand to the plow and looks back is fit for the kingdom of God."

While these exchanges may sound harsh, the point is that loyalty to Christ must take precedence over all other concerns. Jesus is not disrespecting the dead but emphasizing that His followers have the urgent task of spreading the good news of life in Him. There would be no procrastination.[66] In forbidding the other man to say farewell to his family, Jesus is not lecturing on Christian backsliding. Instead, he's stressing that people must not be half-hearted in their discipleship[67] but singularly focused on their work.[68]

JESUS TEACHES IN JERUSALEM (JOHN 7:10–8:11)

Though Jesus tells His disciples He won't go to the Feast of Booths, He later goes privately. The Jews are looking for Him, and many are talking about Him, some positively and some negatively. But people don't speak openly of Him for fear of the religious hierarchy, which can excommunicate them.[69]

About midway through the feast Jesus goes into the Temple and astounds with His teaching. "How is it that this man has learning, when he has never studied" people ask, betraying their arrogance about their exclusive expertise and their ignorance of Jesus' identity. Jesus replies, "My teaching is not mine but his who sent me. If anyone's will is to do God's will, he will know whether the teaching is from God or whether I am speaking on my own authority. The one who speaks on his own authority seeks his own glory; but the one who seeks the glory of him who sent him is true, and in him there is no falsehood. Has not Moses given you the law? Yet none of you keeps the law. Why do you seek to kill me?"

Christ's knowledge and discernment is superior to theirs despite His having no formal rabbinic training. He deftly turns their accusation on them, noting that while boasting of their expertise in the Law, they continually break it and worst of all, plot to kill Him—the very Giver of the Law. Though Jesus' charges are mainly directed at the authorities—the Sanhedrin—the people are hardly innocent, for many of them will eventually clamor, "Crucify Him."[70]

The crowd accuses Jesus of having a demon. He points out their hypocrisy in judging Him for healing on the Sabbath when they perform circumcisions on the Sabbath if it happens to fall on the eighth day after the child's birth, the day on which the Law requires circumcision. If technically violating the Sabbath to perfect one part of the body is permissible, how much more so to heal a sick person? "Do not judge by appearances," cautions Jesus, "but judge with right judgment." Right judgment is wise judgment, which involves far more than mechanically following rules. While they are fastidiously obsessed with every syllable of the Law, they obscure their own vision and blind themselves from recognizing the Messiah. Jesus denounces sanctimonious legalism and demands moral and theological discernment.[71]

Some people ask if Jesus is the One the authorities are seeking to kill. They wonder if they're leaving Him alone because they actually know He's the Messiah. But the people say Jesus can't be the Messiah because they know where He comes from, and no one will know where the Messiah comes from. This is based on their mistaken belief that the Messiah would appear out of nowhere.[72] Though the prophet Micah predicted the Messiah would be born in Bethlehem, some rabbis taught that the Messiah would be completely unknown until He appeared on the scene to deliver them from their oppressors.[73]

Their attitude validates, again, Jesus' declaration that a prophet has no honor in his hometown. They know this lowly Jesus, who comes from ordinary people, so how can He be the Messiah? This exemplifies the widespread human traits of jealousy and arrogance. Jesus responds, "You know me, and you know where I come from. But I have not come of my own accord. He who sent me is true, and him you do not know. I know him, for I come from him, and he sent me." Just as they expected the Messiah to be a military deliverer, they didn't know He would make Himself lowly and experience life like all other human beings do. They didn't realize the Messiah "who, though he was in the form of God, did not count equality with God a thing to be grasped, but emptied himself, by taking the form of a servant, being born in the likeness of men. And being found in human form, he humbled himself by becoming obedient to the point of death, even death on a cross" (Philip. 4:6–8). Though they want to arrest Him, they don't "because his hour had not yet come. Yet many of the people believed in him." God is sovereign and He will not allow Jesus' work to be terminated prematurely.

When the Pharisees hear the crowd talking about Jesus, they send officers to arrest Him. Jesus says, "I will be with you a little longer, and then I am going to him who sent me. You will seek me and you will not find me. Where I am you cannot come." This confounds the Jews, who wonder where He could go that they wouldn't find Him—to the Gentiles, perhaps? Furthermore, as His audience has no idea who sent Him—the Father—they don't understand Jesus will return to Him when He is taken up to a place they can scarcely imagine, much less identify. It's interesting to contrast this with Jesus' teaching that those who seek Him will find Him. Here, those seeking Him will not find Him because they are seeking Him not as their Savior, but to arrest and kill Him.[74]

On the last day of the feast—the most important day—Jesus stands up and cries out, "If anyone thirsts, let him come to me and drink. Whoever believes in me, as the Scripture has said, 'Out of his heart will flow rivers of living water.'" In standing up and speaking loudly, when rabbis normally teach while seated, Jesus is making an emphatic statement.[75] The water He'll provide is the Holy Spirit, Who will indwell believers after He has ascended and infuse them with life. This is consistent with Jesus' teaching to the Samaritan woman that whoever drinks the water He provides will become a spring that bubbles up to everlasting life. Upon hearing this, the people argue among themselves whether Jesus truly is the Messiah. Some want to arrest Him, but no one lays a hand on Him.

When the Pharisees and chief priests ask the officers why they did not arrest Jesus as commanded, they say, "No one ever spoke like this man!" The Pharisees tell them they've been deceived, noting that neither the authorities nor the Pharisees believe in Him. Nicodemus, one of their own who had gone to Jesus before, asks, "Does our law judge a man without first giving him a hearing and learning what he does?" They reply, "Are you from Galilee too? Search and see that no prophet arises from Galilee." The authorities are accusing Nicodemus of being as ignorant as the Galileans—otherwise he would know the Messiah could not be Galilean.[76]

The exclamation, "No one ever spoke like this man!" has always been one of my favorite passages of Scripture. The officers don't arrest Jesus because He is, self-evidently, the Messiah, though they don't see it. It confirms that the Gospels present Jesus as such a unique individual—such a transcendent figure—that no one, even the most gifted author in history, could have fabricated Him. His actions and words make it clear to anyone with an open heart that He is the Son of God. Not only is He sinless, not only does He speak with unparalleled authority, He simply exudes sublime, divine perfection in every aspect of His being. "After reading the doctrine of Plato, Socrates, or Aristotle," says Joseph Parker, "we feel that the specific difference between their words and Christ's is the difference between an inquiry and a revelation."[77]

Arriving at the Temple early in the morning, Jesus sits down and teaches the people. Planning to trip Him up, the scribes and Pharisees bring an adulterous woman before Him and say, "Teacher, this woman has been caught in the act of adultery. Now in the Law, Moses commanded us to stone such women. So what do you say?" Jesus bends down and writes with His finger on the ground. When they persist, He stands up and says, "Let him who is without sin among you be the first to throw a stone at her." He bends down again and writes on the ground. The scribes and Pharisees leave, one by one, and Jesus remains alone with the woman. "Woman, where are they?" he asks. "Has no one condemned you?" She says, "No one, Lord." And He says, "Neither do I condemn you; go, and from now on sin no more."

One striking aspect of this story is that the authorities don't actually care about the woman's sin—they're exploiting her solely to entrap Jesus. Just as He refuses to be ensnared by the Pharisees and Herodians when they ask about the legality of Caesar's taxes, however, He gives them an unexpected answer that penetrates to their souls, forcing them to consider their own motives and hearts, and exposing their hypocrisy and malice. Zealous to condemn the sins of others and to discredit the Savior, they are blind to their own sin. In the face of the Living God, they have no choice but to walk away in shame.

It should be noted that many scholars deny this story was part of John's original Gospel because it was not in the oldest manuscripts.[78] Nevertheless, even if that's true the event still likely occurred, with the story about it circulating as part of the Church's oral tradition.[79] To be sure, it certainly fits with other events where Jesus sees right through the Pharisees' sinister motives and leaves them speechless.

JESUS, THE LIGHT OF THE WORLD (JOHN 8:12–30)

Tensions continue to rise between Jesus and the Pharisees. From this point, says Dr. Joel Willitts, "the ink has all but been dried on Jesus' crucifixion. The religious leaders have had enough of this guy, and they're ready to deal swiftly and violently with him."[80] Jesus repeats that He is the light of the world and that those who follow Him will have the light of life. The Bible reveals God's radiant light, as with the transfiguration, but, as noted, also presents "light" as symbolic of God and His holiness (Psalms 36:9; 1 John 1:5) and Jesus as the light (John 1:4, 9) Who will bring those who believe in Him out of sin and darkness.

The Pharisees accuse Jesus of lying and of bearing witness about Himself, which is anathema according to Rabbinic tradition.[81] After all, Jesus had conceded earlier, "If I alone bear witness about myself, my testimony is not true" (John 5:31). Their charge gives Jesus an opportunity to define Himself as divinely authoritative and to further describe His relationship with the Father, demonstrating He's not merely self-authenticating. Jesus replies, "Even if I do bear witness about myself, my testimony is true, for I know where I came from and where I am going, but you do not know where I come from or where I am going. You judge according to the flesh; I judge no one. Yet even if I do judge, my judgment is true, for it is not I alone who judge, but I and the Father who sent me. In your Law it is written that the testimony of two people is true. I am the one who bears witness about myself, and the Father who sent me bears witness about me."

While Jesus acknowledges that ordinary men cannot vouch for themselves, He is no ordinary man. He is also God and knows things they cannot fathom. He is the light of the world, and light needs no corroborative witnesses. It shows its reality by its radiance.[82] Their perspective, however, is of the flesh, of the world. They are in no position to judge Him because they are ignorant of the two fundamental issues He raises: where He came from and where He's going.[83]

My friend Pastor Donald Fortner, a prolific author who specializes in the Christ-centeredness of Scripture, tells me that in reading the Bible we must focus on six major questions about Jesus Christ:

1. Who is He?
2. Why did He come?
3. What did He accomplish?
4. Why did He die?
5. Where is He now?
6. What is He doing?

Many of these are the same issues Jesus is raising with the Pharisees. They have no idea where He came from because they don't know Who He is. They don't know why He has come because they don't know what

He's going to accomplish. They don't know the real reason He will die, though they have their own reasons for plotting to kill Him. And they certainly don't know where He will be in the future or what He'll be doing.

While Jesus shows He can vouch for Himself, He doesn't need to because the Father sent Him and bears witness about Him. The Pharisees say, "Where is your Father?" and Jesus answers, "You know neither me nor my Father. If you knew me, you would know my Father also." Their question proves they don't know God like they think they do. Yet they are proud because they believe they have special knowledge of Him, and they're surely offended by Jesus' claims.[84] But they don't arrest Him "because his hour had not yet come."

Jesus says He's going away to a place they cannot come and warns they will die in their sins unless they believe in Him. The Jews then wonder whether He means He will kill Himself. They simply don't get it, though they accidentally brush up against a partial truth: Jesus will not kill Himself directly but will voluntarily lay down His life so that we can live (John 10:11, 18).

He is from above, not of this world, and they are from below and of this world. They belong to the world, where Satan rules (1 John 5:19).[85] Unless they believe in Him they will die in their sins. Can you imagine the affront this is to them? They ask Him, "Who are you?" They are asking Him, essentially, "Who do you think you are?" Jesus answers, "Just what I have been telling you from the beginning." Some commentators say Jesus' answer is unclear.[86] Others believe He's just refusing to answer their question directly because it would result in endless argument. He has already told them Who He is, and they are impervious to it (John 8:43).[87] He said He is the bread of life (John 6:35), that He has come from Heaven to do God's will (John 6:38), that by eating His flesh and drinking His blood one may gain eternal life (John 6:54), that those who come to Him and drink will have living water flowing from their hearts (John 7:37–38), and that He is the light of the world (John 8:12).[88] Taken separately, or together, the unmistakable message is that He is the Son of God.

Jesus asserts, "I have much to say about you and much to judge, but he who sent me is true, and I declare to the world what I have heard from him." The Pharisees don't realize He's been speaking to them about the Father. So Jesus says, "When you have lifted up the Son of Man, then you will know that I am he, and that I do nothing on my own authority, but speak just as the Father taught me. And he who sent me is with me. He has not left me alone, for I always do the things that are pleasing to him." Jesus' authority comes from the Father—a concept foreign to them because it involves the Trinity. They won't understand Who He is until He's crucified, resurrected, and ascended—if then. As He teaches, many begin to believe in Him, as difficult as it is for them, which demonstrates the sheer force of Jesus Himself and of His message.

THE TRUTH WILL SET YOU FREE; YOU ARE OF THE FATHER THE DEVIL (JOHN 8:31–47)

Jesus tells the Jews who believe in Him, "If you abide in my word, you are truly my disciples, and you will know the truth, and the truth will set you free." They ask why they need to be freed, as they are Abraham's offspring and have never been slaves. They obviously don't mean that the Jews, as a people, have never been slaves, given their enslavement by Egypt and other powers. More likely they're making a religious statement based on their belief that they're God's spiritual children and Abraham's descendants.[89]

In response Jesus explains, "Truly, truly, I say to you, everyone who practices sin is a slave to sin. The slave does not remain in the house forever; the son remains forever. So if the Son sets you free, you will be free indeed." This is an interesting paradox because it's difficult to see how we'll be freer when Jesus calls us to an even higher standard of living. But when you can't resist the temptation to sin, you're not in control, which is a kind of slavery. Christ can release you from that bondage. To be out from under the controlling influence of sin is to be free. "Truth only can set the mind free from its bondage under ignorance and prejudice and evil habit," writes Rev. H. M. D. Spence. "If the Light of the world shines into the dark places of the heart, the chains [that before were] misunderstood will not only become visible, but will be broken. Godet beautifully says that 'the empire of sin in a human heart is based upon an illusion, a fascination. Let truth shine, and the spell is broken, the will is disgusted with that which seduced it—'the bird escapes from the net of the fowler.'"[90]

Jesus continues, "I know that you are offspring of Abraham; yet you seek to kill me because my word finds no place in you." It's odd, but no less true, that they are descendants of Abraham yet seek to kill Jesus, Who is also Abraham's offspring and the One who fulfills God's covenantal promises to Abraham. They are Abraham's physical descendants, but not his spiritual descendants. As Paul declares, "For not all who are descended from Israel belong to Israel, and not all are children of Abraham because they are his offspring.... This means that it is not the children of the flesh who are the children of God, but the children of the promise are counted as offspring" (Romans 9:6–8; cf. 2:28–29). He further affirms, "And if you are Christ's, then you are Abraham's offspring, heirs according to the promise" (Gal. 3:29).

Jesus says, "I speak of what I have seen with my Father, and you do what you have heard from your father." His words are reinforced by His relationship with the Father, but they listen to a different father—the devil (John 8:44). This "father" is the antithesis of the God of Abraham, the Father of unbounded love.[91] Again, would the passive Jesus depicted in our modern culture dare tell a group of people that their father is the devil?

They insist Abraham is their father but Jesus corrects them: "If you were Abraham's children, you would be doing the works Abraham did, but now you seek to kill me, a man who has told you the truth that I heard from God. This is not what Abraham did. You are doing the works your father did." They continue to protest, saying they aren't sexually immoral because they follow the one Father. Jesus proclaims,

> If God were your Father, you would love me, for I came from God and I am here. I came not of my own accord, but he sent me. Why do you not understand what I say? It is because you cannot bear to hear my word. You are of your father the devil, and your will is to do your father's desires. He was a murderer from the beginning, and does not stand in the truth, because

there is no truth in him. When he lies, he speaks out of his own character, for he is a liar and the father of lies. But because I tell the truth, you do not believe me. Which one of you convicts me of sin? If I tell the truth, why do you not believe me? Whoever is of God hears the words of God. The reason why you do not hear them is that you are not of God.

They are incapable of understanding Him and grasping the truth because they are spiritually dull and follow the devil rather than the true God. William Hendriksen explains that the term "the truth" is far reaching here. It is "used in the sense of that universe of ideas which corresponds with reality as revealed to the Son by the Father."[92] It concerns man's total depravity, the deathly consequences of that condition, and God's plan of redemption through the Son.[93]

BEFORE ABRAHAM WAS, I AM (JOHN 8:48–59)

Now we turn to another one of my favorite passages of Scripture, in which Jesus asserts His deity so powerfully that only hard-hearted readers deny it. The Jews ask Him if He is a Samaritan and has a demon. Jesus answers, "I do not have a demon, but I honor my Father, and you dishonor me. Yet I do not seek my own glory; there is One who seeks it, and he is the judge. Truly, truly, I say to you, if anyone keeps my word, he will never see death."

Indignant, the Jews tell Him they're now sure He has a demon because He's engaging in crazy talk. Abraham died, so how will lesser mortals escape death? They say, "Are you greater than our father Abraham, who died? And the prophets died! Who do you make yourself out to be?" Jesus responds, "If I glorify myself, my glory is nothing. It is my Father who glorifies me, of whom you say, 'He is our God.' But you have not known him. I know him. If I were to say that I do not know him, I would be a liar like you, but I do know him and I keep his word. Your father Abraham rejoiced that he would see my day. He saw it and was glad." The mortified Jews cry out, "You are not yet fifty years old, and have you seen Abraham?" Jesus says, "Truly, truly, I say to you, before Abraham was, I am." They pick up stones to throw at Him, but Jesus hides himself—perhaps supernaturally[94]—and leaves the Temple.

It's as if Jesus is leading them into further revelation, step by step, until they arrive at the inescapable conclusion that He is claiming to be God. When they ask Him how He could have seen Abraham, who lived some two thousand years before, Jesus prefaces His climactic declaration with "Truly, truly," to signify He is about to make a solemn pronouncement. His declaration is jaw dropping. Notice He doesn't say, "Before Abraham was, I was," but "Before Abraham was, I am." He didn't just pre-exist Abraham, He pre-existed all of creation. Had He said, "I was," it could have implied there was a time He didn't exist. But by saying, "I Am," He means He has always existed.

Furthermore, "I am" is the short form of the name God used to identify Himself to Moses—"I am Who I Am" (Exodus 3:14; Deut. 32:39; cf. Isaiah 43:10).

Jesus is indisputably identifying Himself as God. Indeed, John begins His Gospel affirming these truths. "In the beginning was the Word, and the Word was with God, and the Word was God. He was in the beginning with God. All things were made through him, and without him was not any thing made that was made. In him was life, and the life was the light of men" (John 1:1–4). In this context "the Word" (logos) means God, the Son.

The Jews understand Jesus plainly, which is why they want to stone Him. Seventeenth century theologian John Owen writes, "Upon the mentioning of his pre-existence to his incarnation—'Before Abraham was, I am,'...—they fell into a great rage and madness, and took up stones to cast at him." They later clearly state the reason: "It is not for a good work that we are going to stone you but for blasphemy, because you, being a man, make yourself God" (John 10:33).[95] Indeed, if Jesus truly is God, which I believe with all my heart, then His words are the most important ones ever spoken, which is one reason I felt compelled to write this book.

CHAPTER 9

FROM HEALING A BLIND MAN TO MARY'S OINTMENT

It is often overlooked that when Jesus said, "I am the good shepherd," the Jews would inevitably remember that Scripture says, "The Lord (Jehovah) is my shepherd" (John 10:11 and Psalm 23:1). There can be no doubt that Jesus claimed to be God.

—G. BENFOLD[1]

JESUS HEALS A MAN BORN BLIND (JOHN 9:1–34)

As they pass a man with congenital blindness, the disciples ask Jesus whether the man's own sin or his parents' sin caused his condition. "It was not that this man sinned, or his parents," replies Jesus, "but that the works of God might be displayed in him. We must work the works of him who sent me while it is day; night is coming, when no one can work. As long as I am in the world, I am the light of the world." Jesus heals him by anointing his eyes with mud He makes with His own saliva. He then commands the man, "Go wash in the pool of Siloam."

John explains that Siloam means "sent," a prominent concept in John's Gospel. Jesus is "sent" by the Father (John 7:16, 18–29, 33; 8:14, 16, 18, 26, 29, 42), and the disciples are "sent" by Jesus (Matt. 21:2; Mark 11:1; 14:3; Luke 9:2, 52; 10:1).[2] Overall, the issue isn't whether sin caused the man's condition—it's that in the limited time Jesus has left, He can use the man's condition to demonstrate His healing power and advance His ministry.

People who've seen the blind man before question whether it's really him. They take him to the Pharisees, who learn that Jesus healed the man on the Sabbath. Some of them proclaim Jesus is not from God because He violates the Sabbath, while others express doubt that a sinner could do such works. They ask the healed man his opinion, and he says Jesus is a prophet. The Pharisees are probably investigating because curing a congenital condition is more remarkable than healing a temporary condition that could have naturally improved.[3]

The Jewish leaders doubt the man had been blind at all until his parents confirm it. They say their son is "of age," and they should ask him. So the Pharisees ask the man again, encouraging him to confess that Jesus is a sinner. He answers, "Whether he is a sinner I do not know. One thing I do know, that though I was blind, now I see." When they ask him how Jesus healed him, he replies that he's already told them and they won't listen. "Do you also want to become his disciples?" asks the man. They answer rudely that he is Jesus' disciple but they are disciples of Moses—and Moses came from God, but they don't know from where Jesus comes. The man says Jesus must be from God because no one has ever been cured of congenital blindness. "You were born in utter sin, and would you teach us?" they reply indignantly before casting him out.

The Pharisees believe congenital disabilities stem from the sin of the individual or his parents because God would not inflict suffering on the innocent.[4] Their resistance to the truth shows their hard-heartedness— they reject the testimony of the disinterested witnesses, the man, and his parents, preferring darkness to the light.[5]

It's difficult to miss the symbolism in this story, for what better captures a man's conversion to Christ than the avowal, "Though I was blind, now I see?" "That is the testimony of any sinner who has been saved," writes Vernon McGee. "Once I was blind but now I see. Once I was in spiritual darkness but now I am in spiritual light. Once I did not know Christ, but now I know Him as my Savior."[6] "This simple testimony," declares J. E. White, "has been the incontrovertible evidence for the Christian faith for centuries."[7]

I AM THE GOOD SHEPHERD (JOHN 9:35–10:21)

Hearing the Jews had cast out the man, Jesus finds him and asks if he believes in the Son of Man. The man asks who that is, and Jesus says it is He. The man declares, "Lord I believe" and worships Him. Jesus responds, "For judgment I came into this world, that those who do not see may see, and those who see may become blind." Some Pharisees overhearing him ask if they too are blind. Jesus says, "If you were blind, you would have no guilt; but now that you say, 'We see,' your guilt remains." The Pharisees are more culpable than if they were acting in total ignorance. They pride themselves in having knowledge of spiritual things, and yet they are rebelling against Jesus.[8] James reminds us, "Not many of you should become teachers, my brothers, for you know that we who teach will be judged with greater strictness" (James 3:1).

Continuing to address the Pharisees, Jesus says,

Truly, truly, I say to you, he who does not enter the sheepfold by the door but climbs in by another way, that man is a thief and a robber. But he who enters by the door is the shepherd of the sheep. To him the gatekeeper opens. The sheep hear his voice, and he calls his own sheep by name and leads them out. When he has brought out all his own, he goes before them, and the sheep follow him, for they know his voice. A stranger they will not follow, but they will flee from him, for they do not know the voice of strangers. Truly, truly, I say to you, I am the door of the sheep. All who came before me are thieves and robbers, but the sheep did not listen to them. I am the door. If anyone enters by me, he will be saved and will go in and out and find pasture. The thief comes only to steal and kill and destroy. I came that they may have life and have it abundantly.

I am the good shepherd. The good shepherd lays down his life for the sheep. He who is a hired hand and not a shepherd, who does not own the sheep, sees the wolf coming and leaves the sheep and flees, and the wolf snatches them and scatters them. He flees because he is a hired hand and cares nothing for the sheep. I am the good shepherd. I know my own and my own know me, just as the Father knows me and I know the Father; and I lay down my life for the sheep.

And I have other sheep that are not of this fold. I must bring them also, and they will listen to my voice. So there will be one flock, one shepherd. For this reason the Father loves me, because I lay down my life that I may take it up again. No one takes it from me, but I lay it down of my own accord. I have authority to lay it down, and I have authority to take it up again. This charge I have received from my Father.

After hearing this, the Jews remain divided over Jesus, with some claiming He is possessed and others insisting a demon couldn't have healed a blind man.

Jesus is aware that the analogy of the shepherd is richly expressed in the Old Testament (Psalms 23; Ezekiel 34).[9] These scriptures foreshadow His salvation work, for God was Israel's Shepherd (Gen. 49:24; Psalms 23:1; 80:1; Isaiah 40:11). According to Charles Spurgeon, "[Jesus] means us to understand three things; it is as if he said, 'I am a shepherd,' and then 'I am a *good* shepherd,' and, last of all, 'I am *the* good shepherd'—that good shepherd who is spoken of in the Old Testament."[10] Indeed, Christ is here identifying with Jehovah. "This was clearly an affirmation of His absolute Deity," contends Arthur Pink.[11]

Christ is the Shepherd Who protects His sheep (His followers), and they recognize His voice calling, know they are His, and respond by following Him. They instinctively reject and flee from strangers who try to lure them away and destroy them. These are the false prophets and unbelievers who care nothing for the sheep and who work against Jesus and thwart God's work. The Pharisees, in their spiritual darkness, do not recognize Jesus or understand His words. God's kingdom has only one entrance and He is it—He is the gate. Those who enter through Him—via belief in Him—will be saved and will have eternal life. Jesus is the Good Shepherd Who lays down His life for His followers. He knows them, and they know Him, just as He and the Father know one another. This is a weighty revelation because it shows the Son and the Father are perfectly intimate.

In referring to "sheep not of this fold," Jesus has in mind the Gentiles who will enter the kingdom through belief in Him. Jew and Gentile believers alike are part of the same flock and follow one Shepherd—Jesus Christ. Jesus emphasizes that no one, including the Father, is forcing Him to die a substitutionary death on the cross for His sheep, but the Father has given Him the authority to do so and to be resurrected so we may live.

In short, Christ is giving His life for us. "It is for us he lives, and because he lives we live also," writes Charles Spurgeon. "He lives to plead for us. He lives to represent us in heaven. He lives to rule providence for us. He lives to prepare our mansions for us, wither we are going. He lives that he may come again and receive us to himself, that where he is there we may be also. Truly the good shepherd has proved his claim: 'he giveth his life for the sheep.'"[12]

I AND THE FATHER ARE ONE (JOHN 10:22-42)

Jesus is walking in the Temple in Jerusalem during the Feast of Dedication, also known as Hanukkah and the Feast of Lights, which celebrates the cleansing of the Temple after Antiochus Epiphanes desecrated it.[13] The Jews ask Him to state plainly whether He is the Christ. He insists He has already told them and that the works He does for the Father testify that He's the Messiah. But they don't believe, Jesus says, because they're not His sheep. His sheep hear His voice and follow Him, He gives them eternal life, and no one will snatch them away from Him. His Father has given them to Him and He is greater than all. But when Jesus says, "I and the Father are one" (John 10:30), the Jews throw stones at Him. Jesus is not claiming that He and the Father are the same Person, but that their wills are united and that they are of one substance—they are two Persons of the Trinity.[14]

Insisting He has shown them many good works, Jesus demands to know for which one they will stone Him. The Jews say they aren't going to stone Him for good works but for blasphemy—for making Himself God. Jesus says, "Is it not written in your Law, 'I said you are gods'? If he called them gods to whom the word of God came—and Scripture cannot be broken—do you say of him whom the Father consecrated and sent in the world, 'You are blaspheming,' because I said, 'I am the Son of God.' If I am not doing the works of my Father, then do not believe me; but if I do them, even though you do not believe me, believe the works, that you may know and understand that the Father is in me and I am in the Father." They try to arrest Him again, but He escapes across the Jordan River to the place where John had baptized people. Many come to Him and say that everything John said about Him is true, and many believe in Him.

Jesus notes the absurdity of their accusing Him of blasphemy when His works prove He is the Son of God with full authority from the Father, and when their own scriptures, which He affirms cannot be broken, show that God called his appointed agents "gods" when they were only men.[15] Most commentators infer that when Jesus asks, "Is it not written in your Law?" He is referring to Psalm 82, in which God refers to His appointed judges of Israel as "gods."[16]

THE NARROW DOOR (LUKE 13:22–30)

Jesus keeps teaching in the towns on His way to His destiny in Jerusalem. Someone asks Him if only a few people will be saved. He responds with a parable, teaching that they should strive to enter through the narrow door because once the master of the house has shut the door, many will knock and seek to enter in vain, as the master will tell them, "I do not know where you come from." Those denied will protest that they ate and drank with him, but he will repeat that he doesn't know them and declare, "Depart from me, all you workers of evil." Those denied will be cast into a place where there will be weeping and gnashing of teeth, but from there they'll see the Old Testament patriarchs and prophets in God's kingdom. People will come from all directions to enter the kingdom—"some are last who will be first, and some are first who will be last."

By "strive to enter through the narrow door," Jesus doesn't mean people have to earn their way in through good works. Rather, they must repent and believe (Luke 13:3, 5).[17] We must accept Jesus' offer of salvation while we are living on this earth, so we must act while the door is open instead of waiting until it's permanently shut.[18] "The time is short, and there is an hour by which the ordinary householder expects his family to be indoors," notes William Manson, "so there is a time when God will close the gate of life, and those who come knocking after that will be treated as intruders."[19] Salvation is not through kinship or ethnicity, but through saving faith in Him—and His reference to people coming from all directions to enter the kingdom indicates that Jews and Gentiles alike can be saved.[20]

LAMENT OVER JERUSALEM (LUKE 13:31–35)

Some Pharisees warn Jesus to leave because Herod wants to kill Him. He instructs them to tell "that fox" He will cast out demons, heal today and tomorrow, and finish on the third day. But for now He will go on His way, for a prophet should not perish away from Jerusalem. He then laments over Jerusalem—"the city that kills prophets." Jesus declares, "How often would I have gathered your children together as a hen gathers her brood under her wings, and you were not willing! Behold, your house is forsaken. And I tell you, you will not see me until you say, 'Blessed is he who comes in the name of the Lord.'" In bemoaning that He could have taken Jerusalem under His wing, Jesus could be making a veiled reference to His divinity, as God is shown in the Old Testament as protecting His people under His wings (Ruth 2:12; Psalms 17:8; 36:7; 57:1; 61:4; 63:7; 91:4).[21]

Having already ordered the execution of John the Baptist, Herod indeed now has his sights set on Jesus, who is even more popular. Jesus calls Herod a fox, which in the Old Testament represents a petty schemer (Neh. 4:3; Song of Songs 2:15).[22] Jesus must not be captured or killed before He reaches Jerusalem, where He is appointed to die. He reveals His heart and compassion for the city and for His people despite their repeated rejection of Him. After He dies on the cross, is resurrected, and ascends, He will not be seen again until He is welcomed into Jerusalem at His Second Coming as the endtime Messiah (Acts 3:17–21).[23]

JESUS HEALS AGAIN ON THE SABBATH; PARABLES OF THE WEDDING FEAST AND GREAT BANQUET (LUKE 14:1–24)

Again Jesus eats with leery Pharisees. After seeing that a man there has dropsy—excess fluid in the tissues, possibly due to liver or kidney problems[24]—Jesus asks them if it's lawful to heal on the Sabbath. When they don't respond, Jesus heals the man and sends him away. In an argument echoing His remarks about their performance of circumcisions on the Sabbath (John 7:1–24), Jesus asks the Pharisees if they would extricate their son or ox if he fell into a well on the Sabbath. They have no answer, for if they say yes they'd seem like uncompassionate sticklers for the rules, but to admit they would pull him out would openly defy their traditions.

Here, as always, Jesus is in control. Whether it's a question about healing on the Sabbath, stoning an adulterous woman, the disciples washing their hands before eating, or socializing with Samaritans, Jesus confounds the arrogant Pharisees and eludes their attempts to entrap Him.

Next, Jesus challenges their assigned seating order at the dinner table with a parable of a wedding feast. He notes that when invited to such an event you should always sit in the least prestigious spot to avoid being humiliated for picking a place reserved for someone more distinguished. If the host moves you to a higher seat, you will be honored before the guests instead of shamed. "For everyone who exalts himself will be humbled, and he who humbles himself will be exalted." This recalls His earlier teachings that the first will be last and the last, first (Matt. 13:30), and that the meek and poor in spirit shall be blessed (Matt. 5:3–11).

The key to the kingdom of God is saving faith in Jesus Christ. Pride and egotism are mighty obstructions to the humble spirit that accompanies one's surrender, repentance, and faith in Christ to do what one cannot do for himself—earn his way into the kingdom. "For by grace you have been saved through faith," writes the Apostle Paul. "And this is not your own doing; it is the gift of God, not as a result of works, so that no one may boast" (Eph. 2:8). Consider Nebuchadnezzar, whose pride preceded his fall. The Babylonian king said, "Is not this great

Babylon, which I have built by my mighty power as a royal residence and for the glory of my majesty?" (Daniel 4:30). Immediately, "He was driven from among men and ate grass like an ox, and his body was wet with the dew of heaven till his hair grew as long as eagles' feathers, and his nails were like birds' claws" (Daniel 4:33).

Jesus tells his host he shouldn't invite friends, brothers, relatives, or rich neighbors to a dinner party because they'll reciprocate and nullify his good deed. Instead, invite the poor, the crippled, the lame, and the blind, and he will be blessed because they cannot repay him—"for you will be repaid at the resurrection of the just." In the kingdom, God is the host, and no one can repay Him for His grace.[25] We should be good to people because it's the godly thing to do, not to receive something in return. This resembles His instruction that we shouldn't make a public spectacle of prayer, and we shouldn't boast of our good deeds or philanthropy because our real judge is not other men but God.

Jesus relates a parable about the kingdom of God, comparing it to a great banquet to which many are invited, but everyone makes excuses and declines. The master becomes angry and tells his servant to invite the poor, crippled, blind, and lame, which he does, and though they accept, he still doesn't fill the house. The master dispatches the servant to invite more people, noting that none of the previous invitees would taste his banquet. Many of them apparently had legitimate excuses—they needed to work their field, examine their animals, or be with their spouse.[26] But God's kingdom offer—His invitation for us to come to Him in faith—outranks every other priority because it has eternal consequences, and a time will come when the offer will expire (our physical death). We were created to be with Him. As Jesus notes, "For what does it profit a man to gain the whole world and forfeit his soul?" (Mark 8:36).

THE COST OF DISCIPLESHIP (LUKE 14:25-35)

As noted in our discussion of Luke 9:51–62, Jesus is adamant about the high cost of being His disciple. In that passage, He directs one man to follow Him immediately and won't allow Him to first bury his father. Now, Jesus teaches the crowds about the immense sacrifices required to be His disciple. One must hate has own father, mother, wife, children, and even his own life. He must bear his own cross and follow Him. He must calculate the cost before making the decision to follow Him, just as a builder must estimate the cost of building a tower before he begins, lest he be unable to finish and discredit himself. "So therefore, any one of you who does not renounce all that he has cannot be my disciple."

The severe command to hate our loved ones seems inconsistent with Jesus' teachings to love our neighbor and honor our parents. He does not mean this literally, however. Walter Kaiser explains that Jesus uses this language to emphasize that just as material things can interfere with our pursuit of the kingdom of God, so can family ties. A person might be so encumbered with family that he has no time for the kingdom. "The interests of God's kingdom must be paramount with the followers of Jesus, and everything else must take second place to them," writes Kaiser. What better way to make this point than to use such an extreme example showing how Jesus demands a radical reordering of our priorities.[27]

Jesus says, "Salt is good, but if salt has lost its taste, how shall its saltiness be restored? It is of no use either for the soil or for the manure pile. It is thrown away. He who has ears to hear, let him hear." Warren Wiersbe comments, "When a disciple loses his Christian character, he…will eventually be walked on by others and bring disgrace to Christ."[28] John Carroll adds, "In the same way that salt, if it does not remain salty, is set aside, the disciple must persist in the radical commitment that has been undertaken in order to participate in the present-and-future dominion of God."[29]

PARABLES OF THE LOST SHEEP, THE LOST COIN, AND THE PRODIGAL SON (LUKE 15:1–32)

Jesus relates another story, though in a different context, about a man who loses one of his hundred sheep. Matthew related Jesus' story about the joy of finding lost sheep to emphasize His love for children and that He doesn't want to lose any of them (Matt. 18:12–14).[30] Luke uses the metaphor to illustrate God's joy when a sinner repents and finds the kingdom. Jesus reinforces the message with the parable of a woman rejoicing when she finds her lost silver coin. "Just so, I tell you," He says, "there is joy before the angels of God over one sinner who repents."

Jesus next describes a man who divides his property equally between his two sons. The younger son leaves with his property and squanders it all. After suffering in poverty he returns to his father in repentance, determined to tell his father he's no longer worthy to be called his son and should be treated as one of the hired servants. Seeing him coming from far away, the father runs to him and embraces and kisses him. He showers him with gifts and throws a feast for him, exclaiming, "For this my son was dead, and is alive again; he was lost, and is found." The other son, who has played by the rules and conserved his inheritance, is devastated at witnessing his father lavishing attention on his undeserving brother. When he complains the father replies, "Son, you are always with me, and all that is mine is yours. It was fitting to celebrate and be glad, for this your brother was dead, and is alive; he was lost, and is found."

This seems to turn justice on its head—it's as counterintuitive as the notion that we should forsake our parents to follow Christ. But more than property is at stake. The father is determined to restore his family, and that necessitates reconciliation between the brothers.[31] The larger lesson, however, is that God goes and seeks the lost—everyone—and offers His grace to all. Christ is a boundless font of forgiveness and will accept the worst sinner into His fold if He repents, as the younger son clearly does. "How intensely this father loves his son," writes William Hendriksen. "The father cannot have been very young anymore; yet, he runs [to embrace his son upon his return.] In that part of the world it was generally not considered dignified for an elderly man to run; yet, he runs. Nothing can keep him from doing so. He throws his arms around his son's neck. Passionately he embraces his son. Does not this very fact indicate that the father has already in his heart granted forgiveness to his son?"[32]

The parable also implicitly criticizes the Pharisees, who are furious with Jesus' inclusion of outsiders, outcasts, and sinners. But while they strictly obey all the rules, they don't have a humble, contrite spirit and refuse Christ's invitation to the kingdom, which the poor in spirit shall inherit.

Furthermore, this parable makes a strong statement about good works. Note that the older son, though admittedly having lived more righteously than his brother, is still a sinner. The point is, we can't earn entry into the kingdom no matter how many good deeds we do. Admission to heaven, as noted in the previous chapter, isn't based on a test that's graded on a curve. In the end, we are all sinners and don't deserve the kingdom any more than the worst sinners—none of us measures up, so we must simply be grateful for God's grace. "There is no evil that the father's love cannot pardon and cover," explains Timothy Keller. "There is no sin that is a match for his grace."[33] Similarly, John Piper observes, "The elder brother had the mindset of a slave. He worked for the father. He did not rest joyfully in the father's beneficence. And as long as he insisted on treating the commandments of his father as a job description for slaves, he would be cut off from Christ and a stranger to grace. Christ is at the feast with the broken, forgiven sinners who have learned that their service is utterly inadequate. And he invites you and entreats you…to forsake the mindset of a slave and accept the gift of adoption."[34] As John's Gospel asserts, "But to all who did receive him, who believed in his name, he gave the right to become children of God" (1:12).

THE PARABLES OF THE DISHONEST MANAGER AND THE RICH MAN AND LAZARUS; TEACHINGS ON FAITH AND SERVANTHOOD (LUKE 16:1–31; 17:5–10)

Jesus tells of a rich man who fires his financial manager for wasting his assets. While he still can, the manager cuts favorable deals for some of the rich man's debtors, angling to win their favor for later when he'll be unemployed. Oddly, the master praises the dishonest manager for his shrewdness. Jesus comments, "For the sons of this world are more shrewd in dealing with their own generation than the sons of light. And I tell you, make friends for yourselves by means of unrighteous wealth so that when it fails they may receive you into the eternal dwellings."

Jesus uses this unorthodox story to teach a lesson. He isn't praising dishonesty, but teaching that His disciples should use their material goods for spiritual benefit such as caring for the poor and for investing in eternal things.[35] We shouldn't collect treasures on earth but treasures in heaven that can't be destroyed (Matt. 6:19–21). Just because Christians are called to holiness doesn't mean we have to be naïve, helpless, and negligent. Remember, we are to be as shrewd as serpents and as innocent as doves (Matt. 10:16).

That Jesus doesn't endorse every aspect of the manager's behavior is shown in the verses that follow (Luke 16:10–34), in which He stresses honesty and integrity: "One who is faithful [with] very little is also faithful in much, and one who is dishonest [with] very little is also dishonest in much.... No servant can serve two masters, for either he will hate the one and love the other, or he will be devoted to the one and despise the other. You cannot serve God and money."

The Pharisees ridicule Jesus because they love money. Jesus in turn chastises them for exalting themselves before men, which is an abomination to God. He insists they don't understand their own scriptures or they would know that the New Covenant has been inaugurated and the good news of the kingdom of God is being preached. This does not negate the Old Testament, which points to Christ and remains valid: "It is easier for heaven and earth to pass away than for one dot of the Law to become void," He argues. While the Pharisees busy themselves opposing Jesus and missing the boat, others are entering into the kingdom.

Jesus tells the story of Lazarus, a poor man who lays outside a rich man's gate hoping to eat the morsels that fall from the rich man's table. Both the rich man and Lazarus die, with Lazarus going to heaven and the rich man to hell. The rich man begs Father Abraham to mercifully send Lazarus to cool his burning tongue. Abraham refuses, saying the rich man had his chance on earth but greedily consumed himself with his riches, ignoring the plight of others. A great chasm separates heaven and hell, and none may cross it. The rich man begs Abraham to send Lazarus to his five brothers to warn them to avoid the torment of hell. The next verse is sobering: Abraham says that would be fruitless because they already have the scriptures—if they don't believe them, they won't believe a resurrected Lazarus when he warns them.

Notice how this comes together. Jesus affirms the Old Testament scriptures for a reason: they are the inspired, unbreakable Word of God, and we can rely on their promise of a coming Messiah. If people don't come to believe in Jesus, it's not because God hasn't provided us sufficient revelation in Scripture and in general revelation. Something else—pride, sin, or hard-heartedness—may be obstructing their path.

The apostles ask Jesus to enhance their faith, and He again invokes the analogy of a mustard seed, saying if a person had the faith of just one grain of that seed, he could command a mulberry tree to be uprooted and planted in the sea, and it would obey. He probably doesn't means this literally, but rather that even a small amount of genuine faith can yield powerful results.[36]

Next, Jesus asks the apostles whether they would reward a servant coming in from a day's work or order him to prepare dinner for them, noting that you don't thank the servant merely for doing his job. Again, Jesus does not intend every aspect of this story to be accepted literally. He doesn't want us to be ungracious to those working for us. Rather, His message is spiritual: we are unworthy of the kingdom and will only be permitted to enter if we put our trust in Him. It's based solely on His unmerited grace.

THE DEATH OF LAZARUS (JOHN 11:1–45)

In the village of Bethany, two miles east of Jerusalem,[37] a man named Lazarus is ill. He's the brother of Mary, who had anointed Jesus with oil and wiped his feet with her hair. Mary and her sister Martha send word to Jesus that "he whom you love is ill." Jesus assures them the illness will not end in death but is for God's glory so that the Son may be glorified through it. Jesus waits two days before going to Bethany to see Lazarus, who has now died. His disciples warn Him not to go because the Jews there are seeking to stone Him. Jesus assures them He will not be taken until His appointed time, and until then He (and they) must energetically advance the Gospel message. Jesus says He's glad for their sake that Lazarus has died, "so that you may believe." It's remarkable that after all this time He's still concerned about His disciples' faith.

When they arrive in Bethany, they find that Lazarus has been entombed for four days. Martha goes out to meet Jesus while Mary remains at home. Martha tells Jesus that her brother wouldn't have died had He been there, but she knows if He asks God to raise him, God will do so. Jesus insists Lazarus will rise again. Misunderstanding Jesus, Martha says, "I know that he will rise again in the resurrection on the last day." Jesus proclaims that He is the resurrection and the life, and that whoever believes in Him will never die. He asks her if she believes that, and she replies, "Yes, Lord; I believe that you are the Christ, the Son of God, who is coming into the world."

Martha informs Mary that Jesus is calling for her, and Mary quickly goes to Him. The Jews with Mary follow her, thinking she's going to her brother's tomb to mourn. When Mary sees Jesus, she falls at His feet and tells Him that if He'd been there, Lazarus wouldn't have died. When Jesus sees her and the Jews weeping, He is "deeply moved in his spirit and greatly troubled." He asks where they have placed Lazarus, and they tell Him to come see.

John reports that "Jesus wept," which is one of the shortest and most profound passages in the New Testament. It illuminates Jesus' humanity, His compassion, and the pain and suffering He endures because of His unbounded love for us. In a sermon, Charles Spurgeon observes, "Jesus wept.... He was deeply affected, and his tears were the fit expression of his intense emotion. *Love made him weep*: nothing else ever compelled him to tears. I do not find that all the pains he endured, even when scourged or when fastened to the cruel tree, fetched a single tear from him; but for love's sake 'Jesus wept.'"[38] In a separate sermon Spurgeon continues the theme, saying, "You will never forget how 'Jesus wept.' You all know how he suffered, and how at last he died. Treasure up in your mind and heart the assured fact that Christ was most really and truly man; and though the godhead was most mysteriously united to his manhood, yet he was none the less completely and intensely man. Because he was perfectly and supremely God, his godhead did not take away from him his power to suffer and to be wearied."[39]

Some Jews wonder whether Jesus, Who had healed the blind man, could have kept Lazarus from dying. Deeply anguished again, Jesus comes to the tomb, which is inside a cave. He orders them to remove the stone covering the tomb. When they remove it, Jesus lifts up His eyes and says, "Father, I thank you that you have heard me. I knew that you always hear me, but I said this on account of the people standing around, that they may believe that you sent me." He cries out, "Lazarus, come out," and Lazarus emerges with his hands and feet bound with linen strips and his face wrapped in a cloth. Jesus commands them to unbind him. Many of the Jews who came with Mary now believe in Him, but some of them go to the Pharisees and report what Jesus did.

After Jesus wept the Jews proclaim, "See how he loved him!" Pastor Timothy Keller points to this verse as the heart of the message. The Jews are wrong to use the past tense. "The teaching of this passage," says Keller, "is that Jesus' love is never in the past tense. It means if he has set his love on you, his love is always present. It's never in the past tense. It's an eternal love.... Think of that. It never lets you go. Jesus' love is the richest, most powerful, most manifold, wealthy thing you can talk about."[40] Jesus' sorrow should be understood in the context of this resurrection story. Jesus' resurrection of Lazarus is a sign of His own coming resurrection as the culminating event of all salvation history. But it's also symbolic of His everlasting love for us, a love that doesn't end at our physical death.

THE PLOT TO KILL JESUS (JOHN 11:46–54)

When the Jews report Jesus' resurrection of Lazarus to the Pharisees, they join the chief priests in convening the Sanhedrin. They debate what to do, concerned that if He continues to perform signs everyone will believe in Him and the Romans will take away their Temple and their nation. Caiaphas, the high priest, tells them they know nothing. It's better, he says, that one man should die for the people than that the whole nation perish. Caiaphas, unwittingly, has uttered a divine prophecy—that Jesus would die for the nation so it would not perish.[41] From that point, they plot to kill Jesus. Consequently, Jesus no longer walks openly among the Jews but goes to stay with His disciples in Ephraim. "Caiaphas could hardly realize the full meaning of his own words (John 18:14)," writes Charles Ryrie. "He was simply expressing the thought of a political collaborator with Rome; and yet those words express the central doctrine of the Christian faith—the substitutionary atonement of Christ."[42]

CLEANSING OF TEN LEPERS (LUKE 17:11–19)

While passing between Samaria and Galilee, Jesus enters a village and encounters ten lepers who say, "Jesus, Master, have mercy on us." He tells them, "Go and show yourselves to the priests." Jesus means that each of the lepers should go to their respective villages and present themselves for inspection. If they are clean, they may re-enter society.[43] As they go they are cleansed and one of them, a Samaritan, turns back and loudly praises God, falling at Jesus' feet and thanking Him. Jesus asks why he, the "foreigner," was the only one of the ten who praised God. Jesus tells him, "Rise and go your way; your faith has made you well."

This is more than another testimony to Jesus' healing power. It also involves Jesus' concern with the response of those He cures. "Jesus' mercy is offered to all men, but they must acknowledge what God has done through him; to faith must be added thanksgiving," writes I. Howard Marshall. "Moreover, this may be missing from the attitude of Jews, who might be expected to appreciate the obligation more than Samaritans. The person who makes such acknowledgement experiences a salvation which goes beyond merely the physical cure."[44]

THE COMING OF THE KINGDOM (LUKE 17:20–21)

The Pharisees, for once apparently not trying to trick Jesus, ask Him when the kingdom of God will come. He replies, "The kingdom of God is not coming in ways that can be observed, nor will they say, 'Look, here it is!' or 'There!' for behold, the kingdom of God is in the midst of you." The Pharisees don't understand that Jesus has already inaugurated His ministry, recently demonstrated by His healing of the ten lepers. Again, the kingdom of God has both a present and future dimension— it has already arrived, but has not yet come in all its fullness. It begins with His life, death, and resurrection, and will be completed on His coming when He will totally defeat evil. Douglas Moo explains that Jesus is saying, "Don't be looking up to the sky for spectacular signs and wonders. I'm standing right in front of you—the one who in my own person embodies the kingdom of God. I'm right here in your midst....

[The kingdom has already been inaugurated and is] present, [though it] has not yet come to its climax."[45]

JESUS TEACHES HIS DISCIPLES ABOUT THE COMING OF THE KINGDOM (LUKE 17:22–37)

Jesus says the days are coming when the disciples will want to see the return of the Son of Man, but they won't see it. People will claim those days have come, but the disciples shouldn't listen to them—they will know themselves when He has come, for He will be as noticeable as lightning illuminating the entire sky. But first, He must suffer many things and be rejected by this generation.

The Son of Man's coming will be at an unexpected time, just like the flood in Noah's days and like the fire and sulfur that rained from heaven on Sodom and Gomorrah. When that day comes people should not turn back, as Lot's wife did (and became a pillar of salt) (Gen. 19:26). "Whoever seeks to preserve his life will lose it, but whoever loses his life will keep it," Jesus declares. "I tell you, that in that night there will be two in one bed. One will be taken and the other left. There will be two women grinding together. One will be taken and the other left." The disciples ask Jesus, "Where, Lord?" and He replies, "Where the corpse is, there the vultures will gather."

The kingdom has already arrived, but it will come in a different sense in the future with Christ's Second Coming. He will be absent for a while—there will be a time between His ascension and His return (the Church Age) when they will long for His arrival. But they shouldn't listen to people who say He's already here because His coming will be so dramatic they won't need anyone to confirm it.[46] If someone says He has come and they aren't aware of it, they'll be pointing to a false prophet.

We mustn't concern ourselves with the specific time Jesus will come, but should get our houses in order beforehand because once He arrives it will be too late. We will either already believe in Him then or we won't. If we are believers, we will recognize Him. John assures us,

"Beloved, we are God's children now, and what we will be has not yet appeared; but we know that when he appears we shall be like him, because we shall see him as he is" (1 John 3:2; cf. 1 Cor. 15:52–54; Phil. 3:21). Not only will His arrival be unexpected, but He will be coming in judgment, just as God came in judgment in Noah's day and also in Lot's.

TWO PARABLES ON PRAYER (LUKE 18:1–14)

Jesus relates a parable about a widow's repeated attempts to seek justice from an unjust judge who finally relents due to her persistence. How much more will God give justice to His elect who cry to Him day and night! "I tell you," says Jesus, "he will give justice to them speedily. Nevertheless, when the Son of Man comes, will he find faith on earth?" Jesus is encouraging His disciples (and everyone else) to keep the faith and persist in prayer until He comes.

Jesus next compares the respective attitudes of a Pharisee and a tax collector toward prayer. In his prayer, the Pharisee thanks God that he's more righteous than others, including the tax collector. The tax collector is too humble even to look up to heaven, but says, "God, be merciful to a sinner." Jesus says, "I tell you, this man went down to his house justified, rather than the other. For everyone who exalts himself will be humbled, but the one who humbles himself will be exalted."

I marvel at the Bible's thematic consistency. Just as Jesus says the meek and humble will be blessed, that we should not do our "good deeds" conspicuously to win man's approval instead of God's, that we must have the innocence of children, and that we should eschew pride, we must also acknowledge our sinfulness, repent, and come to Him in faith. Righteousness is not a matter of following rules but of the heart. It comes from faith in Him. How affirming for Jesus to explain that it's not our sinfulness that will obstruct our relationship with Him and sabotage our prayers but our pride and conceit. We must not be self-exalted, especially in our prayers—and we should pray that we remain humble.[47]

JESUS ON DIVORCE (MATT. 19:1–12; MARK 10:1–12)

Having decided to kill Jesus (John 11:53) and order His arrest (John 11:57), the Pharisees are even more determined to trap Him in legal questions. Some ask Him whether it's legal for a man to divorce His wife. He replies with a question: "What did Moses command you?" Moses, they reply, allowed a man to divorce his wife. Jesus says Moses permitted it because the Jews' hearts had become hardened. Quoting Genesis 2:24, Jesus explains that since the beginning of time, God has made people male and female, and that they would leave their father and mother and become one flesh. "What therefore God has joined," Jesus declares, "let not man separate." So while God established marriage as permanent, He made allowances for divorce because man's heart became hard.

Later the disciples ask Him again, and He says, "Whoever divorces his wife, except for sexual immorality, and marries another, commits adultery." (Mark's Gospel, however, doesn't include this exception for sexual immorality.) The disciples ask Him whether it would just be better not to marry, which indicates they fully understand the seriousness Jesus is attaching to divorce.[48] While some interpret Jesus' response as recommending celibacy, that would contradict His strong endorsement of marriage as a God-given institution in the preceding verses.[49] Remember that God instituted marriage for mankind, proclaiming, "It is not good that the man should be alone; I will make him a helper fit for him" (Gen. 2:18).

JESUS BLESSES CHILDREN (MATT. 19:13–15; MARK 10:13–16; LUKE 18:15–17)

When people bring children to Jesus to lay His hands on them and pray, the disciples rebuke them. Jesus responds, "Let the little children come to me and do not hinder them, for to such belongs the kingdom of heaven. Truly, I say to you, whoever does not receive the kingdom of God like a child shall not enter it." And He lays His hands on them, and they go away. Jesus is expressing His love for children, praising their innocence, and instructing that all people cultivate such childlike innocence, humility, and trust to inherit the kingdom of God. Thomas Hale explains that when a child receives something, "He holds out his hands. He asks. A little child is helpless. He cannot earn anything. He cannot pay money for what he wants. He cannot say, 'I have worked hard; I deserve to receive a reward.' The child just trusts that what he needs will be given to him. Whatever he asks for he asks in faith.... This is how we must enter the kingdom of God. We do not deserve to enter.... We must receive the kingdom of God by faith like a little child. There is no other way."[50]

JESUS TEACHES ON RICHES (MATT. 19:16–20:16; MARK 10:17–31; LUKE 18:18–30)

A rich man asks Jesus, Whom he calls "Good Teacher," what good deed he must do to have eternal life. Jesus says there is only one who is good—God—and that to enter life the man must keep the commandments. The man says he has done so and asks what he still lacks. Jesus instructs him to sell his possessions and give them to the poor so he will have treasure in heaven, telling him, "Come, follow me." The man leaves heartbroken because he's unwilling to part with his possessions. This is another lesson in the high cost of discipleship.

Surely Jesus isn't endorsing salvation by works in telling this man he must follow the commandments. In saying, "There is only one who is good," He means that no man can live up to the commandments, yet he must to attain eternal life. But if he appropriates the finished work of Christ by placing his saving faith in Him, God will declare him justified on the basis of his trust in Christ (Romans 4:5)—Christ's righteousness, as we earlier observed, will be imputed to him, and it will be as though he did honor all the commandments. Christ's message is consistent, as He demands the same exacting standards in the Sermon on the Mount (Matt. 5:48).

Continuing His talk with the rich man, Jesus avers, "Truly I say to you, only with difficulty will a rich person enter the kingdom of heaven.... It is easier for a camel to go through the eye of a needle than for a rich person to enter the kingdom of God." Hearing these words, His astonished disciples ask, "Who then can be saved?" Jesus responds, "With man this is impossible, but with God all things are possible."

It *is* impossible for a rich man, or any other man, to get to heaven on his own. But with God all things are possible—so we lean on God through faith in Jesus Christ, and heaven opens up to us through God's grace. I'm not dismissing Jesus' reference to rich people, for I think He uses them as an example of a group who is particularly vulnerable to idolatry. If you lust after money or obsess over worldly possessions, you will not have your heart on God, "for the love of money is a root of all kinds of evils" (1 Tim. 6:10).

Peter notes that the disciples have given up everything and asks what they will have. Jesus says that in the "new world," He will sit on His throne and the disciples will sit on twelve thrones, judging the twelve tribes of Israel. And everyone who has left his family or possessions for Jesus' sake will inherit eternal life. "But many who are first will be last, and the last first."

Jesus compares the kingdom of heaven to laborers in the vineyard. The vineyard owner hires laborers who go out early in the morning, and the owner agrees to pay them one denarius a day. Throughout the day he hires additional workers who begin working at different times, but all end work at the same time in the evening and all are paid the same amount. When the laborers who work the longest complain that the arrangement is unfair, the owner argues he's doing nothing wrong because he's honoring his agreement to pay them one denarius. The owner asks, "Am I not allowed to do what I choose with what belongs to me? Or do you begrudge my generosity?" Jesus says, "So the last will be first, and the first last."

As the story of the prodigal son shows, we mustn't worry about the other person, but we should get our own houses in order. The foreman doesn't breach his contract with the laborers but pays them exactly what he promised. If God wants to extend us grace, it's His prerogative to do so, and we have no standing to complain. We shouldn't covet or be jealous.[51] God is in sovereign control of rewards.[52] No one can earn his way to eternal life. No one is worthy on the basis of merit, but only through the substitutionary blood of Jesus Christ. So of course terrible sinners will be admitted into heaven along with those who haven't sinned as much—provided they trust in Christ for their salvation.

When you really think about it, begrudging the other guy's salvation implies that we think we're somehow worthy without God's grace. From a human perspective we may be less *unworthy*, but we're still fallen creatures who fall far short and who cannot earn our salvation.

JESUS AGAIN FORETELLS HIS DEATH (MATT. 20:17–19; MARK 10:32–34; LUKE 18:31–34)

As Jesus heads toward Jerusalem with His twelve disciples He says, "The Son of Man will be delivered over to the chief priests and the scribes, and they will condemn him to death and deliver him over to the Gentiles. And they will mock him and spit on him, and flog him and kill him. And after three days he will rise." Jesus is specific about the phases of suffering He will endure: He will be betrayed, sentenced to death by the Sanhedrin, handed over to the Roman authorities, mocked, spit on, flogged, killed, and resurrected.[53] The disciples are amazed and afraid.

REQUEST OF JAMES AND JOHN (AND THEIR MOTHER) (MATT. 20:20–28; MARK 10:35–45)

Matthew's Gospel relates that the mother of James and John requests that Jesus allow her sons to sit at His right hand and His left hand respectively in His kingdom. (Mark relates that James and John themselves make the request.) Jesus replies, "You do not know what you are asking. Are you able to drink the cup that I drink, or to be baptized with which I am baptized?" They say they are. He says they will drink His cup and be baptized with His baptism. He doesn't have the authority to grant their wishes on seating, however, for the Father will assign such places of honor. Overhearing the discussion, the other ten disciples are indignant at James and John. Jesus reminds them that the rulers of the Gentiles lord their authority over their subjects, but that won't be the case among the disciples. "Whoever would be great among you must be your servant, and whoever would be first among you must be slave of all. For even the Son of Man came not to be served but to serve, and to give his life as a ransom for many."

It's unclear whether Jesus' prediction of His suffering, death, and resurrection fully registers with the disciples. They still may think He's going to establish an earthly kingdom now.[54] Recently, the disciples had argued among themselves as to who among them would be the greatest in the kingdom. Now James and John try to secure the cushiest spots at the table for themselves, but Jesus declines. James and John (as well as the other ten disciples, who are jealous of them) are showing no comprehension of Jesus' message of humility and servanthood. He doesn't scold them, but asks them whether they will drink from His cup and be baptized as He will be baptized. Will they stand by Him and suffer as a result?

Though they cannot possibly understand what they are agreeing to, Jesus doesn't correct them, but affirms they will suffer—a prediction that is fulfilled with James' martyrdom (Acts 12:2) and John's suffering, persecution, banishment, and loneliness in his old age.[55] Jesus is saying that service, not authority or status, will characterize His kingdom. After all, Jesus Christ, the Son of God, is serving human beings and will make the ultimate sacrifice for them on the cross.

JESUS HEALS BARTIMAEUS (MATT. 20:29–34; MARK 10:46:52; LUKE 18:35–43)

Close to Jericho, Jesus walks past a blind man begging on the road-side. When the man hears the crowd he asks what's happening, and people tell him Jesus is passing by. He cries out, "Jesus, Son of David, have mercy on me!" People tell him to be quiet but he cries out all the more. Jesus stops and has the man brought to Him, asking, "What do you want me to do for you?" The man asks Him to return his sight. Jesus says, "Recover your sight; your faith has made you well." Immediately he can see, and he glorifies God and follows Jesus.

Faith again leads to healing and salvation, as the man "follows" Jesus and acknowledges Him as the Messiah—the Son of David—when he asks to be healed. Though initially rebuked by the people, he persists, showing his faith is real. Upon being healed, he gives God the glory. In Matthew's account there are two blind beggars but only one in Mark's and Luke's. Regardless of whether these were two different events, the messages are identical. Warren Wiersbe summarizes the lesson with a contrast between the beggars and the rich young ruler. "The beggars were poor," writes Wiersbe, "yet they became rich, while the young man was rich and became eternally poor. The beggars claimed no special merit and openly admitted their need, while the young man lied about himself and bragged about his character. The young man would not believe, so he went away from Jesus despondent; but the two beggars believed in Jesus and followed Him with songs of praise. 'He hath filled the hungry with good things; and the rich He hath sent empty away' (Luke 1:53)."[56]

JESUS AND ZACCHAEUS (LUKE 19:1–10)

As Jesus enters Jericho, a rich chief tax collector named Zacchaeus is seeking to see Him. The man is too small to see over the crowd, so he climbs a sycamore tree. Jesus notices him and says, "Hurry and come down, for I must stay at your house today." The people grumble that Jesus has gone into the house of a sinner. Zacchaeus tells Jesus, "Behold, Lord, the half of my goods I give to the poor. And if I have defrauded anyone of anything, I restore it fourfold." Jesus tells him, "Today salvation has come to this house, since he also is a son of Abraham. For the Son of Man came to seek and to save the lost."

Tax collectors are hated and widely regarded as corrupt. Jesus doubtlessly chooses this man to show that His grace is available to the worst of sinners provided they are repentant, which Zacchaeus obviously is. Notice that Jesus already knows his name and says, "I must stay at your house today," which suggests a divine priority to extend His grace to Zacchaeus. After all, as Jesus attests, "The Son of Man came to seek and save the lost" (Luke 19:10).[57]

This statement summarizes Jesus' entire mission and is probably the key verse in Luke's Gospel.[58] Peter comments, "The Lord is not slow to fulfill his promise as some count slowness, but is patient toward you, not wishing that any should perish, but that all should reach repentance" (2 Peter 3:9). "None are too sinful, too base, too vile, or too far gone for Christ to save," writes Donald Fortner. "His arm is not shortened that he cannot save. Oh, no! His mighty arm is omnipotent in the operations of his grace! None are beyond the reach of omnipotent mercy!... Here is a notorious publican, one of the most well known of the despised tax-collectors dwelling near Jericho, transformed into a child of God.... Here is a covetous man transformed instantaneously into a self-sacrificing philanthropist!"[59] Indeed, let us not overlook the extent of his wickedness when Jesus meets him or the radical transformation in his character after Jesus completes His work in him.

THE PARABLE OF THE TEN MINAS (LUKE 19:11–28)

Jesus tells of a nobleman who is about to travel to a far country to be crowned king. He calls ten of his servants and, giving them each ten minas (a mina is equal to one hundred denari, about one hundred times a typical day's wage),[60] says to them, "Engage in business until I come." But the people hate him and send a delegation after him to say they don't want him to reign over them. When he returns, he orders the servants to report how they have fared with the minas. The first says he made ten minas more. The nobleman says, "Well done, good servant! Because you have been faithful in very little, you shall have authority over ten cities." The second one made five minas, and the nobleman says to him, "And you are to be over five cities."

Another servant returns his mina, saying he'd kept it in a handker-chief because he was afraid of the nobleman. The nobleman tells him, "I will condemn you with your own words, you wicked servant! You knew that I was a severe man, taking what I did not deposit and reaping what I did not sow? Why then did you not put my money in the bank, and at my coming I might have collected it with interest?" He orders those standing by to take the mina from him and give it to the servant with ten minas. They say, "Lord, he has ten minas!" The nobleman replies, "I tell you that to everyone who has, more will be given, but from the one who has not, even what he has will be taken away. But as for these enemies of mine, who did not want me to reign over them, bring them here and slaughter them before me."

Jesus probably presents this parable because the people think He's going to reinstitute His kingdom immediately. But the parable shows the kingdom will not reach its fullness until His return.[61] The various elements in the story suggest it's pointing to Jesus, Who will be reviled and rejected by His people, intensely opposed when His kingship is announced, and called away for a time (after He dies, is resurrected, and ascended). He will later return in power and glory, and demand an accounting from those to whom He has entrusted responsibility and resources.[62]

If those elements point to Jesus, the rest of the story points to Christians, all of whom are accountable for their lives, with some acquitting themselves as good stewards and the others as poor ones. The poor steward, having been disobedient and inattentive to the nobleman's directions, suffers the consequences. Just as we don't know when we will be called home or when Christ will return, we have to believe in Him and fulfill the responsibilities attendant to Christian living.

Matthew relates a similar parable that differs in certain details but conveys the same message. Matthew's version has three servants, not ten, and they receive talents rather than minas. In Matthew the worthless servant is cast into the outer darkness and in Luke the enemies are slain before the king.

TALK OF ARRESTING JESUS AS PASSOVER APPROACHES (JOHN 11:55–57)

As the Passover is at hand, many Jews have come to Jerusalem before the feast to purify themselves. Looking for Jesus, they are wondering if He will come to the feast, and the chief priests and Pharisees order people to inform them if Jesus appears so they can arrest Him.

ANOINTING OF JESUS AT BETHANY
(MATT. 26:6–13; MARK 14:3–9; JOHN 12:1–8)

Jesus is sitting at the table at Simon the leper's house when Mary, sister of Martha and Lazarus,[63] approaches Him with an alabaster flask of expensive ointment and pours it on His head. (John's Gospel says she anoints His feet and wipes His feet with her hair.) The disciples, including Judas Iscariot, are appalled that she has "wasted" ointment that could have been sold for a large sum and given to the poor. Jesus asks, "Why do you trouble the woman? For she has done a beautiful thing to me. For you always have the poor with you, but you will not always have me. In pouring this ointment on my body, she has done it to prepare me for burial. Truly, I say to you, wherever this gospel is proclaimed in the whole world, what she has done will also be told in memory of her."[64] Judas, the disciples' treasurer, is pretending to be altruistic to mask his greed.

It might appear that Jesus is downplaying any concern for the poor, but that's absurd in light of His ministry. Instead, He's using this event to highlight urgent priorities. We will always have the poor, and we should always show them love and mercy and be charitable. But Jesus' time on earth is coming to an end, and He is drawing their attention to His impending death and the precious time left for the disciples (and others) to spend with Him. "The gift of the woman was a tremendous memorial, wonderfully preservable in the light of the forthcoming death of Jesus," Gerald Borchert writes. "It was an anointing fit for a king who came to save the world."[65] Though some might view Mary's act as wasteful, she's demonstrating her love and commitment to Him. Jesus, for good reason, emphasizes her act of sacrifice motivated by her deep love.

CHAPTER 10

FROM THE PLOT TO KILL LAZARUS TO PETER'S ILL-FATED VOW

How different it is to read a passage from a gospel. It scarcely matters where, whether Jesus is debating with the Pharisees in Capernaum or standing by the bedside of Jairus's daughter. He meets us in the story. It is the divine genius of the gospel writer that he draws the readers existentially into the narrative, to involve us, so that we find ourselves making decisions about Jesus and therefore about ourselves.... The gospel... draws us into a drama that Christ himself is directing. In the gospel Christ himself meets us and requires the answer, "Who do you say I am?"

—P. BARNETT[1]

THE PLOT TO KILL LAZARUS (JOHN 12:9–11)

L earning Jesus is in Bethany, a large crowd of Jews comes to see Him and Lazarus, whom He'd raised from the dead. The chief priests conspire to kill Lazarus too, because his resurrection is causing many to believe in Jesus. Their hardness of heart leads them to conceal evidence rather than accept it, and they're willing to murder an innocent man just to preserve their authority and their belief system—for the chief priests are mostly Sadduccees,[2] who do not believe in the resurrection, and Lazarus' resurrection not only is leading people to Christ, but is a standing condemnation of their doctrine.[3]

THE TRIUMPHAL ENTRY (MATTHEW 21:1–11; MARK 11:1–10; LUKE 19:29–40; JOHN 12:12–19)

When Jesus and His disciples come to the Mount of Olives near Jerusalem, Jesus sends two disciples into the village to get Him a donkey and a colt. "If anyone says anything to you," Jesus instructs them, "you shall say, 'The Lord needs them,' and he will send them at once." This fulfills the Old Testament prophecy of Zechariah, "Say to the daughter of Zion, 'Behold, your king is coming to you, humble, and mounted on a donkey, on a colt, the foal of a beast of burden'" (Zech. 9:9). The disciples don't understand the significance of this until Jesus is glorified, and then they remember these things had been written about Him.

The disciples obey His command, and Jesus enters Jerusalem on the donkey. Many spread their cloaks on the road while others lay down cut branches. Those preceding Him and following Him shout, "Hosanna to the Son of David! Blessed is he who comes in the name of the Lord! Hosanna in the highest!" When He enters Jerusalem the entire city is stirred up and is asking, "Who is this?" And the crowds say, "This is the prophet Jesus, from Nazareth of Galilee." After indignant Pharisees urge Jesus to rebuke His disciples for this blasphemy, He says, "I tell you, if these were silent, the very stones would cry out."

Jesus astounds the Pharisees by embracing the crowds' claim that He's the Messiah, noting that if the crowds hadn't done so, God's creation itself would have. The time has come to reveal this irrepressible truth. "Indeed, 'stones' would pick up the chorus of joyful praise were these people silenced," writes Joel Green, "signaling the cosmic repercussions of the consummation of God's salvific plan signified in this event."[4]

Jesus' statement is interesting in terms of salvation history. Ever since the Fall, creation has been tainted. "For we know that the whole creation has been groaning together in the pains of childbirth until now" (Romans 8:18), writes Paul. But Jesus will eventually inaugurate a new heaven and a new earth, and the entire creation will be glorified through Him. Philip Ryken argues,

> By saying this, Jesus was claiming that he deserved the worship of the whole creation. Even if human beings stop singing his praises, he will still have the glory that he deserves. Jesus was riding down the Mount of Olives when he said this, and if necessary, every stone on that mountainside would join his choir. The very stones of the ground would open their mouths to declare their Maker's praise. The Bible says that the creation "waits with eager longing" for the day of salvation, when it will be "set free from its bondage to decay and obtain the freedom of the glory of the children of God" (Rom. 8:19, 21). Here Jesus gives us the sense that in that painful longing, the creation is almost bursting to sing its song. The rocks are ready at any moment to break their stony silence and shout for joy that Jesus is the King.[5]

Matthew's account mentions a donkey and a colt, whereas the other Gospels mention only the colt, probably because Matthew, with his messianic emphasis, wants to focus on Zechariah's prophecy of the coming Messiah. As Jesus walks almost everywhere during His ministry, He probably chooses to ride into Jerusalem to make a statement—that He is the King Who is fulfilling the prophecy.[6] Consider the irony of a king voluntarily entering the city—in triumph, no less—knowing He will die there instead of conquering it. Consider as well the exemplary humility of Jesus Christ Who, as creator of the Universe, chooses to come into the city on a donkey's back rather than in some spectacular fashion.

The variations in the Gospel accounts of the Triumphal Entry illustrate the value of having four separate Gospels. "Overall, the Gospel accounts are seldom identical," writes Bruce Barton. "The differences usually have to do with perspective and priorities. Under the inspiration of the Holy Spirit, each writer told his story. The Gospels maintain a balance between shared similarities and independent entries. The similarities in language indicate the later writers were aware of and used material from the earlier ones and that they were all writing about the same life. The dissimilarities show they wrote independently and that each one had a slightly different purpose and audience in mind while composing his version."[7]

JESUS WEEPS OVER JERUSALEM (LUKE 19:41–44)

When Jesus draws near Jerusalem, He weeps over it, exclaiming, "Would that you, even you had known on this day the things that make for peace! But now they are hidden from your eyes. For the days will come upon you, when your enemies will set up a barricade around you and surround you and hem you in on every side and tear you down to the ground, you and your children with you. And they will not leave one stone upon another in you, because you did not know the time of your visitation."

Jesus here shows His humanity again. Like Jeremiah, "the weeping prophet" (Jer. 9:1; 13:17; 48:32; Lam 1:16), He deeply wants the people to repent and thereby remove the impending judgment on His beloved holy city.[8] He is anguished because Israel rejects Him as the Messiah and because Jerusalem will be annihilated due to its unbelief. In fulfillment of His prophecy, Rome would besiege and destroy Jerusalem, including the Temple, in 70 AD, some forty years later. After all the time Jesus has spent with His people they still reject Him, yet He willingly goes to the cross anyway, plainly illustrating God's unbroken patience, grace, mercy, and love.

JESUS VISITS THE TEMPLE; HE CURSES THE FIG TREE (MATT. 21:18–22; MARK 11:11–14, 20–26)

Once in Jerusalem, Jesus enters the Temple and looks around, then leaves for Bethany with His twelve disciples. In the morning, on the way back to Jerusalem, He's hungry and sees a fig tree with nothing on it but leaves, "for it was not the season for figs." He says, "May no one ever eat fruit from you again," and the tree withers at once. God, a spiritual being, doesn't get hungry, but the Son of God, also fully human, experiences hunger as acutely as any other person. This is part of Christ's humiliation and suffering on behalf of His people (2 Cor. 8:9; Gal. 3:13; Phil 2:8).[9]

Some commentators suggest the fig tree represents Israel, whose ritual religion is like the leaves of the tree, lacking the "fruit" of righteousness God requires[10]—and like the fig tree, it will perish unless it repents.[11] In other words, Jesus is cursing the fig tree figuratively—His curse is really for His people who are rejecting Him. However, the lesson applies not just to Israel—all who do not repent and believe will perish.[12]

Peter and the disciples ask Jesus how the fig tree withered at once. Jesus says if they have faith "and do not doubt," they can accomplish such things as moving mountains into the sea. Whatever they ask in prayer they will receive if they have faith. He cautions, however, "And whenever you stand praying, forgive, if you have anything against anyone, so that your Father also who is in heaven may forgive you your trespasses."

I don't believe Jesus means God will answer our arbitrary, selfish prayers, but that we really should pray and that it really matters. We must have faith in God as a pre-condition and pray in accordance with His will. An unforgiving spirit will short-circuit the power of prayer,[13] however, since one can hardly align with God's will if he's actively holding a grudge as he prays. "People must *not* be left with the impression that Jesus teaches that we can get whatever we want by strenuous prayer," writes Douglas Hare. "…Implicit in this teaching…is the conviction that all our prayer requests are subject to the proviso, 'Not my will but thine be done.'"[14]

Hare makes two other valuable points. Just because Jesus says in this passage "if you have faith and do not doubt," it doesn't mean that only perfect faith is acceptable to God. We all have our ups and downs, and God does not want us to approach Him only at our moments of greatest faith. Additionally, Hare observes that we are not to infer "that only the greatest heroes of the faith can move mountains. Many ordinary Christians, brought to their knees by impossible circumstances, have found through prayer the strength to do what they thought they could never do."[15]

JESUS CLEARS THE TEMPLE; RELIGIOUS LEADERS CONSPIRE AGAINST HIM (MATT. 21:12–13; MARK 11:15–19; LUKE 19:45–48; 21:37–38)

Entering the Temple (probably the next morning),[16] Jesus drives out all who sell and buy, and He overturns the tables of the money-changers and the seats of those who sell pigeons. Quoting from Isaiah (56:7) He declares, "It is written, 'My house shall be called a house of prayer,' but you make it a den of robbers."[17] Jesus is lashing out against a market with merchants and money-changers that was authorized by the high priests to operate in the Court of the Gentiles, the Temple's huge outer court. This is the only place Gentile converts are permitted to worship, but these activities are consuming all the space, making worship impossible. The money-changers convert international currency into special Temple coins, which is the only currency the merchants accept. Jesus is offended that the sacred house of worship has been transformed into a house of extortion and idolatry. To the chagrin of the chief priests and the scribes, who fear His growing renown and are seeking a way to destroy Him, He begins teaching daily in the Temple.

SOME GREEKS SEEK JESUS (JOHN 12:20–26)

Some who go to worship at the feast are Greeks, probably converts to Judaism.[18] They come to Philip and ask to see Jesus. Philip tells Andrew, and together they inform Jesus. He replies, "The hour has come for the Son of Man to be glorified. Truly, truly, I say to you, unless a grain of wheat falls into the earth and dies, it remains alone; but if it dies, it bears much fruit. Whoever loves his life loses it, and whoever hates his life in this world will keep it for eternal life. If anyone serves me, he must follow me; and where I am, there will my servant be also. If anyone serves me, the Father will honor him." Jesus' time to die is approaching, and His death will lead many others to life. To find eternal life, one must die to himself and live for Christ. His disciples must follow and serve Him, and if they do the Father will honor them.

This passage puts into stark relief why Jesus must die. "Without the 'death' of the seed, no crop;" notes C. H. Dodd, "without the death of Christ, no worldwide gathering of mankind. This strikes the key-note of the whole discourse."[19]

Syrian theologian Theodore of Mopsuestia supposes Jesus is telling His disciples His death should not upset them. Jesus is saying, essentially,

> As indeed a grain of wheat is just a single grain before falling into the earth, [and] after it has fallen and decomposed, it sprouts forth in great glory and produces double fruit by showing before everyone its riches in its ears and displaying the spectacle of its beauty to those looking on. This is the same way you should think about me. Now I am alone, and just one more man among obscure people without any glory. But when I undergo the passion of the cross, I will be raised in great honor. And when I produce much fruit, then everyone will know me—not only the Jews but also the people of the entire world will call me their Lord. Then, not even the spiritual powers will refuse to worship me.[20]

The people continue to resist Jesus' message, however. "That the crucifixion of a man should be the ultimate manifestation of the glory of God is as scandalous to Jewish religious messianism as it is absurd to Greek philosophy (1 Cor. 1:22–24)," declares Lesslie Newbigin. "But it is true, for the glory of God is the outpouring of love which is supremely revealed in the obedience of Jesus to death and in the action of the Father who gives his only Son for the life of the world."[21]

THE SON OF MAN MUST BE LIFTED UP
(JOHN 12:27–36)

Jesus tells His disciples, "Now is my soul troubled. And what shall I say? 'Father, save me from this hour'? But for this purpose I have come to this hour. Father, glorify your name." Then a voice from heaven says, "I have glorified it, and I will glorify it again." The crowd hears the voice and some think it has thundered; others think an angel has spoken to Him. "This voice has come for your sake, not mine," Jesus explains. "Now is the judgment of this world; now will the ruler of this world be cast out. And I, when I am lifted up from the earth, will draw all people to myself."

The confused crowd asks, "We have heard from the Law that the Christ remains forever. How can you say that the Son of Man must be lifted up? Who is this Son of Man?" Jesus replies, "The light is among you for a little while longer. Walk while you have the light, lest darkness overtake you. The one who walks in the darkness does not know where he is going. While you have the light, believe in the light, that you may become sons of light." Jesus then leaves and hides Himself.

Here we see Jesus' humanity again. He admits He's troubled, as He's preparing to experience incomparable agony including unbearable physical suffering and intolerable separation and wrath from the Father for taking on all mankind's sins. Nevertheless, He won't ask to be spared because He has come for the purpose of dying. This is a foretaste of what He would experience in the Garden of Gethsemane when He asks that the cup be taken from Him, then immediately follows with, "Thy will be done." In both instances, His humanity is screaming to escape this torment, but His divinity immediately overrules it and says, essentially, "No, of course not. This is the very reason I came. And, in the process I will glorify the Father, so Father, please proceed and glorify your name."

The people again reveal their misapprehension of the role of the true Messiah, Who has come to die so that we can live. They still don't understand that the kingdom of God has both present and future components and that the Messiah, Who ushers in the kingdom in both respects, has present and future functions. They believe Jesus has come to establish the kingdom now and reign forever (Daniel 7:13–14). They don't grasp He has come first as a Suffering Servant to die a substitutionary death for us. Yes, He has inaugurated His kingdom, but it will not come to full fruition until He returns at His Second Coming, when He will reign forever. But for now, He—the light—will only be with them a little longer. They must believe in Him to become sons of light, and live.

Jesus does not answer the people when they ask, "Who is this Son of Man?" We have seen this term throughout the Gospels. It is the title Jesus uses most often to refer to Himself, but its precise meaning is subject to debate. The Old Testament prophet Ezekiel uses the term ninety-three times, mostly to refer to himself as a human being.[22] Daniel also uses the term, as a divine title, when he describes a vision of one "like a son of man" who "comes with the clouds" and is given glory and a kingdom over all peoples and nations (Daniel 7:13–14). Some mistakenly argue that Jesus uses the title only to refer to His human nature, perhaps because they contrast it with "Son of God," which shows His deity. In fact, the term encompasses both Jesus' mysterious manifestation in human form and His heavenly origin and divine dignity.[23]

In the Gospels Jesus uses "Son of Man" some eighty times to refer to Himself.[24] Commentators sort these uses into three basic categories, which include both His earthly and divine natures: 1) to refer to Himself in His earthly life, and His authority and earthly ministry; 2) to anticipate His suffering, death, and resurrection; and 3) to anticipate His future exaltation, when the Son of Man will come in glory.[25] Philip Comfort argues that Jesus uses this "enigmatic title" as a way of identifying Himself as the Messiah without saying it directly.[26]

It seems to me, then, that Jesus uses "Son of Man" to describe His uniqueness both as God and man, and the uniqueness of His functions in each capacity, both of which are indispensable to His messianic role and His work as the agent of salvation history. "Son of Man" connotes the full import of all aspects of Jesus' messiahship—His incarnation and suffering servanthood in His earthly life, ministry, suffering, death, and resurrection, and His future glory when He returns to judge mankind and establish His permanent earthly kingdom. Professor Douglas Moo remarks, "As 'Son of Man,' then, Jesus claims to be the fulfillment of God's purposes in the creation and work through His people Israel—one Who will suffer, be vindicated, and bring in an eternal kingdom."[27]

THE UNBELIEF OF THE PEOPLE (JOHN 12:37–43)

Though Jesus has done many signs for them, the people still don't believe in Him, and He hides Himself from them. This fulfills Isaiah's prophecy, "Lord, who has believed what he heard from us, and to whom has the arm of the Lord been revealed? … He has blinded their eyes and hardened their heart, lest they see with their eyes, and understand with their heart, and turn, and I would heal them" (Isaiah 53:1; 6:10). John notes that Isaiah says these things because He sees Christ's glory and speaks of Him. "The implication," writes E. A. Blum, "is startling: Jesus is Yahweh. Jesus in His nature is God (but God the Son is distinct in person from God the Father and God the Spirit). Isaiah spoke about Him, for many of Isaiah's prophecies predicted the coming Messiah, Jesus of Nazareth."[28]

Despite the prevalence of unbelief, many do believe in Him, even many of the authorities, but they won't admit it because they fear the Pharisees will put them out of the synagogue, which proves they love glory from man more than glory from God (John 12:41–43).

I think this passage also shows that unbelief is often not intellectually grounded. It's a lesson for us today. If many people who witnessed Jesus' signs and teaching still rejected Him, we must not be surprised that some still reject abundant evidence that Christianity is true and that Jesus is Who He claimed to be. I'm not suggesting that doubt is illegitimate; Who doesn't experience doubt? But I'm saying some people are so hard-hearted that they can't even consider the probity of Christianity's truth claims, and so they reject them outright without giving them a fair hearing. Their "light" has been dimmed; their receptiveness to truth has been dulled. It's as if the Gospel is an unintelligible foreign language to them. "Unbelief is not a polite unwillingness to assent to some fact," writes Merrill Tenney, "but is a flat refusal to listen to His truth and to acknowledge His claims on one's personal life."[29] One question you can ask an unbeliever to test his receptiveness to the Gospel is, "If Christianity were true, would you become a Christian?" If the person says no, it indicates his resistance is not intellectual but in his heart. Never forget, however, that many people so disposed at one point in their lives have later become believers, so let's not give up hope or discontinue prayers on their behalf.

JESUS CAME TO SAVE THE WORLD
(JOHN 12:44–50)

Jesus says, "Whoever believes in me, believes not in me but in him who sent me. And whoever sees me sees him who sent me. I have come into the world as light, so that whoever believes in me may not remain in darkness. If anyone hears my words and does not keep them, I do not judge him; for I did not come to judge the world but to save the world. The one who rejects me and does not receive my words has a judge; the word that I have spoken will judge him on the last day. For I have not spoken on my own authority, but the Father who sent me has himself given me a commandment—what to say and what to speak. And I know that his commandment is eternal life. What I say, therefore, I say as the Father has told me."

This succinctly summarizes the message Jesus has been communicating. To believe in Jesus is to believe in God, and to heed and obey His words is to be obedient to God, just as Jesus, the Son, is obedient to God, the Father, and does everything to glorify Him. Those who reject Him are choosing death, though He came not to impose that judgment. He came to save people from the sentence already pronounced on them because of their own sin.

Note that in this passage Jesus again identifies Himself as "light," Who will bring those who believe in Him out of darkness. Faith in Christ does not mean the abandonment of the intellect, but it will expand our understanding because it will deliver us from darkness—and from vulnerability to the allures of evil—and illuminate the truth. "The images of light and darkness are used metaphorically with many different meanings in the [New Testament]," writes Colin Kruse. "Here the light is the revelation of the Father, which Jesus brought into the world, and the darkness is the ignorance about God in which people languish, and which leaves them prey to the evil one (1 John 5:19)."[30]

RELIGIOUS LEADERS CHALLENGE JESUS' AUTHORITY (MATT. 21:23–22:14; MARK 11:27–12:12; LUKE 20:1–19)

When Jesus is teaching and "preaching the Gospel" in the Temple, the religious leaders ask Him, "By what authority are you doing these things, and who gave you this authority?" Jesus tells them He will answer them if they answer His question: Did John's baptism come from heaven or from man? Talking among themselves, they realize they're trapped. If they say heaven Jesus will ask why they didn't believe John, but if they say from man, it will upset the crowd, who believe John was a prophet. So they tell Him they don't know, and He replies, "Neither will I tell you by what authority I do these things."

The leaders are essentially demanding to see Jesus' credentials. If He can produce none He'll be discredited, but if He claims God authorizes Him, they'll accuse Him of blasphemy. While it might appear He's evading their question with His counter-question, in fact, the correct answer to His question *would* answer their question: His authority comes from God. They're the ones being evasive and dishonest.[31]

Jesus relates the parable of a man asking his two sons to work in the vineyard. The first one says no but then changes his mind and goes. The second one says yes but does not go. Jesus asks which one is doing the will of his father. "The first," they answer. Jesus says, "Truly, I say to you, the tax collectors and the prostitutes go into the kingdom of God before you. For John came to you in the way of righteousness, and you did not believe him, but the tax collectors and the prostitutes believed him. And even when you saw it, you did not afterward change your minds and believe him."

Jesus compares the first son to the tax collectors and the prostitutes because he initially refuses to go and then repents, which represents the initial sinfulness of the tax collectors and prostitutes and their subsequent repentance. These were sinners among sinners, and yet they believed John and repented and received forgiveness, illustrating God's endless mercy. The religious leaders, by contrast, are like the son who initially says yes because they purport to be religious and faithful to the Law, yet they outright reject the Giver of that Law and His forerunner when they appear. The first son is obedient and does his father's will, just as the tax collectors and the prostitutes do the Father's will and thereby are permitted to enter the kingdom.

Jesus next recounts the parable of the tenants. The owner plants a vineyard, encloses it with a fence, digs a winepress in it, and builds a tower. He then leases it to tenants and leaves for another country. He later sends his servants to the tenants to get his fruit. The tenants kill one servant and severely injure the others. The owner sends more servants, and the tenants do the same to them. Then he sends his son to them, and the tenants kill him for his inheritance. Jesus asks, "When therefore the owner of the vineyard comes, what will he do to those tenants?" They reply that the owner would kill the tenants and find other ones to give him the fruits in their seasons.

Jesus says, "Have you never read in the Scriptures: 'The stone that the builders rejected has become the cornerstone; this was the Lord's doing, and it is marvelous in our eyes'? Therefore, I tell you, the kingdom of God will be taken away from you and given to a people producing its fruits. And the one who falls on this stone will be broken to pieces; and when it falls on anyone, it will crush him." The Pharisees perceive Jesus is referring to them and again want to arrest Him, but they fear the crowds, who believe He's a prophet. Jesus, however, might be referring to the whole nation of Israel, which God had prepared to be His fruitful vineyard, but the religious leaders were poor stewards and disobedient toward God and mistreated His prophets and messengers.

The parable reaches its climax when Jesus asks if they've ever read in the scriptures about the rejected stone. He's quoting Psalms 118:22–23, which is a messianic prophecy. Though the religious leaders boast of their expertise in the scriptures, they are unaware Isaiah prophesied that the nation would not only reject God and His prophets, but would reject and kill His one and only Son in order to enrich themselves.[32] John writes, "He came to his own, and his own people did not receive him" (John 1:11).

By getting rid of the Son they would retain their prominence as religious leaders. But the stone they rejected would become the cornerstone: they would crucify Christ and He would rise again, providing salvation for those who believe in Him and judgment for those who reject

Him. The Psalmist encapsulates this parable's message: "Kiss the Son, lest he be angry, and you perish in the way, for his wrath is quickly kindled. Blessed are all who take refuge in him" (Psalms 2:12).[33]

Jesus relates the parable of the wedding feast, which is similar to His parable of the great banquet in Luke 14:15–24. Here, a king gives a feast for his sons and sends his servant to invite guests, but none will come and some even kill the servants. The furious king destroys the killers and burns their cities. Deciding that those he has invited are not worthy, he orders his servants to bring others, good and bad, as many as they can find.

When the king arrives at the banquet he surveys the guests and notices a man without a wedding garment. The king has him bound head and foot and cast into the outer darkness where there is weeping and gnashing of teeth. Jesus says, "For many are called, but few are chosen," which means that those who reject God's call are lost and those who respond to it and believe are accepted and enter into the kingdom. God will invite many, good and bad, and some will only respond outwardly (the man with no wedding garment). God will see through them and reject them as well.

Belief requires more than just going through the motions. One must sincerely place his trust in Christ. As we have stressed throughout, people must not pridefully assume they can earn salvation. "The reason many are called but few chosen," declares Charles Price, "is that many of those who are called do not allow the one who called them to do it. They rely on their own ability, their own righteousness, and their own resources, rather than on God and his working. When the king comes, they are rejected. They are in the banquet hall, they fellowship with those dressed in the genuine wedding garment, but they are exposed and cast out."[34]

PAYING TAXES TO CAESAR (MATT. 22:15–22; MARK 12:13–17; LUKE 20:20–26)

The Pharisees, seeking again to entrap Jesus, send their disciples and the Herodians to Him to ask whether paying taxes to Caesar is proper. Jesus sees through their malice and rebukes them as hypocrites for testing Him. He tells them to show Him a denarius, and asks whose likeness and inscription is on it. They respond, "Caesar," and He says, "Therefore render to Caesar the things that are Caesar's, and to God the things that are God's." They marvel and go away. Ravi Zacharias argues that the questioners' failure to ask a second question proves their disingenuousness. They should have asked, "What belongs to God?" Jesus then would have responded, "Whose image is on you?" Ravi concludes, "Give to Caesar that which belongs to Caesar; give to God that which belongs to God. God's image is on you."[35]

The Pharisees and Herodians are mutual enemies, but they're so desperate to get rid of Jesus that they're conspiring together to ensnare Him. It's a convenient union for grilling Jesus about taxes because the Herodians are loyal to Herod, who is sympathetic to the Roman authorities, and if Jesus instructs people not to pay taxes they'll declare Him lawless toward Rome. But if He agrees to pay taxes, then the Pharisees will adjudicate Him disloyal to God. Jesus threads the needle, saying taxes should be paid but not in a way that compromises people's loyalty and duties to God.

Jesus' antagonists aren't as clever as they imagine, for Jesus has been telling them He's not the type of Messiah they have expected. He does not intend to establish political rule in opposition to Rome, and that's reflected in His remarks about paying taxes. "Devotion to God demands a higher allegiance to him than to anything else," insists Craig Keener, "but it is not an excuse to avoid our other responsibilities that do not conflict with it."[36] Merely paying taxes is not inconsistent with a person's spiritual duties.

THE SADDUCEES ASK JESUS ABOUT THE RESURRECTION (MATT. 22:23–33; MARK 12:18–27; LUKE 20:27–40)

Despite not believing in the resurrection, the Sadducees try to trip up Jesus by asking a question on the topic. According to Moses, they say, if a man dies without children his brother must marry the widow and raise the children. They then pose a hypothetical in which there are seven brothers who die in succession and the wife marries each of them in turn. They ask Him, "In the resurrection, of the seven, whose wife shall she be? For they all had her."

Jesus tells them they know neither the scriptures nor the power of God. "The sons of this age marry and are given in marriage," He says, "but those who are considered worthy to attain to that age and to the resurrection from the dead neither marry nor are given in marriage, for they cannot die anymore, because they are equal to angels and are sons of God, being sons of the resurrection. But that the dead are raised, even Moses showed, in the passage about the bush, where he calls the Lord the God of Abraham and the God of Isaac and the God of Jacob. Now he is not God of the dead, but of the living, for all live to him." All are amazed at His teaching, and some of the scribes say, "Teacher, you have spoken well." They don't dare ask Him further questions.

Jesus affirms, contrary to their beliefs, that the resurrection of the dead is a reality and that marriage will not be part of that life—people will be like undying angels and will not need to have children to ensure mankind's future.[37] Had they known the scriptures, they would have understood Moses is speaking of the resurrection when he depicts God as presently being the God of Abraham, Isaac, and Jacob (Exodus 3:1–6, 15), all of whom had long since died but are still alive. God only has a relationship with those who are presently alive.[38] Thus God's promise to the patriarchs that He is and will be their God means He will maintain them in life.[39] By denying the resurrection, the Sadducees are denying the power of God.

THE GREAT COMMANDMENT (MATT. 22:34–40; MARK 12:28–34)

A scribe asks Jesus which commandment is most important. Jesus responds, "The most important is, 'Hear, O Israel: The Lord our God, the Lord is one. And you shall love the Lord your God with all your heart and with all your soul and with all your mind and with all your strength.' The second is this: 'You shall love your neighbor as yourself.' There is no other commandment greater than these." Recognizing that Jesus has summarized the entirety of the Law by reciting the first two commandments, the scribe notes that the love mandated in those commandments is worth much more than all the Old Testament sacrifices. Jesus approvingly replies, "You are not far from the kingdom of God."

While Jesus technically cites two commandments instead of the requested one, these two are inseparable because the love of God is demonstrated in His love for man, whom He created in His image, and love of humanity cannot exist without love of God as its basis. As M. Eugene Boring writes, "The double commandment of love transcends all the others as their essence and meaning."[40]

WHOSE SON IS THE CHRIST (MATT. 22:41–46; MARK 12:35–37; LUKE 20:41–44)

Jesus asks the Pharisees how they can say the Messiah is the son of David when David himself, relating a conversation between God and the Messiah, says in the Book of Psalms, "The Lord said to my Lord, 'Sit at my right hand, until I put your enemies under your feet.'" How can the Messiah be David's son, Jesus asks, if David is calling him "Lord"? No one can answer, and from that day forward no one asks Him any more questions.

Jesus is asking how Christ can be both David's son and his Lord. Throughout the Old Testament the coming Messiah is described as the Son of David, meaning the Messiah will be a king in the line of David—that is, David's direct descendant. But Jesus is pointing out that this psalm, written by David under the inspiration of the Holy Spirit, means the Messiah is not only David's descendant but his Lord.

The quoted psalm is a messianic prophecy that includes two Persons of the Trinity—God the Father and God the Son ("The Lord says to my Lord"). Jesus is explaining He is the Messiah—a human being, but also God eternal, Who pre-existed creation and, in fact, was the agent in the creation (John 1:3; 1 Cor. 8:6; Col. 1:16; Heb. 1:2). He is also David's Lord (God).

This short exchange encapsulates the Pharisees' fundamental misunderstanding about the nature, identity, and purpose of the Messiah. Again in this passage, Jesus is consciously declaring that He is the

Messiah.[41] William Hendriksen maintains that Jesus is referring to Himself when He says "the Christ," but in such a veiled way (referring to Himself in the third person) that the Pharisees can answer the question without affirming that Jesus is the Christ—a notion that's repugnant to them.[42]

SEVEN WOES TO THE SCRIBES AND PHARISEES (MATT. 23:1–36; MARK 12:38–40; LUKE 20:45–47)

Addressing the crowds and His disciples, Jesus unleashes a stunning denunciation of the scribes and Pharisees that's worth reproducing at length:

The scribes and the Pharisees sit on Moses' seat, so do and observe whatever they tell you, but not the works they do. For they preach, but do not practice. They tie up heavy burdens, hard to bear, and lay them on people's shoulders, but they themselves are not willing to move them with their finger.

They do all their deeds to be seen by others. For they make their phylacteries broad and their fringes long, and they love the place of honor at feasts and the best seats in the synagogues and greetings in the marketplaces and being called rabbi by others.

But you are not to be called rabbi, for you have one teacher, and you are all brothers. And call no man your father on earth, for you have one Father, who is in heaven. Neither be called instructors, for you have one instructor, the Christ. The greatest among you shall be your servant. Whoever exalts himself will be humbled, and whoever humbles himself will be exalted.

But woe to you, scribes and Pharisees, hypocrites! For you shut the kingdom of heaven in people's faces. For you neither enter yourselves nor allow those who would enter to go in.

Woe to you, scribes and Pharisees, hypocrites! For you travel across sea and land to make a single proselyte, and when he becomes a proselyte, you make him twice as much a child of hell as yourselves.

Woe to you, blind guides, who say, "If anyone swears by the temple, it is nothing, but if anyone swears by the gold of the temple, he is bound by his oath." You blind fools! For which is greater, the gold or the temple that has made the gold sacred? And you say, "If anyone swears by the altar, it is nothing, but if anyone swears by the gift that is on the altar, he is bound by his oath." You blind men! For which is greater, the gift or the altar that makes the gift sacred? So whoever swears by the altar swears by it and by everything on it. And whoever swears by the temple swears by it and by him who dwells in it. And whoever swears by heaven swears by the throne of God and by him who sits upon it.

Woe to you, scribes and Pharisees, hypocrites! For you tithe mint and dill and cumin, and have neglected the weightier matters of the law: justice and mercy and faithfulness. These you ought to have done, without neglecting the others. You blind guides, straining out a gnat and swallowing a camel!

Woe to you, scribes and Pharisees, hypocrites! For you clean the outside of the cup and the plate, but inside they are full of greed and self-indulgence. You blind Pharisee! First clean the inside of the cup and the plate, that the outside also may be clean.

Woe to you, scribes and Pharisees, hypocrites! For you are like whitewashed tombs, which outwardly appear beautiful, but within are full of dead people's bones and all uncleanness. So you also outwardly appear righteous to others, but within you are full of hypocrisy and lawlessness.

Woe to you, scribes and Pharisees, hypocrites! For you build the tombs of the prophets and decorate the monuments of the righteous, saying, "If we had lived in the days of our fathers, we would not have taken part with them in shedding the blood of the prophets." Thus you witness against yourselves that you are sons of those who murdered the prophets. Fill up, then, the measure of your fathers.

You serpents, you brood of vipers, how are you to
escape being sentenced to hell? Therefore I send you prophets and wise men and scribes, some of whom you will kill
and crucify, and some you will flog in your synagogues and
persecute from town to town, so that on you may come all
the righteous blood shed on earth, from the blood of righteous Abel to the blood of Zechariah the son of Barachiah,
whom you murdered between the sanctuary and the altar.
Truly, I say to you, all these things will come upon this
generation (Matt. 23:1–36).

Jesus is saying the religious leaders occupy important positions,
and they talk the talk but don't walk the walk. They preach the right
words and appear to be righteous, but their hearts are filled with
envy, hatred, and malice.[43] Through their rules they lay heavy burdens
on the people, but they're unwilling to take those burdens upon
themselves. Jesus came to free us from such legalism and the burdens
that accompany it, saying, "My yoke is easy and my burden is light"
(Matt. 11:30).

The scribes and Pharisees seek prestigious positions and honor,
and they're called rabbi, a term of great respect. But Jesus tells them
they have no competent teachers among them—they have only one
rabbi, Jesus Christ. He repeats that they must have a servant's heart
and that the humble, rather than the proud, will be exalted. He condemns those who puff themselves up with their religious knowledge
or trappings of power and praises those who recognize their failings,
have a repentant heart, and approach Him in humility and faith.

Jesus, in this passage, then turns His attention to the leaders and
declares seven woes upon them. A "woe" is an exclamation denoting
pain or displeasure.[44] Some commentators say the seven woes Jesus
declares on the scribes and Pharisees should be seen in contrast to the
first seven blessings in the Sermon on the Mount.[45] It's true that these
woes seem harsh, but the Sermon on the Mount includes hard sayings
as well. Besides, Jesus directs these woes to the people who are trying
to sabotage Him and His ministry every step of the way and who are,
through their false teachings, leading people away from Him and

from eternal life. Ironically, though, in conspiring to kill Him they're ultimately serving His purpose, for He was born to die for our salvation.

In the first two woes Jesus rebukes the leaders for the harm they've caused others, and in the last five He condemns their character and behavior.[46] In the first woe, Jesus says that through their false teachings, the Pharisees are leading people away from the kingdom when they should be leading them toward it. In the second, Jesus says they strive hard to convert people to their brand of religion with all its burdensome rules and end up sending them to hell—the exact opposite of what their goal should be.

In the third woe Jesus chastises the Pharisees for teaching that oaths made by the gold of the Temple and the gift on the altar are binding, but those made by the Temple and altar themselves are not. The leaders are more interested in the gold and the gifts than the actual Temple and the altar, which shows they're preoccupied with material things. They are engrossed with the human to the exclusion of the divine—as the Temple itself is the dwelling place of God, and the gold would have no significance apart from it. Similarly, the altar represents God's interests whereas the gift on it is purely the human response.[47]

In the fourth woe, Jesus condemns them for tithing while neglecting "the weightier matters of the law: justice, and mercy and faithfulness." To borrow a cliché, they can't see the forest (the overarching spiritual truths) for the trees (their rules and traditions). With the fifth and sixth woes, Jesus rebukes them for appearing pure while ignoring their sinful hearts. They're like whitewashed tombs, externally beautiful but internally corrupt. In the seventh woe, Jesus condemns them for pretending they're more righteous than their ancestors who killed the prophets, while they're no better because they're doing the same thing by suppressing the Gospel message, which fulfills the Old Testament prophecies. They're snakes and vipers who are destined for hell and justly so, for they're rejecting the truth. They're responsible for the innocent blood of Old Testament prophets, wise men, and teachers, from the first martyr, Abel (Gen. 4:8), to the last one, Zechariah (2 Chron. 24:20–22).[48]

THE WIDOW'S OFFERING (MARK 12:41–44; LUKE 21:1–4)

Jesus observes people making their offerings to the Temple treasury, with the rich putting in large sums and a poor widow giving two small copper coins. He tells His disciples, "Truly, I say to you, this poor widow has put in more than all those who are contributing to the offering box. For they all contributed out of their abundance, but she out of her poverty has put in everything she had, all she had to live on." James Edwards captures the lesson: "In purely financial terms, the value of her offering is negligible—and unworthy of compare to the sums of the wealthy donors. But in the divine exchange rate things look differently. That which made no difference in the books of the temple is immortalized in the Book of Life.... Everything about this woman has been described in terms of *less*, particularly in comparison to the scribes and wealthy crowd. And yet, the contrast between her genuine piety and faith and the pretense of the wealthy is beyond compare. For Jesus, the value of the gift is not the amount given, but the cost to the giver."[49]

JESUS AGAIN PREDICTS THE TEMPLE'S DESTRUCTION (MATT. 24:1–2; MARK 13:1–2; LUKE 21:5–6)

As Jesus emerges from the Temple, one of His disciples calls attention to the wonderful stones and buildings. "Do you see these great buildings?" Jesus asks. "There will not be left here one stone upon another that will not be thrown down."

Jewish historian Josephus describes the Temple as lavish, made of large, white marble stone, with wonderful roofs, long beams, splendorous ornaments, and a great number of rooms filled with a prodigious variety of figures and furniture, and vessels filled with silver and gold.[50] Jesus does not explain His prophecy, but He's surely predicting the utter annihilation of the Temple by the Romans in 70 AD.[51] In describing the totality of the corruption, Josephus says, "It was so thoroughly laid even with the ground by those that dug it up to the foundation, that there was left nothing to make those that came thither believe it had ever been inhabited."[52] Similarly, William Lane writes, "Isolated fragments of the substructures and of the old city wall which have been recognized by archaeological research only confirm the degree to which Jesus' prophecy was fulfilled."[53]

Some commentators believe God allowed the Temple's destruction because the Temple and the sacrificial system it maintained were part of the old order that was passing away.[54] But the destruction should be viewed as God's judgment upon His rebellious people, and not simply the reaction of Imperial Rome to Jewish insurrection. In fact, a body of Jewish literature teaches that Jerusalem's fall was due to the sins of her people.[55]

JESUS' RETURN AND THE END OF THE AGE (MATT. 24:3–25:46; MARK 13:3–37; LUKE 21:7–36)

As Jesus and His disciples sit on the Mount of Olives, the disciples ask when Jerusalem and the Temple will be destroyed, and also what will be the signs of His Second Coming and of the end of the age. His response is sometimes called the Olivet Discourse.

Jesus warns them not to be misled by anyone who falsely claims to be Christ. Before He returns there will be wars and rumors of wars, nation rising against nation, and famines and earthquakes. These are just the birth pains—just as a pregnant woman has birth pains when her child is about to be born, so these events will signify the end of the age is near but has not yet arrived.[56] John MacArthur observes that the fallen world has always experienced these calamities, but by calling them "the beginning" of birth pains, Jesus is implying conditions will get much worse toward the end of the age.[57]

People will be persecuted and killed because they follow Christ. Many will fall away and hate one another. False prophets will arise and lead people astray. Lawlessness will increase, and love will grow cold. But he who endures to the end will be saved. This does not mean people will earn their salvation through perseverance, but God will superintend our salvation and protect us. People mustn't be passive in the process, but one way God secures us is to issue these warnings about the many challenges we'll face. Those who fall away were probably never true believers.[58]

The risen Jesus will issue the command to make disciples of all nations (Matt. 28:16–20), and this Great Commission will continue until the end of the age when the Gospel will have been proclaimed throughout the world. Jesus does not say every person will hear the Gospel but that it will be proclaimed to all nations.[59]

Those in Judea who see the abomination of desolation standing in the holy place, as Daniel predicted, must flee to the mountains. No one should waste any time or look back. There will be great tribulation unlike anything seen before. Unless God cuts short those days, no one will be spared. But for the sake of the elect, He will cut them short.

Many believe Jesus is referring in these passages to the tribulation— the time of trouble or distress that precedes His Second Coming, which many think will be a seven-year period. The abomination of desolation refers to the profaning of the Temple. The term originally applied to the Temple's desecration by Syrian ruler Antiochus Epiphanes, who invaded Jerusalem in 168 BC and dedicated the Temple to the Greek God Zeus. But Jesus is probably speaking of a future abomination when the Antichrist establishes an image in the Temple during the tribulation. This clearly implies, observes John MacArthur, "that the temple will be rebuilt in the future and that the daily sacrificial system will be reinstated."[60] Some believe, however, that this prophecy was finally fulfilled when Rome sacked Jerusalem and the Temple in 70 AD, as mentioned above, and that there won't be a future fulfillment.[61]

Jesus warns that during the tribulation, false christs and false prophets will appear all over, doing great signs and wonders, to lead people astray. We'll be able to recognize such imposters because the coming of the Son of Man will be like lightning from east to west, for immediately after the tribulation the sun and moon will be darkened and stars will fall from heaven. Then the sign of the Son of Man will appear in heaven. All the tribes on earth will mourn, and they will see the Son of Man coming on the clouds of heaven with power and great glory. He will send out His angels with a loud trumpet call, and they'll gather His elect from all directions. This corresponds to Daniel's prophecy of the Son of Man coming with the clouds of heaven (Daniel 7:13–14).

Jesus tells them to learn from the fig tree—as soon as its branch becomes tender and puts out its leaves, they'll know summer is near, so when they see the events He has described they shall know the end is near.

But no one, says Jesus, knows the exact day and hour of His return—not the angels, not the Son, but only the Father. He repeats that this day will come unexpectedly, as Noah's flood did. Therefore, they must always be ready.

In the meantime, blessed is the faithful and wise servant who tends to the master's household when he's gone. But if the servant doesn't take care of the estate or beats his fellow servants, the master will return without warning, cut him in pieces, and put him with the hypocrites, where there will be weeping and gnashing of teeth.

Jesus likens the kingdom of heaven to ten virgins who take their lamps to meet their bridegroom. Five are foolish and take no oil, and the other five are wise and take flasks of oil. When the bridegroom is delayed, the virgins fall asleep. At midnight, the bridegroom's coming is announced and they are called to meet him. The foolish ones ask to borrow oil from the wise ones, who refuse because there isn't enough. The wise ones tell them to go buy more for themselves. But while they're gone, the bridegroom comes and takes the five wise ones with him to the marriage feast and shuts the door. When the foolish ones come and ask the lord to open the door, he says, "Truly, I say to you, I do not know you." Summing up the lesson, Jesus warns, "Watch, therefore, for you know neither the day nor the hour." The point is that people must be vigilant and always be ready for Christ's return because only those who are prepared (those who have come to faith in Him) will enter His kingdom.[62]

Jesus next tells the parable of the talents, which closely resembles the parable of the minas we discussed in Chapter 9. A man entrusts his three servants with his property, each according to his ability—one with five talents, one with two, and the other with one. The first two use the talents to earn more, and the man blesses them as "good and faithful servants" and entrusts more to them. The servant given one talent buries it in the ground and gives it back to the man, saying he was afraid of him because he's a hard man. Rebuking this servant as wicked and slothful, the man takes his only talent and gives it to the one who has ten, saying, "For to everyone who has will more be given, and he will have an abundance. But from the one who has not, even what he has will be taken away. And he cast the worthless servant into the outer darkness. In that place there will be weeping and gnashing of teeth."

Stewardship is an important Christian concept. Faithful stewardship in our lives will lead to greater responsibility and stewardship in the life to come.[63] We must use our spiritual gifts wisely and exploit the opportunities for service that God gives us, doing our part to advance His kingdom. We are given these opportunities in accordance with our gifts from God. Negligence is punished and diligence is rewarded.[64]

Jesus says when the Son of Man comes in His glory with all the angels, He'll sit on His glorious throne. The nations will be gathered before Him and He'll separate the "sheep" from the "goats." He—as king—will tell the sheep that because they fed Him when He was hungry, clothed Him, gave Him something to drink when thirsty, welcomed Him though a stranger, and came to Him when He was sick and when He was in prison, they are blessed by the Father and are inheriting the kingdom prepared for them since the foundation of the world. When the righteous ask Him when they did these things for Him, He will respond, "Truly, I say to you, as you did it to one of the least of these my brothers, you did it to me."

When we show acts of kindness toward other believers, especially the poor and those otherwise in need, we are showing kindness to Christ Himself. Some scholars believe this passage applies not just to acts of kindness toward other believers but to all who are hungry, in distress, or needy.[65] But even if the passage only applies to believers, the Bible is elsewhere clear that God is deeply concerned for all the poor (Deut. 15:11; Matt. 22:37–40; 26:1; Gal. 2:10).[66]

The goats will receive a much different command: "Depart from me, you cursed, into the eternal fire prepared for the devil and his angels"— for they didn't give Him food or water, welcome Him, clothe Him, or visit Him. They protest that they never saw Him hungry, thirsty, as a stranger, naked, sick, or in prison, and He replies, "Truly, I say to you, as you did not do it to one of the least of these, you did not do it to me." Then He adds, "And these will go away into eternal punishment, but the righteous into eternal life." This passage is clear and firm about the final judgment, which is permanent and eternal.[67]

JESUS PREDICTS HIS CRUCIFIXION IN TWO DAYS; RELIGIOUS LEADERS PLOT TO ARREST AND KILL HIM; JUDAS BETRAYS HIM (MATT. 26:1–5, 14–16; MARK 14:1–2, 10–11; LUKE 22:1–6)

When Jesus finishes His discourse, He says, "You know that after two days the Passover is coming, and the Son of Man will be delivered up to be crucified." While Jesus has predicted His passion several times before, He adds here the specific day—in two days, the beginning of the Passover,[68] an annual Jewish feast commemorating the Israelites' deliverance from slavery in Egypt (Exodus 12–13). It's divinely fitting that Jesus will be killed on the day the Passover lamb is to be sacrificed at the Jewish feast, since Jesus *is* the Passover Lamb (1 Cor. 5:7).[69] Remember John the Baptist's words, "Behold, the Lamb of God, who takes away the sin of the world!" (John 1:29).

While Jesus is preparing His disciples for His death, the religious leaders are gathered in high priest Caiaphas' palace secretly plotting to arrest and kill Him—but not during the feast, which would cause an uproar. The plotters aren't some fringe cabal but the people's highest spiritual leaders—and they're planning His death in the name of spiritual purity, no less. Their evil and hypocrisy are seen in their clandestine scheming in the darkness of Caiaphas' home, and in their caution to avoid being seen or heard in the light of day for fear that forces for good would foil their evil plan.

One of Jesus' apostles, Judas Iscariot, goes to the chief priests and asks how much they will pay him for turning over Jesus to them. After receiving thirty pieces of silver, he begins looking for an opportunity to betray Him. Just contemplate the magnitude of this treachery: Judas is one of twelve special people chosen by the Son of God to work with Him intimately in the turning point of salvation history, and he betrays Him for just thirty pieces of silver. His greed blinds him to the truth. He followed Christ for a time, but he's not a genuine believer who trusts his eternal life to Him.[70]

DISCIPLES PREPARE FOR THE LAST SUPPER; JESUS WASHES HIS DISCIPLES' FEET (MATT. 26:17–25; MARK 14:12–25; LUKE 22:7–21, 31–34; JOHN 13:1–35)

On the first day of the Feast of Unleavened Bread,[71] the disciples ask Jesus where they should prepare the Passover meal. He directs them to go into Jerusalem and tell a certain man, "The Teacher says, my time is at hand. I will keep the Passover at your house with my disciples." The disciples obey and prepare the Passover.

Jesus knows His time has come to go to the Father. He has demonstrated His love for His own to the very end. Aware Judas will betray Him, Jesus rises from supper, lays aside His outer garments, and ties a towel around His waist. He pours water into a basin and begins to wash His disciples' feet and wipe them with His towel. Peter asks Him why He's washing *his* feet, and Jesus says, "What I am doing you do not understand now, but afterward you will understand." Peter protests, "You shall never wash my feet." Jesus responds, "If I do not wash you, you have no share with me." Peter says, "Lord, not my feet only but also my hands and my head." Jesus replies, "The one who has bathed does not need to wash, except for his feet, but is completely clean. And you are clean, but not every one of you"—a reference to Judas.

After He has washed their feet and resumed His seat, Jesus asks if they understand what He's just done. He explains that if He, their teacher, has washed their feet, then they should wash one another's feet, using His action as an example. "Truly, truly, I say to you, a servant is not greater than the one who sent him," He declares. "If you know these things, blessed are you if you do them."

The irony couldn't be more pronounced. Jesus, the Son of God, is about to be flogged and crucified—that's the gratitude He'll receive from an evil world for which He's giving His life. Instead of using His divine power to prevent His fate, however, He calmly breaks bread with His disciples and washes *their* feet—a profound and symbolic act of humble service.

How this stands culture on its head! Peers rarely washed one another's feet except as an act of great love. Because sandals were commonly worn at the time, people's feet were full of dirt, dust, and traces of waste found on the ground. So washing feet, note Jim Dixon and Lee Strobel, "was a dirty, horrible, and thankless job, and nobody but the lowest of the low did it."[72] Some Jews even refused to make their Jewish slaves wash their feet; the job was reserved for Gentile slaves, women, children, or pupils.[73] The disciples are exceedingly uncomfortable with this role reversal, but it probably brings home to them, in shocking fashion, the gravity of the situation—the impending death of their Messiah. Unlike the ordinary person, Jesus is not humiliated by His own act of condescension. He does not wash their feet as a matter of surrender to His fate but as a display of unfettered love and as a quintessential demonstration of selfless Christian service.

Consider Jesus' response to Peter's objection—He assures Peter he'll understand later (meaning after Jesus' death and resurrection),[74] but warns him that unless he permits Jesus to wash his feet, he would have no part with Him. Jesus came to serve and to sacrifice His life for them. If Peter doesn't believe Jesus should serve him in a small matter like washing his feet, how could he accept that Jesus will die for him on the cross? Without this understanding, Peter can't be part of Jesus' program because he's rejecting the Gospel.[75] If Peter and the disciples reject Christ's offer to wash their feet, they're not only rejecting Him but the Father who sent Him (John 13:20).

In showing humility initially, Peter is presuming to know better than his Savior how matters should proceed—something he'll do again before the crucifixion.[76] This is instructive for people who reject the Gospel because they can't get past the idea that God loves us so much He gave His one and only Son for us. Their own sense of unworthiness, ironically, keeps them from accepting the One who can save them—even believers put barriers between themselves and Christ because they have difficulty believing they're worthy enough to be forgiven. In fact, we *are not* worthy of forgiveness, which is the whole point, and which demonstrates

God's grace so resoundingly. But with Christ's stern rejoinder, Peter wholly embraces the concept and then some, asking Jesus to wash not only his feet, but his hands and head as well.

When He has finished washing their feet, Jesus says He's given them an example: if their Lord and teacher has washed their feet, how much more should they serve others. Humble service is essential to Christianity, because it mirrors Christ's life and death on our behalf and because it draws more people to Christ.

JESUS CELEBRATES PASSOVER WITH HIS DISCIPLES; HE DECLARES HE'LL BE BETRAYED (MATT. 26:17–29; MARK 14:18–25; LUKE 22:14–23; JOHN 13:21–35)

As they're eating, Jesus takes bread and blesses it, breaks it, gives it to His disciples, and says, "Take, eat, this is my body." He takes a cup of wine, gives thanks, and hands it to them, saying, "Drink of it, all of you, for this is my blood of the covenant, which is poured out for many for the forgiveness of sins. I tell you I will not drink again of this fruit of the vine until that day when I drink it new with you in my Father's kingdom."

Here Jesus institutes the Lord's Supper, in which He gives bread and wine a special meaning: the bread is His body and the wine is His blood of the New Covenant. The bread prefigures His body figuratively broken and literally killed in His upcoming crucifixion. Theologians differ on the significance of this. The doctrine of transubstantiation holds that the bread and wine become Christ's actual body and blood.[77] Catholics believe that through transubstantiation, the risen Christ becomes truly present in the Eucharist.

Protestants subscribe to numerous other views, including consubstantiation, the memorial view, and the dynamic view. Developed by Martin Luther,[78] consubstantiation holds that Christ is really present "in, with, and under" the elements[79]—that is, Christ penetrates and permeates the bread and the wine. The bread and wine don't become Christ's body and blood, but the body and blood are present in addition to the bread and wine.[80] The memorial view, held by most Baptists and independent churches,[81] holds that the Communion service is mainly a commemoration of Christ's death on the cross, though Christ is not physically or spiritually present. The bread and cup are a figurative memorial to Christ's death.[82] Another view, sometimes called the dynamic view, to which John Calvin subscribed and which is followed by Reformed and Presbyterian churches,[83] is that Christ is not literally present in the elements but is spiritually present.[84]

When Jesus and His disciples are eating, He says to them, "Truly, I say to you, one of you will betray me." Disheartened, each asks, "Is it I, Lord?" Jesus replies, "He who has dipped his hand in the dish with me will betray me. The Son of Man goes as it is written of him, but woe to that man by whom the Son of Man is betrayed! It would have been better for that man if he had not been born." Judas says, "Is it I, Rabbi?" Jesus retorts, "You have said so."

After Judas leaves, Jesus says, "Now is the Son of Man glorified, and God is glorified in him. If God is glorified in him, God will also glorify him in himself, and glorify him at once. Little children, yet a little while I am with you. You will seek me, and just as I said to the Jews, so now I also say to you, 'Where I am going you cannot come.' A new commandment I give to you, that you love one another: just as I have loved you, you also are to love one another. By this all people will know that you are my disciples, if you have love for one another."

Judas' departure on the way to betraying Christ marks the beginning of the end, which will culminate in Jesus' saving act on the cross. As such, Christ's glorification has begun and is all but complete.

The statement, "Now is the Son of Man glorified" is rich in irony, for the event that will consummate Jesus' glorification—His death on the cross—is not what man would consider glorification. Jesus clarifies that His glory and the Father's glory are the same—they're of one mind in their intention to implement their redemption plan for mankind.[85] God will also glorify Jesus in Himself—that is, He'll glorify Him in heaven in His own presence with the glory They shared before the world existed (John 17:5).

The requirement to love is not altogether new, as it's part of the first two commandments and is integral to everything Jesus has taught. In fact, He included it in His identification of "the great commandment" (Matt. 22:34–40) discussed earlier. But His life and sacrifice exhibit a new kind of love Christians share because they have experienced the incomparable love of Christ.[86] Christ commands them to love one another as He has loved them because their mutual bond of love will embolden them to evangelize and draw more people to Christ, as love is inherently attractive.

JESUS PREDICTS PETER'S DENIAL (MATT. 26:30–35; MARK 14:26–31; LUKE 22:31–34; JOHN 13:36–38)

After they sing a hymn together, Jesus and His disciples go out to the Mount of Olives along the eastern edge of Jerusalem. Peter asks Jesus, "Where are you going?" Jesus replies, "Where I am going you cannot follow me now, but you will follow afterward." Jesus would go to the Father in His death and again in His ascension, but neither Peter nor other believers can come with Him (cf. John 7:33–34; 8:21) until they are reunited with Him in eternal life. Then He says to them, "You will all fall away because of me this night. For it is written, 'I will strike the shepherd, and the sheep of the flock will be scattered.' But after I am raised up, I will go before you to Galilee."

Jesus is quoting an Old Testament prophecy of Zechariah, "Strike the shepherd, and the sheep will be scattered" (Zech. 13:7). Peter promises he will never fall away even if the others do, and Jesus replies, "Will you lay down your life for me? Truly, I tell you, this very night, before the rooster crows, you will deny me three times." Peter proclaims, "Even if I must die with you, I will not deny you!" The other disciples say the same.

CHAPTER 11

FROM JESUS' REASSURANCE TO PILATE'S JUDGMENT

Now if there is any reality within the whole sphere of human experience that is by its very nature worthy to challenge the mind, charm the heart and bring the total life to a burning focus, it is the reality that revolves around the Person of Christ. If He is who and what the Christian message declares Him to be, then the thought of Him should be the most exciting, the most stimulating, to enter the human mind.

—A. W. TOZER[1]

JESUS SPEAKS WITH HIS DISCIPLES; I AM THE WAY, AND THE TRUTH, AND THE LIFE (JOHN 14:1–17:26)

Continuing His discussion at the Last Supper, Jesus reassures His disciples that even though He's leaving, He'll come back for them:

"Let not your hearts be troubled. Believe in God; believe also in me. In my Father's house are many rooms. If it were not so, would I have told you that I go to prepare a place for you? And if I go and prepare a place for you, I will come again and will take you to myself, that where I am you may be also. And you know the way to where I am going."

Thomas said to him, "Lord, we do not know where you are going. How can we know the way?"

Jesus said to him, "I am the way, and the truth, and the life. No one comes to the Father except through me. If you had known me, you would have known my Father also. From now on you do know him and have seen him."

Philip said to him, "Lord, show us the Father, and it is enough for us."

Jesus said to him, "Have I been with you so long, and you still do not know me, Philip? Whoever has seen me has seen the Father. How can you say, 'Show us the Father'? Do you not believe that I am in the Father and the Father is in me? The words that I say to you I do not speak on my own authority, but the Father who dwells in me does his works. Believe me that I am in the Father and the Father is in me, or else believe on account of the works themselves. Truly, truly, I say to you, whoever believes in me will also do the works that I do; and greater works than these will he do, because I am going to the Father. Whatever you ask in my name, this I will do, that the Father may be glorified in the Son. If you ask me anything in my name, I will do it."

Jesus never ceases to amaze. As He's about to be lawlessly crucified, the victim of the worst injustice in human history, He seeks to comfort His disciples. It's not that Jesus is impervious to pain and suffering—His full humanity guarantees, and His experience proves, He suffers more than any other person could. He even acknowledges His agony directly, exclaiming, "Now is my soul troubled. And what shall I say? Father, save me from this hour? But for this purpose I have come to this hour" (John 12:27). Additionally, recall that when predicting His betrayal, Jesus said He was "troubled in his spirit" (John 13:21). While Jesus is assuring His disciples, His gentle spirit speaks to all who face troubling times. We must abide in Him, as He will go on to say.

His disciples are distressed over Jesus' imminent departure, not understanding that He must die for their benefit and for the benefit of all believers. He needs to go prepare a place for us before He can come back for us. He has to die on the cross for us to have a path to salvation.

When Thomas expresses confusion over Christ's destination and how believers will get there, Jesus says, "I am the way, and the truth and the life. No one comes to the Father except through me." Where He's going is not as much a location as a spiritual state. We are going to be with Him wherever He is. But the only route to the Father—to eternal life—is through faith in the Son. Those who say all religions are similar because they all lead to God, though through different paths, directly contradict Scripture and Christ's unambiguous words. "Jesus," says D. A. Carson, "is the way to God, precisely because he is the truth of God and the life of God. Jesus is the truth, because he embodies the supreme revelation of God...He is His Word made flesh.... Jesus is the life, the one who has 'life in himself' (5:26), 'the resurrection and the life' (11:25), 'the true God and eternal life' (1 John 5:20). Only because he is the truth and the life can Jesus be the way for others to come to God."[2] Jesus is the only way to eternal life because He is the only sinless person who can pay for our sins, and our perfectly just God cannot allow sin to go unpunished. He punishes an innocent substitute in our place—His only Son.

Since Jesus is the way to the Father, Philip asks Jesus to show the Father to them. Having previously stated, "I and the Father are one" (John 10:30), Jesus declares that He and the Father are mirror images. The writer of Hebrews explains, "He is the radiance of the glory of God and the exact imprint of his nature" (1:3). They have already seen the Father because they have seen *Him*, lived with Him, and worked with Him.

When I was a new believer, I was particularly moved by this passage because it assures us we know exactly what the Father is like if we know what Jesus is like—and we know what He is like because Scripture reveals Him to us—we meet Him in the Gospels. Yes, the mysteries of God are beyond our ability to fathom, but we also have a personal God we can know and with Whom we can have an eternal relationship. We don't have to wonder about the Father's nature. If we know Christ, then we can't envision the Father as an angry old man with a flowing beard. He is exactly like Christ—an infinitely loving and merciful being Who created us in His image.

JESUS PROMISES THE HOLY SPIRIT (JOHN 14:15–31)

Jesus further engages His disciples in a compelling discussion about the Holy Spirit:

> "If you love me, you will keep my commandments. And I will ask the Father, and he will give you another Helper, to be with you forever, even the Spirit of truth, whom the world cannot receive, because it neither sees him nor knows him. You know him, for he dwells with you and will be in you. I will not leave you as orphans; I will come to you. Yet a little while and the world will see me no more, but you will see me. Because I live, you also will live. In that day you will know that I am in my Father, and you in me, and I in you. Whoever has my commandments and keeps them, he it is who loves me. And he who loves me will be loved by my Father, and I will love him and manifest myself to him."
>
> Judas (not Iscariot) said to him, "Lord, how is it that you will manifest yourself to us, and not to the world?"
>
> Jesus answered him, "If anyone loves me, he will keep my word, and my Father will love him, and we will come to him and make our home with him. Whoever does not love me does not keep my words. And the word that you hear is not mine but the Father's who sent me.
>
> "These things I have spoken to you while I am still with you. But the Helper, the Holy Spirit, whom the Father will send in my name, he will teach you all things and bring to your remembrance all that I have said to you. Peace I leave with you; my peace I give to you. Not as the world gives do I give to you. Let not your hearts be troubled, neither let them be afraid.

"You heard me say to you, 'I am going away, and I will come to you.' If you loved me, you would have rejoiced, because I am going to the Father, for the Father is greater than I. And now I have told you before it takes place, so that when it does take place you may believe. I will no longer talk much with you, for the ruler of this world is coming. He has no claim on me, but I do as the Father has commanded me, so that the world may know that I love the Father. Rise, let us go from here."

When Jesus is gone, He'll ask the Father to send them a helper, or an advocate. He's referring to the third Person of the Trinity, the Holy Spirit. As the disciples later learn, Jesus will send them the Holy Spirit on Pentecost after He ascends into heaven. The Holy Spirit will indwell them and all believers, empowering them to overcome sin (Romans 8:9; 1 Cor. 12:13). The Holy Spirit will work silently through believers when they evangelize and transform them into new creatures in Christ.[3] Those who love Him will keep His word as a natural outgrowth of their love. The Holy Spirit will also teach the apostles and remind them of everything He's taught them. But for the inspiration and promptings of the Holy Spirit, the apostles could not have written the New Testament.[4]

It's hard to overstate the significance of Christ's assurances about the Holy Spirit. "It will make a great deal of difference in your own life," John Piper writes, "if you believe that you are being indwelt and led and purified not by impersonal forces from a distant God, but a person who in his essence is the love of God" (Romans 5:5; 1 John 4:12–13). It's a most glorious truth, Piper adds, "that when the Holy Spirit comes into our lives, he comes not merely as the Spirit of the Son, nor merely as the Spirit of the Father, but as the Spirit of infinite love between the Father and the Son, so that we may love the Father with the very love of the Son, and love the Son with the very love of the Father."[5]

The Holy Spirit indeed comes to us as love, but as J. I. Packer laments, "The average Christian is in a complete fog as to what work the Holy Spirit does."[6] Theologian James Montgomery Boice helps to clarify the issue, explaining that the Holy Spirit reproduces Christ in believers by leading Christians to greater victory over sin, praying for them, teaching them to pray, and showing them God's will for their lives and enabling them to walk in it.[7]

Jesus reassures His disciples again not to be troubled that He's going away because He will return. But for now, He's going to the Father, Who is greater than He. Jesus, as we've pointed out, is not a lesser being than the Father, however—He and the Father are equal in essence (John 1:1; 8:58; 10:30; 20:28). Norman Geisler and Ron Rhodes point out, "The Father is greater than the Son by *office*, not by *nature*, since both are God. Just as an earthly father is equally human but holds a higher office than his son, even so the Father and the Son in the Trinity are equal in *essence*, but different in *function*."[8]

I AM THE TRUE VINE (JOHN 15:1–17)

Jesus describes Himself to His disciples as the True Vine:

I am the true vine, and my Father is the vinedresser. Every branch in me that does not bear fruit he takes away, and every branch that does bear fruit he prunes, that it may bear more fruit. Already you are clean because of the word that I have spoken to you. Abide in me, and I in you. As the branch cannot bear fruit by itself, unless it abides in the vine, neither can you, unless you abide in me.

I am the vine; you are the branches. Whoever abides in me and I in him, he it is that bears much fruit, for apart from me you can do nothing. If anyone does not abide in me he is thrown away like a branch and withers; and the branches are gathered, thrown into the fire, and burned. If you abide in me, and my words abide in you, ask whatever you wish, and it will be done for you. By this my Father is glorified, that you bear much fruit and so prove to be my disciples. As the Father has loved me, so have I loved you. Abide in my love. If you keep my commandments, you will abide in my love, just as I have kept my Father's commandments and abide in his love. These things

I have spoken to you, that my joy may be in you, and that your joy may be full.

This is my commandment, that you love one another as I have loved you. Greater love has no one than this, that someone lay down his life for his friends. You are my friends if you do what I command you. No longer do I call you servants, for the servant does not know what his master is doing; but I have called you friends, for all that I have heard from my Father I have made known to you. You did not choose me, but I chose you and appointed you that you should go and bear fruit and that your fruit should abide, so that whatever you ask the Father in my name, he may give it to you. These things I command you, so that you will love one another.

As the vinedresser, or gardener, the Father removes unfruitful branches and prunes the others to maximize fruit production. We are to abide in Christ by having a personal relationship with Him through the study of Scripture, trust, prayer, obedience, and joy.[9] Jesus says His word makes the disciples clean, and His word is memorialized for us in the Bible. God's primary way of pruning us (making us more fruitful) is working in us through His word,[10] which is why we must habitually read and study Scripture. We're unable to bear fruit on our own, but when we abide in Christ, we bear much fruit and glorify the Father (Philip. 1:11). We must abide in His love, just as He abides in the Father's love, so that His joy may be in us. It follows that as Christ is love, we will become more like Him and thus more loving and joyful by abiding in Him.

We must love one another as Christ has loved us, and He proved His love by laying down His life for us, the greatest possible act of love. Though the disciples do not fully understand His message at the time, they will when the Holy Spirit reminds them of the things Jesus said to them (John 14:26).[11] Placing the interests of others above our own is the model of sacrificial Christian love. "The command is not—abide *with* me—abide *near* me—abide *under* me; but, abide *in* me," British theologian and pastor John Brown notes. "The fruit-bearing branch is not only in the same place with the vine—near it, under its shadow—it is *in* it, and it *abides* in it. It is difficult—it is impossible—to bring all out that is in the expression. It is not the obscurity of the expression, but the magnitude of the thought, that perplexes us. The statement, though perfectly clear, is unfathomably deep. Let us endeavor to draw from a fountain we cannot exhaust."[12]

THE HATRED OF THE WORLD (JOHN 15:18–16:4)

Jesus warns His disciples of the hardships and persecution they will encounter as they spread the Gospel:

> If the world hates you, know that it has hated me before it hated you. If you were of the world, the world would love you as its own; but because you are not of the world, but I chose you out of the world, therefore the world hates you. Remember the word that I said to you: "A servant is not greater than his master." If they persecuted me, they will also persecute you. If they kept my word, they will also keep yours. But all these things they will do to you on account of my name, because they do not know him who sent me. If I had not come and spoken to them, they would not have been guilty of sin, but now they have no excuse for their sin. Whoever hates me hates my Father also. If I had not done among them the works that no one else did, they would not be guilty of sin, but now they have seen and hated both me and my Father. But the word that is written in their Law must be fulfilled: "They hated me without a cause."
>
> But when the Helper comes, whom I will send to you from the Father, the Spirit of truth, who proceeds from the Father, he will bear witness about me. And you also will bear witness, because you have been with me from the beginning.
>
> I have said all these things to you to keep you from falling away. They will put you out of the synagogues. Indeed, the hour is coming when whoever kills you will think he is offering service to God. And they will do these things because they

have not known the Father, nor me. But I have said these things to you, that when their hour comes you may remember that I told them to you.

As the world is under Satan's power (John 14:30), it's no surprise that it's hostile to Christians, yet Peter suggests Christians might be surprised at the fiery trial they will endure (1 Peter 4:12–13). The world into which Jesus came hated Him from His birth and will hate His followers for their obedience to Him and for spreading His message.

Recall that Jesus told his "brothers" He would not go to the Jews' Feast of Booths because they hated Him and were trying to kill Him. The world hates Him because He is the light of the world and He shines brightly on man, testifying as to his evil deeds (John 7:7). People who are friends with the world—the system of evil in the world under Satan's control—are enemies of God (James 4:4). Those who organize themselves against God love the darkness rather than the light because their works are evil (John 3:20).[13] Some people feel threatened by those who adhere to the truth and honor God's standards. They oppose those standards because they expose their darkness. The world organized under Satan's control is hostile to the Father, the Son, and the Son's disciples.

Since a servant is not greater than his master, the world will surely hate Jesus' disciples because it hated Him. It will hate them for following Him and for emulating His behavior. "Jesus modeled the standard of God (15:10, etc.)," Gerald Borchert writes, "and that meant his very presence in the world was a reminder to the world of its evil works and God's resultant judgment."[14] R. Kent Hughes explains that Jesus' "inner righteousness drew [the people's] abiding hostility because it revealed the shabbiness of their external goodness."[15]

Jesus says if He had not done unique works among the people and had not come and spoken to them, they would not be guilty of sin. This doesn't mean man was sinless before He came; the Bible clearly teaches that all of us are sinners (Romans 3:23). Rather, those who reject Him after hearing His word and witnessing His actions are guilty of the sin of rejecting Him and God's revelation manifested in Him.[16] Those who hate Him also hate His Father.

Jesus' message is unmistakable: if you reject Him you reject the Father. Your attitude toward Him will necessarily be your attitude toward the Father. This is another way of saying, "I am the way, and the truth, and the life. No one comes to the Father except through me" (John 14:6). Faith in Jesus Christ is the exclusive path to God. Jesus says this hatred of Him "without a cause" is in fulfillment of Old Testament prophecy (Psalms 35:19; 69:4).

The Holy Spirit will come to them from the Father and bear witness to the world about Christ—just as they will. Knowing this will comfort them and keep them from falling away when they are hated and persecuted by those who don't know Jesus or the Father.

THE WORK OF THE HOLY SPIRIT (JOHN 16:4–15)

Jesus then expounds on the benefits the Holy Spirit will bring:

I did not say these things to you from the beginning, because I was with you. But now I am going to him who sent me, and none of you asks me, "Where are you going?" But because I have said these things to you, sorrow has filled your heart. Nevertheless, I tell you the truth: it is to your advantage that I go away, for if I do not go away, the Helper will not come to you. But if I go, I will send him to you. And when he comes, he will convict the world concerning sin and righteousness and judgment: concerning sin, because they do not believe in me; concerning righteousness, because I go to the Father, and you will see me no longer; concerning judgment, because the ruler of this world is judged.

I still have many things to say to you, but you cannot bear them now. When the Spirit of truth comes, he will guide you into all the truth, for he will not speak on his own authority, but whatever he hears he will speak, and he will declare to you the things that are to come. He will glorify me, for he will take what is mine and declare it to you. All that the Father has is mine; therefore I said that he will take what is mine and declare it to you.

The Holy Spirit will be such help to them that His coming will justify Jesus' departure—while Jesus is on earth He can only be in one place at a time, but the Holy Spirit will work in believers throughout the world at all times.[17] He'll be their best asset in spreading the Gospel. Not only will He indwell believers and empower them to defeat sin in their daily lives, but He'll also convict the world concerning sin, righteousness, and judgment—that is, He'll bring truth to the world and more people will be convicted of their own fallen condition, which will lead to their repentance and trust in Christ. He will guide them into all the truth which, writes E. A. Blum, "was a promise to the apostles that their partial understanding of the person and work of Jesus as the Messiah would be completed as the Spirit would give them insight into the meanings of the soon-to-come Cross and the Resurrection as well as truths about Jesus' return (cf. 1 Cor. 2:10). The New Testament books are the fulfillment of this teaching ministry of the Spirit."[18]

YOUR SORROW WILL TURN INTO JOY (JOHN 16:16–24)

As the disciples grow concerned about Jesus' remarks, He consoles them with a glimpse of what's to come after his departure:

"A little while, and you will see me no longer; and again a little while, and you will see me."

So some of his disciples said to one another, "What is this that he says to us, 'A little while, and you will not see me, and again a little while, and you will see me'; and, 'because I am going to the Father?'" So they were saying, "What does he mean by 'a little while?' We do not know what he is talking about."

Jesus knew that they wanted to ask him, so he said to them, "Is this what you are asking yourselves, what I meant by saying, 'A little while and you will not see me, and again a little while and you will see me?' Truly, truly, I say to you, you will weep and lament, but the world will rejoice. You will be sorrowful, but your sorrow will turn into joy. When a woman is giving birth, she has sorrow because her hour has come, but when she has delivered the baby, she no longer remembers the anguish, for joy that a human being has been born into the world. So also you have sorrow now, but I will see you again, and your hearts will rejoice, and no one will take your joy from you. In that day you will ask nothing of me. Truly, truly, I say to you, whatever you ask of the Father in my name, he will give it to you. Until now you have asked nothing in my name. Ask, and you will receive, that your joy may be full."

Shortly, Jesus will die on the cross and within no time be resurrected, and they will see Him again. They'll be inconsolable over His death, but the world will rejoice—including even the authorities and His other opponents, who will believe that they've finally stopped this menace.

Jesus' analogy of a woman giving birth is fitting because she goes through intense pain in childbirth, but once the baby is born she forgets her anguish. In the same way, once Christ returns the disciples' joy will overshadow their sorrow because His death and resurrection will finally bring God's salvation plan to fruition, and they will come to understand all that has happened and its eternal significance. Their joy will be permanent—"no one will take your joy from you."[19]

Jesus says they will no longer ask anything of Him. "When Christ has promised the disciples 'joy' from their unshaken firmness and courage, he talks about another grace of the Spirit which will be given to them," explains John Calvin. "They will receive such a light of understanding that they will be raised to heavenly mysteries. At the time they were so slow that the slightest difficulty of any kind made them hesitate; as children learning the alphabet cannot read a single line without many pauses, so the disciples stumbled at almost everything Christ said. But a little later, when they had been enlightened by the Holy Spirit, they no longer suffered any delay in becoming familiar and acquainted with the wisdom of God, so as to progress among the mysteries of God without stumbling."[20]

Leon Morris states that in prayer Christians generally approach the Father on the basis of Christ's atoning work on their behalf. "The words do not, of course, exclude the possibility of prayer to the Son," argues Morris. "But they remind us that, for Christians, prayer is normally addressed to the Father in the name of the Son."[21] We should be careful that when we say we are praying in Jesus' name we are not just throwing His name in by rote. *The ESV Study Bible* offers wise counsel on this subject: "Praying in Jesus' name means praying in a way consistent with his character and his will (a person's name in the ancient world represented what the person was like); it also means coming to God in the authority of Jesus. Adding 'in Jesus' name' at the end of every prayer is neither required nor wrong. Effective prayer must ask for and desire what Jesus delights in."[22]

I HAVE OVERCOME THE WORLD (JOHN 16:25–33)

Jesus proceeds to speak more directly about Himself and His fate:

"I have said these things to you in figures of speech. The hour is coming when I will no longer speak to you in figures of speech but will tell you plainly about the Father. In that day you will ask in my name, and I do not say to you that I will ask the Father on your behalf; for the Father himself loves you, because you have loved me and have believed that I came from God. I came from the Father and have come into the world, and now I am leaving the world and going to the Father."

His disciples said, "Ah, now you are speaking plainly and not using figurative speech! Now we know that you know all things and do not need anyone to question you; this is why we believe that you came from God." Jesus answered them, "Do you now believe? Behold, the hour is coming, indeed it has come, when you will be scattered, each to his own home, and will leave me alone. Yet I am not alone, for the Father is with me. I have said these things to you, that in me you may have peace. In the world you will have tribulation. But take heart; I have overcome the world."

Throughout Jesus' ministry, the disciples had difficulty grasping the complete salvation plan and continually faltered in their faith. He spoke to them in ways they could understand at the time, but He knew they would understand more after witnessing His death and resurrection. As noted earlier, in His resurrection appearances He opens the scriptures to them and improves their grasp of redemptive history and His central role in it. The disciples' response in this passage shows they're coming to understand the whole picture even though they will falter again during His trial and crucifixion and desert Him (Matt. 26:56; John 18:17, 25–26).

Jesus repeatedly reinforces these themes because even if they don't fully understand yet, they will when the events unfold, and especially when the Holy Spirit comes and assists them in remembering. Jesus assures them that while they'd abandon Him for a time, He would not be alone because the Father is with Him (John 8:29)—though the Father would forsake Him during His passion to consummate their salvation plan. He brings them peace and comfort by reinforcing their faith in Him and assuring them victory is at hand, though they would experience tribulation. They must take heart because He has overcome the world and defeated Satan and his evil forces.

THE HIGH PRIESTLY PRAYER (JOHN 17:1–26)

In front of His disciples, Jesus utters what Warren Wiersbe calls "the greatest prayer ever prayed":[23]

> When Jesus had spoken these words, he lifted up his eyes to heaven, and said, "Father, the hour has come; glorify your Son that the Son may glorify you, since you have given him authority over all flesh, to give eternal life to all whom you have given him. And this is eternal life, that they know you, the only true God, and Jesus Christ whom you have sent. I glorified you on earth, having accomplished the work that you gave me to do. And now, Father, glorify me in your own presence with the glory that I had with you before the world existed.

"I have manifested your name to the people whom you gave me out of the world. Yours they were, and you gave them to me, and they have kept your word. Now they know that everything that you have given me is from you. For I have given them the words that you gave me, and they have received them and have come to know in truth that I came from you; and they have believed that you sent me. I am praying for them. I am not praying for the world but for those whom you have given me, for they are yours. All mine are yours, and yours are mine, and I am glorified in them. And I am no longer in the world, but they are in the world, and I am coming to you. Holy Father, keep them in your name, which you have given me, that they may be one, even as we are one. While I was with them, I kept them in your name, which you have given me. I have guarded them, and not one of them has been lost except the son of destruction, that the Scripture might be fulfilled. But now I am coming to you, and these things I speak in the world, that they may have my joy fulfilled in themselves. I have given them your word, and the world has hated them because they are not of the world, just as I am not of the world. I do not ask that you take them out of the world, but that you keep them from the evil one. They are not of the world, just as I am not of the world. Sanctify them in the truth; your word is truth. As you sent me into the world, so I have sent them into the world. And for their sake I consecrate myself, that they also may be sanctified in truth.

"I do not ask for these only, but also for those who will believe in me through their word, that they may all be one, just as you, Father, are in me, and I in you, that they also may be in us, so that the world may believe that you have sent me. The glory that you have given me I have given to them, that they may be one even as we are one, I in them and you in me, that they may become perfectly one, so that the world may know that you sent me and loved them even as you loved me. Father, I desire that they also, whom you have given me, may be with me where I am, to see my glory that you have given me because you loved me before the foundation of the world. O righteous Father, even though the world does not know you, I know you, and these know that you have sent me. I made known to them your name, and I will continue to make it known, that the love with which you have loved me may be in them, and I in them."

Jesus has just finished teaching His disciples—giving them His word—and now He's praying for them. Prayer and the Bible go hand in hand. If we just read the Bible and don't pray, we have the truth but forego the power prayer can give. If we have prayer without Bible teaching, we rely too much on our subjective experiences. We need to be anchored in the word.[24] As Paul writes, "We will devote ourselves to prayer and to the ministry of the word" (Acts 6:4). Warren Wiersbe comments, "The only way the Word of God can become real in our lives is through prayer and obedience."[25] If Jesus needed prayer, how much more do we need it!

In the first five verses of this passage, Jesus prays for Himself. Though He needs strength to finish the greatest work ever performed by a human being, His work is for us. Unless He receives the Father's glory and returns to Him in heaven, our salvation will be impossible. His prayer is for us. In His greatest distress, He petitions the Father to fill us with Jesus' joy. What an awesome display of His sacrificial love for us. In His greatest hour of need, He focuses on His followers, not Himself.

For me, the most moving part of this wonderful prayer is when Jesus asks that His followers all be united as one, and united in the Father and Son like He and the Father are united. Timothy Keller elucidates God's desire to share His glory with us:

In that incredible statement we learn something. As lofty as this is, we know what he's talking about because we're made in the image of God. There is nothing more incredible and wonderful than to be in love with someone and simply to affirm each other's gifts and strengths and beauty, just enjoy each other, just build each other up, just be ravished with each other. What we have known in drops, the Father, Son, and the Holy Spirit have known in infinite oceans. From all eternity they've been glorifying each other, which is what you do when you're in love, building each other up, doting on each other, enjoying each other, appreciating each other, loving each other, rejoicing in one another. They've been doing it from all eternity, and there is nothing better. You know that, except we've only had drops and they have had the ocean.

This is the answer to the big, philosophical question. If it's true God is a Trinity, then when he created us, he wouldn't have created us because he needed us to glorify him. Right? It couldn't be. He already had that. Then why would he have done it? Jesus actually says so. "Father, I want them, my disciples, to see my glory, the glory you gave me from the foundation of the world because you loved me."

The only reason God could've created you and me is not because he needed glory, but to share it. He didn't need this incredible circle of rejoicing in and loving in and glorifying in one another. He already had it, so why would he have created us? Only because he wants to make us capable of reflecting his glory, capable of praising his glory, capable of also giving and reflecting love and joy and glory. He made us capable of entering into the cosmic joy of the Godhead.[26]

I want to add something to these wise words. Please reread the entire prayer and notice how many times and in how many different ways Jesus expresses His desire that we share with Him and the Father. He wants us all to be one: *"I in them and you in me, that they may become perfectly one."* He wants us to bask in the joy of our mutual love. Though He, the Father, and the Holy Spirit are infinitely superior to us, they want to delight in us and for us to delight in them. They want us to radiate their infinite love. We just have to believe it, accept it, and live it.

As His people are *in* the world but not *of* the world, He asks the Father not to take them out of the world, but to protect them from Satan. He's not trying to remove us from life on earth and immediately zap us into heaven—we will remain here until we die. So He asks the Father to protect us from Satan, and to make us holy in the truth—the word of God. We should immerse ourselves in the Bible and in prayer, but not puff ourselves up with Bible knowledge. God blesses us for doing His will, not for being faithful Bible students. Prayer and reading the scriptures, however, are necessary to understand and do His will. "But the one who looks into the perfect law, the law of liberty, and perseveres, being no hearer who forgets but a doer who acts, he will be blessed in his doing" (James 1:25).

JESUS PRAYS IN GETHSEMANE (MATT. 26:36–46; MARK 14:32–42; LUKE 22:39–46; JOHN 18:1)

Jesus goes with His disciples to the Garden of Gethsemane, where He takes Peter, James, and John aside and begins to pray. His soul is sorrowful as He asks them to stay with Him and keep watch. He falls on His face and pleads, "My Father, if it be possible, let this cup pass from me; nevertheless not as I will, but as you will." An angel then appears from heaven to strengthen Him.

This is one of the most arresting passages in all of Scripture, for it demonstrates Christ's acute agony and His raw humanity followed by His expression of unreserved obedience and commitment. He asks the Father to remove Him from this unbearable situation. But in the next breath, He says, "Not as I will, but as you will."

Jesus' humanity is wrestling with His divinity. Though He knows He'll be reunited with the Father in a matter of days, and notwithstanding that He was a co-planner of these events from before creation, He is truly suffering—He's literally sweating blood, and His flesh wants to escape. He knows He cannot, but He's undergoing indescribable physical and spiritual torture. His anguish is exacerbated when He returns to His disciples and finds them sleeping instead of keeping watch.

Thus, just as He's about to be betrayed, just as the Father is about to visit His wrath upon Him for all the sins of mankind, and just as He's about to be forsaken by the Father and separated from Him for the first time, He finds Himself alone. Yet, He selflessly instructs His disciples to rise and pray that they may not enter into temptation—temptation to abandon Him when

He's arrested and put on trial, and then again after He is ascended, when they will be persecuted for preaching the Gospel on His behalf.

The Bible provides many other examples of Jesus sharing human experiences: He was born as a human being (Luke 2:5, 120); He grew physically and intellectually (Luke 2:40, 52; Matt. 26:39); He experienced human emotions—anger (Mark 3:5), grief (John 11:35), close affection (John 13:23), and agony (Luke 22:44); and He became hungry (Matt. 4:2), thirsty (John 4:7; 19:28), grew weary (John 4:6), and slept (Matt. 8:24). Then He suffered and died.[27]

It's clear Jesus was fully human as well as fully God, though certain cults throughout history have denied His humanity. John, in his first epistle, stresses the importance of believing Jesus came in the flesh, insisting that to deny His humanity is to be in concert with the devil: "Beloved, do not believe every spirit, but test the spirits to see whether they are from God, for many false prophets have gone out into the world. By this you know the Spirit of God: every spirit that confesses that Jesus Christ has come in the flesh is from God, and every spirit that does not confess Jesus is not from God. This is the spirit of the antichrist, which you heard was coming and now is in the world already" (1 John 4:1–3). I find this particularly interesting because in His Gospel John strongly stresses Christ's deity. This, coupled with his emphasis on Christ's humanity in his first epistle, underscores the necessity of grasping His dual nature.

I wonder if Christians often consider this. Sure, we commonly acknowledge that unless we believe He's divine we do not have faith. But it's equally important that we confess His humanity, for if He hadn't become one of us, we could not be saved. "For there is one God, and there is one mediator between God and men, the man Christ Jesus" (1 Tim. 2:5).

JESUS IS BETRAYED AND ARRESTED (MATT. 26:47–56; MARK 14:43–52; LUKE 22:47–53; JOHN 18:2–14, 19–24)

While Jesus is still speaking, Judas comes with a great crowd carrying swords and clubs, sent by the religious leaders. Approaching Jesus and calling out, "Greetings, Rabbi," Judas kisses Him, thereby identifying Jesus to His captors. Jesus says, "Friend, do what you came to do." They seize Jesus, and Peter strikes the high priest's servant, cutting off his ear. Jesus commands Peter to put his sword away. "Shall I not drink the cup that the Father has given me?" asks Jesus. "For all who take the sword will perish by the sword. Do you think that I cannot appeal to my Father, and he will at once send me more than twelve legions of angels? But how then should the Scriptures be fulfilled, that it must be so?" Jesus tells the crowds, "Have you come out as against a robber, with swords and clubs to capture me? Day after day I sat in the temple teaching, and you did not seize me. But all this has taken place that the Scriptures of the prophets might be fulfilled." Then all the disciples leave Him and flee—which is such an embarrassing admission that it's highly unlikely any writer would have made it up.

God is in control, but Peter still hasn't caught on. Jesus could have summoned legions of angels to rescue Him, but His decision to "drink the cup" the Father has given Him was made in eternity past, and nothing would interfere with the sovereign design for man's salvation. Jesus is always a willing participant (John 10:18) in their plan that He lay down His life in a supreme act of sacrificial love (John 15:13; 10:11).

They lead Jesus to Annas, the father-in-law of the high priest Caiaphas, who questions Jesus about His disciples and His teaching. "I have spoken openly to the world," declares Jesus. "I have always taught in synagogues and in the temple, where all Jews come together. I have said nothing in secret. Why do you ask me? Ask those who have heard me what I said to them; they know what I said." One of the officers strikes Jesus for talking disrespectfully to the high priest. Jesus responds, "If what I said is wrong, bear witness about the wrong, but if what I said is right, why do you strike me?" Annas then sends Him bound to Caiaphas.

Jesus tells His arrogant adversaries that His teaching and actions have been public, not secret. They invent false scenarios to justify their malicious deeds, which is a testament to the monumental injustice they're inflicting upon Him. But Jesus will have no part in it—He has nothing to hide. His accusers have no case, and by demanding they specify their allegations against Him, Jesus exposes their wrongdoing.

PETER DENIES JESUS (MATT. 26:58, 69-70, 71-75; MARK 14:54, 66-72; LUKE 22:54-62; JOHN 18:15-18, 25-26)

Peter and another disciple follow as they lead Jesus to Annas. The unnamed disciple enters with Jesus into the courtyard of the high priest while Peter stands outside the door. This disciple goes out to get Peter, and when they're at the door a servant girl asks Peter, "You also are not one of this man's disciples, are you?" Peter replies, "I am not." He goes out into the gateway and the rooster crows. The servant girl sees him again and says to the bystanders, "This man is one of them," and Peter denies it again. A little later the bystanders say to Peter, "Certainly you are one of them, for you are a Galilean." (Except for Judas, Jesus' disciples are Galileans, and Judeans living in Jerusalem recognize their accent.)[28] Peter invokes a curse on himself and swears, "I do not know the man." And the rooster crows a second time. Peter then remembers Jesus' prediction, "Before the rooster crows twice, you will deny me three times." And he goes out and weeps bitterly.

Peter acts differently than he'd planned. He genuinely believed he would stand up for Jesus and willingly go to prison or die for Him (Luke 22:33-34; Mark 14:29-31). When the time comes, however, he loses his courage and so thoroughly betrays his friend and Lord that he weeps in anguish, disgusted with himself and disgraced. Before harshly judging Peter's betrayal, however, we must ask ourselves whether we've ever failed to stand up for Jesus when it was uncomfortable or inconvenient. This story reminds us that because Jesus died for us, we must stand by Him even when it's difficult.

JESUS BEFORE CAIAPHAS AND THE SANHEDRIN (MATT. 26:57, 59-68; MARK 14:53, 55-65; 15:1; LUKE 22:54, 63-71; JOHN 18:24)

Jesus' captors lead Him to Caiaphas, who is with the chief priests, the scribes, and the elders. The entire council seeks false testimony against Jesus to justify His execution. Though many false witnesses come forward, no two can agree on any charges against Him until finally two men declare, "This man said, 'I am able to destroy the temple of God, and to rebuild it in three days.'" The high priest asks Jesus if He has an answer, and Jesus remains silent. The high priest says, "I adjure you by the living God, tell us if you are the Christ, the Son of God." Jesus responds, "You have said so. But I tell you, from now on you will see the Son of Man seated at the right hand of Power and coming on the clouds of heaven."

The high priest tears his robes and declares, "He has uttered blasphemy. What further witnesses do we need? You have now heard his blasphemy. What is your judgment?" They reply, "He deserves death." They spit in His face and strike Him. They blindfold Him, and some slap and mock Him, saying, "Prophesy to us, you Christ! Who is it that struck you?"

In the morning, the chief priests consult with the elders, scribes, and the whole council. Deciding to put Jesus to death, they bind Him and lead Him away to be delivered to Pilate.

Many false witnesses came before the council, but the law requires two witnesses before putting someone to death (Num. 35:30; Deut. 19:15). The witnesses were each called separately, which made collaboration more difficult.[29] Two witnesses finally leveled a charge against Him—that He said He could destroy the Temple and rebuild it in three days. But Jesus didn't say that—He said if *they* destroyed the Temple He could rebuild it (John 2:19). Furthermore, He was not referring to the Temple in Jerusalem but to His body—His death and resurrection after three days. Jesus' silence in the face of His false accusers frustrates Caiaphas, but it's in fulfillment of Isaiah's prophecy, "He was oppressed, and he was afflicted, yet he opened not his mouth; like a lamb that is led to slaughter, and like a sheep that before its shearers is silent" (Isaiah 53:7). This is yet another depiction of Jesus as a lamb, as discussed earlier.

When Jesus finally spoke He plainly asserted His deity, which the religious leaders considered blasphemous. Moreover, since He admitted it, they felt no need for corroborating witnesses. But He hadn't committed blasphemy because it's impossible for Jesus, being God, to commit blasphemy.

The Sanhedrin can't, by itself, condemn Jesus to death because the Romans prohibit the Jews from inflicting capital punishment, which requires the sentence of a Roman authority. But blasphemy is not a capital crime in a secular Roman court, so they would have to find another angle. This would be to frame Jesus for treason—for claiming to be king of the Jews.[30] Jesus' prediction that He would be crucified (Matt. 10:19; 26:2; John 12:32–33) is all the more amazing because, despite the prohibition against Jewish executions, the Jews did carry out some death sentences—but they were through stoning, not crucifixion (cf. Acts 6:8–7:60). The Romans, however, used crucifixion to execute foreigners and traitors.[31]

JUDAS HANGS HIMSELF (MATT. 27:3–10)

After Jesus is sentenced to death, Judas remorsefully brings back the thirty pieces of silver to the religious leaders, saying he has sinned against an innocent man. They respond, "What is that to us? See to it yourself." He then throws the silver into the Temple and goes and hangs himself.

The leaders say they can't keep the silver because it's blood money, so they use it to buy a potter's field as a burial place for strangers. This fulfills the Old Testament prophecy, "And they took the thirty pieces of silver, the price of him on whom a price had been set by some of the sons of Israel, and they gave them to the potter's field, as the Lord directed me." Matthew attributes the prophecy to Jeremiah, but its wording more closely resembles Zechariah's prophecy (Zech. 11:12–13), which has caused some confusion and debate over the years. D. A. Carson explains, "The quotation appears to refer to Jeremiah 19:1–13 along with phraseology drawn mostly from Zechariah 11:12–13.... Jeremiah alone is mentioned, perhaps because he is the more important of the two prophets, and perhaps also because, though Jeremiah 19 is the less obvious reference, it is the more important as to prophecy and fulfillment."[32]

PILATE AND HEROD QUESTION JESUS (MATT. 27:2; 27:11–14; MARK 15:1–5; LUKE 23:1–12; JOHN 18:28–38)

Jesus is led from Caiaphas' house to the governor's headquarters. Pilate goes outside and asks what charges they bring against Jesus. They answer, "If this man were not doing evil, we would not have delivered him over to you." Pilate orders them to take Him and judge Him by their own law. The Jews say, "It is not lawful for us to put anyone to death." So Pilate asks Jesus if He's the king of the Jews. Jesus responds, "Do you say this of your own accord, or did others say it to you about me?" Pilate replies, "Am I a Jew? Your own nation and the chief priests have delivered you over to me. What have you done?" Jesus says, "My kingdom is not of this world. If my kingdom were of this world, my servants would have been fighting, that I might not be delivered over to the Jews. But my kingdom is not from the world." Pilate asks, "So you are a king?" Jesus says, "You say that I am a king. For this purpose I was born and for this purpose I have come into the world—to bear witness to the truth. Everyone who is of the truth listens to my voice." After scornfully asking, "What is truth?" Pilate goes back outside to the Jews and reports, "I find no guilt in him."

When the chief priests and elders accuse Him, Jesus gives no answer. Pilate asks, "Do you not hear how many things they testify against you?" Jesus does not reply to any of the charges, which amazes Pilate. But the religious leaders persist, saying, "He stirs up the people, teaching throughout all Judea, from Galilee even to this place." Pilate then asks if Jesus is a Galilean, under the jurisdiction of Herod Antipas. Discovering that He is, Pilate sends Him to Herod in Jerusalem.

Jesus' arrival pleases Herod, who has long heard about Him and wants to see Him perform a sign. Herod questions Jesus at length, and Jesus doesn't answer while the religious leaders stand by vehemently accusing Him. Herod and his soldiers mock Him, and Herod arrays Him in splendid clothing and sends Him back to Pilate. Though they'd been enemies, on this day Pilate and Herod become friends. "The irony here should not be lost," notes Robert Stein. "Jesus' passion brings reconciliation even between such people as Herod and Pilate."[33]

Pilate's cryptic question to Jesus, "What is truth?" is rich with spiritual significance. Pilate is cynically mocking Jesus, as if to say, "Is there any such thing as absolute truth? Who are you, Jesus, to say what truth is?" If only he had known. People today may think moral relativism is a new construct, but Pilate is an early practitioner. Absolute truth does exist—Jesus is Truth. He tells us so: "I am the way, the truth, and the life" (John 14:6). He is the source of all truth. He embodies truth, and He represents and commands the absolute moral standard against which to measure our hearts, actions, and intentions.

Truth is not what we wish it to be. We cannot manipulate it to conform to our standards. "For the Christian, the starting point is God," Ravi Zacharias writes. "*He* is the eternally existent one, the absolute, from whom we draw all definitions for life's purpose and destiny.... Truth by definition is exclusive. If truth were all-inclusive, nothing would be false. And if nothing were false, what would be the meaning of truth?... Therefore, when Jesus said, 'I am the way and the truth and the life. No man comes to the father except through me,' He was making a very reasonable statement by affirming truth's exclusivity."[34]

Moreover, if truth doesn't matter, why do we describe Satan as the father of lies? Deceit leads people away from eternal life and into death, for it distorts the nature of reality, obscures man's vision, and obstructs his spiritual path. It steers people away from He that is truth and from the salvation He offers. Satan fundamentally attacked God's word and the truth itself to seduce Adam and Eve into sin. Let us never underestimate the divine significance of truth or fail to see that our Savior Himself is the Way, the Truth, and the Life.

PILATE DELIVERS JESUS TO BE CRUCIFIED (MATT. 27:15–26; MARK 15:6–15; LUKE 23:13–25; JOHN 18:38–19:16)

Calling together the religious leaders and the people, Pilate says, "You brought me this man as one who was misleading the people. And after examining him before you, behold, I did not find this man guilty of any of your charges against him. Neither did Herod, for he sent him back to us. Look, nothing deserving death has been done by him. I will therefore punish and release him."

They all cry out together, "Away with this man, and release to us Barabbas"—a man in prison for insurrection and murder. The governor's custom is to release one prisoner at the Passover Feast at the people's request, and the religious leaders had persuaded the crowd to ask for Barabbas instead of Jesus. When Pilate asks them whether they want him to release the "King of the Jews" or Barabbas, the people cry out again, "Not this man, but Barabbas!"

Pilate is reluctant to condemn Jesus because he believes He is innocent. Adding to his consternation, his wife had sent word to him not to do anything to "that righteous man" because she had suffered much because of Him that day in a dream—during these times people placed great importance on dreams and sometimes considered them to be oracles from the gods.[35] Pilate asks again, but they continue shouting, "Crucify, crucify him." Pilate reiterates, "What evil has he done? I have found in him no guilt deserving of death. I will therefore punish and release him." But the people insist on His crucifixion.

Pilate's soldiers take Jesus into Pilate's headquarters to flog Him before the whole battalion. They strip Him and put a purple robe on Him, then twist together a crown of thorns and put it on His head. They kneel before Him and mock Him, saying, "Hail, King of the Jews!"

Pilate goes out to the crowd again and says he finds no guilt in Him. When Jesus comes out wearing the crown of thorns and the purple robe, Pilate declares, "Behold the man!" On seeing Him, the religious leaders shout out again, "Crucify him, crucify him!" Pilate again insists he finds no basis to charge Him and tells *them* to crucify Him. The Jews say their law requires that He be executed because He claims to be the Son of God.

Upon hearing this, Pilate becomes afraid and goes back inside his palace. He might have become scared when considering he could actually be dealing with a god, especially when factoring in his wife's ominous dream. Or he could have been fearful that a riot was about to ensue among the Jews.[36] He asks Jesus where He comes from, and Jesus refuses to answer. Pilate taunts, "Do you not know that I have authority to release you and authority to crucify you?" Jesus says, "You would have no authority over me at all unless it had been given to you from above. Therefore he who delivered me over to you has the greater sin." "From then on Pilate seeks to release Him, but the Jews cry out, 'If you release this man, you are not Caesar's friend. Everyone who makes himself a king opposes Caesar.'" Pilate brings Jesus back out to them and says, "Behold, your king." But they shout, "Away with him, away with him, crucify him!" Pilate asks, "Shall I crucify your king?" The chief priests reply, "We have no king but Caesar."

Pilate, realizing he's getting nowhere and that a riot is erupting, washes his hands with water before the crowd and proclaims, "I am innocent of this man's blood; see to it yourselves." The people answer, "His blood be on us and on our children!" Pilate then releases Barabbas and sends Jesus to be crucified alongside two criminals.

Pilate is not a Jew; he's not the one charging Jesus. When Jesus won't fall into the trap and admit He's asserting His political kingship—as opposed to His divine kingship—Pilate finds no guilt in Him because he knows Jesus does not plan to oust the Roman authorities. Pilate tries to pass the buck and asks the Jews whether they want him to release Jesus to them. Pilate could have released Him outright—because He is innocent—and still allowed them to free the guilty Barabbas. But he takes the cowardly way out, proving that to display apathy or indecision in the face of evil, and failing to prevent evil when you can, are themselves evil acts.

While the Jewish leaders certainly schemed to have Jesus crucified by the Roman authorities, it's a horrible injustice that Jews have suffered centuries of persecution due to these events. Jews may have been the active agents, but as others have noted, we are all responsible for Jesus' fate. Jesus, Himself a Jew, died for all people's sins, and it was God's sovereign will for Him to die to enable our salvation. Jesus chose not to summon the Father's angels to rescue Him. He came to earth to die so that we could live. No one should ever use this momentous history—or any other excuse—to justify infernal prejudice against the Jewish people.

CHAPTER 12

FROM THE FLOGGING OF JESUS TO HIS ASCENSION

The angel rolled away the stone from Jesus' tomb, not to let the living Lord out but to let the unconvinced outsiders in.

—D. G. BARNHOUSE[1]

Jesus has forced open a door that had been locked since the death of the first man. He has met, fought and beaten the King of Death. Everything is different because he has done so.

—C. S. LEWIS[2]

JESUS IS MOCKED AND BEATEN (MATT. 27:27–32; MARK 15:16–21; LUKE 23:27–31; JOHN 19:16–17)

Pilate's soldiers strip Jesus of the robe and put His own clothes back on Him. Then they take Him out, bearing His own cross, to a place called the Place of a Skull, which in Aramaic is called Golgotha. Jesus soon grows too weak to carry the cross because of the severe beating He's taken.[3] So the soldiers find a passerby called Simon of Cyrene and force him to carry it. This adds meaning to Jesus' warning to His disciples that "if anyone would come after me, let him deny himself and take up his cross daily and follow me" (Luke 9:23).[4]

Turning to the great multitudes of mourners following Him, Jesus says, "Daughters of Jerusalem, do not weep for me, but weep for yourselves and for your children. For behold the days are coming when they will say, 'Blessed are the barren and the wombs that never bore and the breasts that never nursed.' Then they will begin to say to the mountains, 'Fall on us,' and to the hills, 'Cover us.' For if they do these things when the wood is green, what will happen when it is dry?"

Jesus is predicting the coming judgment of Jerusalem. Even while being judged He's still in control, pronouncing His own judgment on His judges.[5] Robert H. Stein translates Jesus' metaphorical words into plain language: "If God has not spared his innocent Son from such tribulation [by permitting his crucifixion] how much worse will it be for a sinful nation when God unleashes his righteous wrath upon it."[6] The Romans would fulfill this prophecy by destroying Jerusalem and its Temple in 70 AD.

THE CRUCIFIXION (MATT. 27:33–44; MARK 15:22–32; LUKE 23:32–38; JOHN 19:18–27)

When they come to Golgatha Jesus is offered wine mixed with gall, but He tastes it and declines. It's not clear who offers Him the drink but it's probably the Jews, since the drink has a pain-relieving effect, and the Roman tradition is to inflict maximum pain. As Jesus has come to suffer and die, He likely refuses the drink because He doesn't want to alleviate His own pain and because He wants to be in full control of His faculties during His suffering.[7]

At the third hour (9:00 a.m.) they crucify Jesus and the two criminals, one on each side of Him. Many women who've followed Jesus from Galilee—including Mary Magdalene, Mary the mother of James and Joseph, and Salome the mother of Zebedee's sons James and John[8]—look on from a distance. Jesus cries out, "Father, forgive them, for they know not what they do." Instead of feeling sorry for Himself, Jesus displays a spirit of forgiveness, the spirit that led Him to His incarnation in the first place. His statement, "They know not what they do" does not mean they are blameless for their horrendous act, but that they don't understand the magnitude of evil they are perpetrating.[9] As Paul writes, "None of the rulers of this age understood this, for if they had, they would not have crucified the Lord of glory" (1 Cor. 2:8).

One of the criminals mockingly tells Jesus to save Himself. But the other one rebukes him, saying, "Do you not fear God, since you are under the same sentence of condemnation? And we indeed justly, for we are receiving the due reward of our deeds; but this man has done nothing wrong." He then turns to Jesus and says, "Jesus, remember me when you come into your kingdom." Jesus replies, "Truly, I say to you, today you will be with me in paradise."

Does this not demonstrate God's endless capacity for forgiveness and the power of repentance? Does it not destroy the myth that something beyond faith is required for our salvation? "Do not delude yourself with the idea that there is a great deal for you to do and to feel in order to fit yourself for coming to Christ," Charles Spurgeon writes. "All such fitness is nothing but unfitness. All that you can do to make yourself ready for Christ to save you is to make yourself more unready.... This is a faithful saying, and worthy of all acceptation, that Christ Jesus came into the world to save sinners; and to that declaration we may add our Lord's own words, 'he that believeth on him is not condemned.' Oh, that God would give all of you the grace to receive this gracious gospel, whose requirements are so tenderly and so mercifully brought down to your low estate!"[10]

This robber, a duly convicted sinner, doesn't change his ways and doesn't acquire a repentant heart until he's on the cross hours from death. He's unable to offer anything in exchange for his desperate request for forgiveness and life. But all he has to do is believe in Jesus Christ. That he does—and he is saved. Anglican bishop of Liverpool, J. C. Ryle discusses the man's fate:

> If ever there was a soul hovering on the brink of hell, it was the soul of this thief. If ever there was a case that seemed lost, gone, and past recovery, it was his. If ever there was a child of Adam whom the devil made sure of as his own, it was this man....

And then mark what kind of answer he received. Some would have said he was too wicked a man to be saved; but it was not so. Some would have fancied it was too late: the door was shut, and there was no room for mercy; but it proved not too late at all. The Lord Jesus returned him an immediate answer—spoke kindly to him—assured him he should be with Him that day in paradise—pardoned him completely—cleansed him thoroughly from his sins—received him graciously—justified him freely—raised him from the gates of hell—gave him a title to glory. Of all the multitude of saved souls, none ever received so glorious an assurance of his own salvation as did this penitent thief. Go over the whole list, from Genesis to Revelation, and you will find none who had such words spoken to him as these—"Today shalt thou be with Me in paradise." ... Have I not a right to say, By grace ye may be saved through faith, not of works: fear not, only believe? Behold the proof of it. This thief was never baptized: he belonged to no visible Church; he never received the Lord's Supper; he never did any work for Christ; he never gave money to Christ's cause! *But he had faith, and so he was saved.*[11]

Even in His hour of greatest anguish, Jesus is not too weak or distraught to exercise His gracious power of salvation. Few things could be more encouraging to us as sinners than this story, which God placed in Scripture for us to read, savor, and treasure for our own eternal security.

The soldiers divide Jesus' clothes and cast lots for them, in fulfillment of the Old Testament Scripture, "They divided my garments among them, and for my clothing they cast lots" (Psalms 22:18). Jesus' mother, His mother's sister Mary (the wife of Clopas), and Mary Magdalene are near the cross. When Jesus sees His mother and John, "the disciple whom He loved," standing nearby, He says to His mother, "Woman, behold, your son!" Then He says to John, "Behold, your mother!" From that time onward, John would care for her in his own home. It was Jewish tradition that the eldest son would provide for the mother's care when the Husband or father could not, and through this gesture, Jesus is fulfilling His responsibility.[12]

Pilate had placed an inscription on the cross in Aramaic, Latin, and Greek reading, "Jesus of Nazareth, the King of the Jews." The chief priests protested that he should have written instead, "This man said, I am King of the Jews," but Pilate insisted, "What I have written I have written." Many Jews read the inscription because Jesus is crucified near the city. They're mortified that the inscription contradicts the claim for which they're executing Jesus. They could abide a reference to Jesus claiming to be the Messiah, but not that He *is* the Messiah. This beautifully illustrates who's in charge: it's not the Jews, who initiate this process, nor the Romans who carry it out, but God Himself Who has the final word. It was our sovereign God Who superintended Pilate's insistence on leaving the subscription as He had written it[13] because Jesus is, in fact, the King of the Jews, the Messiah in the line of David Whom God promised at the beginning of salvation history as recorded from Genesis forward.

The religious leaders and bystanders deride Jesus, saying, "He saved others; let him save himself, if he is the Christ of God, his Chosen One! Come down from the cross." The soldiers also mock Him, offering Him sour wine and calling out, "If you are the King of the Jews, save yourself!" The irony is staggering. These weak groups of haters are ridiculing Jesus for His supposed inability to save Himself when He, in foregoing His use of divine powers, is making it possible for *them* to be saved. Had He done what they ordered, our salvation and eternal life would have been nipped in the bud. "They consider it a joke," comments William Hendriksen. "Scornfully they exclaim that the way for the crucified One to prove his claim to being the Son of God will be for him to descend from the cross. They imply that it is weakness that keeps him there. Actually, however, it was strength, the strength of his love for sinners. But these bypassers have made up their minds to defy the testimony of all the miracles, all the mercy shown to those in need, all the marvelous discourses, yes, the entire beautiful life of the Son of God on earth. All of this they have rejected. They prefer to jeer, to blaspheme!"[14]

What a beautiful demonstration by Jesus of love for one's enemies—proving once again that He practices what He preaches (Matt. 5:44).

JESUS' DEATH ON THE CROSS (MATT. 27:45–56; MARK 15:33–41; LUKE 23:44–49; JOHN 19:28–37)

There is darkness over all the land from the sixth hour (noon) until the ninth hour (3:00 p.m.), when Jesus cries out, "Eloi, Eloi, lema sabach-thani," which means, "My God, my God, why have you forsaken me?"

In *Jesus on Trial* I noted that in my skeptical days I was puzzled by Jesus asking God why He'd forsaken Him. If He were God, he would know everything the Father knows, so why ask such a question? Years later I came to cherish this verse for affirming rather than undermining my faith. As a stranger to Scripture, I had no inkling of Christ's dual nature—fully human and fully divine—nor was I aware He'd decided to forego the use of certain divine attributes during His incarnation. For "Christ Jesus, who, though he was in the form of God, did not count equality with God a thing to be grasped, but emptied himself, by taking the form of a servant, being born in the likeness of men. And being found in human form, he humbled himself by becoming obedient to the point of death, even death on a cross" (Philip. 2:5–8). Most conservative theologians believe that "emptied Himself" means Jesus left His preincarnate position, took on a servant-humanity, and voluntarily surrendered the use of some of the attributes of deity.[15] In order to effectuate God's salvation plan, Christ became a man while still being fully God.

Of course Christ understood that the Father would have to forsake Him. This too was part of their salvation plan. He became sin for us (2 Cor. 5:21), bore the curse of the Law by becoming a curse for us (Gal. 3:13), received God's wrath for all of mankind's sins, and suffered immeasurably for it both in His human and divine nature. Christ "died forsaken by God," writes J. D. Grassmick, "so that His people might claim God as their God and never be forsaken."[16] The writer of Hebrews attests that with His sacrifice, Jesus ensured we would not be forsaken. "Keep your life free from love of money, and be content with what you have, for he has said, 'I will never leave you nor forsake you.' So we can confidently say, 'The Lord is my helper; I will not fear; what can man do to me'" (Heb. 13:5–6; cf. Joshua 1:5; Psalms 37:25; 2 Cor. 4:9).

What was once a nagging obstacle to my faith became a foundational pillar fortifying it. By becoming fully human at the point of His incarnation, Christ experiences suffering on a far greater scale than we can imagine. In retaining His deity, He suffers incomprehensible separation from the Father. He suffers so intensely on the cross—both physically, in ways we can't begin to fathom,[17] and spiritually—that He asks the Father why He abandoned Him. Of course, He already knows the answer, and He also knows that within hours He'll return to the Father in paradise. His deity doesn't insulate Him from excruciating pain. Having suffered on our behalf, Christ can personally relate to us, and we can relate to Him. Such is the glory of God's plan of redemption.

Knowing He is nearing the end, Jesus says, "I thirst," which yet again fulfills Scripture (Psalms 69:21). A man from the crowd puts a sponge full of the sour wine on a hyssop branch and holds it to his mouth. When Jesus receives it, He says, "It is finished," and He calls out loudly, "Father, into your hands I commit my spirit!" And then He breathes His last breath. The centurion facing Him sees that He has died and declares, "Certainly this man was innocent!" and "Truly this man was the Son of God." The crowds observing the crucifixion return home beating their breasts.

Notice Christ doesn't say, "I am finished," but "It is finished." He doesn't mean His life is finished, but that His redemptive work is complete so that people, through faith in Him, can attain eternal life. As we've said, He was born to die, and at this moment that crucial occasion is seconds away. He has accomplished the saving work He planned to do before creation by paying the penalty for our sins. This is what Christians mean by "the finished work of Christ." His death is the perfect, one-time sacrifice. "For the death he died he died to sin, once for all, but the life he lives he lives to God," writes Paul. "So you also must consider yourselves dead to sin and alive to God in Christ Jesus" (Romans 6:9–10). The writer of Hebrews expresses the same truth: "He has no need, like those high priests, to offer sacrifices daily, first for his own sins and then for those of the people, since he did this once for all when he offered up himself" (7:27; cf. 9:12; 10:10). Christ, in committing His spirit to the Father, underscores that His self-sacrifice is voluntary, as will be His resurrection (John 2:19; 10:17).[18]

When Jesus dies the tombs open. Many bodies of saints are raised, and they go into Jerusalem and appear to many. Moreover, the earth shakes, the rocks are split, and the Temple's curtain is torn from top to bottom. That last event is imbued with spiritual significance. The Temple curtain separates the Holy Place from the Most Holy Place (Heb. 9:2–3). The priests regularly go into the Holy Place to perform their ritual duties, but only the high priest is permitted to enter the Most Holy Place, and just once a year, to offer blood sacrifices for himself and for the people's unintentional sins (Heb. 9:6–8). The tearing of the curtain signifies the removal of this separation between God and the people,[19] and its tearing from top to bottom symbolizes that God is the One ripping it. At the precise moment Christ dies, God tears the curtain to show that access to Him no longer requires a priest, but is now available to everyone. The writer of Hebrews explains,

> Since then we have a great high priest who has passed through the heavens, Jesus, the Son of God, let us hold fast our confession. For we do not have a high priest who is unable to sympathize with our weaknesses, but one who in every respect has been tempted as we are, yet without sin. Let us then with confidence draw near to the throne of grace, that we may receive mercy and find grace to help in time of need (4:14–16).... Therefore, brothers, since we have confidence to enter the holy places by the blood of Jesus, by the new and living way that he opened for us through the curtain, that is, through his flesh, and since we have a great priest over the house of God, let us draw near with a true heart in full assurance of faith, with our hearts sprinkled clean from an evil conscience and our bodies washed with pure water (10:19–22).

The Law requires the body of a hanged man to be buried on the day he dies (Deut. 21:22–23), and bodies are not supposed to remain on the cross on the Sabbath. So the Jews ask Pilate for permission to break the dying men's legs in order to remove the bodies before the Sabbath—this hastened death because it prevented crucifixion victims from pushing themselves up to breathe, leading to asphyxiation. The soldiers break the legs of the two criminals, but they avoid Jesus because they see He's already dead. John, in his Gospel, reports that these events fulfill the Old

Testament prophecies, "Not one of his bones will be broken" (Exodus 12:46; Num. 9:12; Psalms 34:20) and, "They will look on him whom they have pierced" (Zech. 12:10).

Blood and water pour out when one of the soldiers pierces Jesus' side with a spear, proving Jesus is a real human being Who has died a real death. This would later help to dispel the claims of Gnostics, Docetists, and other heretical groups that Jesus was not human but only a spiritual being.[20] Such specious claims would also be discredited by eyewitness testimony that Jesus, in His resurrected body, showed that His hands and side had been pierced (John 20:20).[21]

JESUS' BURIAL (MATT. 27:57–66; MARK 15:42–47; LUKE 23:50–56; JOHN 19:38–42)

Though a respected member of the Sanhedrin, Joseph of Arimathea is a follower of Jesus who opposed His execution.[22] In the evening he goes to ask for Jesus' body from Pilate, who is surprised to learn Jesus has already died. After calling for the centurion to confirm Jesus' death, Pilate grants the corpse to Joseph. It's unusual for a body to be released to anyone other than a relative, but Joseph may be the only person willing and able to bury Jesus.[23] Nicodemus accompanies Joseph, bringing a mixture of myrrh and aloes weighing about seventy-five pounds. Joseph wraps the body in a clean linen shroud and lays it in his new tomb, which he's cut in the rock in a garden where Jesus was crucified. He rolls a great stone against the entrance of the tomb and leaves. Mary Magdalene and Mary the mother of Joses are sitting opposite the tomb, having followed Joseph and Nicodemus to see where His body is laid so they could return later with spices and ointments to anoint Jesus' body.[24]

The next day, the chief priests and the Pharisees gather before Pilate and say, "Sir, we remember how that imposter said, while he was still alive, 'After three days I will rise.' Therefore order the tomb to be made secure until the third day, lest his disciples go and steal him away and tell the people, 'He has risen from the dead,' and the last fraud will be worse than the first." Pilate obligingly grants them soldiers who seal the stone and set a guard.

The religious leaders fear if Jesus' disciples can steal the body, they can invent a resurrection story to legitimize their cult. The allegation that Christ's disciples stole His body, in fact, was one of the main early challenges to the Christian faith, but the theory doesn't hold water. In addition to all the other evidence refuting the claim, it's noteworthy that no early writer—Jew, Greek, or Roman—ever identified a tomb where Jesus' body remained. The Romans and especially the Jews had every motive to produce the body—they desperately wanted to stop the spread of Christianity, and placing guards at the tomb was designed to do just that. So if Jesus didn't rise from the dead, why didn't the Jews simply go to their own tomb (Joseph owned it) and display the body? It would have ended Christianity right there and then. Though there are fanciful theories that Jesus "swooned" rather than died and then recovered in the tomb and left, these have been thoroughly discredited despite modern efforts to revive them.

The details of Christ's burial are an important part of the Gospel message (1 Cor. 15:4). It's beyond the scope of this book to address in-depth the theories challenging the burial and resurrection, but see the exhaustive treatment by Norman Geisler and Frank Turek in *I Don't Have Enough Faith to be an Atheist*.[25] "It's one thing to concoct an alternative theory to the Resurrection," declare Geisler and Turek, "but it's another thing to actually find first-century evidence for it. A theory is not evidence. Reasonable people demand evidence, not just theories."[26] All the alternative resurrection theories are fatally flawed, and strong eyewitness and circumstantial evidence corroborates Jesus' actual bodily resurrection.[27]

THE RESURRECTION (MATT. 28:1–15; MARK 16:1–11; LUKE 24:1–12; JOHN 20:1–23)

Carrying spices they've prepared to anoint Jesus, Mary Magdalene, Mary mother of James, and Salome go to the tomb and discover that the stone has been rolled away. (Matthew reports that an earthquake strikes and an angel descends who rolls away the stone.) When they enter the tomb, they're perplexed that Jesus' body is not there. Two angels appear in "dazzling apparel" (though some of the Gospel accounts say it was one angel).[28] The frightened women bow their faces to the ground as the angels say, "Why do you seek the living among the dead? He is not here, but has risen. Remember how he told you, while he was still in Galilee, that the Son of Man must be delivered into the hands of sinful men and crucified and on the third day rise." And they remember Jesus' words.

The angels instruct the women to go tell Peter and the other disciples that Jesus is going before them to Galilee where they will see Him, just as He had told them. Trembling, they joyously flee from the tomb and tell the disciples, "They have taken the Lord out of the tomb, and we do not know where they have laid him." But the disciples don't believe them. Peter and John run toward the tomb, with John outpacing Peter.[29]

The Gospel of John only mentions Mary Magdalene as going to the tomb. It relates that as soon as she sees that Jesus' body is not there, she runs to tell Peter and John that Jesus' body has been removed and "we do not know where they have laid him." It's possible that Mary, seeing that the tomb was empty, quickly runs away before the angels appear and tells Peter and John about the empty tomb.[30] In that case she would have missed the angels' explanation to the others that Jesus had risen, which would explain why she thinks Jesus' body had been removed.

John, arriving at the tomb first, looks in and sees the linen cloths but does not enter. Then Peter arrives, enters the tomb, and sees the cloths. However, the face cloth that had been on Jesus' head is not lying with the linen cloths but is folded up by itself. Then John goes in, and he sees and believes, even though "as yet they did not understand the Scripture, that he must rise from the dead." The disciples then return to their homes.

At this point, while John believes that no grave robber would have left the scene in this condition (with the face cloth nicely folded and placed separately) and that Jesus must have risen, He still does not fully grasp the theological significance of what he's witnessed. John probably relates this misunderstanding to show that the disciples would not have made up this story to validate the prophecies.[31] This further confirms what we've been saying all along: they are confused about Jesus' mission, even now.

Having apparently followed Peter and John back to the tomb, Mary Magdalene weeps outside it after Peter and John leave. Stooping to look in, she sees two angels in white sitting where Jesus' body had been lain, one where His head had been and the other at the feet. They say to her, "Woman, why are you weeping?" She replies, "They have taken away my Lord, and I do not know where they have laid him." She turns around and sees Jesus but doesn't recognize Him. Jesus asks, "Woman, why are you weeping? Whom are you seeking?" Assuming He's the gardener, she asks Him where he's taken Jesus. He says to her, "Mary" and she turns to Him and cries out, "Teacher!" Jesus says, "Do not cling to me, for I have not yet ascended to the Father; but go to my brothers and say to them, 'I am ascending to my Father and your Father, to my God and your God.'" Mary goes and tells the disciples, "I have seen the Lord," and shares what He told her.

Notice that only two angels appear to Mary, not a multitude, probably because only two are required to bear witness to the word. The angels ask her, as does Jesus later, why she's weeping when she should be joyful, which could be a way of easing her into what she is about to discover. Mary's affection is so deep that she wants to know where His body has been taken so she can move it to a proper place, though she's not strong enough to move it by herself, especially considering the weight of the spices. When she learns she's talking to Jesus she's overcome with joy, but He cautions her not to embrace Him. He's only going to remain on the earth for forty more days before He ascends, and He probably doesn't want to give her the impression he'll be there longer. "He forbids her to dote upon his bodily presence," notes Welsh Minister Matthew Henry, "to set her heart on this, or expect its continuance, and leads her to the spiritual converse and communion which she should have with him after he was ascended to his Father; for the greatest joy of his resurrection was that it was a step towards his ascension.... Mary must not stay to talk with her Master, but must carry his message; for it is a day of good tidings, which she must not engross the comfort of, but hand it to others."[32]

Matthew reports that on their way to the disciples, a group of women who'd been at the tomb encounter Jesus, who says, "Greetings!"[33] And they take hold of His feet and worship Him. Jesus then tells them, "Do not be afraid; go and tell my brothers to go to Galilee, and there they will see me."

After the women leave the tomb, some of the guardsmen go into the city and tell the chief priests all that has occurred. The priests assemble with the elders and pay the soldiers to tell the people Jesus' disciples stole His body at night while they were sleeping. Matthew says the Jews were still spreading this story as he was writing his Gospel. As the truth is often harder to believe than a lie, many embraced the falsehood.[34] But the tale is a clumsy fabrication—how would the soldiers have known what happened if they were asleep? Moreover, sleeping on watch was punishable by death, so it's unlikely the soldiers would have admitted to it barring some conspiracy. Finally, note that this claim implicitly admits the tomb was in fact empty, which is powerful testimony by Christianity's opponents that Jesus rose from the dead.[35]

Admittedly, some of the accounts of the initial resurrection appearances in the various Gospels can be confusing. In the *Apologetics Study Bible*, Ted Cabal explains, "The Gospels record several resurrection appearances that are at once similar and difficult to reconcile with one another. Matthew's account seems the most summarized, whereas the accounts in Luke and John are the most detailed (they appear to use a common source for some of their material). Any relative discrepancies can be accounted for by the different focuses and the necessary summarizing tendencies of all the Gospel writers."[36]

THE EMMAUS ROAD (MARK 16:12–13; LUKE 24:13–32)

Jesus next appears to Peter (Luke 24:33–34; 1 Cor. 15:4–5) and then to two of His disciples who are on their way to the village of Emmaus, about seven miles from Jerusalem. As they're talking about the dramatic events that have just occurred, Jesus appears and starts to walk with them, though they're kept from recognizing Him. He asks what they're discussing. Looking despondent, one of them, named Cleopas, answers, "Are you the only visitor to Jerusalem who does not know the things that have happened there in these days?" When Jesus asks them to explain, they relate to Him the facts about His crucifixion and burial and that His body is missing from the tomb. Jesus declares, "O foolish ones, and slow of heart to believe all that the prophets have spoken! Was it not necessary that the Christ should suffer these things and enter into his glory?" And beginning with Moses and all the prophets, He interprets to them in all the scriptures the things concerning himself.

Later, while Jesus is eating with the disciples, He blesses and breaks the bread and gives it to them. At once their eyes are opened and they recognize Him. He then vanishes from their sight. They say to each other, "Did not our hearts burn within us while he talked to us on the road, while he opened to us the Scriptures?"

This is one of the most remarkable stories of the Bible because the resurrected Christ, the greatest Bible teacher in history, gives the most profound Bible lesson in history to these disciples, walking them through the entirety of the Old Testament and demonstrating how it all points to Him. Even today, many Christians aren't sufficiently aware of the unity of Scripture and how Jesus Christ is the thread running through the Old and New Testaments. Some regard it as a radical, fanciful notion that Jesus is foreshadowed, typified, and prophesied in the Old Testament, yet this is no twenty-first century construct of zealous Christians looking to find Jesus behind every rock. Jesus Himself affirms it in this passage (Luke 24:13–32) and in a similar one a few verses later (Luke 24:44–49). Those who deny it reject Jesus' own testimony. I can't conceive of a more enriching experience than sitting at the Savior's feet listening to Him unfold His presence in God's promise plan throughout the pages of the Old Testament.

When the disciples reflect on their experience, they are beside themselves with joy and wonder. He opened their eyes, and they finally understand everything He has taught them from the beginning. Like nearly all Jews at the time, they expected an entirely different type of Messiah and were devastated when Christ not only didn't lead them to political and military victory, but died a humiliating death. They now understand He came to offer salvation, which is much more sublime—so much so that their hearts are aglow. Now the Old Testament makes sense, now Jesus' teachings make sense, and now His life, death, and resurrection make sense. Now they are immovable believers who will give the remainder of their lives to Him and to spreading the Gospel. This story is so meaningful to me that I wrote the book *The Emmaus Code* to detail the many ways the Old Testament points to Christ, hoping to reconstruct, in some insufficient way, just a glimpse of what Christ might have revealed to these disciples on the Emmaus road.

Charles Spurgeon captures the essence of the event. "Your hearts will burn too," he declares, "and your whole spiritual system will flame and glow if you walk in the company of Jesus. I recommend constant fellowship with God as one of the best remedies for spiritual sloth."[37] Though we didn't walk physically with Jesus during His incarnation, we have both Testaments available to us. The New Testament reveals the entirety of God's redemptive plan, and with both Testaments we have a panoramic view of salvation history. We see Christ throughout the Bible—the Gospels share His person, life, and teachings, and the other New Testament writers explain their significance.

If we want our own Emmaus road experience, we must go to the word ourselves and savor it and absorb it. Spurgeon proclaims, "Oh, to get one verse or perhaps only a few words in it—into your mouth, and keep it there, and roll it under your tongue as a sweet morsel. At first, it tastes like wafers made with honey, and as you press it between the lips of meditation, and turn it over and over on the palate of mental discernment, at last you say, 'How sweet are thy words unto my taste!... So the Word begins to warm your heart.... Your faith, which seemed to be in a swoon, suddenly revives, and gains new vigor. Ah brethren, read the Scriptures diligently, when you are passing through these cold seasons, keep close to the fire of the precious promises and the other divine messages, and you will not be frostbitten. That is one fire."[38] Another fire is equally effective, says Spurgeon—to warm your soul in prayer. These words are no less true today than when Spurgeon preached them over a century ago. If we want our hearts to burn within us for God, we must frequently read and study His word and go to Him in prayer.

JESUS APPEARS TO THE DISCIPLES (MARK 16:14; LUKE 24:36–43; JOHN 20:19–23)

The disciples to whom Jesus appeared on the Emmaus road return to Jerusalem. They find the apostles and others gathered together behind locked doors for fear of the Jews. Referring to Peter by his original name, the duo exclaims to the group, "The Lord has risen indeed, and has appeared to Simon!"[39] Then the two share what happened on the road, and how Christ became known to them when they broke bread. As they are conversing, Jesus appears, stands among them, and says, "Peace to you," and, "As the Father has sent me, even so I am sending you." He breathes on them—reminiscent of God breathing into Adam's nostrils the breath of life (Gen. 2:7)—and says, "Receive the Holy Spirit. If you forgive the sins of any, they are forgiven them; if you withhold forgiveness from any, it is withheld."

His followers are startled and frightened, thinking they have seen a spirit. So Jesus says to them, "Why are you troubled, and why do doubts arise in your hearts? See my hands and my feet, that it is I myself. Touch me, and see. For a spirit does not have flesh and bones as you see that I have." Then He shows them His hands and feet. As they marvel, He says, "Have you anything here to eat?" They give Him a piece of broiled fish, which He eats before them.

This is a lot for the disciples to take in. Before we judge them for their skepticism, we have to honestly consider how we might react to something entirely out of our realm of experience. Jesus wants to prove that He isn't an apparition but a sentient human being who can touch and be touched and can eat. People sometimes so strongly emphasize Christ's deity in the face of doubters that they overlook the equally important reality of His humanity, as we've noted. Jesus shows He is every bit as human as we are. His resurrection was a bodily resurrection as ours will be, as Scripture promises (1 Cor. 15:35–49).

Just as the Father conferred authority on Jesus and sent Him to us, Jesus is empowering the apostles and sending them to spread the Gospel and bring salvation to the world.[40] They are to preach the good news of His atoning sacrifice and that those who believe in Him will be saved and those who don't will be judged.

"MY LORD AND MY GOD" (JOHN 20:24–30)

Thomas, one of the disciples, is not with the others when Jesus comes, so the others tell him afterward they have seen the Lord. Thomas says that unless he sees the nail marks in Jesus' hands, places his finger into them, and places his hand into His side, He will never believe. Eight days later the disciples, including Thomas, are inside again and though the doors are locked, Jesus appears and stands by them, saying "Peace be with you." He then tells Thomas, "Put your finger here, and see my hands; and put out your hand, and place it in my side. Do not disbelieve, but believe." Thomas declares, "My Lord and my God!" Jesus says to him, "Have you believed because you have seen me? Blessed are those who have not seen and yet have believed."

The disciples have been transformed from skeptics into incomplete believers, back to doubters, then to stronger believers, and finally to authentic believers in Jesus Christ. Thomas' experience illustrates the culmination of this evolution. While Thomas holds out as a doubter, He eventually displays His complete faith, saying, "My Lord and my God." According to Beauford Bryant and Mark Krause, "It is among a very small number of places in the New Testament where Jesus is [directly] referred to as 'God.' Thus Thomas, the one accused of unbelief, is radically transformed and becomes a mouthpiece for the highest possible confession of faith in Jesus. In some ways this is the climax of the Book of John."[41]

Indeed, it is "the high point of confession in the Gospel," observes Gerald Borchert. "What it does is bring the Gospel full circle from the Prologue, where it is emphatically said that the 'Word was God' (John 1:1), to this confession, 'My Lord and my God.'"[42] To be sure this is a turning point, for not only does Thomas realize Jesus rose from the dead, but he understands its profound significance. "Mere men do not rise from the dead in this fashion," writes Leon Morris. "The One who was now so obviously alive, although he had died, could be addressed in the language of adoring worship."[43]

Immediately following the story of Thomas' encounter with Jesus, John relates, "Now Jesus did many other signs in the presence of the disciples, which are not written in this book; but these are written so that you may believe that Jesus is the Christ, the Son of God, and that by believing you may have life in his name."

This short paragraph tells us two important things. First, John's main purpose in writing his Gospel is to inspire people to believe in Jesus

Christ so that they may have eternal life by putting their trust in Him. Second, while he could have shared plenty more with us, he has provided more than enough for us to become believers.

Recall Jesus' story about the rich man who died, went to hell in torment, and begged Abraham to warn his five brothers so they wouldn't end up there. Abraham told him that if they didn't hear Moses and the prophets, neither would they be convinced if someone should rise from the dead. The scriptures give us more than enough evidence to believe. We must choose what we do with this information. This is instructive because it reminds us either of our own experiences as doubters, if we had them, or those of others. People will often try to pick the Bible apart, going out of their way to find little discrepancies or problematic areas that reinforce their doubt. But oftentimes doubt is not a matter of the intellect, too little information, troublesome areas of Scripture, or other issues such as the pervasiveness of evil in the world. Sometimes it's simply a matter of the heart, pride, or sin we don't want to forego, and we would do well to communicate this to recalcitrant friends who resist the word. The scriptures are in no way inadequate; they reveal Christ to us plainly if we'll just open our hearts and minds.

A MIRACULOUS CATCH OF FISH; JESUS RECONCILES WITH PETER (JOHN 21:1–25)

Jesus next appears to seven disciples by the Sea of Tiberias: Peter, Thomas, Nathanael of Cana in Galilee, the sons of Zebedee, and two others. Peter announces he's going fishing, and the others join him, but they catch nothing that night. Just as day is breaking, Jesus is standing on the shore, but the disciples don't recognize Him. Jesus says to them, "Children, do you have any fish?" (The term "children" is to convey an intimacy akin to that of a parent for his or her child).[44] They tell Him no, and He says, "Cast the net on the right side of the boat, and you will find some." So they cast it and catch so many fish that they can't haul them in.

John then says to Peter, "It is the Lord!" When Peter hears this he puts on his outer garment and throws himself into the sea. The others come into the boat, dragging the net full of fish. When they get to shore they see bread and a charcoal fire with fish laid out on it. Jesus says, "Bring some of the fish that you have just caught." Peter goes aboard and hauls the net ashore, full of 153 large fish. Nevertheless, the net is not torn. Jesus says, "Come and have breakfast." None of the disciples dare ask who He is, for they already know. Jesus comes and gives the bread and fish to them.

Jesus demonstrates His supernatural powers in supplying abundant fish when His disciples had failed to catch any throughout the night. The specific number of fish—153—adds credence to the story, since fisher-men ordinarily counted their fish before selling them at market.[45] Jesus uses this resurrection appearance and the others to embolden the disci-ples to spread the Gospel message—and the strategy works. The Book of Acts reports Peter saying, "They put him to death by hanging him on a tree, but God raised him on the third day and made him to appear, not to all the people but to us who had been chosen by God as witnesses, who ate and drank with him after he rose from the dead. And he com-manded us to preach to the people and to testify that he is the one appointed by God to be judge of the living and the dead" (10:39–42).

After they eat breakfast, Jesus asks Peter a question about his fellow disciples: "Simon, son of John, do you love me more than these?" Peter replies, "Yes, Lord you know that I love you." Jesus says, "Feed my lambs." Then He asks again, "Simon, son of John, do you love me?" Peter answers, "Yes, Lord; you know that I love you." Jesus asks him a third time, "Do you love me?" Troubled by the repeated questioning, Peter says to Jesus, "Lord you know everything; you know that I love you." Jesus responds, "Feed my sheep. Truly, truly, I say to you, when you were young you used to dress yourself and walk wherever you wanted, but when you are old, you will stretch out your hands, and another will dress you and carry you where you do not want to go." Then Jesus says, "Follow me."

Many commentators believe Jesus asks Peter whether he loves Him more than the other disciples because Peter had said he would never abandon Jesus. In asking Peter three times, Jesus surely intends to give him the opportunity to repent for each of his three betrayals and to demonstrate His abundant forgiveness. Christ doesn't doubt the

genuineness of Peter's love, and He knows He'll be persecuted and crucified for it, which explains Christ's reference to Peter stretching out his
hands and being carried where he doesn't want to go when he's old. By
instructing Peter to follow Him, Jesus means Peter's fate on earth will
be difficult, but by following Jesus he'll reap an eternal reward.

Turning and seeing John following them, Peter says, "Lord, what
about this man?" Jesus replies, "If it is my will that he remain until I
come, what is that to you? You follow me!" Peter shouldn't worry about
John or anyone else but should simply obey and follow Jesus. Whether
or not John lives longer than Peter or faces the same kind of persecution
is no concern of Peter's—that's up to Jesus.

In his Gospel, John says the word spread among the brothers that
John was not to die even though Jesus did not actually say that. John
identifies himself in his Gospel, saying, "This is the disciple who is bearing witness about these things, and who has written these things, and
we know that his testimony is true." John closes his book averring that
he is the author of this Gospel, that he was an eyewitness of all that he
wrote, and we can therefore rely on its historical accuracy. He makes
another reference to the many other things Christ did that he didn't
include in his Gospel because "were every one of them to be written, I
suppose that the world itself could not contain the books that would be
written" (John 21:25). While John may be exaggerating, just consider
the millions of pages written about Christ's life and its unparalleled
significance.

THE GREAT COMMISSION (MATT. 28:16–20; MARK 16:15–18)[46]

The eleven apostles meet Jesus at a mountain in Galilee where He
previously directed them to go. They worship Him, and Jesus tells them,
"All authority in heaven and on earth has been given to me. Go therefore
and make disciples of all nations, baptizing them in the name of the
Father and of the Son and of the Holy Spirit, teaching them to observe
all that I have commanded you. And behold, I am with you always to
the end of the age."

Matthew reports that some of the apostles still doubt Jesus. It's unlikely, however, that any of them really disbelieve at this point that Jesus is the Messiah and the Son of God, for by now they're all believers in the resurrected Christ (John 20:19–28).[47] Some commentators suggest Matthew might be referring to others present besides the eleven. Others propose that some simply might not have recognized Him at first. In any event, if there are any lingering doubts, they're soon dispelled.[48]

R. T. France declares that these last five verses bring most of the themes of Matthew's Gospel to their final resolution. Jesus' disciples, who had previously abandoned Him (Matt. 26:56), are now at His side again in positions of complete trust and authority, ready to embark on the mission for which they'd been called (Matt. 10:1–15). Jesus had prophesied He would return in His glory and now He's done so. His mission to reach His people—the "lost sheep of the house of Israel" (Matt. 10:6; 15:24)—has now been expanded to all nations, as He previously indicated would happen (Matt. 24:14). "And, perhaps most remarkably of all," writes France, "the human Jesus of the hills of Galilee is now to be understood not as the preacher and promoter of the faith, but as himself its object."[49]

The last verse (Matt. 28:20)—"And behold, *I am with you always*, to the end of the age"—gives full meaning to the words proclaimed by the angel of the Lord who appeared to Joseph in a dream: "Do not fear to take Mary as your wife, for that which is conceived in her is from the Holy Spirit. She will bear a son, and you shall call his name Jesus, for he will save his people from their sins." All this took place to fulfill what the Lord had spoken by the prophet: 'Behold, the virgin shall conceive and bear a son, and they shall call his name Immanuel,' (which means, God with us)" (Matt 1:20–23). Earl Radmacher observes, "'I am with you always' demonstrates that Jesus is the true Immanuel, 'God with us.'"[50]

Craig Blomberg likewise argues that these last few verses represent the climax of Matthew's Gospel. Jesus is passing the torch to His disciples, though He promises to continue to be with them spiritually based on authority He is given by the Father. "Jesus can make this claim," writes Blomberg, "only if he is fully God, inasmuch as the whole universe is embraced in the authority delegated to him."[51]

Jesus commands His disciples to "make disciples," which means more than just spreading the Gospel and turning people into believers. It means instructing new Christians on how to follow and submit to Him as Master and Lord and to obey His commands.[52] By making disciples—those fully committed to Jesus—more people will be converted and more evangelists will emerge to spread the word, teach, and train more disciples.

FINAL APPEARANCES AND ASCENSION (1 COR. 15:6–7; MARK 16:19–20; LUKE 24:44–53; ACTS 1:4–11)

Paul reports in his first letter to the Corinthians that Jesus appeared to more than five hundred brothers at one time—most of whom were still alive at the time he wrote his letter—and then appeared to James separately (1 Cor. 15:7). This is powerful evidence for the historicity of this account because Paul was making this bold assertion to people who could have come forward and contradicted him, and he would have had no reason to discredit himself in this way if his story were untrue. Jesus also dramatically appears to Saul (later Paul) on the Damascus Road (Acts 9:1–19; 1 Cor. 15:8).

Jesus gives parting instructions to His apostles, mirroring what He had told the disciples on the Emmaus road. "These are my words that I spoke to you while I was still with you," He says, "that everything written about me in the Law of Moses and the Prophets and the Psalms must be fulfilled." Then He opens their minds to understand the scriptures and declares, "Thus it is written, that the Christ should suffer and on the third day rise from the dead, and that repentance for the forgiveness of sins should be proclaimed in his name to all nations, beginning from Jerusalem. You are witness of these things. And behold, I am sending the promise of my Father upon you. But stay in the city until you are clothed with power from on high."

Leading them out as far as Bethany, He lifts up His hands and blesses them. During this blessing, Jesus is lifted up, and a cloud takes Him out of their sight into heaven, where He sits down at the right hand of God.[53]

As they are gazing into heaven, two men stand by them in white robes and say, "Men of Galilee, why do you stand looking into heaven? This Jesus, who was taken up from you into heaven, will come in the same way as you saw him go into heaven." And they worship Jesus and return to Jerusalem with great joy, and are continually in the Temple blessing God.

This final act punctuates Jesus' divine mission and ignites a fire under the disciples to honor His commission and make disciples of all nations. "So grand and mighty was the revelation of His divine Sonship in His majestic ascension," Norval Geldenhuys writes, "that the disciples spontaneously worshipped Him as Lord and King. To His disciples His ascension in divine glory was the final proof that He was truly the Christ, the Son of God, and that He as the Almighty was able to fulfill His promises. In addition, the angel (Acts 1:11) once more gave the joyful assurance that...He would return in person, not in order to suffer once again, but to bring the sovereign dominion of God to complete and everlasting realization, and to establish His heavenly kingdom in perfection."[54]

Though Jesus leaves His disciples to sit at the right hand of God, His work is just beginning—His apostles and disciples, through the power of the Holy Spirit, will establish the Church and spread the Gospel to the ends of the earth. The exciting history of the inauguration and early development of the Church—from Jerusalem to Rome—is recorded in the Book of Acts, to which we shall turn in my next book, *Founding: Jesus and the Christian Church from Acts to Revelation.*

CONCLUSION

I n the introduction I explained that this book is not a polemic. It's not primarily a book on Christian apologetics, though I do address certain challenges to the reliability and accuracy of the New Testament. I also expressed my conviction that the Bible is its own apologetic because if one reads it with an open heart he will ultimately see that it's inspired—that it truly is the Word of God and that Jesus is the Son of God. Along these lines, John Piper describes how Scripture is "self-authenticating;"

> It would seem strange if God revealed himself in his Son Jesus Christ and inspired the record of that revelation in the Bible, but did not provide a way for ordinary people to know it. Stated most simply, the common path to sure knowledge of

the real Jesus is this: Jesus, as he is revealed in the Bible, has a glory—an excellence, a spiritual beauty—that can be seen as self-evidently true. It is like seeing the sun and knowing that it is light and not dark, or like tasting honey and knowing that it is sweet and not sour. There is no long chain of reasoning from premises to conclusions. There is a direct apprehension that this person is true and his glory is the glory of God.[1]

In these pages I have sought to introduce you to the true Jesus of the Gospels. Like no other books of Scripture, the Gospels take us into the life of Jesus where we see His teachings and His actions as if we are eyewitnesses. The epistles interpret these messages and their theological significance, but the Gospels present Jesus speaking for Himself and interacting with His disciples, the religious authorities, and others. In fact, when we read the Gospels we're more than eyewitnesses—we are in a sense a part of the story, and we're in Jesus' presence because His message applies to us as well. We're not simply reading about Him—we're virtually walking with Him and sitting at His feet. The Gospel, explains Lynn Cohick, "invites us to enter into, to walk alongside, to get our own feet dusty as the story unfolds. It connects...Jesus' teachings and Jesus' deeds, and it invites us to come along."[2]

The Gospels alone transport us to Jesus' world and reveal His distinctiveness. No other human being in history compares to Him in any important way—He is manifestly God in the flesh. This conclusion is unavoidable if you read the Gospels because they give us the real Jesus. Christianity is all about Jesus Himself, not just His teachings and wondrous acts. It is grounded in His *person*. Jesus does infinitely more than teach moral lessons. He *is* the message. "It must be obvious to any thoughtful reader of the Gospels," writes Kenneth Scott Latourette, "that Jesus regarded himself and *his* message as inseparable.... If you take away the things Jesus said about himself, directly or indirectly, his teaching loses virtually all of its impact."[3]

Yes, when you read the Gospels, you will know Jesus is the Son of God because His divine reality jumps off the pages in a way that's difficult to describe. This isn't a cop-out; Christianity's truth claims stand up to rigorous scrutiny, but that's an entirely separate point. No mere human writer could have fabricated such a being, and if you immerse yourselves in these writings, putting your cynicism aside, you too will recognize you are reading about God's only Son—and if you open your mind you will come to know Him. Please take the time to read the Gospels from beginning to end and see if you come away with a greater appreciation for His uniqueness, His deity, His humanity, and His glory.

Again, Piper poignantly expresses the point: "I do not ask you to pray for a special whisper from God to decide if Jesus is real. Rather I ask you to look at the Jesus of the Bible. Look at him. Don't close your eyes and hope for a word of confirmation. Keep your eyes open and fill them with the full portrait of Jesus provided in the Bible."[4]

Does any great figure in history or fiction possess a fraction of His qualities—this curious mixture of paradoxical attributes—what Jonathan Edwards calls "an admirable conjunction of diverse excellencies"?[5] Is there a single idealized historical or fictional figure who is portrayed as supremely powerful yet incomparably humble? As morally exacting but merciful? As equal with God—the exact imprint of His nature—yet perfectly obedient to the Father? As divine and yet utterly human? As unfathomably complex, but simply and intimately personal?[6] Indeed, Jesus is described in Scripture as both a lion and a lamb,[7] and He demonstrates the qualities of each.

As we've seen, Jesus' diverse qualities are tied to His diverse callings—even in the unfolding of both aspects of the kingdom of God. In His incarnation He ushered in the kingdom, but this aspect of it was altogether unconventional. During His life on earth He had no physical kingdom. He had no standing armies. He conquered no territory. He had no castle. He didn't even have a place He could call home. He died a humiliating death, but in so doing, He conquered Satan, sin, and death itself, and on His return He will establish a permanent kingdom where He will be sovereign in every respect—not just in our hearts.

It's true that the intertestamental Jews did not anticipate that their Messiah would first be a Suffering Servant. But it's also highly doubtful that the human mind could have ever conceived of a figure with such "diverse excellencies," or of a salvation plan in which the God of the universe would become a human being and die for our sins. At first blush it seems so strange, but with years of reflection and meditation, I have come to believe it's the best, and probably the only, possible salvation scheme to reconcile and satisfy God's perfect justice and His infinite love, grace, and mercy. Perhaps, in his infinite wisdom, God could have devised another salvation plan to accomplish those purposes, but two things are clear: if another plan could have avoided the suffering of His Son, surely He would have chosen it; and He chose to send His Son, and faith in Him is *the only way* to salvation.

As you read through the Gospels, I respectfully urge you not only to open yourself up to Christ revealing Himself as God in the flesh, but also to be mindful of how Jesus completes the story of the Bible beginning in Genesis and how He consummates salvation history. The New Testament reveals Christ as the fulfillment of the hopes and promises of the Old Testament Law and the prophets.[8] "All the promises of God find their Yes in him. That is why it is through him that we utter our Amen to God for his glory" (2 Cor. 1:20).

In one sense Jesus changed nothing; in another He changed everything. His incarnation, life, and death were planned and promised from the beginning. Nothing in the course of history changed His divine mission. But as part of that mission He fulfilled all the Old Testament promises and prophecies, and He brought to fruition God's promise to Abraham that He'd make a nation out of him through which He'd bless all nations. Yes, He changes everything for those who believe in Him. The Bible is a miraculous work of unity because it is God's revelation of His perfectly unified salvation plan for human beings He created in His image. Jesus is the perfect answer for every question raised in the Old Testament. He is the perfect fulfillment of every prophecy recorded in the Old Testament. He is the perfect Servant and King, and He is our perfect salvation, if we will just trust in Him.

Finally, Christ's offer of salvation is not exclusive, but the path He offers to salvation is. *He* is the exclusive path. Therefore, no one in the end can remain neutral. If you don't decide to trust Him, then you have made your decision. It may be hard to contemplate a change in lifestyle or to accept truths that popular culture rejects and ridicules. Like Adam, however, we are all sinners and we all will die. There is no escaping it. As such, we all need forgiveness—no matter how much our pride might impede our clarity and our willingness to come to terms with this.

But there is a remedy for hopelessness—the resurrection of Jesus Christ, which makes possible our own resurrection. "Blessed be the God and Father of our Lord Jesus Christ! According to his great mercy, he has caused us to be born again to a living hope through the resurrection of Jesus from the dead, to an inheritance that is imperishable, undefiled, and unfading" (1 Peter 1:3–4). As Paul writes, "We do not want you to be uninformed, brothers, about those who are asleep, that you may not grieve as others do who have no hope. For since we believe that Jesus died and rose again, even so, through Jesus, God will bring with him those who have fallen asleep" (1 Thess. 4:13).

Remember always that Jesus' resurrection was an actual historical event, and it means everything for us. Because He lives, those who trust in Him will also be resurrected to eternal life. Christ's resurrection leads to our resurrection and our eternal communion with the Lord.[9] "But in fact Christ has been raised from the dead, the firstfruits of those who have fallen asleep. For as by a man came death, by a man has come also the resurrection of the dead. For as in Adam all die, so also in Christ shall all be made alive" (1 Cor. 15:20–22). "As sin reigned in death, grace also might reign through righteousness leading to eternal life through Jesus Christ our Lord" (Romans 5:21).

Let's return to Jesus' vital question: "Who do you say that I am?" He asks us not as a group but individually. And so, who do *you* say He is? I say He's the living Son of God who has died for my sins so that through faith in Him I can have eternal life. How about you? If you are not yet sure—and even if you are—I ask you again to read the Gospels and see the glory of Jesus unfold before your eyes. In one of his revival addresses, American evangelist R. A. Torrey puts this message to his listeners quite bluntly:

Men and women, Christ is a Saviour. God offers Him to you; you take Him and it is done. Feeling or no feeling, will you take Him tonight?

No one has a good reason for not coming to Christ. There are a thousand reasons why you ought to come. Every year that you have lived has brought you one year nearer to eternity, and is a reason for coming to Christ tonight; every year that you have still to live and that might be a year of service is a reason for coming to Christ tonight. Every saved friend you have is a reason for coming to Christ tonight, that you may spend eternity with him in Heaven. Every unsaved friend that you have is a reason why you should come to Christ tonight, that you may bring him with you. Every thorn in the Savior's crown, every nail in the Savior's hands and feet, every stroke laid upon the Savior's back, when He was wounded for your transgressions and bruised for your iniquities, and the chastisement of your peace was laid upon Him, is a reason for accepting Christ tonight. Will you do it? Oh, there is an awful risk in delay.[10]

The same point comes across in this short anecdote:

Once I heard this story concerning King Edward VII of England. He and his queen were out walking late one afternoon when suddenly she stumbled and sprained an ankle. In great pain, and with considerable difficulty, she limped along, holding to her husband's shoulder. At dusk, they approached the home of a humble man. The king knocked on the door. "Who's there?" came the query.

"It is Edward. It is the king. Let me in."

The man on the inside shouted back, "Enough of your pranks now. Be off...."

The king, not being accustomed to such language, was shocked. He hardly knew what to do, but he knocked a second time. The cottager inquired, "What do you want?"

"I tell you it is the king! It is Edward, your king. Let me in."

In anger the man shouted, "I'll teach you to torment an honest man trying to get his sleep." He threw open the door in disgust, only to see that indeed it was his king! With profuse apologies the laborer invited the royal visitors in and sent for help to attend his queen.

Years later, when the Britisher was too old to work, he would spend much time rocking on the porch and visiting with neighbors. He took great delight in reviewing that experience, always concluding with the same words: "And to think, to think, I almost didn't let him in! To think I almost didn't let him in!"

"Behold, I stand at the door and knock; if any one hears my voice and opens the door, I will come in to him and eat with him, and he with me" (Rev. 3:20).

Not until you open your heart and let Jesus in will you know what God is like.[11]

Indeed, He is knocking at your door and I pray that you let Him in, for God wants all people to be saved and to come to the knowledge of the truth (1 Tim. 2:1). He wants no one to perish (2 Peter 3:9). Everyone who believes in Jesus Christ will be saved (John 3:16; Romans 10:9–10).

Are you still waiting? Wait no more.

ACKNOWLEDGMENTS

As always, a sincere thank you to Regnery Publishing and everyone there who worked on this project, from editors to designers to the marketing and sales team. Many thanks to Marji Ross for her steadfast support, encouragement, openness to new book ideas, and flexibility and cooperation throughout the process. From the beginning, Harry Crocker has been a rock and a loyal friend whose wisdom and guidance have been invaluable. No one in the writing and publishing business is harder working or more talented. Again, Maria Ruhl was extraordinarily proficient in copy editing and proofing the manuscript, always made the extra effort to accept changes throughout the process, and made herself accessible despite the constant pressure her position entails.

I feel repetitive complimenting Jack Langer, who is uniquely gifted in all aspects of writing and editing. He conscientiously reads and rereads—again and again. He tightens, clarifies, polishes, and sometimes even restructures certain portions of the text, and he challenges me to rework certain paragraphs or sentences when he thinks they might confuse the reader. My writing has improved so much over the years just watching him work with my manuscripts. As I've mentioned before, he does magic without ever insinuating himself into the text. It's never about ego with him; it's never about advocating his own point or ideas. It's only about trying to help me better express the ideas I am trying to convey, and he has a knack for making suggestions that neither alter the meaning nor my voice. He is one of the hardest workers I've ever encountered. On more than one occasion we were trading emails and calls significantly past midnight my time in Missouri, and he is in D.C. I hope that he will continue to edit my books as long as I continue to write them.

Sincere thanks to my longtime friend Greg Mueller and his team at Creative Response Concepts for quarterbacking the promotion and marketing of this book along with the excellent marketing staff at Regnery. Thanks again to Greg for first recruiting me as a Regnery author, which has been life-changing for me. Greg's reliable judgment and support are very important to me.

My wife Lisa, my best friend and mother of our five children, was patient and prayerful during the early years that I would come to faith in Christ, and her confidence and persistence finally paid off. Her support throughout is impossible to adequately express.

My friend Frank Turek read this book as he did *Jesus on Trial* and *The Emmaus Code*, vetting it for theological accuracy and making many helpful suggestions. Frank is always solid and if he doesn't know the answer—which is rare—he'll admit it and push me in the right direction to find it. I am proud to be a board member of his organization, CrossExamined.org, which is doing amazing apologetics work on our college campuses, combating the secular message that dominates America's universities.

My longtime friend Sean Hannity has always been supportive of all my books and other professional endeavors. Sean remains a humble, kind, and generous man despite his celebrity and phenomenal success. I am proud to call him my very close friend and am eternally appreciative of his encouragement.

Mark Levin is a very close friend whose loyalty exceeds anything any friend would ever deserve. As usual, he has been extremely supportive of this project for which I am grateful.

Again, special thanks and gratitude to my brother Rush for inspiring me, for opening up doors for me directly and indirectly, and for doing wonderful work for this nation we both love from the bottom of our hearts. He has always supported me and my career pursuits, unfailingly encouraging and cheering me on. I am blessed and grateful to have such a generous, caring, and thoughtful brother, who makes a difference every day in working to keep this nation true to its founding principles. He doesn't get nearly the credit he deserves and takes way more heat than anyone should have to endure.

Most of all, I am grateful to God for pursuing me until He captured me and opening my eyes and heart to the Truth and to the reality of His love. I must confess that I am blessed to have been born in a wonderful family in the greatest nation in the history of the world.

NOTES

INTRODUCTION

1. Graeme Goldsworthy, *Preaching the Whole Bible as Christian Scripture* (Grand Rapids, MI: William B. Eerdman's Publishing Company, 2000), 5, 19.
2. Mark Dever, & John F. MacArthur Jr., *The Message of the New Testament: Promises Kept* (Wheaton, IL: Crossway Books, 2005).
3. John Piper, *Seeing and Savoring Jesus Christ* (Wheaton, IL: Crossway Books, 2004), 9.
4. John MacArthur Jr., "Jesus Plus Nothing Equals Everything," *John MacArthur Sermon Archive* (Panorama City, CA: Grace to You, 2004).
5. Faithlife Staff, *Rediscover the Original Jesus*, Faithlife Today, August 8, 2016, https://today.faithlife.com/2016/08/11/rediscover-the-original-jesus/?utm_medium=feed&utm_source=feedpress.me&utm_campaign=Feed%3A+faithlife-today-6.

CHAPTER 1: THE OVERLOOKED ERA: LIFE BETWEEN THE OLD AND NEW TESTAMENTS

1. I. L. Jensen, *Jensen's Survey of t: he Old Testament: Search and Discover* (Chicago: Moody Press, 1978), 471–72.
2. Thomas D. Lea and David Alan Black, *The New Testament: Its Background and Message*, 2nd ed. (Nashville, TN: Broadman & Holman Publishers 2003), 8.
3. Craig A. Evans, *NT311 The World of Jesus and the Gospels* (Bellingham, WA: Lexham Press, 2014), segment 1.
4. Mark L. Strauss, *Four Portraits, One Jesus: A Survey of Jesus and the Gospels* (Grand Rapids, MI: Zondervan, 2007), 94; Joel Willitts, *NT202 A Survey of Jewish History and Literature from the Second Temple Period* (Bellingham, WA: Lexham Press, 2015), segment 1.
5. Richard L. Pratt Jr., *1 and 2 Chronicles: A Mentor Commentary* (Fearn, Tain, Ross-shire, Great Britain: Mentor, 2006), 11.
6. R. K. Harrison, "Canon of the OT," in G. W. Bromiley, ed., *The International Standard Bible Encyclopedia, Revised* (Wm. B. Eerdmans), vol. 1, 598.
7. Josephus wrote that since Artaxerxes' age the succession of prophets had ceased. Harrison, "Canon of the OT," in Bromiley, ed., *The International Standard Bible Encyclopedia*, vol. 1, 598.
8. Paul N. Benware, *Survey of the New Testament (Revised)* (Chicago: Moody Press, 1990), 22.
9. Paul J. Achtemeier, Harper & Row and Society of Biblical Literature, in *Harper's Bible Dictionary*, 1st ed. (San Francisco: Harper & Row, 1985), 219. The apocrypha—a word derived from the Greek word for "hidden"—is a collection of books that are rejected as non-canonical by Protestants but most of them—referred to as the deuterocanonical books—are accepted by the Roman Catholics as part of the Old Testament Canon. Craig L. Blomberg. *Jesus and the Gospels: An Introduction and Survey* (Nashville, TN: Broadman & Holman Publishers, 1997), 8.
10. Robert A. Morey, *The Trinity: Evidence and Issues* (Iowa Falls, IA: World Pub, 1996), 230.

11. J. Sidlow Baxter, *Explore the Book* (Grand Rapids, MI: Academie Books, Zondervan Publishing House, 1960), vol. 5, 12.

12. Pratt Jr., *1 and 2 Chronicles*, 11.

13. Baxter, *Explore the Book*, vol. 5, 11.

14. Blomberg, *Jesus and the Gospels*, 8.

15. John F. MacArthur Jr., ed., *The MacArthur Study Bible*, electronic ed. (Nashville, TN: Word Pub, 1997), 1,369.

16. Ronald F. Youngblood, F. F. Bruce, and R. K. Harrison, Thomas Nelson Publishers, eds., in *Nelson's New Illustrated Bible Dictionary* (Nashville, TN: Thomas Nelson, Inc., 1995).

17. L. K. Crocker, "Temple, Solomon's," in J. D. Barry et al., eds., *The Lexham Bible Dictionary* (Bellingham, WA: Lexham Press, 2016); Strauss, *Four Portraits*, 94.

18. Elmer Towns and Ben Gutierrez, *The Essence of the New Testament* (Nashville: B&H, 2012).

19. John A. Martin, "Ezra," in J. F. Walvoord and R. B. Zuck, eds., *The Bible Knowledge Commentary: An Exposition of the Scriptures* (Wheaton, IL: Victor Books, 1985), vol. 1, 660.

20. H. W. Hoehner, "Between the Testaments," in F. E. Gaebelein, ed., *The Expositor's Bible Commentary: Introductory Articles* (Grand Rapids, MI: Zondervan Publishing House, 1979), vol. 1, 179; Baxter, *Explore the Book*, vol. 5, 13.

21. Earl D. Radmacher et al., *Nelson's New Illustrated Bible Commentary* (Nashville: T. Nelson Publishers, 2009).

22. MacArthur Jr., ed., *The MacArthur Study Bible*, 1,369.

23. Ibid., 1,369.

24. David S. Dockery et al. and Holman Bible Publishers, *Holman Bible Handbook* (Nashville, TN: Holman Bible Publishers, 1992), 505.

25. Blomberg, *Jesus and the Gospels*, 13.

26. Benware, *Survey of the New Testament*, 24.

27. Henry Hampton Halley, *Halley's Bible Handbook with the New International Version*, completely rev. and expanded (Grand Rapids, MI: Zondervan Publishing House, 2000), 508.

28. Benware, *Survey of the New Testament*, 24.

29. Crossway Bibles, *The ESV Study Bible* (Wheaton, IL: Crossway Bibles, 2008), 1,783.

30. Strauss, *Four Portraits*, 98, 100; Benware, *Survey of the New Testament*, 24.

31. D. F. Payne, "Jerusalem," in D. R. W. Wood et al., eds., *New Bible Dictionary*, 3rd ed. (Leicester, England; Downers Grove, IL: InterVarsity Press, 1996), 560.

32. R. A. Batey, "Jerusalem," in Craig A. Evans and Stanley E. Porter, eds., *Dictionary of New Testament Background: A Compendium of Contemporary Biblical Scholarship*, electronic ed. (Downers Grove, IL: InterVarsity Press, 2000), 560.

33. Hoehner, "Between the Testaments," in Gaebelein, ed., *The Expositor's Bible Commentary*, vol. 1, 184.

34. Batey, "Jerusalem," in Evans and Porter, eds., *Dictionary of New Testament Background*, 560.

35. Towns and Gutierrez, *The Essence of the New Testament*.

36. Hoehner, "Between the Testaments," in Gaebelein, ed., *The Expositor's Bible Commentary*, vol. 1, 184; R. C. Kashow, "Judas Maccabeus," in Barry et al., eds., *The Lexham Bible Dictionary*.

37. Batey, "Jerusalem," in Evans and Porter, eds., *Dictionary of New Testament Background*, 560.

38. J. Kampen, "Judas Maccabeus," in D. N. Freedman, A. C. Myers, and A. B. Beck, eds., *Eerdmans Dictionary of the Bible* (Grand Rapids, MI: W.B. Eerdmans, 2000).

39. D. P. Fuller, "Satan," in G. W. Bromiley, ed., *The International Standard Bible Encyclopedia, Revised* (Wm. B. Eerdmans, 1979–1988), vol. 4, 341; Craig G. Bartholomew and Michael W. Goheen, *The Drama of Scripture: Finding Our Place in the Biblical Story* (Grand Rapids, MI: Baker Academic, 2004), 121.

40. Bartholomew and Goheen, *The Drama of Scripture*, 122.

41. Kampen, "Judas Maccabeus," in Freedman, Myers, and Beck, eds., *Eerdmans Dictionary of the Bible*.

42. Batey, "Jerusalem," in Evans and Porter, eds., *Dictionary of New Testament Background*, 560.

43. Gary M. Burge, *The New Testament in Antiquity* (Grand Rapids, MI: Zondervan, 2009), 19.

44. Crossway Bibles, *The ESV Study Bible*, 1,784.

45. Strauss, *Four Portraits*, 105.

46. Dockery et al. and Holman Bible Publishers, *Holman Bible Handbook*, 513.

47. Walter A. Elwell and B. J. Beitzel, in *Baker Encyclopedia of the Bible* (Grand Rapids, MI: Baker Book House, 1988), 1,065.

48. Paul J. Achtemeier, Harper & Row, and Society of Biblical Literature, in *Harper's Bible Dictionary*, 1st ed. (San Francisco: Harper & Row, 1985), 1,028.

49. M. H. Gracey, "Herodian Army," in D. N. Freedman, ed., *The Anchor Yale Bible Dictionary* (New York: Doubleday, 1992), vol. 3, 172, and Dockery et al. and Holman Bible Publishers, *Holman Bible Handbook*, 513.

50. Charles Caldwell Ryrie, *Ryrie Study Bible: New International Version*, expanded ed. (Chicago: Moody Publishers, 1994), 1,430–31.

51. Crossway Bibles, *The ESV Study Bible*, 1,784.

52. Alfred A. Plummer, *A Critical and Exegetical Commentary on the Gospel According to St. Luke* (London: T&T Clark International, 1896), 440.

53. Crossway Bibles, *The ESV Study Bible*, 1784.

54. S. W. Lemke, "Hellenism," in C. Brand et al., eds., *Holman Illustrated Bible Dictionary* (Nashville, TN: Holman Bible Publishers. 2003), 746. Another philosophy at the time was Pythagoreanism, which was founded in southern Italy in the latter half of the sixth century BC by Pythagoras, a devotee of Apollo. If he produced any writings, none survived, but poets, philosophers, and historians say that he believed in metempsychosis—the transmigration of the soul. He thought the soul was a fallen divinity that was imprisoned in the body and condemned to a cycle of reincarnation. Only followers of Apollo had any chance of escaping. He also believed in interpreting the world through numbers. N. C. Croy, "Neo-Pythagoreanism," in C. A. Evans and S. E. Porter, eds., *Dictionary of New Testament Background: A Compendium of Contemporary Biblical Scholarship*, electronic ed. (Downers Grove, IL: InterVarsity Press, 2000), 739.

55. Ibid.

56. Lea and Black, *The New Testament*, 54.

57. N. C. Croy, "Epicureanism," in Evans and Porter, eds., *Dictionary of New Testament Background*, 324.

58. Ibid., 326.

59. Lea and Black, *The New Testament*, 54.

60. Archibald T. Robertson, *Word Pictures in the New Testament* (Nashville, TN: Broadman Press, 1933), and Croy, "Epicureanism," in Evans and Porter, eds., *Dictionary of New Testament Background*, 326.

61. Walter E. Elwell, in *Evangelical Dictionary of Theology: Second Edition* (Grand Rapids, MI: Baker Academic, 2001), 887.

62. J. C. Thom, "Stoicism," in Evans and Porter, eds., *Dictionary of New Testament Background*, 1,139–40; Lea and Black, *The New Testament*, 54.

63. H. B. Alexander et al., "Ethics and Morality," in J. Hastings, J. A. Selbie, and L. H. Gray, eds., *Encyclopedia of Religion and Ethics* (Edinburgh; New York: T. & T. Clark; Charles Scribner's Sons, 1908–1926), vol. 5, 490.

64. Andreas Graeser, "Greek Philosophy," in *The Encyclopedia of Christianity* (Grand Rapids, MI; Leiden, Netherlands: Wm. B. Eerdmans; Brill, 1999–2003), vol. 2, 467.

65. "Mercurius," in Brand et al., eds., *Holman Illustrated Bible Dictionary*, 1,105.

66. Harold L. Willmington, *Willmington's Book of Bible Lists* (Wheaton, IL: Tyndale, 1987), 154.

67. Benware, *Survey of the New Testament*, 29.

68. Ibid.

69. Ibid., 30.

70. Craig S. Keener, *The IVP Bible Background Commentary: New Testament* (Downers Grove, IL: InterVarsity Press, 1993).

71. Christopher Catherwood, *Church History: A Crash Course for the Curious* (Wheaton, IL: Crossway, 2007).

72. Youngblood, Bruce, and Harrison, Thomas Nelson Publishers, eds., in *Nelson's New Illustrated Bible Dictionary*.

73. Josh McDowell and Sean McDowell, *The Unshakable Truth, How You Can Experience the 12 Essentials of a Relevant Faith* (Eugene, OR: Harvest House, 2010).

74. Walter A. Elwell and Philip W. Comfort, in *Tyndale Bible Dictionary* (Wheaton, IL: Tyndale House Publishers, 2001), 430.

75. Benware, *Survey of the New Testament*, 32–33.

76. Elwell and Beitzel, in *Baker Encyclopedia of the Bible*, 719.

77. Evans, *NT311 The World of Jesus*; Benware, *Survey of the New Testament*, 32–41.

78. N. T. Wright, *The New Testament and the People of God* (London: Society for Promoting Christian Knowledge, 1992), 209.

79. Ibid., 210.

80. Evans, *NT311 The World of Jesus*.

81. Wright, *The New Testament and the People of God*, 210–11.

82. Robert Gromacki, *New Testament Survey* (Grand Rapids, MI: Baker Academic, 1974), 31.

83. Benware, *Survey of the New Testament*, 40–41.

84. Gromacki, *New Testament Survey*, 30–31.

85. M. G. Easton, in *Easton's Bible Dictionary* (New York: Harper & Brothers, 1893).

86. Gary M. Burge, *The New Testament in Antiquity* (Grand Rapids, MI: Zondervan, 2009), 70.

87. Benware, *Survey of the New Testament*, 38.

88. Burge, *The New Testament in Antiquity*, 70.

89. J. Julius Scott Jr., *Jewish Backgrounds of the New Testament* (Grand Rapids, MI: Baker Academic, 2000), 202.

90. MacArthur Jr., ed., *The MacArthur Study Bible*, 1,371.

91. Everett Ferguson, *Backgrounds of Early Christianity*, 3rd ed. (Grand Rapids, MI; Cambridge, UK: William B. Eerdmans Publishing Company, 2003), 514; Elwell and Beitzel, in *Baker Encyclopedia of the Bible*, 719.

92. Wright, *The New Testament and the People of God*, 182.

93. Burge, *The New Testament in Antiquity*, 63.

94. Blomberg, *Jesus and the Gospels*, 47.

95. Flavius Josephus, *The Works of Josephus: Complete and Unabridged*, William Whiston, trans. (Peabody: Hendrickson, 1987), Wars of the Jews, 1.2.

96. Scott Jr., *Jewish Backgrounds of the New Testament*, 203.

97. Lea and Black, *The New Testament*, 57–58.

98. Ryrie, *Ryrie Study Bible*, 1,431.

99. Josephus, *The Works of Josephus*, Whiston, trans., Antiquities, 18.1.4.

100. Benware, *Survey of the New Testament*, 36.

101. Ferguson, *Backgrounds of Early Christianity*, 520.

102. Benware, *Survey of the New Testament*, 36.

103. Easton, in *Easton's Bible Dictionary*. Some speculate that they may have been referred to in Matt. 19:11, 12, Col. 2:8, 18, 23.

104. F. C. Conybeare, "Essenes," in J. Hastings et al., eds., *A Dictionary of the Bible: Dealing with Its Language, Literature, and Contents Including the Biblical Theology* (New York; Edinburgh: Charles Scribner's Sons; T. & T. Clark, 1911–1912), vol. 1, 768.

105. F. L. Cross and E. A. Livingstone, eds., in *The Oxford Dictionary of the Christian Church*, 3rd ed. rev. (Oxford; New York: Oxford University Press, 2005), 565.

106. E. M. Cook, "Dead Sea Scrolls, Nonbiblical," in Barry et al., eds., *The Lexham Bible Dictionary*.

107. A. Schofield, "Dead Sea Scrolls, Biblical," in Barry et al., eds., *The Lexham Bible Dictionary*.

108. Lea and Black, *The New Testament*, 58; Benware, *Survey of the New Testament*, 36–37.

109. Craig S. Keener et al., *NT146 The Arrival of Christ and His Kingdom* (Bellingham, WA: Lexham Press, 2016).

110. Ryrie, *Ryrie Study Bible*, 1,431.

111. W. H. Franzmann, *Bible History Commentary: New Testament*, electronic ed. (Milwaukee, WI: WELS Board for Parish Education, 1998).

112. Mark Allan Powell, *Introducing the New Testament: A Historical, Literary, and Theological Survey* (Grand Rapids, MI: Baker Academic, 2009), 21–22.

113. Benware, *Survey of the New Testament*, 35.

114. Scott Jr., *Jewish Backgrounds of the New Testament*, 234.

115. Wright, *The New Testament and the People of God*, 213–14.

116. Scott Jr., *Jewish Backgrounds of the New Testament*, 235.

117. Ibid., 139.

118. Bartholomew and Goheen, *The Drama of Scripture*, 114.

119. Wright, *The New Testament and the People of God*, 157.

120. Scott Jr. *Jewish Backgrounds of the New Testament*, 267.

121. Blomberg, *Jesus and the Gospels*, 9.

122. Scott Jr., *Jewish Backgrounds of the New Testament*, 267.

123. Bartholomew and Goheen, *The Drama of Scripture*, 119.

124. Scott Jr., *Jewish Backgrounds of the New Testament*, 267.

125. Bartholomew and Goheen, *The Drama of Scripture*, 114–15.

126. Ibid., 115–16.

127. George Eldon Ladd, *I Believe in the Resurrection of Jesus* (Grand Rapids: William B. Eerdmans Publishing Company, 1975), 62.

128. Bartholomew and Goheen, *The Drama of Scripture*, 123.

129. Ibid., 124.

130. Towns and Gutierrez, *The Essence of the New Testament*.

131. Bartholomew and Goheen, *The Drama of Scripture*, 124.

132. F. F. Bruce, *New Testament History* (New York: Doubleday, 1969), 133.

133. Michael Heiser, "Why Didn't the Israelites Know Jesus Was the Messiah?" Faithlife Videos, August 24, 2016, https://today.faithlife.com/2016/08/24/why-didnt-the-israelites-know-jesus-was-the-messiah/?utm_medium=feed&utm_source=feedpress.me&utm_campaign=Feed%3A+faithlife-today-6.

134. George Eldon Ladd, *I Believe in the Resurrection of Jesus* (Grand Rapids: William B. Eerdmans Publishing Company, 1975), 61–62.

135. Ibid., 64, 66.

136. Ibid., 66.

137. Ibid., 61.

138. Ibid., 66.

139. Ibid., 71.

140. Ibid., 71–72.

141. Ibid., 72.

142. Wright, *The New Testament and the People of God*, 153.

143. "Pax Romana," in *Encyclopedia Britannica*, Noet ed. (Chicago, IL: EncyclopÊdia Britannica, 2016).

144. Philip W. Comfort and Walter A. Elwellm, in *Tyndale Bible Dictionary* (Wheaton, IL: Tyndale House Publishers, 2001), 876.

145. Wright, *The New Testament and the People of God*, 154.

146. Craig R. Koester, vol. 38A, *Revelation: A New Translation with Introduction and Commentary*, J. J. Collins, ed. (New Haven; London: Yale University Press, 2014), 471.

147. Mark A. Noll, "The Fullness of Time," R. F. Ingram, ed., *Tabletalk Magazine*, December 1990, 13.

148. Ibid., 11.

149. Larry R. Helyer, *Exploring Jewish Literature of the Second Temple Period: A Guide for New Testament Students* (Downers Grove, IL: InterVarsity Press, 2002), 497.

150. Gary H. Everett, *The Epistle of Galatians*, 2011, 80.

151. Origen, "Origen against Celsus," in A. Roberts, J. Donaldson, and A. C. Coxe, eds., F. Crombie, trans., vol. 4, *Fathers of the Third Century: Tertullian, Part Fourth; Minucius Felix; Commodian; Origen, Parts First and Second* (Buffalo, NY: Christian Literature Company, 1885), 443–44.

152. Everett Ferguson, *Backgrounds of Early Christianity*, 3rd ed. (Grand Rapids, MI; Cambridge, UK: William B. Eerdmans Publishing Company, 2003), 1.

153. Ibid., 49.

154. Ibid., 67.

155. Craig S. Keener, *The IVP Bible Background Commentary: New Testament* (Downers Grove, IL: InterVarsity Press, 1993).

156. David A. Fiensy, *New Testament Introduction* (Joplin, MO: College Press Pub. Co., 1997), 182.

157. Moyer V. Hubbard, *Christianity in the Greco-Roman World: A Narrative Introduction* (Grand Rapids, MI: Baker Academic, 2010), 197.

158. Ibid., 200.

159. Fiensy, *New Testament Introduction*, 182.

160. Craig S. Keener, *The IVP Bible Background Commentary: New Testament* (Downers Grove, IL: InterVarsity Press, 1993).

161. Fiensy, *New Testament Introduction*, 183.
162. Ibid., 84.
163. Lea and Black, *The New Testament*, 32.
164. Ibid., 34–35.
165. Ibid., 35.

CHAPTER 2: NEW TESTAMENT BASICS: BUILDING BLOCKS OF THE REVELATION

1.   F. F. Bruce, *The New Testament Documents: Are They Reliable?*, 5th rev. ed. (Downers Grove, IL: InterVarsity Press, 1997), 15.
2.   The Roman Catholic Bible includes additional Old Testament books, which Catholics refer to as "deuterocanonical" and Protestants call "the Apocrypha."
3.   John D. Barry, "New Testament, Title of," in J. D. Barry et al., eds., *The Lexham Bible Dictionary* (Bellingham, WA: Lexham Press, 2016).
4.   George Thomas Kurian, in *Nelson's New Christian Dictionary: The Authoritative Resource on the Christian World* (Nashville, TN: Thomas Nelson Publishers, 2001); J. E. Miller, "Codex Sinaiticus," in J. D. Barry et al., eds., *The Lexham Bible Dictionary*.
5.   J. E. Miller, "Codex Vaticanus," in J. D. Barry et al., eds., *The Lexham Bible Dictionary*.
6.   F. F. Bruce, *The Canon of Scripture* (Downers Grove, IL: InterVarsity Press, 1988), 16.
7.   S. T. Raquel, "Canon, New Testament," in J. D. Barry et al., eds., *The Lexham Bible Dictionary*.
8.   Bruce, *The Canon of Scripture*, 16.
9.   Ibid., 116.
10. Arthur G. Patzia, *The Making of the New Testament: Origin, Collection, Text & Canon* (Downers Grove, IL: InterVarsity Press, 2011), 168.
11. Ibid.
12. Josh McDowell, *Evidence for Christianity* (Nashville, TN: Thomas Nelson Publishers, 2006), 44.

13. Lee Martin McDonald, *The Biblical Canon: Its Origin, Transmission, and Authority* (Grand Rapids, MI: Hendrickson Publishers, 2011), 245.

14. R. M. Raymer, 1 Peter. In J. F. Walvoord & R. B. Zuck (Eds.), *The Bible Knowledge Commentary: An Exposition of the Scriptures* (Wheaton, IL: Victor Books, 1985), Vol. 2, 844.

15. McDonald, *The Biblical Canon*, 246.

16. McDowell, *Evidence for Christianity*, 42.

17. Bruce, *The Canon of Scripture*, 123.

18. Patzia, *The Making of the New Testament*, 170.

19. Raquel, "Canon, New Testament," in J. D. Barry et al., eds., *The Lexham Bible Dictionary*.

20. Norman L. Geisler and William E. Nix, *A General Introduction to the Bible*, rev. and expanded (Chicago: Moody Press, 1986), 276–78.

21. Ibid., 282.

22. Norman L. Geisler, in *Baker Encyclopedia of Christian Apologetics* (Grand Rapids, MI: Baker Books, 1999), 147.

23. Thomas D. Lea and David Alan Black, *The New Testament: Its Background and Message*, 2nd ed. (Nashville, TN: Broadman & Holman Publishers 2003), 51–52.

24. Joe Blair, *Introducing the New Testament* (Nashville, TN: Broadman & Holman, 1994), 5.

25. Gary Habermas, *The Historical Jesus* (Joplin, Mo.: College Press, 1996), 152–57.

26. Geisler and Nix, *A General Introduction to the Bible*, 284.

27. William Lane Craig, *On Guard* (Colorado Springs, CO: David C. Cook, 2010).

28. Mark Roberts, *Can We Trust the Gospels? Investigating the Reliability of Matthew, Mark, Luke, and John* (Wheaton, IL: Crossway, 2007).

29. W. H. Kelber, "Oral Tradition: New Testament," in D. N. Freedman, ed., *The Anchor Yale Bible Dictionary* (New York: Doubleday, 1992), 31.

30. Darrell L. Bock and Daniel B. Wallace, *Dethroning Jesus: Exposing Popular Culture's Quest to Unseat the Biblical Christ* (Nashville: Thomas Nelson, 2010).

31. Roberts, *Can We Trust the Gospels?*

32. Valesius. Life of Eusebius Pamphilus, in Parker S. E., trans., *An Ecclesiastical History to the 20th Year of the Reign of Constantine* (London: Samuel Bagster and Sons, 1847), Eus. Hist. eccl. 339.

33. Bruce, *The Canon of Scripture*, 118.

34. Alex McFarland and Lee Strobel, *The 10 Most Common Objections to Christianity* (Ventura, CA: Regal Books, 2007).

35. List compiled by Gary Habermas, *The Historical Jesus: Ancient Evidence for the Life of Christ*, pp. 146–152, in ibid.

36. Bruce, *The Canon of Scripture*, 118.

37. Ibid., 118–19.

38. D. A. deSilva, *An introduction to the New Testament: contexts, methods and ministry formation* (p. 32). (Downers Grove, IL: InterVarsity Press, 2004).

39. Geisler and Nix, *A General Introduction to the Bible*, 284–87.

40. Ibid., 288.

41. C. D. Hamilton, "The Development of the Canon," E. Harrell, ed., *Christianity Magazine*, 2(9), 1985, 14.

42. Geisler and Nix, *A General Introduction to the Bible*, 295.

43. Norman L. Geisler and Frank Turek, *I Don't Have Enough Faith to Be An Atheist* (Wheaton, IL: Crossway Books, 2004), 236.

44. Darrell L. Bock, *NT211 Introducing the Gospels and Acts: Their Background, Nature, and Purpose* (Bellingham, WA: Lexham Press, 2014).

45. F. L. Cross and E. A. Livingstone, eds., in *The Oxford Dictionary of the Christian Church*, 3rd ed. rev. (Oxford; New York: Oxford University Press, 2005), 281.

46. John D. Barry and R. V. Noord, "Canon, Timeline of Formation of," J. D. Barry et al., eds., *The Lexham Bible Dictionary*.

47. Frank A. James III, *CH101 Introducing Church History I: Obscurity to Christendom* (Bellingham, WA: Lexham Press, 2016).

48. H. Gamble, "Canonical Formation of the New Testament," in C. A. Evans and S. E. Porter, eds., *Dictionary of New Testament*

Background: A Compendium of Contemporary Biblical Scholarship, electronic ed. (Downers Grove, IL: InterVarsity Press, 2000), 190; Hamilton, "The Development of the Canon," 14.

49. Geisler and Nix, *A General Introduction to the Bible*, 231.

50. Patzia, *The Making of the New Testament*, 166.

51. Lee Strobel, *Finding the Real Jesus*, Kindle ed. (Grand Rapids, MI: Zondervan, 2008), location 212.

52. Ibid., location 215.

53. Steve Walton and David Wenham, *Exploring the New Testament: The Gospels and Acts*, 2nd ed., vol. 1 (London: Society for Promoting Christian Knowledge, 2011), 58.

54. John P. Meier, *A Marginal Jew: Rethinking the Historical Jesus: The Roots of the Problem and the Person, Vol. 1* (New York, New York: Doubleday, 1991), 115.

55. Habermas, *The Historical Jesus*, 16.

56. Albert Schweitzer, *The Quest of the Historical Jesus: A Critical Study of its Progress from Reimarus to Wrede*, trans. by J. W. Montgomery from the first German edition of 1906 (New York: Macmillan, 1968), 38–39.

57. Habermas, *The Historical Jesus*, 18.

58. Ibid.

59. C. S. Lewis, *Mere Christianity* (C.S. Lewis Pte. Ltd., 1952), 55.

60. R. J. Morgan, *Nelson's Complete Book of Stories, Illustrations, and Quotes*, electronic ed. (Nashville: Thomas Nelson Publishers, 2000), 484.

61. Habermas, *The Historical Jesus*, 25–26.

62. R. G. Howe, "The New Testament, Jesus Christ, and the Da Vinci Code," in N. L. Geisler and C. V. Meister, eds., *Reasons for Faith: Making a Case for the Christian Faith* (Wheaton, IL: Crossway Books, 2007), 271.

63. Ibid., 271–72.

64. Robert Payne, "Heresy in the Early Church," *Christian History Magazine*, issue 51, 1996.

65. Bruce Barton, *John*, in Life Application Commentary (Wheaton, IL: Tyndale House, 1993), 4.

66. Howe, "The New Testament, Jesus Christ, and the Da Vinci Code," 273.

67. John Henry Newman, *The Arians of the Fourth Century* (London: J. G. & F. Rivington, 1983), 218–19.

68. Howe, "The New Testament, Jesus Christ, and the Da Vinci Code," 275.

69. Ibid., 280.

70. Thomas W. H. Griffith, *How We Got Our Bible* (Chicago, IL: Moody Publishers, 2013).

71. Norman L. Geisler, *Christian Apologetics* (Grand Rapids: Baker Book House, 1976), 305.

72. Craig L. Blomberg, *Making Sense of the New Testament: Three Crucial Questions* (Grand Rapids, MI: Baker Academic, 2004), 26; Geisler, *Christian Apologetics*, 313.

73. Blomberg, *Making Sense of the New Testament*, 33–36.

74. Ibid., 27.

75. Ibid., 145.

76. Philip Schaff, *Companion to the Greek Testament and the English Version* (New York: Harper and Brothers, 1883), 86.

77. Elmer L. Towns and Ben Gutierrez, *The Essence of the New Testament* (Nashville: B&H, 2012).

78. Bruce Metzer in an interview with Lee Strobel, in *Lee Strobel, The Case for Christ: A Journalist's Personal Investigation of the Evidence for Jesus* (Grand Rapids, MI: Zondervan, 1998), chapter 3.

79. Blomberg, *Making Sense of the New Testament*, 145.

80. Crossway Bibles, *The ESV Study Bible* (Wheaton, IL: Crossway Bibles, 2008), 2,587.

81. Ibid.

82. Ibid.

83. Geisler, *Christian Apologetics*, 307.

84. Carl F. H. Henry, *God, Revelation, and Authority* (Wheaton, IL: Crossway Books, 1999), vol. 2, 14.

85. Norman L. Geisler, "Updating the Manuscript Evidence for the New Testament," September 2013.

86. Philip Schaff, *Companion to the Greek Testament and the English Version* (New York: Harper and Brothers, 1883), 178.

87.   Ed Komoszewski, M. James Sawyer, and Daniel B. Wallace, *Reinventing Jesus, How Contemporary Skeptics Miss the Real Jesus and Mislead Popular Culture*, Kindle ed. (Grand Rapids, MI: Kregel Publications, 2006), location 1103.

88.   Henry, *God, Revelation, and Authority*, vol. 2, 14.

89.   John A. T. Robinson, *Can We Trust the New Testament?* (Grand Rapids, MI: William B. Eerdmans Publishing Company, 1977), 36.

90.   Norman L. Geisler, "The New Testament Is Historically Reliable," PowerPoint presentation, 2014.

91.   Frederic Kenyon, *The Bible and Archaeology* (New York: Harper, 1940), 288. Limbaugh, David (2014-09-08).

92.   Geisler, "The New Testament Is Historically Reliable."

93.   Irving L. Jensen, *Jensen's Survey of the New Testament: Search and Discover* (Chicago: Moody Press, 1981), 137.

94.   Paul N. Benware, Survey of the New Testament, rev. ed. (Chicago, IL: Moody Press, 1990), 285, and Geisler, "The New Testament is Historically Reliable."

95.   Mark L. Strauss, *Four Portraits, One Jesus: A Survey of Jesus and the Gospels* (Grand Rapids, MI: Zondervan, 2007), 387.

96.   F. F. Bruce, *The New Testament Documents, Are They Reliable?*, Kindle ed. (Grand Rapids, MI; Cambridge, U.K.: William B. Eerdmans Publishing Company, 1943), location 517.

97.   J. P. Moreland, *Scaling the Secular City: A Defense of Christianity* (Grand Rapids, MI: Baker Academic, 1987), 138.

98.   Habermas, *The Historical Jesus*, 172.

99.   Moreland, *Scaling the Secular City*, 138; Dan Story, *Defending Your Faith* (Grand Rapids, MI: Kregel Publications, 1997), 43.

100. Habermas, *The Historical Jesus*, 172.

101. Story, *Defending Your Faith*, 44.

102. Robert G. Gromacki, *New Testament Survey* (Grand Rapids, MI: Baker Academic, 1974), 50.

103. Ibid.

104. Norman L. Geisler, *Baker Encyclopedia of Christian Apologetics* (Grand Rapids, MI: Baker Books, 1999), 100.

105. I discuss these sources in more depth in *Jesus on Trial*, Chapter 10

CHAPTER 3: MIRACULOUS: THE LITERARY WONDER OF THE NEW TESTAMENT

1. J. L Resseguie, "Literature, New Testament as," in D. N. Freedman, A. C. Myers, and A. B. Beck, eds., *Eerdmans Dictionary of the Bible* (Grand Rapids, MI: W.B. Eerdmans, 2000), 815.

2. William W. Klein, *BI260 Interpreting New Testament Genres* (Bellingham, WA: Lexham Press, 2015).

3. Leland L. Ryken, *Words of Delight: A Literary Introduction to the Bible*, 2nd ed. (Grand Rapids, MI: Baker Academic, 1992), 12.

4. Ibid., 16.

5. Ibid., 14.

6. J. Sidlow Baxter, *Explore the Book* (Grand Rapids: MI: Zondervan Publishing House, 1960), Vol. 5, 101.

7. S. W. Crawford, "Apocalyptic," in Freedman, Myers, and Beck, eds., *Eerdmans Dictionary of the Bible*, 72.

8. Ibid.

9. Norman L. Geisler and William E. Nix, *A General Introduction to the Bible*, rev. and expanded (Chicago: Moody Press, 1986), 29.

10. Jason S. DeRouchie, "Jesus' Bible: An Overview," in J. S. DeRouchie, ed., *What the Old Testament Authors Really Cared About: A Survey of Jesus' Bible* (Grand Rapids, MI: Kregel Academic, 2013), 48.

11. Norman L. Geisler, *To Understand the Bible Look for Jesus: The Bible Student's Guide to the Bible's Central Theme* (Eugene, OR: Wipf and Stock Publishers, 1979), 72.

12. James D. Dunn, "The History of the Tradition: New Testament," in J. D. G. Dunn and J. W. Rogerson, eds., *Eerdmans Commentary on the Bible* (Grand Rapids, MI; Cambridge, UK: William B. Eerdmans Publishing Company 2003), 950.

13. Louis Berkhof, *New Testament Introduction* (Grand Rapids, MI: Eerdmans-Sevensma Co, 1915), 133.

14. James D. Dunn, "The History of the Tradition: New Testament," in Dunn and Rogerson, eds., *Eerdmans Commentary on the Bible*, 950.

15. David Wenham and Steve Walton, *Exploring the New Testament: The Gospels and Acts*, 2nd ed., Vol. 1 (London: Society for Promoting Christian Knowledge, 2011), 50.
16. Ibid.
17. Ibid.
18. Klein, *BI260 Interpreting New Testament Genres*.
19. Ibid.
20. Ibid.
21. Plutarch. *The Lives of the Noble Grecians and Romans: The Dryden Translation*, M. J. Adler and P. W. Goetz, eds. (Chicago; Auckland; Geneva; London; Madrid; Manila; Paris; Rome; Seoul; Sydney; Tokyo; Toronto: Robert P. Gwinn; Encyclopædia Britannica, Inc., 1990), 2nd ed., vol. 13, 540–41.
22. Wenham and Walton, *Exploring the New Testament*, 2nd ed., vol. 1, 52.
23. Ibid.
24. Ibid., 54.
25. Ibid.
26. Earl D. Radmacher, Ronald Barclay Allen, and H. Wayne House, *The Nelson Study Bible: New King James Version* (Nashville: T. Nelson Publishers, 1997).
27. Norman L. Geisler and Frank Turek, *I Don't Have Enough Faith to Be an Atheist* (Wheaton, IL: Crossway Books, 2004), 290.
28. Klein, *BI260 Interpreting New Testament Genres*.
29. William W. Klein, Craig L. Blomberg, and Robert L. Hubbard Jr., *Introduction to Biblical Interpretation* (Nashville, TN: Thomas Nelson, 2004), 400–1.
30. Klein, *BI260 Interpreting New Testament Genres*.
31. Elmer Towns and Ben Guitierrez, *The Essence of the New Testament* (Nashville: B&H, 2012).
32. Ben Witherington III, *The Acts of the Apostles: A Socio-rhetorical Commentary* (Grand Rapids, MI: Wm. B. Eerdmans Publishing Co, 1998), 31.
33. John W. Drane, *Introducing the New Testament*, completely rev. and updated (Oxford: Lion Publishing plc, 2000), 254.

34. Spiros Zodhiates and Warren Baker, *The Complete Word Study Bible: King James Version*, electronic ed. (Chattanooga: AMG Publishers, 2000).

35. Walter A. Elwell and B. J. Beitzel, in *Baker Encyclopedia of the Bible* (Grand Rapids, MI: Baker Book House, 1988), 1,633.

36. Ray C. Stedman, *Adventuring through the New Testament* (Grand Rapids, MI: Discovery House Publishers, 2011), Kindle ed., location 1984.

37. Bruce Barton says the book is not about the life of Paul but about the spread of the gospel. Bruce B. Barton and G. R. Osborne, *Acts* (Wheaton, IL: Tyndale House, 1999), 457.

38. David G. Peterson, *The Acts of the Apostles* (Grand Rapids, MI; Nottingham, England: William B. Eerdmans Publishing Company, 2009), 12.

39. Klein, *BI260 Interpreting New Testament Genres*.

40. Harold L. Willmington, *Willmington's Bible Handbook* (Wheaton, IL: Tyndale House Publishers, 1997), 632.

41. Ibid.

42. D. A. Carson and Douglas J. Moo, *Introducing the New Testament: A Short Guide to Its History and Message* (Grand Rapids, MI: Zondervan, 2010), 65–66.

43. Norman L. Geisler, *A Popular Survey of the New Testament* (Grand Rapids, MI: Baker Books, 2014), 123.

44. Berkhof, *New Testament Introduction*, 135.

45. Klein, *BI260 Interpreting New Testament Genres*.

46. Walter A. Elwell and Robert W. Yarbrough, *Encountering the New Testament: A Historical and Theological Survey*, 2nd ed. (Grand Rapids, MI: Baker Academic, 2005), 348.

47. Berkhof, *New Testament Introduction*, 138.

48. Geisler, *A Popular Survey of the New Testament*, 123; Jeannine K. Brown, *BI131 Introducing Literary Interpretation* (Bellingham, WA: Lexham Press, 2015).

49. Klein, *BI260 Interpreting New Testament Genres*.

50. Ibid.

51. Ibid.

52. Paul N. Benware, *Survey of the New Testament (Revised)* (Chicago: Moody Press, 1990), 18–19.

53. John F. Walvoord, "Revelation," in J. F. Walvoord and R. B. Zuck, eds., *The Bible Knowledge Commentary: An Exposition of the Scriptures* (Wheaton, IL: Victor Books, 1985), vol. 2, 925.

54. G. K. Beale, *The Book of Revelation: A Commentary on the Greek Text* (Grand Rapids, MI; Carlisle, Cumbria: W.B. Eerdmans; Paternoster Press, 1999), 37.

55. Ryken, *Words of Delight*, 480.

56. Ibid.

57. Bruce B. Barton, *Revelation*, G. R. Osborne, ed. (Wheaton, IL: Tyndale House Publishers, 2000), 1.

58. Beale, *The Book of Revelation*, 37.

59. Ibid., 39.

60. J. Ramsey Michaels, *Interpreting the Book of Revelation*, vol. 7 (Grand Rapids, MI: Baker Book House, 1992), 31–32.

61. William W. MacDonald, *Believer's Bible Commentary: Old and New Testaments*, A. Farstad, ed. (Nashville: Thomas Nelson, 1995).

62. Baxter, *Explore the Book*, vol. 5, 102.

63. Ibid., 104.

64. Ibid., 104–5.

65. Ibid., 105.

66. Ibid., 106.

67. Klein, Blomberg, and Hubbard Jr., *Introduction to Biblical Interpretation*, 114.

68. Edgar J. Goodspeed, *The Formation of the New Testament*, 2nd ed. (Chicago: University of Chicago Press, 1927), 35, cited in Arthur G. Patzia, *The Making of the New Testament: Origin, Collection, Text & Canon* (Downers Grove, IL: InterVarsity Press, 2011), 177.

69. Baxter, *Explore the Book*, vol. 5, 1,202.

70. Ibid.

71. Ibid., 107–9.

72. Dale Leschert, *The Flow of the New Testament* (Fearn, Great Britain: Christian Focus Publications, 2002), 21.

73. Baxter, *Explore the Book*, vol. 5, 110.

74. Kenneth O. Gangel, *John*, vol. 4 (Nashville, TN: Broadman & Holman Publishers, 2000), 23.

75. Benware, *Survey of the New Testament (Revised)*, 18.

76. Roy B. Zuck, *A Biblical Theology of the Old Testament*, electronic ed. (Chicago: Moody Press, 1991), 32.

77. John F. MacArthur Jr., "The Sabbath of Moses," in *John MacArthur Sermon Archive* (Panorama City, CA: Grace to You, 2014).

78. Larry Richards, *The 365 Day Devotional Commentary* (Wheaton, IL: Victor Books, 1990), 54; Paul P. Enns, *The Moody Handbook of Theology* (Chicago, IL: Moody Press, 1989), 57; Charles Fred Lincoln, The Biblical Covenants, Part 2, Bibliotheca Sacra, 1943, 100: 448.

79. John F. MacArthur Jr., "The Sabbath Question: The Nature of the Old Covenant," in *John MacArthur Sermon Archive*.

80. Arnold G. Fruchtenbaum, *The Messianic Bible Study Collection* (Tustin, CA: Ariel Ministries, 1983), vol. 21, 18.

81. Vern S. Poythress, *The Shadow of Christ in the Law of Moses* (Phillipsburg, NJ.... Publishing, 1991), 43.

82. David M. Howard, "The Historical Books," in John D. Barry et al., Faithlife Study Bible (Bellingham, WA: Logos Bible Software, 2012).

83. Craig A. Blaising and Darrell L. *Progressive Dispensationalism* (Grand Rapids, MI: Baker Books, 1993), 194.

84. M. S. Mills, *Genesis: A Study Guide to the Book of Genesis* (Dallas: 3E Ministries, 1998).

85. Michael P. V. Barrett, *Beginning at Moses: A Guide to Finding Christ in the Old Testament* (Greenville, SC; Belfast, Northern Ireland: Ambassador-Emerald International, 2001), 125.

86. Mark Dever and Graeme Goldsworthy, *The Message of the Old Testament: Promises Made* (Wheaton, IL: Crossway, 2006).

87. Paul R. Williamson, *Sealed with an Oath* (Downers Grove, IL: InterVarsity Press, 2007), 94.

88. Craig A. Blaising and Darrell L. Bock, *Progressive Dispensationalism* (Grand Rapids, MI: Baker Books, 1993), 151.

89. Walter C. Kaiser, *The Promise-Plan of God: A Biblical Theology of the Old and New Testaments* (Grand Rapids, MI: Zondervan, 2008), 393.
90. Benware, *Survey of the New Testament (Revised)*, 19.
91. Kaiser, *The Promise-Plan of God*, 19.
92. Roy B. Zuck et al., *A Biblical Theology of the Old Testament*, electronic ed. (Chicago, IL: Moody Press, 1991), 12–13.
93. Willis Judson Beecher, *The Prophets and the Promise*, (Ancaster, ON: Alev Books, 2011), 99–102.
94. Ibid., 100–1.
95. Ibid.
96. Ibid.
97. Ibid., 101.
98. Ibid.
99. Ibid., 102.
100. Ibid., 103.

CHAPTER 4: THE GOSPELS: FOUR PERSPECTIVES, ONE MESSAGE

1. John Blanchard, in *The Complete Gathered Gold: A Treasury of Quotations for Christians* (Webster, New York; Darlington, England: Evangelical Press, 2006), 263.
2. J. Sidlow Baxter, Baxter's *Explore the Book*, Kindle ed. (Zondervan, 2010), 1,210.
3. Ibid.
4. Benjamin Franklin, The Autobiography of Benjamin Franklin, in C. W. Eliot, ed., *The Harvard Classics 1: The Autobiography of Benjamin Franklin, The Journal of John Woolman, and the Fruits of Solitude by William Penn* (New York: P. F. Collier & Son, 1909), 106.
5. George Whitefield, *The Works of the Reverend George Whitefield* (London: Edward and Charles Dilly. 1772), vol. 6, 79–81.
6. Ibid., 81–83.
7. Carl F. H. Henry, *God, Revelation and Authority* (Wheaton, IL: Crossway Books, 1999), vol. 2, 17.

8. Baxter's *Explore the Book*, 1,213.
9. Norman L. Geisler and Frank Turek, *I Don't Have Enough Faith to Be an Atheist* (Wheaton, IL: Crossway Books, 2004), 285.
10. Ibid.
11. J. Warner Wallace, *Cold-Case Christianity: A Homicide Detective Investigates the Claims of the Gospels* (David C. Cook, 2013), 82–83.
12. Michael Licona, *AP113 Objections to the Gospels* (Bellingham, WA: Lexham Press, 2016), Segment 43.
13. Darrell L. Bock, *NT211 Introducing the Gospels and Acts: Their Background, Nature, and Purpose* (Bellingham, WA: Lexham Press, 2014), Segment 29.
14. Charles H. Scobie, *Ways of Our God: An Approach to Biblical Theology* (Grand Rapids, MI: Wm. B. Eerdmans Publishing Co., 2002), 10.
15. Irenaeus of Lyons, "IrenÊus against Heresies," in A. Roberts, J. Donaldson, and A. C. Coxe, eds., *The Apostolic Fathers with Justin Martyr and Irenaeus* (Buffalo, NY: Christian Literature Company, 1885), vol. 1, 3.11.8, page 428.
16. Ray Stedman, *Adventuring through the New Testament*, Kindle ed. (Discovery House Publishers, 2011), Kindle Location 167–182.
17. Robert Hawker, in *The Poor Man's Concordance and Dictionary to the Sacred Scriptures* (London: Ebenezer Palmer, 1828), 92.
18. Henry, *God, Revelation, and Authority*, vol. 2, 17.
19. Stedman, *Adventuring through the New Testament*, Kindle Location 182.
20. Paul J. Achtemeier, Harper & Row and Society of Biblical Literature, in *Harper's Bible Dictionary*, 1st ed. (San Francisco: Harper & Row, 1985), 286.
21. Simon J. Kistemaker and William Hendriksen, *Exposition of the Book of Revelation* (Grand Rapids: Baker Book House, 1953–2001), vol. 20, 190.
22. Dale Leschert, *The Flow of the New Testament* (Fearn, Great Britain: Christian Focus Publications, 2002), 29.
23. Baxter's *Explore the Book*, 1,215.

24. Arthur W. Pink, *Why Four Gospels?* (Swengel, PA: Bible Truth Depot, 1921).

25. Stedman, *Adventuring through the New Testament*, Kindle Location 216.

26. Ibid., Kindle Location 231.

27. Leschert, *The Flow of the New Testament*, 29.

28. Richard B. Gardner, *Matthew* (Scottdale, PA: Herald Press, 1991), 428.

29. Ronald F. Youngblood, F. F. Bruce, and R. K. Harrison, Thomas Nelson Publishers, eds., in *Nelson's New Illustrated Bible Dictionary* (Nashville, TN: Thomas Nelson, Inc., 1995); Joe Blair, *Introducing the New Testament* (Nashville, TN: Broadman & Holman, 1994), 49.

30. Bock, *NT211 Introducing the Gospels and Acts*, Segment 29.

31. Douglas Mangum, *The Lexham Glossary of Theology* (Bellingham, WA: Lexham Press, 2014).

32. James D. G. Dunn and John W. Rogerson, eds., *Eerdmans Commentary on the Bible* (Grand Rapids, MI; Cambridge, U.K.: William B. Eerdmans Publishing Company 2003), 995.

33. K. R. Hughes, Markan Hypothesis, in J. D. Barry et al., eds., *The Lexham Bible Dictionary* (Bellingham, WA: Lexham Press, 2016).

34. Cliff McManis, *Christian Living Beyond Belief: Biblical Principles for the Life of Faith* (The Woodlands, TX: Kress Christian Publications, 2006), 132–37.

35. R. Kent Hughes, *Luke: That You May Know the Truth* (Wheaton, IL: Crossway Books, 1998), 336–37.

36. Walter A. Elwell and Philip W. Comfort, "Atonement," in *Tyndale Bible Dictionary* (Wheaton, IL: Tyndale House Publishers, 2001), 129.

37. Eugene E. Carpenter and Philip W. Comfort, in *Holman Treasury of Key Bible Words: 200 Greek and 200 Hebrew Words Defined and Explained* (Nashville, TN: Broadman & Holman Publishers, 2000), 370. Alan Cairns, in *Dictionary of Theological Terms* (Belfast; Greenville, SC: Ambassador Emerald International, 2002), 348.

38. M. G. Easton, in *Easton's Bible Dictionary* (New York: Harper & Brothers, 2016).

39. Cliff McManis, *Christian Living Beyond Belief: Biblical Principles for the Life of Faith* (The Woodlands, TX: Kress Christian Publications, 2006), 134.

40. Charles H. Spurgeon, *Christ in the Old Testament: Sermons on the Foreshadowing of Our Lord in Old Testament History, Ceremony, and Prophecy*, electronic ed. (Chattanooga, TN: AMG Publishers, 1997), 370.

41. John Blanchard, in *The Complete Gathered Gold: A Treasury of Quotations for Christians* (Webster, New York; Darlington, England: Evangelical Press, 2006), 343.

42. Ibid.

43. Ibid., 201.

44. Ibid.

45. B. Kennedy Repentance, in J. D. Barry et al., eds., *The Lexham Bible Dictionary*.

46. Walter A. Elwell and B. J. Beitzel, in *Baker Encyclopedia of the Bible* (Grand Rapids, MI: Baker Book House, 1988).

47. Elmer L. Towns, "Salvation by Grace through Faith," *Conservative Theological Journal* 7, no. 20, (2003), 38.

48. John F. MacArthur Jr., *The MacArthur Bible Handbook* (Nashville, TN: Thomas Nelson Publishers, 2003), 303.

49. Craig L. Blomberg, *Matthew* (Nashville: Broadman & Holman Publishers, 1992), vol. 22, 34.

50. John Nolland, "Preface," in *The Gospel of Matthew: A Commentary on the Greek text* (Grand Rapids, MI; Carlisle: W.B. Eerdmans; Paternoster Press, 2005), 18.

51. Craig A. Evans, *NT314 Book Study: The Gospel of Matthew in Its Jewish Context* (Bellingham, WA: Lexham Press, 2014), Segment 5.

52. Donald A. Hagner, *Matthew 1–13* (Dallas: Word, Incorporated, 1998), vol. 33A, ixiv.

53. H. N. Ridderbos, Kingdom of God, "Kingdom of Heaven," in D. R. W. Wood et al., eds., *New Bible Dictionary*, 3rd ed. (Leicester, England; Downers Grove, IL: InterVarsity Press, 1996), 647.

54. L. A. Barbieri Jr., "Matthew," in J. F. Walvoord and R. B. Zuck, eds., *The Bible Knowledge Commentary: An Exposition of the Scriptures* (Wheaton, IL: Victor Books, 1985).

55. O. Brooks, "Matthew, Gospel of," in C. Brand et al., eds., *Holman Illustrated Bible Dictionary* (Nashville, TN: Holman Bible Publishers, 2003), 1,091.

56. Roger Hahn, *Matthew: A Commentary for Bible Students* (Indianapolis, IN: Wesleyan Publishing House, 2007), 34.

57. J. Cate, "Matthew, Gospel of," in J. D. Barry et al., eds., *The Lexham Bible Dictionary.*

58. J. D. Grassmick, "Mark," in Walvoord and Zuck, eds., *The Bible Knowledge Commentary*, vol. 2, 95.

59. MacArthur Jr., *The MacArthur Study Bible* (Nashville, TN: Word Pub., 1997), 1,452.

60. Geisler and Turek, *I Don't Have Enough Faith to Be an Atheist*, 241.

61. David Smith, *Mark: A Commentary for Bible Students* (Indianapolis, IN: Wesleyan Publishing House, 2007), 33; J. D. Grassmick, "Mark," in Walvoord and Zuck, eds., *The Bible Knowledge Commentary*, vol. 2, 99, and Crossway Bibles *The ESV Study Bible* (Wheaton, IL: Crossway Bibles, 2008), 1,890.

62. *Word in Life Study Bible*, electronic ed. (Nashville, TN: Thomas Nelson, 1996).

63. MacArthur Jr., *The MacArthur Bible Handbook*, 288.

64. Edmond D. Hiebert, *The Gospel of Mark: An Expositional Commentary* (Greenville, SC: Bob Jones University Press, 1994), 12.

65. Crossway Bibles *The ESV Study Bible*, 1,890.

66. Ibid.

67. K. R. MacGregor, "Mark, Gospel of," in J. D. Barry et al., eds., *The Lexham Bible Dictionary.*

68. John D. Barry et al., *Faithlife Study Bible* (Bellingham, WA: Lexham Press, 2012–1016).

69. MacGregor, "Mark, Gospel of," in J. D. Barry et al., eds., *The Lexham Bible Dictionary.*

70. Crossway Bibles *The ESV Study Bible*, 1,935.

71. Geisler and Turek *I Don't Have Enough Faith to Be an Atheist*, 240.

72. Craig A. Evans, *NT319 Book Study: The Gospel of Luke in Its Gentile Context* (Bellingham, WA: Lexham Press, 2016), Segment 2.

73. MacArthur Jr., *The MacArthur Bible Handbook*, 290.

74. Stedman, *Adventuring through the New Testament*, Kindle Locations 1055–56.

75. Evans, *NT319 Book Study: The Gospel of Luke*, Segment 3.

76. Ibid.

77. D. S. Huffman, "Luke, Gospel of," in J. D. Barry et al., eds., *The Lexham Bible Dictionary*.

78. Evans, *NT319 Book Study: The Gospel of Luke*, Segment 3.

79. MacArthur Jr., *The MacArthur Study Bible*, 1,505.

80. E. A. Blum, "John," in Walvoord and Zuck, eds., *The Bible Knowledge Commentary*, vol. 2, 266.

81. MacArthur Jr., *The MacArthur Bible Handbook*, 341; E. A. Blum, "John," in Walvoord and Zuck, eds., *The Bible Knowledge Commentary*, vol. 2, 266.

82. Leon Morris, *The Gospel According to John* (Grand Rapids, MI: Wm. B. Eerdmans Publishing Co., 1995), 29.

83. Bruce B. Barton, *John* (Wheaton, IL: Tyndale House, 1993), xiii.

84. John D. Barry et al., *Faithlife Study Bible* (Bellingham, WA: Lexham Press, 2012–1016).

85. MacArthur Jr., *The MacArthur Bible Handbook*, 290; Blum, "John," in Walvoord and Zuck, eds., *The Bible Knowledge Commentary*, vol. 2, 266.

86. Barry et al., *Faithlife Study Bible* (Bellingham, WA: Lexham Press, 2012–1016).

87. Bruce B. Barton, *John* (Wheaton, IL: Tyndale House, 1993), viii–ix.

88. Fulton J. Sheen, *Life of Christ* (Doubleday Religious Publishing Group, Kindle Edition, 2008), 6.

89. Bock, *NT211 Introducing the Gospels and Acts*, Segments 11–16.

90. I got much of the material for this summary from several sources other than the Bible itself: D. S. Dockery et al. and Holman Bible Publishers, *Holman Bible Handbook* (Nashville, TN: Holman

Bible Publishers, 1992), 572; T. D. Lea and D. A. Black, *The New Testament: Its Background and Message*, 2nd ed. (Nashville, TN: Broadman & Holman Publishers, 2003).

91. L. O. Richards, *The Bible Reader's Companion*, electronic ed. (Wheaton: Victor Books, 1991), 600.
92. Henry Hampton Halley, *Halley's Bible Handbook with the New International Version*, completely rev. and expanded (Grand Rapids, MI: Zondervan Publishing House, 2000), 513.
93. Ibid., 514.
94. Halley, *Halley's Bible Handbook*, 513–514.
95. Ibid.
96. Bruce B. Barton and G. R. Osborne, *Life Application Bible Commentary.... Corinthians* (Wheaton, IL: Tyndale House, 1999), 37.
97. Mark Dever and John F. MacArthur Jr., *The Message of the New Testament: Promises Kept* (Wheaton, IL: Crossway Books, 2005).
98. Bruce Edward Gordon, *The Life of Jesus Christ, Promised Messiah, Servant of God, Son Of Man, Son of God* (Self Published through Lulu Publishing, 2011), 11.
99. Powell, *Introducing the New Testament*, 77.
100. D. A. Carson, ed., *NIV Zondervan Study Bible: Built on the Truth of Scripture and Centered on the Gospel Message* (Grand Rapids, MI: Zondervan, 2015), 2,876.

CHAPTER 5: FROM JESUS' BIRTH TO HIS INITIAL TEACHINGS

1. John Blanchard, in *The Complete Gathered Gold: A Treasury of Quotations for Christians* (Webster, New York; Darlington, England: Evangelical Press, 2006), 262.
2. S. Hahn, "Covenant," in J. D. Barry et al., eds., *The Lexham Bible Dictionary* (Bellingham, WA: Lexham Press, 2012, 2013, 2014); Charles C. Ryrie, *Ryrie Study Bible: New International Version*, expanded ed. (Chicago, IL: Moody Publishers, 1994), 462.
3. J. A. Martin, "Luke," in J. F. Walvoord and R. B. Zuck, eds., *The Bible Knowledge Commentary: An Exposition of the Scriptures* (Wheaton, IL: Victor Books, 1985), vol. 2, 212–13.

4. Ibid., 213.
5. Donald S. Fortner, *Discovering Christ in All the Scriptures* (Danville, KY: Don Fortner, 2007), 440.
6. Mark E. Moore, *The Chronological Life of Christ* (Joplin, MO: College Press Publishing Company, 2011), 49.
7. Ibid., 51.
8. Thomas A. Golding, "The Imagery of Shepherding in the Bible," Part 1, *Bibliotheca Sacra, 163* (Dallas Theological Seminary, 2011).
9. Robert H. Stein, *Luke*, vol. 24 (Nashville: Broadman & Holman Publishers, 1992), 117.
10. Roy E. Gingrich, *The Earthly Life of Christ (Volume II)* (Memphis, TN: Riverside Printing, 2002), 7.
11. E. A. Blum, "John," in Walvoord and Zuck, eds., *The Bible Knowledge Commentary*, vol. 2, 300.
12. Moore, *The Chronological Life of Christ*, 66.
13. Frederic Louis Godet, *A Commentary on the Gospel of St. Luke*, E. W. Shalders and M. D. Cusin, trans. (New York: I. K. Funk & co, 1881), vol. 1, 147.
14. Moore, *The Chronological Life of Christ*, 70.
15. John F. Walvoord, *Jesus Christ Our Lord* (Galaxie Software, 2008), 98.
16. Gerhard A. Krodel, *Acts* (Minneapolis, MN: Augsburg Publishing House, 1986), 32.
17. Wayne A. Grudem, *The Gift of Prophecy*, (Wheaton: IL: Crossway, 2000).
18. Gingrich, *The Earthly Life of Christ*, 5.
19. David M. Levy, *Malachi: Messenger of Rebuke and Renewal* (Bellmawr, NJ: Friends of Israel Gospel Ministry, 1992); Robert J. Utley, *Hope in Hard Times—The Final Curtain: Revelation* (Marshall, TX: Bible Lessons International, 2001), vol. 12, 6; Gingrich, *The Earthly Life of Christ (Volume Two)*, 3.
20. F. F. Bruce, *New Testament History* (New York, New York: Doubleday, 1969), 155.
21. Ibid., 156.

22. John Nolland, "Preface," in *The Gospel of Matthew: A Commentary on the Greek Text* (Grand Rapids, MI; Carlisle: W.B. Eerdmans; Paternoster Press, 2005), 175.

23. Paul J. Achtemeier, Harper & Row and Society of Biblical Literature, in *Harper's Bible Dictionary*, 1st ed. (San Francisco: Harper & Row Crossway Bibles, 1985), 528; *The ESV Study Bible* (Wheaton, IL: Crossway Bibles, 2008); J. D. Barry et al., *Faithlife Study Bible* (Bellingham, WA: Lexham Press, 2012, 2016).

24. S. M. Sheeley, Kingdom of God, Kingdom of Heaven, in D. N. Freedman, A. C. Myers, and A. B. Beck, eds., *Eerdmans Dictionary of the Bible* (Grand Rapids, MI: W.B. Eerdmans 2000), 768.

25. D. A. Carson, "Matthew," in T. Longman III and D. E. Garland, eds., *The Expositor's Bible Commentary: Matthew–Mark (Revised Edition)* (Grand Rapids, MI: Zondervan, 2010), vol. 9, 128.

26. K. A. Kitchen and T. C. Mitchell, "Chronology of the Old Testament," in D. R. W. Wood et al., eds., *New Bible Dictionary*, 3rd ed. (Leicester, England; Downers Grove, IL: InterVarsity Press, 1996).

27. Ibid.

28. F. F. Bruce, *New Testament History* (New York, NY: Doubleday, 1969), 158.

29. Donald S. Fortner, *Discovering Christ in All the Scriptures* (Danville, KY: Don Fortner, 2007), 443.

30. Other New Testament illustrations of the Trinity are: Matt. 28:19; John 15:26; 1 Cor. 12:4–13; 2 Cor. 13:13; Eph. 2:18; 1 Thess. 1:2–5; 1 Peter 1:2. Bruce B. Barton, D. Veerman, L. C. Taylor, and G. R. Osborne, *Luke* (Wheaton, IL: Tyndale House Publishers, 1997), 76.

31. Robert H. Stein, *Luke* (Nashville: Broadman & Holman Publishers, 1992), vol. 24, 139.

32. Norval Geldenhuys, *Commentary on the Gospel of Luke: The English Text with Introduction, Exposition and Notes* (Grand Rapids, MI: Wm. B. Eerdmans Publishing Co., 1952), 146.

33. William Hendriksen, and S. J. Kistemaker, *Exposition of the Gospel According to Luke* (Grand Rapids: Baker Book House, 1953–2001), vol. 11, 217.

34. Bruce Barton et al., *Life Application New Testament Commentary* (Wheaton, IL: Tyndale, 2001), 255.

35. John J. MacArthur, ed., *The MacArthur Study Bible*, electronic ed. (Nashville, TN: Word Pub., 1997), 19; Patricia A. Ennis, Clyde P. Greer, Jr., Grant Horner, John A. Hughes, Taylor B. Jones, John F. MacArthur, Jr., et al *Think Biblically! Recovering a Christian Worldview* (Wheaton, IL: Crossway, 2003); Bruce Barton, Philip W. Comfort, Grant R. Osborne, Linda K. Taylor and Dave Veerman, *Life Application New Testament Commentary* (Wheaton, IL: Tyndale, 2001), 19.

36. Bruce Barton, Philip W. Comfort, Grant R. Osborne, Linda K. Taylor and Dave Veerman, *Life Application New Testament Commentary* (Wheaton, IL: Tyndale, 2001), 1085–1086.

37. Daniel L. Akin, *The New American Commentary, 1, 2, 3 John* (Nashville: Broadman & Holman Publishers, 2001), vol. 38, 213.

38. Walvoord and Zuck, *The Bible Knowledge Commentary*, vol. 2, 891.

39. Charles C. Ryrie, Ryrie Study Bible: New International Version, expanded ed. (Chicago: Moody Publishers, 1994), 1927; and MacArthur Jr., *The MacArthur Study Bible*, electronic ed., 1974.

40. Werner H. Franzmann, *Bible History Commentary: New Testament*, electronic ed. (Milwaukee, WI: WELS Board for Parish Education, 1998), 67.

41. Thomas Hale, *The Applied New Testament Commentary* (Colorado Springs, CO; Ontario, Canada; East Sussex, England: David C. Cook, 1996), 143.

42. Edersheim is not suggesting here that Satan is of equal but opposite power with God, just that He persistently opposes God and His Kingdom.

43. Alfred Edersheim, *The Life and Times of Jesus the Messiah* (New York: Longmans, Green, and Co, 1896), Volume 1, 291.

44. Ibid., 292.

45. Ibid., 292.

46. Charles Foster Kent, *The Life and Teachings of Jesus: According to the Earliest Records* (New York; Chicago; Boston: Charles Scribner's Sons, 1913), 69.

47. Ibid.

48. Bruce L. Shelley, *Church History in Plain Language*, updated 2nd ed. (Dallas, TX: Word Pub., 1995), 3.

49. E. A. Blum, "John," in Walvoord and Zuck, eds., *The Bible Knowledge Commentary*, vol. 2, 275.

50. Ibid., 275–276.

51. Gerald L. Borchert, *John 1–11* (Nashville: Broadman & Holman Publishers, 1996), vol. 25A, 157.

52. Ibid., 155–56.

53. Kenneth O. Gangel, *John* (Nashville, TN: Broadman & Holman Publishers, 2000), vol. 4, 29–30.

54. Moore, *The Chronological Life of Christ*, 90.

55. M. B. Winstead, "Capernaum," in J. D. Barry et al., eds., *The Lexham Bible Dictionary* (Bellingham, WA: Lexham Press, 2016).

56. Moore, *The Chronological Life of Christ*, 91.

57. Borchert, *John 1–11*, vol. 25A, 161.

58. MacArthur Jr., ed., *The MacArthur Study Bible*, electronic ed., 1,579.

59. Leon Morris, *The Gospel According to John* (Grand Rapids, MI: Wm. B. Eerdmans Publishing Co., 1995), 167–168.

60. E. A. Blum, "John," in Walvoord and Zuck, eds., *The Bible Knowledge Commentary*, vol. 2, 280.

61. Bruce B. Barton *John* (Wheaton, IL: Tyndale House, 1993), 47.

62. Walter A. Elwell, and B. J. Beitzel, In *Baker Encyclopedia of the Bible* (Grand Rapids, MI: Baker Book House, 1988).

63. Robert G. Tuttle, *Sanctity without Starch* (Bristol Books, 1992), 127.

64. E. A. Blum, "John," in Walvoord and Zuck, eds., *The Bible Knowledge Commentary*, vol. 2, 282.

65. Kenneth O. Gangel, *John* (Nashville, TN: Broadman & Holman Publishers, 2000), vol. 4, 54.

66. Bruce B. Barton *John* (Wheaton, IL: Tyndale House, 1993), 63.

67. Gangel, *John*, vol. 4, 55.

68. Paul J. Achtemeier, Harper & Row and Society of Biblical Literature, (1985). In *Harper's Bible Dictionary*, 1st ed. (San Francisco: Harper & Row, 1985), 207.

69. E. A. Blum, "John," in Walvoord and Zuck, eds., *The Bible Knowledge Commentary*, vol. 2, 272.

70. MacArthur, ed., *The MacArthur Study Bible*, electronic ed., 1582; E. A. Blum, "John," in Walvoord and Zuck, eds., *The Bible Knowledge Commentary*, vol. 2, 282.

71. E. A. Blum, "John," in Walvoord and Zuck, eds., *The Bible Knowledge Commentary*, vol. 2, 283.

72. See MacArthur, ed., *The MacArthur Study Bible*, electronic ed., 1582.

73. Moore, *The Chronological Life of Christ*, 104.

74. Borchert, *John 1–11*, vol. 25A, 206–7.

75. A. H. J. Gunneweg, M. Awerbuch, and C. A. Kimball, "Israel," in *The Encyclopedia of Christianity* (Grand Rapids, MI; Leiden, Netherlands: Wm. B. Eerdmans; Brill, 1999–2003), vol. 2, 772; Moore, *The Chronological Life of Christ*, 107.

76. E. A. Blum, "John," in Walvoord and Zuck, eds., *The Bible Knowledge Commentary*, vol. 2, 286.

77. Morris, *The Gospel According to John*, 241.

78. Lee Martin McDonald, *The Story of Jesus in History and Faith* (Grand Rapids, MI: Baker Academic, 2013), 205.

79. Warren W. Wiersbe, *Wiersbe's Expository Outlines on the New Testament* (Wheaton, IL: Victor Books, 1992), 156.

80. Robert H. Stein, *Luke* (Nashville: Broadman & Holman Publishers, 1992), vol. 24, 156.

81. John A. Martin, "Luke," in Walvoord and Zuck, eds., *The Bible Knowledge Commentary*, vol. 2, 214.

82. Darrell L. Bock, *Luke: 1:1–9:50* (Grand Rapids, MI: Baker Academic, 1994), vol. 1, 419.

83. Moore, *The Chronological Life of Christ*, 117–18.

84. Alfred Edersheim, *The Life and Times of Jesus the Messiah* (New York: Longmans, Green, and Co, 1896), Volume 1, 451.

85. James R. Edwards, *The Gospel according to Mark* (Grand Rapids, MI; Leicester, England: Eerdmans; Apollos, 2002), 64.

86. M. A. Powell, ed., in *The HarperCollins Bible Dictionary (Revised and Updated, Third Edition)* (New York: HarperCollins, 2011), 628, 629.

87. James R. Edwards, *The Gospel according to Mark* (Grand Rapids, MI; Leicester, England: Eerdmans; Apollos, 2002), 64.

88. Sigurd Grindheim, *God's Equal: What Can We Know about Jesus' Self-Understanding?*, M. Goodacre, ed. (London; New York: T&T Clark, 2011), vol. 446, 1.

89. Ibid., 2–3.

90. Paul W. Barnett, *Jesus and the Rise of Early Christianity: A History of New Testament Times* (Downers Grove, IL: IVP Academic, 1999), 202.

91. Ibid.

92. Moore, *The Chronological Life of Christ*, 119.

93. Nolland, "Preface," in *The Gospel of Matthew*, 175.

94. K. A. Kitchen, and T. C. Mitchell, "Chronology of the Old Testament," in D. R. W. Wood et al., eds., *New Bible Dictionary*, 3rd ed. (Leicester, England; Downers Grove, IL: InterVarsity Press, 1996).

95. Paul J. Achtemeier, Harper & Row and Society of Biblical Literature, In *Harper's Bible Dictionary*, 1st ed. (San Francisco: Harper & Row.Crossway Bibles, 1985), 528.

96. Walter A. Elwell, B. J. Beitzel, In *Baker Encyclopedia of the Bible* (Grand Rapids, MI: Baker Book House, 1988), Volume 2, 1269.

97. Ibid., 1,275.

98. Ibid.

99. Douglas J. Moo, *NT305 New Testament Theology* (Bellingham, WA: Lexham Press), Segment 23.

100. Douglas J. Moo, *NT305 New Testament Theology* (Bellingham, WA: Lexham Press), Segment 23.

101. C. C. Caragounis, "Kingdom of God/Kingdom of Heaven," in J. B. Green and S. McKnight, eds., *Dictionary of Jesus and the Gospels* (Downers Grove, IL: InterVarsity Press, 1992), 417.

102. J. Daniel Hays, et al, In *Dictionary of Biblical Prophecy and End Times* (Grand Rapids, MI: Zondervan Publishing House, 2007), 22.

103. This idea is partially expressed in Stan Norman with Peter Gentry, "Kingdom of God," in C. Brand et al., eds., *Holman Illustrated Bible Dictionary* (Nashville, TN: Holman Bible Publishers, 2003), 989.

104. Craig S. Keener et al, *NT146 The Arrival of Christ and His Kingdom* (Bellingham, WA: Lexham Press, 2016), Segment 19.

105. J. Daniel Hays, et al, In *Dictionary of Biblical Prophecy and End Times* (Grand Rapids, MI: Zondervan Publishing House, 2007), 22.

106. Ibid., 23.

107. See Charles Price, *Matthew: Can Anything Good Come Out of Nazareth?* (Fearn, Great Britain: Christian Focus Publications. 1998), 54; Arthur K. Robertson, *Matthew.* (Chicago, IL: Moody Press, 1983), 34; L. A. Barbieri Jr., "Matthew," in Walvoord and Zuck, eds., *The Bible Knowledge Commentary*, vol. 2, 27; D. A. Carson, "Matthew," in T. Longman III and D. E. Garland, eds., *The Expositor's Bible Commentary: Matthew–Mark (Revised Edition)* (Grand Rapids, MI: Zondervan, 2010), vol. 9, 147.

108. H. I. Hester, *The Heart of the New Testament* (Nashville, TN: Broadman & Holman Publishers, 1963), 139.

109. Crossway Bibles, *The ESV Study Bible.*

110. Hester, *The Heart of the New Testament*, 139.

111. Leon Morris, *The Gospel According to Matthew* (Grand Rapids, MI; Leicester, England: W.B. Eerdmans; Inter-Varsity Press, 1992), 84.

112. Ajith Fernando, The Supremacy of Christ (Wheaton, IL: Crossway Books, 1995), 39.

113. W. W. Wessel and M. L. Strauss, "Mark," in T. Longman III and D. E. Garland, eds., *The Expositor's Bible Commentary: Matthew–Mark (Revised Edition)* (Grand Rapids, MI: Zondervan, 2010), vol. 9, 716.

114. William Hendriksen and S. J. Kistemaker, *Exposition of the Gospel According to Mark* (Grand Rapids: Baker Book House, 1953–2001), vol. 10, 71–72.

CHAPTER 6: FROM "CATCHING MEN" TO THE GOLDEN RULE

1. David Martyn Lloyd-Jones, *From Fear to Faith* (London: Intervarsity Press, 1953), 23–24.
2. R. A. Cole, "Mark," in D. A. Carson, R. T. France, J. A. Motyer, and G. J. Wenham, eds., *New Bible Commentary: 21st Century Edition*, 4th ed. (Leicester, England; Downers Grove, IL: Inter-Varsity Press, 1994), 953.
3. J. A. Martin, "Luke," in J. F. Walvoord and R. B. Zuck, eds., *The Bible Knowledge Commentary: An Exposition of the Scriptures* (Wheaton, IL: Victor Books, 1985), vol. 2, 215–16.
4. "Leprosy," in *Compton's Encyclopedia* (Chicago, IL: Compton's Encyclopedia, 2015).
5. William Hendriksen and S. J. Kistemaker *Exposition of the Gospel According to Matthew* (Grand Rapids: Baker Book House, 1953–2001), vol. 9, 388.
6. L. A. Barbieri Jr., "Matthew," in Walvoord and Zuck, eds., *The Bible Knowledge Commentary*, vol. 2, 37.
7. Craig S. Keener, *The IVP Bible Background Commentary: New Testament* (Downers Grove, IL: InterVarsity Press, 1993).
8. Paul, for example, heals a cripple at Lystra (Acts 14:10). Robert H. Stein, *Luke* (Nashville: Broadman & Holman Publishers, 1992), vol. 24, 177.
9. John F. MacArthur Jr., ed., *The MacArthur Study Bible* (electronic ed.) (Nashville, TN: Word Pub, 1997), 1,522.
10. Stein, *Luke*, vol. 24, 177.
11. Kurt A. Richardson, *James* (Nashville: Broadman & Holman Publishers, 1997), vol. 36, 233–34; J. Reiling and J. L. Swellengrebel, *A Handbook on the Gospel of Luke* (New York: United Bible Societies, 1993), 241.
12. Richardson, *James*, vol. 36, 233–34.
13. G. H. Twelftree, Signs and Wonders. In T. D. Alexander and B. S. Rosner (Eds.), *New Dictionary of Biblical Theology* (electronic ed.) (Downers Grove, IL: InterVarsity Press, 2000), 778.

14. Larry Richards, *Every Miracle in the Bible* (Nashville: T. Nelson, 1998), 261.

15. Gerhard A. Krodel, *Acts* (Minneapolis, MN: Augsburg Publishing House, 1986), 28.

16. Crossway Bibles. *The ESV Study Bible* (Wheaton, IL: Crossway Bibles, 2008), 1831, 1837.

17. Bruce B. Barton, et al, *Life Application New Testament Commentary* (Wheaton, IL: Tyndale, 2001), 44.

18. R. T. France, *The Gospel of Matthew* (Grand Rapids, MI: Wm. B. Eerdmans Publication Co, 2007), 351–352.

19. Bruce B. Barton, et al, *Life Application New Testament Commentary* (Wheaton, IL: Tyndale, 2001), 44.

20. David L. Turner, *Matthew* (Grand Rapids, MI: Baker Academic, 2008), 252.

21. Douglas Sean O'Donnell, *Matthew: All Authority in Heaven and on Earth* (R. K. Hughes, Ed.), (Wheaton, IL: Crossway, 2013), 241.

22. James Luther Mays, (Ed.), *Harper's Bible Commentary* (San Francisco: Harper and Row, 1988), 1022.

23. John D. Barry, et al, *Faithlife Study Bible* (Bellingham, WA: Lexham Press, 2012, 2016).

24. H. Ronald Vandermey and Gary Cohen, (1981). *Hosea and Amos* (Chicago, IL: Moody Press, 1981), 47; R. Carroll, M. D., "Hosea," in T. Longman III and D. E. Garland, eds., *The Expositor's Bible Commentary: Daniel–Malachi (Revised Edition)* (Grand Rapids, MI: Zondervan 2008), vol. 8, 257.

25. Douglas R. A. Hare, *Matthew* (Louisville, KY: John Knox Press, 1993), 102.

26. Crossway Bibles, *The ESV Study Bible* (Wheaton, IL: Crossway Bibles, 2008), 1837.

27. L. A. Barbieri, Matthew, in Walvoord and Zuck, eds., *The Bible Knowledge Commentary*, vol. 2, 39.

28. D. A. Carson, "Matthew," in T. Longman III and D. E. Garland, eds., *The Expositor's Bible Commentary: Matthew–Mark (Revised Edition)* (Grand Rapids, MI: Zondervan, 2010), vol. 9, 266.

29. Ibid.

30. Ibid.

31. Ibid.

32. William Hendriksen and S. J. Kistemaker *Exposition of the Gospel According to Matthew* (Grand Rapids: Baker Book House, 1953–2001), vol. 9, 428.

33. Crossway Bibles. *The ESV Study Bible* (Wheaton, IL: Crossway Bibles, 2008), 1837.

34. Craig S. Keener, *The Gospel of John: A Commentary & 2* (Grand Rapids, MI: Baker Academic, 2012), vol. 1, 646.

35. Charles H. Spurgeon, *Spurgeon's Sermons*, electronic ed. (Albany, OR: Ages Software, 1998), vol. 44, no. 2568.

36. Crossway Bibles. *The ESV Study Bible* (Wheaton, IL: Crossway Bibles, 2008), 2031.

37. William Hendriksen and S. J. Kistemaker *Exposition of the Gospel According to John* (Grand Rapids: Baker Book House, 1953–2001), vol. 1–2, 195.

38. E. A. Blum, "John," in Walvoord and Zuck, eds., *The Bible Knowledge Commentary*, vol. 2, 290.

39. Ibid., 291–92.

40. Crossway Bibles. *The ESV Study Bible* (Wheaton, IL: Crossway Bibles, 2008), 2032.

41. Ibid.

42. R. C. H. Lenski, *The Interpretation of St. Luke's Gospel* (Minneapolis, MN: Augsburg Publishing House, 1961), 326.

43. A. K. Robertson, *Matthew* (Chicago, IL: Moody Press, 1983), 64.

44. Crossway Bibles. *The ESV Study Bible* (Wheaton, IL: Crossway Bibles, 2008), 1844.

45. L. A. Barbieri Jr., "Matthew," in Walvoord and Zuck, eds., *The Bible Knowledge Commentary*, vol. 2, 45.

46. John G. Butler, *Analytical Bible Expositor: Matthew* (Clinton, IA: LBC Publications, 2008), 201.

47. Bruce B. Barton, *Matthew* (Wheaton, IL: Tyndale House Publishers, 1996), 234.

48. Lynn H. Cohick, *NT101 Introducing New Testament: Its Structure and Story* (Bellingham, WA: Lexham Press, 2013), Segment 8.

49. Spurgeon, *Spurgeon's Sermons*, electronic ed. vol. 44, no. 2568.

50. Mark E. Moore, *The Chronological Life of Christ* (Joplin, MO: College Press Publishing Company, 2011), 155.

51. Hendriksen and Kistemaker *Exposition of the Gospel According to Matthew*, vol. 9, 522.

52. Walter A. Elwell, and Douglas Buckwalter, *Topical Analysis of the Bible: with the New International Version* (Grand Rapids, MI: Baker Book House, 1996), vol. 5.

53. See Matt. 3:16–17; Matt. 12:18; Matt. 12:28; Matt. 22:43–44; Matt. 28:19; Luke 1:35; Luke 3:21; Luke 24:49; John 1:33–34; John 3:34–35; John 14:11–26; John 15:26; John 16:7–15; John 20:21–22; Acts 2:32–33, 38–39; Acts 10:36–38; Rom. 8:9–11, 26–27; Rom. 15:16; 1 Cor. 6:15, 19; 1 Cor. 12:4–6; 2 Cor. 1:20–22; 2 Cor. 13:14; Gal. 4:4, 6; Eph. 2:13, 18, 22; Eph. 3:14–19; Eph. 4:4–6; 2 Thess. 2:13–14; Titus 3:4–6; Heb. 9:14; 1 Pet. 1:2; 1 Pet. 3:18; 1 John 4:2, 13–14; Jude 20–21, cited in Elwell and Buckwalter, *Topical Analysis of the Bible*, vol. 5.

54. Crossway Bibles. *The ESV Study Bible* (Wheaton, IL: Crossway Bibles, 2008), 1,827.

55. Craig S. Keener, *Matthew*, vol. 1, IN IVP New Testament Commentary (Downers Grove, IL: InterVarsity Press, 1997).

56. Ibid.

57. Timothy J. Keller, "The Love of Christ," August 25, 1991, In *The Timothy Keller Sermon Archive* (New York City: Redeemer Presbyterian Church, 2013).

58. Samuel L. Hoyt, *Michigan Theological Journal*, (Michigan Theological Seminary, Electronic Copyright, 2009), vol. 3, no. 2, 177.

59. T. P. Jenney, Sanctify, Sanctification, In D. N. Freedman, A. C. Myers, and A. B. Beck (Eds.), *Eerdmans Dictionary of the Bible* (Grand Rapids, MI: W.B. Eerdmans, 2000) 1165.

60. J. C. Kuo, Sermon on the Mount/Plain, In J. D. Barry, D. Bomar, D. R. Brown, R. Klippenstein, D. Mangum, C. Sinclair Wolcott, … W. Widder (Eds.), *The Lexham Bible Dictionary* (Bellingham, WA: Lexham Press, 2016).

61. D. A. Carson, D. *Jesus' Sermon on the Mount and His Confrontation with the World: An Exposition of Matthew 5–10* (Grand Rapids, MI: Baker Academic, 1999), 12.

62. Ibid.

63. Ibid., 14.

64. Leon Morris, *The Gospel According to Matthew* (Grand Rapids, MI; Leicester, England: W.B. Eerdmans; Inter-Varsity Press, 1992), 179.

65. Crossway Bibles. *The ESV Study Bible* (Wheaton, IL: Crossway Bibles, 2008), 1827.

66. Leland Ryken, et al Ryken, In *Dictionary of biblical imagery* (electronic ed.) (Downers Grove, IL: InterVarsity Press, 2000), 82.

67. Crossway Bibles. *The ESV Study Bible* (Wheaton, IL: Crossway Bibles, 2008), 1827.

68. John D. Barry, et al, *Faithlife Study Bible* (Bellingham, WA: Lexham Press, 2012, 2016).

69. John F. MacArthur, Jr. (Ed.), *The MacArthur Study Bible* (electronic ed.) (Nashville, TN: Word Pub, 1997), 1399.

70. Barbieri Jr., "Matthew," in Walvoord and Zuck, eds., *The Bible Knowledge Commentary*, vol. 2, 29.

71. Crossway Bibles. *The ESV Study Bible* (Wheaton, IL: Crossway Bibles, 2008), 1827; D. A. Carson, D. *Jesus' Sermon on the Mount and His Confrontation with the World: An Exposition of Matthew 5–10* (Grand Rapids, MI: Baker Academic, 1999), 17–18.

72. D. A. Carson, D. *Jesus' Sermon on the Mount and His Confrontation with the World: An Exposition of Matthew 5–10* (Grand Rapids, MI: Baker Academic, 1999), 18.

73. Ibid.,19.

74. John D. Barry, et al, *Faithlife Study Bible* (Bellingham, WA: Lexham Press, 2012, 2016).

75. D. A. Carson, D. *Jesus' Sermon on the Mount and His Confrontation with the World: An Exposition of Matthew 5–10* (Grand Rapids, MI: Baker Academic, 1999), 20.

76. Ibid., 23.

77. Ibid., 24.

78. Crossway Bibles. *The ESV Study Bible* (Wheaton, IL: Crossway Bibles, 2008), 1828.
79. Bruce Barton et al., *Life Application New Testament Commentary* (Wheaton, IL: Tyndale, 2001), 24.
80. D. A. Carson, "The Gospels and Acts," in D. A. Carson, ed., *NIV Zondervan Study Bible: Built on the Truth of Scripture and Centered on the Gospel Message* (Grand Rapids, MI: Zondervan, 2015), 1,937.
81. Barton et al., *Life Application New Testament Commentary*, 24.
82. D. A. Carson, D. *Jesus' Sermon on the Mount and His Confrontation with the World: An Exposition of Matthew 5–10* (Grand Rapids, MI: Baker Academic, 1999), 27.
83. Barbieri Jr., "Matthew," in Walvoord and Zuck, eds., *The Bible Knowledge Commentary*, vol. 2, 29.
84. D. A. Carson, D. *Jesus' Sermon on the Mount and His Confrontation with the World: An Exposition of Matthew 5–10* (Grand Rapids, MI: Baker Academic, 1999), 29.
85. Craig Blomberg, *Matthew* (Nashville: Broadman & Holman Publishers, 1992), vol. 22, 101.
86. Craig A. Evans, *NT314 Book Study: The Gospel of Matthew in Its Jewish Context* (Bellingham, WA: Lexham Press, 2014), Segment 23.
87. Crossway Bibles. *The ESV Study Bible* (Wheaton, IL: Crossway Bibles, 2008), 1829.
88. Moore, *The Chronological Life of Christ*, 177.
89. Ibid., 185.
90. Bryan Chapell, *Praying Backwards: Transform Your Prayer Life By Beginning in Jesus' Name* (Grand Rapids, MI: Baker, 2005), 187.
91. Derek W. H. Thomas, *Acts.* (R. D. Phillips, P. G. Ryken, and D. M. Doriani, Eds.) (Phillipsburg, NJ: P&R Publishing, 2011), 108.
92. Bob Utley, *The Gospel According to Luke* (Marshall, TX: Bible Lessons International, 2004), vol. 3A.
93. D. A. Carson, D. *Jesus' Sermon on the Mount and His Confrontation with the World: An Exposition of Matthew 5–10* (Grand Rapids, MI: Baker Academic, 1999), 91.

94. Ibid., 92.
95. John R. W. Stott, *The Message of the Sermon On the Mount (Matthew 5–7): Christian Counter-culture* (Leicester; Downers Grove, IL: InterVarsity Press, 1985), 175.
96. Frank Turek, *Stealing from God: Why Atheists Need God to Make Their Case* (NavPress, Kindle Edition, 2014), Kindle Location 3181.
97. Ibid., Kindle Location 3176.
98. John R. W. Stott, *The Message of the Sermon On the Mount (Matthew 5–7): Christian Counter-culture* (Leicester; Downers Grove, IL: InterVarsity Press, 1985), 175-176.
99. Ibid., 176.
100. Ibid.
101. Ibid., 177.
102. Ibid., 188-189.
103. John R. W. Stott, *The Message of the Sermon On the Mount (Matthew 5-7): Christian Counter-culture* (Leicester; Downers Grove, IL: InterVarsity Press, 1985), 189.
104. *The Sermon on the Mount* by Joachim Jeremias (the Ethel M. Wood Lecture delivered before the University of London on 7 March 1961: University of London, Athlone Press, 1961), 96, 97, as quoted in John R. W. Stott, *The Message of the Sermon On the Mount (Matthew 5-7): Christian Counter-culture* (Leicester; Downers Grove, IL: InterVarsity Press, 1985), 185.
105. John R. W. Stott, *The Message of the Sermon On the Mount (Matthew 5-7): Christian Counter-culture* (Leicester; Downers Grove, IL: InterVarsity Press, 1985), 185.
106. Ibid.
107. Brennan Manning, and Jon Foreman, *Abba's Child: the Cry of the Heart for Intimate Belonging* (Colorado Springs, CO: NavPress, 2015).
108. Joachim Jeremias, *The Parables of Jesus* (New York: Scribner, 1970), 128.
109. Manning, and Foreman, *Abba's Child.*
110. Ibid.

111. Henri J. M. Nouwen, *Life of the Beloved: Spiritual Living in a Secular World* (New York: Crossroad, 1992), 21.

112. Manning, and Foreman, *Abba's Child*.

113. Georges Bernanos, *Diary of a Country Priest* (New York: Sheed and Ward, 1936), 178; Brennan Manning, and Jon Foreman, *Abba's Child: the Cry of the Heart for Intimate Belonging* (Colorado Springs, CO: NavPress, 2015).

114. Brennan Manning, *Ruthless Trust, the Ragamuffin's Path to God*, (San Francisco, CA: HarperSanFrancisco, 2000), 15.

115. Manning, and Foreman, *Abba's Child*.

116. Moore, *The Chronological Life of Christ*, 195.

117. Barbieri Jr., "Matthew," in Walvoord and Zuck, eds., *The Bible Knowledge Commentary*, vol. 2, 34.

CHAPTER 7: FROM HEALING A CENTURION'S SERVANT TO CONFRONTATIONS WITH PHARISEES

1. Will Durant, *The Story of Civilization, Vol. 3, Caesar and Christ* (New York: Simon and Schuster, 1972), 557.

2. Bruce B. Barton, *Matthew* (Wheaton, IL: Tyndale House Publishers, 1996), 155.

3. *NIV Cultural Backgrounds Study Bible*, (Grand Rapids, MI: Zondervan, 2016), 1759.

4. Bruce B. Barton, D. Veerman, L. C. Taylor, and G. R. Osborne, *Luke* (Wheaton, IL: Tyndale House Publishers, 1997), 177.

5. Valesius, Life of Eusebius Pamphilus. In Parker S.E. (Trans.), *An Ecclesiastical History to the 20th Year of the Reign of Constantine* (London: Samuel Bagster and Sons, 1847), 146.

6. Mark E. Moore, *The Chronological Life of Christ* (Joplin, MO: College Press Publishing Company, 2011), 204.

7. R. Kent Hughes, *Luke: That You May Know the Truth* (Wheaton, IL: Crossway Books, 1998), 262.

8. L. A. Barbieri Jr., "Matthew," in J. F. Walvoord and R. B. Zuck, eds., *The Bible Knowledge Commentary: An Exposition of the Scriptures* (Wheaton, IL: Victor Books, 1985), vol. 2, 43.

9. Craig L. Blomberg, *Matthew* (Nashville: Broadman & Holman Publishers, 1992), vol. 22, 185.

10. John Peter Lange and J. J. van Oosterzee, *A Commentary on the Holy Scriptures: Luke* (P. Schaff and C. C. Starbuck, Trans.) (Bellingham, WA: Logos Bible Software, 2008), 59.

11. Bruce B. Barton, Matthew (Wheaton, IL: Tyndale House Publishers, 1996), 222, and Crossway Bibles, *The ESV Study Bible* (Wheaton, IL: Crossway Bibles, 2008), 1,843.

12. John D. Barry, *Faithlife Study Bible* (Bellingham, WA: Lexham Press, 2012, 2016).

13. Thomas Hale, *The Applied New Testament Commentary* (Colorado Springs, CO; Ontario, Canada; East Sussex, England: David C. Cook. Crossway Bibles, 1996), 227; Crossway Bibles, *The ESV Study Bible*, 1,843.

14. David L. Turner, *Matthew* (Grand Rapids, MI: Baker Academic, 2008), 330.

15. John F. MacArthur, Jr. (Ed.), *The MacArthur Study Bible* (electronic ed.) (Nashville, TN: Word Pub, 1997), 1416.

16. C. H. Dodd, *The Parables of the Kingdom* (London: Nisbet, 1935; New York: Scribner's 1936), 16.

17. J. E. Miller, "Jesus, Parables of," in J. D. Barry et al., eds., *The Lexham Bible Dictionary* (Bellingham, WA: Lexham Press, 2016).

18. Craig L. Blomberg, *Interpreting the Parables* (Downers Grove, IL: InterVarsity Press, 1990), 30.

19. D. A. Carson, D. A. The Gospels and Acts. In D. A. Carson (Ed.), *NIV Zondervan Study Bible: Built on the Truth of Scripture and Centered on the Gospel Message* (Grand Rapids, MI: Zondervan, 2015), 1956.

20. D. A. Carson, in F. E. Gaebelein, ed., *The Expositor's Bible Commentary: Matthew, Mark, Luke* (Grand Rapids, MI: Zondervan Publishing House), vol. 8, 310.

21. Mark E. Moore, *The Chronological Life of Christ* (Joplin, MO: College Press Publishing Company, 2011), 226.

22. D. R. Sunukjian, "Amos," in Walvoord and Zuck, eds., *The Bible Knowledge Commentary*, vol. 1, 1,448.

23. Michael P. Green, *The Message of Matthew: the Kingdom of Heaven* (Leicester, England; Downers Grove, IL: InterVarsity Press, 2001), 153.
24. Crossway Bibles, *The ESV Study Bible*, 1,848–49.
25. G. Campbell Morgan, *The Parables of the Kingdom* (New York; Chicago; Toronto; London; Edinburgh: Fleming H. Revell Company, 1907), 73–79.
26. Ibid., 82.
27. Ibid.
28. Ibid., 77.
29. D. A. Carson, Matthew, In F. E. Gaebelein (Ed.), *The Expositor's Bible Commentary: Matthew, Mark, Luke* (Grand Rapids, MI: Zondervan Publishing House, 1984), vol. 8, 317–318.
30. Arthur K. Robertson, *Matthew* (Chicago, IL: Moody Press, 1983), 73.
31. Daniel M. Doriani, *NT252 Parables of Jesus* (Bellingham, WA: Lexham Press, 2014), Segment 9.
32. Arthur K. Robertson, *Matthew* (Chicago, IL: Moody Press, 1983), 73
33. Barbieri Jr., "Matthew," in Walvoord and Zuck, eds., *The Bible Knowledge Commentary*, vol. 2, 51.
34. Daniel M. Doriani, *NT252 Parables of Jesus* (Bellingham, WA: Lexham Press, 2014), Segment 11.
35. Barbieri Jr., "Matthew," in Walvoord and Zuck, eds., *The Bible Knowledge Commentary*, vol. 2, 51.
36. Daniel M. Doriani, *NT252 Parables of Jesus* (Bellingham, WA: Lexham Press, 2014), Segment 11.
37. Barbieri Jr., "Matthew," in Walvoord and Zuck, eds., *The Bible Knowledge Commentary*, vol. 2, 52.
38. Craig L. Blomberg, *Matthew* (Nashville: Broadman & Holman Publishers, 1992), vol. 22, 224.
39. Crossway Bibles, *The ESV Study Bible*, 1,849.
40. Ibid., 1850.
41. Charles H. Spurgeon, *The Gospel of the Kingdom: A Commentary on the Book of Matthew* (London: Passmore and Alabaster, 1893). 52.

42. Michael P. Green, *The Message of Matthew: The Kingdom of Heaven* (Leicester, England; Downers Grove, IL: InterVarsity Press, 2001), 119.
43. Crossway Bibles, *The ESV Study Bible*, 1,836.
44. John F. MacArthur, Jr. (Ed.), *The MacArthur Study Bible* (electronic ed.) (Nashville, TN: Word Pub, 1997), 1407.
45. D. M. May, Decapolis. In J. D. Barry, D. Bomar, D. R. Brown, R. Klippenstein, D. Mangum, C. Sinclair Wolcott, ... W. Widder (Eds.), *The Lexham Bible Dictionary* (Bellingham, WA: Lexham Press, 2016).
46. Crossway Bibles, *The ESV Study Bible*, 1,848, 1,902.
47. John D. Barry, *Faithlife Study Bible* (Bellingham, WA: Lexham Press, 2012, 2016).
48. J. D. Grassmick, "Mark," in Walvoord and Zuck, eds., *The Bible Knowledge Commentary*, vol. 2, 126.
49. John F. MacArthur, Jr. (Ed.), *The MacArthur Study Bible* (electronic ed.) (Nashville, TN: Word Pub, 1997), 1470.
50. Bruce B. Barton, *Matthew* (Wheaton, IL: Tyndale House Publishers, 1996), 194.
51. Barbieri Jr., "Matthew," in Walvoord and Zuck, eds., *The Bible Knowledge Commentary*, vol. 2, 41.
52. Bruce B. Barton, *Matthew* (Wheaton, IL: Tyndale House Publishers, 1996), 196.
53. Crossway Bibles, *The ESV Study Bible*, 1,848, 1,975.
54. Earl D. Radmacher, Ronald Barclay Allen, and H. Wayne House, *The Nelson Study Bible: New King James Version* (Nashville: T. Nelson Publishers, 1997).
55. Ibid..
56. Barbieri Jr., "Matthew," in Walvoord and Zuck, eds., *The Bible Knowledge Commentary*, vol. 2, 41.
57. G, F, Hasel, Dove. In G. W. Bromiley (Ed.), *The International Standard Bible Encyclopedia, Revised* (Wm. B. Eerdmans, 1979–1988), vol. 1, 988.
58. Marshall Shelley, *Well-intentioned Dragons: Ministering to Problem People in the Church* (Carol Stream, IL; Waco, TX: Christianity Today; Word Books, 1985), vol. 1, 62.

59. Crossway Bibles, *The ESV Study Bible*, 1,848, 1,840.

60. Craig Blomberg, *Matthew* (Nashville: Broadman & Holman Publishers, 1992), vol. 22, 176.

61. A. Gamble, December 14th: Christ the Divider of Households (Micah 7:6). In I. Steeds (Ed.), *Day by Day: Christ Foreshadowed: Glimpses in the Old Testament* (West Glamorgan, UK: Precious Seed, 2002), 363.

62. F. F. Bruce, *New Testament History* (New York, New York: Doubleday, 1969), 152.

63. Flavius Josephus, *The Works of Josephus: Complete and Unabridged*, William Whiston, trans., Antiquities, (Peabody: Hendrickson, 1987) 18.116–118.

64. H. W. Hoehner, Chronology, In J. B. Green and S. McKnight (Eds.), *Dictionary of Jesus and the Gospels* (Downers Grove, IL: InterVarsity Press, 1992), 119; Walter A. Elwell, and B. J. Beitzel, In *Baker Encyclopedia of the Bible* (Grand Rapids, MI: Baker Book House, 1988), 1183.

65. P. Borgen, *Bread from Heaven* (Leiden: Brill, 1965).

66. Barbieri Jr., "Matthew," in Walvoord and Zuck, eds., *The Bible Knowledge Commentary*, vol. 2, 54.

67. Larry Chouinard, *Matthew* (Joplin, MO: College Press, 1997).

68. Warren W. Wiersbe, *Wiersbe's Expository Outlines on the New Testament* (Wheaton, IL: Victor Books, 1992), 57–58.

69. Ray C. Stedman, *Adventuring Through the New Testament*, (Grand Rapids, MI: Discovery House Publishers, 2011), Kindle Location 1528 of 7729.

70. Grassmick, "Mark," in Walvoord and Zuck, eds., *The Bible Knowledge Commentary*, vol. 2, 132.

71. J. C. Ryle, *Matthew* (Wheaton, IL: Crossway Books, 1993), 121.

72. William Hendriksen and S. Kistemaker, *Exposition of the Gospel According to Mark* (Grand Rapids: Baker Book House, 1953–2001), vol. 10, 264.

73. William L. Lane, *The Gospel of Mark* (Grand Rapids, MI: Wm. B. Eerdmans Publishing Co, 1974), 240–241.

74. William Hendriksen and S. Kistemaker, *Exposition of the Gospel According to John* (Grand Rapids: Baker Book House, 1953–2001), vol. 1, 232.

75. Bruce B. Barton, *John* (Wheaton, IL: Tyndale House, 1993), 139.

76. Gerald L. Borchert, *John 1–11* (Nashville: Broadman & Holman Publishers, 1996), vol. 25A, 272.

77. Mark E. Moore, *The Chronological Life of Christ* (Joplin, MO: College Press Publishing Company, 2011), 280.

78. Matthew Henry and Thomas Scott, *Matthew Henry's Concise Commentary* (Oak Harbor, WA: Logos Research Systems, 1997).

79. Grassmick, "Mark," in Walvoord and Zuck, eds., *The Bible Knowledge Commentary*, vol. 2, 133.

80. Ronald F. Youngblood, F. F. Bruce, and R. K. Harrison, Thomas Nelson Publishers (Eds.), In *Nelson's New Illustrated Bible Dictionary* (Nashville, TN: Thomas Nelson, Inc. Crossway Bibles, 1995); *The ESV Study Bible*, 1,907.

81. John D. Barry et al., *Faithlife Study Bible* (Bellingham, WA: Lexham Press, 2012–2016).

82. Bruce B. Barton, *Mark* (Wheaton, IL: Tyndale House Publishers, 1994), 209.

83. Alfred Edersheim, *The Life and Times of Jesus the Messiah* (New York: Longmans, Green, and Co., 1896), vol. 2, 41–42.

84. Donald English, *The Message of Mark: the Mystery of Faith* (Leicester, England; Downers Grove, IL: InterVarsity Press, 1992), 150–152.

85. Earl D. Radmacher, Ronald Barclay Allen, and H. Wayne House, *The Nelson Study Bible: New King James Version* (Nashville: T. Nelson Publishers, 1997).

86. Bruce B. Barton, *Matthew* (Wheaton, IL: Tyndale House Publishers, 1996), 311–312.

87. Walter W. Wessel, Mark. In F. E. Gaebelein (Ed.), *The Expositor's Bible Commentary: Matthew, Mark, Luke* (Grand Rapids, MI: Zondervan Publishing House, 1984), vol. 8, 686.

88. John F. MacArthur, Jr. (Ed.), *The MacArthur Study Bible* (electronic ed.) (Nashville, TN: Word Pub, 1997), 1475.

89. Ted Cabal et al., *The Apologetics Study Bible: Real Questions, Straight Answers, Stronger Faith* (Nashville, TN: Holman Bible Publishers, 2007), 1482.

90. Crossway Bibles, *The ESV Study Bible*, 1908.

91. P. F. Wilbanks, Magadan. In D. N. Freedman, A. C. Myers, and A. B. Beck (Eds.), *Eerdmans Dictionary of the Bible* (Grand Rapids, MI: W.B. Eerdmans, 2000), 843.

92. Crossway Bibles, *The ESV Study Bible*, 1,854.

93. Leadership Ministries Worldwide. *The Gospel according to Matthew: Chapters 1:1–16:12* (Chattanooga, TN: Leadership Ministries Worldwide, 2004), vol. 1, 364.

94. Blaise Pascal, *The Provincial Letters; PensÈes; Scientific Treatises*, M. J. Adler and R. McHenry, eds., W. F. Trotter, trans., second ed. (Chicago; Auckland; London; Madrid; Manila; Paris; Rome; Seoul; Sydney; Tokyo; Toronto: EncyclopÊdia Britannica, Inc, 1990), vol. 30, 336.

95. Bruce B. Barton et al., *Life Application New Testament Commentary* (Wheaton, IL: Tyndale, 2001), 74–75.

96. K. J. Udd, and M. B. Winstead, Bethsaida. In J. D. Barry, D. Bomar, D. R. Brown, R. Klippenstein, D. Mangum, C. Sinclair Wolcott, … W. Widder (Eds.), *The Lexham Bible Dictionary* (Bellingham, WA: Lexham Press, 2016).

97. Crossway Bibles, *The ESV Study Bible*, 1,909.

98. Lamar Williamson Jr., *Mark* (Atlanta, GA: J. Knox Press, 1983), 148.

99. Geoffrey W. Grogan, *Mark: Good News from Jerusalem* (Ross-shire, Scotland: Christian Focus Publications, 2003), 154.

100. M. G. Easton, In *Easton's Bible dictionary* (New York: Harper & Brothers, 1893).

101. William Hendriksen and S. Kistemaker, *Exposition of the Gospel According to Matthew* (Grand Rapids: Baker Book House, 1953–2001), vol. 9, 646.

102. Crossway Bibles, *The ESV Study Bible*, 1,855.

103. Earl D. Radmacher, R. B. Allen, and H. W. House, *The Nelson Study Bible: New King James Version* (Nashville: T. Nelson

Publishers, 1997); Hendriksen and Kistemaker, *Exposition of the Gospel According to Matthew,* vol. 9, 649.

104. John D. Barry, *Faithlife Study Bible* (Bellingham, WA: Lexham Press, 2012, 2016).

105. Fulton J. Sheen, *Life of Christ* (New York: McGraw-Hill Book Company, Inc., 1958), 20.

106. Charles H. Spurgeon, *Spurgeon's Sermons,* electronic ed. (Albany, OR: Ages Software, 1998), vol. 9.

CHAPTER 8: FROM THE TRANSFIGURATION TO AN ARGUMENT OVER ABRAHAM

1. Philip Schaff, in Robert J. Morgan, *Nelson's Complete Book of Stories, Illustrations, and Quotes,* electronic ed. (Nashville: Thomas Nelson Publishers, 2000), 479.

2. Mark E. Moore, *The Chronological Life of Christ* (Joplin, MO: College Press Publishing Company, 2011), 310.

3. John G. Butler, *Jesus Christ: His Praying* (Clinton, IA: LBC Publications, 2004), vol. 6, 86; Crossway Bibles, *The ESV Study Bible* (Wheaton, IL: Crossway Bibles, 2008), 1,973.

4. Butler, *Jesus Christ: His Praying,* vol. 6, 86.

5. Crossway Bibles, *The ESV Study Bible* (Wheaton, IL: Crossway Bibles, 2008), 1973.

6. James R. Edwards, *The Gospel According to Mark* (Grand Rapids, MI; Leicester, England: Eerdmans; Apollos, 2002), 269.

7. Walter A. Elwell and B. J. Beitzel, in *Baker Encyclopedia of the Bible* (Grand Rapids, MI: Baker Book House, 1988), 2,098.

8. H. J. R. Marston, "Christ All in All," in *The Church Pulpit Commentary: St. Mark–St. Luke 7* (London: J. Nisbet & Co, 1908), 148.

9. Butler, *Jesus Christ: His Praying,* vol. 6, 81.

10. John D. Barry et al., *Faithlife Study Bible* (Bellingham, WA: Lexham Press, 2012, 2016).

11. Crossway Bibles, *The ESV Study Bible,* 1,857.

12. Ibid., 1,858.

13. Michael P. Green, *The Message of Matthew: The Kingdom of Heaven* (Leicester, England; Downers Grove, IL: InterVarsity Press, 2001), 196; Frank E. Gaebelein et al., *The Expositor's Bible Commentary: Matthew, Mark, Luke* (Grand Rapids, MI: Zondervan Publishing House, 1984), vol. 8, 403; Bruce Barton et al., *Life Application New Testament Commentary* (Wheaton, IL: Tyndale, 2001), 83; William Hendriksen and S. J. Kistemaker, *Exposition of the Gospel According to Matthew* (Grand Rapids: Baker Book House, 2001), vol. 9, 703; John F. MacArthur, *The MacArthur Study Bible: New American Standard Bible* (Nashville, TN: Thomas Nelson Publishers, 2006).

14. J. D. Grassmick, "Mark," in J. F. Walvoord and R. B. Zuck, eds., *The Bible Knowledge Commentary: An Exposition of the Scriptures* (Wheaton, IL: Victor Books, 1985), vol. 2, 146.

15. Larry Richards, *The Teacher's Commentary* (Wheaton, IL: Victor Books, 1987), 572.

16. William Barclay, *The Gospel of Matthew*, 3rd ed. (Edinburgh: Saint Andrew Press, 2001), 225.

17. In Mark Water, *The New Encyclopedia of Christian Quotations* (Alresford, Hampshire: John Hunt Publishers Ltd., 2000), 470–71.

18. Barry et al., *Faithlife Study Bible.*

19. L. A. Barbieri Jr., "Matthew," in Walvoord and Zuck, eds., *The Bible Knowledge Commentary*, vol. 2, 45.

20. R. T. France, *Matthew: an Introduction and Commentary* (Downers Grove, IL: InterVarsity Press, 1985), vol. 1, 203.

21. Crossway Bibles, *The ESV Study Bible*, 1,843.

22. Kenneth Daughters, *"The Trinity and the Christian*, in *Emmaus Journal* vol. 14 (2005), 69.

23. R. C. Sproul, *Essential Truths of the Christian Faith* (Wheaton, IL: Tyndale House, 1992), chapter 26.

24. Robert H. Stein, *Luke* (Nashville: Broadman & Holman Publishers, 1992), vol. 24, 313.

25. Michael Green, *The Message of Matthew: the Kingdom of Heaven* (Leicester, England; Downers Grove, IL: InterVarsity Press, 2001), 143.

26. Charles F. Stanley, *Finding Peace: God's Promise of a Life Free from Regret, Anxiety, and Fear* (Nashville, TN: Thomas Nelson Publishers, 2003), 25.

27. Stein, *Luke*, vol. 24, 316.

28. MacArthur Jr., *The MacArthur Study Bible.*

29. John G. Butler, *Jesus Christ: His Parables* (Clinton, IA: LBC Publications. 2002), vol. 3, 388–92.

30. Crossway Bibles, *The ESV Study Bible*, 1,977.

31. Michael Wilcock, *The Savior of the World: the Message of Luke's Gospel* (Downers Grove, IL: InterVarsity Press, 1979), 124.

32. D. Michael Martin, *1, 2 Thessalonians*, vol. 33 (Nashville: Broadman & Holman Publishers, 1995), 61.

33. Barbieri Jr., "Matthew," in Walvoord and Zuck, eds., *The Bible Knowledge Commentary*, vol. 2, 47.

34. Crossway Bibles, *The ESV Study Bible*, 1,899.

35. Ibid., 1,982.

36. Wilcock, *The Savior of the World*, 132.

37. Crossway Bibles, *The ESV Study Bible*, 1,846.

38. Earl D Radmacher, Ronald Barclay Allen, and H. Wayne House, *The Nelson Study Bible: New King James Version* (Nashville: T. Nelson Publishers, 1997).

39. Barton et al., *Life Application New Testament Commentary*, 61.

40. John G. Butler, *Analytical Bible Expositor: Matthew* (Clinton, IA: LBC Publications, 2008), 211.

41. Radmacher, Barclay, and H. Wayne House, *The Nelson Study Bible: New King James Version.*

42. M. G. Easton, in *Easton's Bible Dictionary* (New York: Harper & Brothers, 1893); John T. Carroll, *Luke: A Commentary*, C. C. Black and M. E. Boring, eds., 1st ed. (Louisville, KY: Westminster John Knox Press, 2012), 261.

43. William Hendriksen and S. J. Kistemaker, *Exposition of the Gospel According to Luke* (Grand Rapids: Baker Book House, 1953–2001), vol. 11, 650.

44. Leon Morris, *Luke: An Introduction and Commentary* (Downers Grove, IL: InterVarsity Press, 1988), vol. 3, 228.

45. Warren W. Wiersbe, *The Bible Exposition Commentary* (Wheaton, IL: Victor Books, 1996), vol. 1, 219.

46. M. G. Easton, M. G. In *Easton's Bible Dictionary* (New York: Harper & Brothers, 1893)

47. Walter A. Elwell and B. J. Beitzel, In *Baker Encyclopedia of the Bible* (Grand Rapids, MI: Baker Book House), vol. 1, 539.

48. Wiersbe, *The Bible Exposition Commentary*, vol. 1, 221.

49. Crossway Bibles, *The ESV Study Bible*, 1,982.

50. Joel B. Green, *The Gospel of Luke* (Grand Rapids, MI: Wm. B. Eerdmans Publishing Co., 1997), 494.

51. William Hendriksen and S. J. Kistemaker, *Exposition of the Gospel According to Luke* (Grand Rapids: Baker Book House, 1953–2001), vol. 11, 669.

52. Frank E. Gaebelein et al., *The Expositor's Bible Commentary: Matthew, Mark, Luke* (Grand Rapids, MI: Zondervan Publishing House, 1984), vol. 8, 963.

53. Andrew W. Pitts, *NT316 Book Study: The Gospel of Luke* (Bellingham, WA: Lexham Press, 2015), Segment 94.

54. Bruce B. Barton et al., *Luke* (Wheaton, IL: Tyndale House Publishers, 1997), 331.

55. Arthur W. Pink, *The Arthur Pink Anthology* (Bellingham, WA: Logos Bible Software, 2005).

56. J. C. Ryle, *Expository Thoughts on Luke* (New York: Robert Carter & Brothers, 1879), vol. 2, 103–104.

57. Matthew Henry, *Matthew Henry's Commentary on the Whole Bible: Complete and Unabridged in One Volume* (Peabody: Hendrickson, 1994), 1871.

58. Crossway Bibles, *The ESV Study Bible*, 1,985.

59. Wiersbe, *The Bible Exposition Commentary*, vol. 1, 225.

60. B. M. Austin, "Booths, Feast of," in J. D. Barry, D. Bomar, D. R. Brown, R. Klippenstein, D. Mangum, C. Sinclair Wolcott, ... W. Widder (Eds.), *The Lexham Bible Dictionary* (Bellingham, WA: Lexham Press, 2016).

61. Colin G. Kruse, *John: an Introduction and Commentary* (Downers Grove, IL: InterVarsity Press, 2003), vol. 4, 182.

62. Barry et al., *Faithlife Study Bible*.

63. J. A. Martin, "Luke," Walvoord and Zuck, eds., *The Bible Knowledge Commentary*, vol. 2, 232.

64. Morris, *Luke*, vol. 3, 199.

65. John T. Carroll, *Luke: A Commentary*. (C. C. Black and M. E. Boring, Eds.) (First Edition) (Louisville, KY: Westminster John Knox Press, 2012), 230.

66. Jack Hayford et al., eds., *New Spirit-Filled Life Bible: Notes* (Nashville, TN: Thomas Nelson Bibles, 2002), 1,406.

67. Ibid.

68. Barry et al., *Faithlife Study Bible*.

69. Mark E. Moore, *The Chronological Life of Christ* (Joplin, MO: College Press Publishing Company, 2011), 336.

70. Ibid., 338.

71. MacArthur, *The MacArthur Study Bible*.

72. Bruce B. Barton, *John* (Wheaton, IL: Tyndale House, 1993), 158.

73. Crossway Bibles, *The ESV Study Bible*, 2,037.

74. J. Ramsey Michaels, *The Gospel of John* (Grand Rapids, MI; Cambridge, UK: William B. Eerdmans Publishing Company, 2010), 456.

75. E. A. Blum, "John," Walvoord and Zuck, eds., *The Bible Knowledge Commentary*, vol. 2, 301.

76. Ibid., 302.

77. John Blanchard, In *The Complete Gathered Gold: A Treasury of Quotations for Christians* (Webster, New York; Darlington, England: Evangelical Press, 2006), 351.

78. Crossway Bibles, *The ESV Study Bible*, 2,039.

79. MacArthur, *The MacArthur Study Bible*.

80. Joel Willitts, *NT323 Book Study: The Gospel of John* (Bellingham, WA: Lexham Press, 2014), Segment 60.

81. Blum, "John," Walvoord and Zuck, eds., *The Bible Knowledge Commentary*, vol. 2, 303.

82. Merrill Chapin Tenney, *John: The Gospel of Belief* (Grand Rapids, MI; Cambridge, U.K.: Wm. B. Eerdmans Publishing Co, 1976), 144–145.

83. Gerald L. Borchert, *John 1–11* (Nashville: Broadman & Holman Publishers, 1996), vol. 25A, 297.

84. Andreas J. Kostenberger, *John* G(rand Rapids, MI: Baker Academic, 2004), 257.

85. Leon Morris, *The Gospel According to John* (Grand Rapids, MI: Wm. B. Eerdmans Publishing Co., 1995), 397.

86. Leon Morris, *The Gospel According to John* (Grand Rapids, MI: Wm. B. Eerdmans Publishing Co., 1995), 398.

87. Bruce B. Barton, *John* (Wheaton, IL: Tyndale House, 1993), 158.

88. R. H. Mounce, John. In T. Longman III and D. E. Garland (Eds.), *The Expositor's Bible Commentary: Luke–Acts (Revised Edition)* (Grand Rapids, MI: Zondervan, 2007), vol. 10, 477.

89. Borchert, *John 1–11*, vol. 25A, 303–304.

90. H. D. M. Spence-Jones, Ed.), *St. John* (London; New York: Funk & Wagnalls Company, 1909), vol. 1, 360.

91. Ibid., 363–364.

92. William Hendriksen and S. J. Kistemaker, *Exposition of the Gospel According to John* (Vol. 1–2) (Grand Rapids: Baker Book House, 1953–2001), vol. 2, 61.

93. Ibid.

94. John MacArthur says that this verse most likely indicates Jesus escaped by miraculous means. John F. MacArthur Jr., *The MacArthur Study Bible.*

95. John Owen, *The Works of John Owen*, W. H. Goold, ed. (Edinburgh: T&T Clark), vol. 17, 566.

CHAPTER 9: FROM HEALING A BLIND MAN TO MARY'S OINTMENT

1. Gary Benfold, *Why Lord? The Book of Job for Today* (Epsom, Surrey: Day One, 1998), 90.

2. Leon Morris, *The Gospel According to John* (Grand Rapids, MI: Wm. B. Eerdmans Publishing Co, 1995), 428.

3. Warren W. Wiersbe, *The Bible Exposition Commentary* (Wheaton, IL: Victor Books, 1996), vol. 1, 325.

4. John D. Barry et al, *Faithlife Study Bible* (Bellingham, WA: Lexham Press, 2012, 2016).

5.   Colin G. Kruse, C. G. (2003). *John: an Introduction and Commentary* (Vol. 4) ⸀Downers Grove, IL: InterVarsity Press, 2003), 226.

6.   J. Vernon McGee, *Thru the Bible Commentary* (electronic ed.) (Nashville: Thomas Nelson, 1997), Volume 4, 426–427.

7.   J. E. White, John. In D. S. Dockery (Ed.), *Holman Concise Bible Commentary* (Nashville, TN: Broadman & Holman Publishers, 1998), 477.

8.   Leon Morris, *The Gospel According to John* (Grand Rapids, MI: Wm. B. Eerdmans Publishing Co, 1995), 442.

9.   Walter A. Elwell and B. J. Beitzel, In *Baker Encyclopedia of the Bible* (Grand Rapids, MI: Baker Book House, 1988), Volume 2, 2091.

10. Charles H. Spurgeon, "Whose Goodness Faileth Never", No. 2919, *Spurgeon's Sermons* (electronic ed., Vol. 51) (Albany, OR: Ages Software, 1998).

11. Arthur W. Pink, A. W. (1923–1945). *Exposition of the Gospel of John* (Swengel, PA: Bible Truth Depot, (1923–1945), 529.

12. Charles H. Spurgeon, "Whose Goodness Faileth Never", No. 2919, *Spurgeon's Sermons* (electronic ed., Vol. 51) (Albany, OR: Ages Software, 1998).

13. Ronald F. Youngblood, F. F. Bruce, R. K. Harrison, Thomas Nelson Publishers (Eds.). In *Nelson's New illustrated Bible Dictionary* (Nashville, TN: Thomas Nelson, Inc., 1995).

14. Grant R. Osborne and Philip W. Comfort, *Cornerstone Biblical Commentary, Vol 13: John and 1, 2, and 3 John* (Carol Stream, IL: Tyndale House Publishers, 2007), 157.

15. Bruce B. Barton, *John* (Wheaton, IL: Tyndale House, 1993), 218.

16. Not all scholars agree. Dr. Michael Heiser, whose book, *The Unseen Realm*, deals with these types of questions, argues in a scholarly paper that God, in Psalm 82, was talking not to human beings but lesser divine beings. Michael S. Heiser, Jesus' Quotation of Psalm 82:6 in John 10:34: A Different View of John's Theological Strategy; See also Michael S. Heiser, *The Unseen Realm: Recovering the Supernatural Worldview of the Bible* (First Edition) (Bellingham, WA: Lexham Press, 2015). But for the majority view,

see Leon Morris, *The Gospel According to John* (Grand Rapids, MI: Wm. B. Eerdmans Publishing Co, 1995), 467; E. A. Blum, John. In J. F. Walvoord and R. B. Zuck, eds., *The Bible Knowledge Commentary: An Exposition of the Scriptures* (Wheaton, IL: Victor Books, 1985), Volume 2, 312; Gerald L. Borchert, *John 1–11* (Nashville: Broadman & Holman Publishers, 1996), vol. 25A, 343; William Hendriksen and S. J. Kistemaker, *Exposition of the Gospel According to John* (Vol. 1–2) (Grand Rapids: Baker Book House, 1953–2001), Volume 2, 128; Bruce Milne *The Message of John: Here is Your King!: with study guide* (Leicester, England; Downers Grove, IL: InterVarsity Press, 1993), 155.

17. Robert H. Stein, *Luke* (Vol. 24) (Nashville: Broadman & Holman Publishers, 1992), 379.

18. Norval Geldenhuys, *Commentary on the Gospel of Luke: The English Text with Introduction, Exposition and Notes* (Grand Rapids, MI: Wm. B. Eerdmans Publishing Co., 1952), 380.

19. William Manson, *The Gospel of Luke* (J. Moffatt, Ed.) (New York; London: Harper and Brothers Publishers, 1930), 167.

20. Leon Morris, *Luke: an Introduction and Commentary* (Vol. 3) (Downers Grove, IL: InterVarsity Press, 1988), 244.

21. Bruce B. Barton et al, *Life Application New Testament Commentary* (Wheaton, IL: Tyndale, 2001), 315.

22. Mark E. Moore, *The Chronological Life of Christ* (Joplin, MO: College Press Publishing Company, 2011), 415–416.

23. John Nolland, *Luke 9:21–18:34* (Vol. 35B) (Dallas: Word, Incorporated, 1998), 743–744.

24. Moore, *The Chronological Life of Christ*, 418.

25. Fred B. Craddock, *Luke* (Louisville, KY: John Knox Press, 1990), 177.

26. Ibid., 178–179.

27. Walter C. Kaiser, Jr. et al, *Hard Sayings of the Bible* (Downers Grove, IL: Intervarsity, 1996), 475.

28. Wiersbe, *The Bible Exposition Commentary*, vol. 1, 232.

29. John T. Carroll, *Luke: A Commentary*, (C. C. Black and M. E. Boring, Eds.) (First Edition) (Louisville, KY: Westminster John Knox Press, 2012), 308.

30. L. A. Barbieri Jr., "Matthew," in Walvoord and Zuck, eds., *The Bible Knowledge Commentary*, vol. 2, 62.

31. John T. Carroll, *Luke: A Commentary*, (C. C. Black and M. E. Boring, Eds.) (First Edition) (Louisville, KY: Westminster John Knox Press, 2012), 318.

32. William Hendriksen and S. J. Kistemaker, *Exposition of the Gospel According to Luke* (Grand Rapids: Baker Book House, 1953–2001), Volume 11, 755.

33. Timothy J, Keller, *The Prodigal God: Recovering the Heart of the Christian Faith* (1st ed.) (New York: Dutton, 2008), 24.

34. John Piper, "Our Hope: Righteousness," June 1, 1986, *Sermons from John Piper (1980–1989)* (Minneapolis, MN: Desiring God, 2007).

35. Moore, *The Chronological Life of Christ*, 432.

36. Crossway Bibles, *The ESV Study Bible* (Wheaton, IL: Crossway Bibles, 2008), 1992.

37. Paul J. Achtemeier, "Bethany," in *Harper's Bible Dictionary* (1st ed.) (San Francisco: Harper & Row, 1985).

38. Charles H. Spurgeon, "Might Have Been, or May Be," *Spurgeon's Sermons* (electronic ed., Vol. 33) (Albany, OR: Ages Software, 1998).

39. Charles H. Spurgeon, "Jesus Sitting On the Well," *Spurgeon's Sermons* (electronic ed., Vol. 44) (Albany, OR: Ages Software, 1998).

40. Timothy J. Keller, "The Love of Christ," August 25, 1991, In *The Timothy Keller Sermon Archive* (New York City: Redeemer Presbyterian Church, 2013).

41. Wiersbe, *The Bible Exposition Commentary*, vol. 1, 338.

42. Charles C. Ryrie, *Ryrie Study Bible: New International Version* (Expanded ed.) (Chicago: Moody Publishers, 1994), 1643.

43. Craig A. Evans, *NT319 Book Study: The Gospel of Luke in Its Gentile Context* (Bellingham, WA: Lexham Press, 2016), Segment 59.

44. I. Howard Marshall, *The Gospel of Luke: a Commentary on the Greek Text* (Exeter: Paternoster Press, 1978), 649.

45. Douglas J. Moo, *NT305 New Testament Theology* (Bellingham, WA: Lexham Press, 2015), Segment 23.

46. Francois Bovon, *Luke 2: A Commentary on the Gospel of Luke 9:51–19:27.* (H. Koester, Ed., D. S. Deer, Trans.) (Minneapolis, MN: Fortress Press, 2013), 527.

47. Norval Geldenhuys, *Commentary on the Gospel of Luke: The English Text with Introduction, Exposition and Notes* (Grand Rapids, MI: Wm. B. Eerdmans Publishing Co., 1952), 451.

48. J. Knox Chamblin, J. K. (2010). *Matthew: A Mentor Commentary.* Ross-shire, Great Britain: Mentor, 2010), 930.

49. R. T. France, *Matthew: an introduction and commentary* (Vol. 1) (Downers Grove, IL: InterVarsity Press 1985), 286.

50. Thomas Hale, *The Applied New Testament Commentary* (Colorado Springs, CO; Ontario, Canada; East Sussex, England: David C. Cook, 1996), 252.

51. Larry Chouinard, *Matthew* (Joplin, MO: College Press, 1997).

52. Barbieri Jr., "Matthew," in Walvoord and Zuck, eds., *The Bible Knowledge Commentary*, vol. 2, 66.

53. Ralph Earle, *Mark: the Gospel of Action* (Chicago: Moody Press, 1970), 89.

54. D. Edmond Hiebert, *The Gospel of Mark: An Expositional Commentary* (Greenville, SC: Bob Jones University Press, 1994), 297.

55. Ibid., 299–300.

56. Wiersbe, *The Bible Exposition Commentary*, vol. 1, 251.

57. Robert H. Stein, *Luke* (Vol. 24) (Nashville: Broadman & Holman Publishers, 1992), 467.

58. W. L. Leifeld, Luke. In F. E. Gaebelein (Ed.), *The Expositor's Bible Commentary: Matthew, Mark, Luke* (Vol. 8) (Grand Rapids, MI: Zondervan Publishing House, 1984), 1007.

59. Donald S. Fortner, *Discovering Christ in the Gospel of Luke* (Vol. 2) (Durham, England: Go Publications, 2012), 218–219.

60. M. M. Schaub, Pottery. In M. A. Powell (Ed.), *The HarperCollins Bible Dictionary (Revised and Updated)* (Third Edition) (New York: HarperCollins, 2011), 824.

61. Crossway Bibles, *The ESV Study Bible*, 1,997.

62. Allison A. Trites and William J. Larkin, *Cornerstone Biblical Commentary, Vol 12: The Gospel of Luke and Acts* (Carol Stream, IL: Tyndale House Publishers, 2006), 255.
63. Borchert, *John 1–11*, vol. 25A, 32.
64. In Chapter 7 we discussed a similar incident reported in the Gospel of Luke (7:36–50). Most scholars believe these are separate incidents because they occur at different times and locations in Jesus' ministry and teach different lessons. Additionally, Luke describes the woman anointing Jesus as a sinner. See Crossway Bibles, *The ESV Study Bible*, 2,047, and Gerald L. Borchert, *John 1–11* (Vol. 25A) (Nashville: Broadman & Holman Publishers, 1996), 32–33.
65. Borchert, *John 1–11*, vol. 25A, 37.

CHAPTER 10: FROM THE PLOT TO KILL LAZARUS TO PETER'S ILL-FATED VOW

1. Paul Barnett, *Finding the Historical Christ* (Grand Rapids, MI; Cambridge, U.K.: William B. Eerdmans Publishing Company, 2009), Vol. 3, 270.
2. Tokunboh Adeyemo, *Africa Bible commentary* (Nairobi, Kenya; Grand Rapids, MI: WordAlive Publishers; Zondervan, 2006), 1303.
3. Leon Morris, *The Gospel According to John* (Grand Rapids, MI: Wm. B. Eerdmans Publishing Co, 1995), 517.
4. Joel B. Green, *The Gospel of Luke* (Grand Rapids, MI: Wm. B. Eerdmans Publishing Co., 1997) 688.
5. Philip Graham Ryken, *Luke*. (R. D. Phillips, P. G. Ryken, & D. M. Doriani, Eds.) (Vol. 1 & 2) (Phillipsburg, NJ: P&R Publishing. 2009), Volume 2, 335–336.
6. Bruce B. Barton, *Matthew* (Wheaton, IL: Tyndale House Publishers, 1996), 404–5.
7. Ibid., 407.
8. Allison Trites, & J. William Larkin. *Cornerstone Biblical Commentary, Vol 12: The Gospel of Luke and Acts* (Carol Stream, IL: Tyndale House Publishers, 2006), 260.

9. William Hendriksen, & S. J. Kistemaker, *Exposition of the Gospel According to Mark* (Vol. 10) (Grand Rapids: Baker Book House, 1953–2001), 441.

10. J. D. Grassmick, Mark. In J. F. Walvoord & R. B. Zuck (Eds.), *The Bible Knowledge Commentary: An Exposition of the Scriptures* (Wheaton, IL: Victor Books, 1985), Volume 2, 157.

11. Craig L. Blomberg, *Matthew* (Vol. 22) (Nashville: Broadman & Holman Publishers, 1992), 318.

12. Ralph Earle, The Gospel according to St. Luke, In *Matthew-Acts* (Vol. 4) (Grand Rapids, MI: William B. Eerdmans Publishing Company, 1966), 284.

13. J. Vernon McGee, *Thru the Bible commentary: The Gospels (Mark)* (electronic ed., Vol. 36) (Nashville: Thomas Nelson, 1991), 137.

14. Douglas R. A. Hare, *Matthew* (Louisville, KY: John Knox Press, 1993), 244.

15. Ibid.

16. L. A. Barbieri, Jr. Matthew, In J. F. Walvoord & R. B. Zuck (Eds.), *The Bible Knowledge Commentary: An Exposition of the Scriptures* (Wheaton, IL: Victor Books, 1985), Volume 2, 68.

17. Bruce Barton, et al, *Life Application New Testament Commentary* (Wheaton, IL: Tyndale, 2001), 92.

18. William Hendriksen, & S. J. Kistemaker, *Exposition of the Gospel According to John* (Vol. 1–2) (Grand Rapids: Baker Book House, 1953–2001), Volume 2, 193.

19. C. H. Dodd, *The Interpretation of the Fourth Gospel*, 372, In Frederick Dale Bruner, Bruner, *The Gospel of John: A Commentary* (Grand Rapids, MI;Cambridge, U.K.: Eerdmans, 2012), 712.

20. Theodore of Mopsuestia, *John*, 5:12:24, in ACCS NT 4/b: 60, In Frederick Dale Bruner, Bruner, *The Gospel of John: A Commentary* (Grand Rapids, MI;Cambridge, U.K.: Eerdmans, 2012), 711.

21. Lesslie Newbigin, *The Light Has Come*, 156, In Frederick Dale Bruner, Bruner, *The Gospel of John: A Commentary* (Grand Rapids, MI;Cambridge, U.K.: Eerdmans, 2012), 712.

22. P. Garcìa, Son of God Text, Aramaic. In J. D. Barry, D. Bomar, D. R. Brown, R. Klippenstein, D. Mangum, C. Sinclair Wolcott, … W.

Widder (Eds.), *The Lexham Bible Dictionary* (Bellingham, WA: Lexham Press, 2016).

23. Walter A. Elwell, & B. J. Beitzel, In *Baker encyclopedia of the Bible* (Grand Rapids, MI: Baker Book House, 1988), Volume 2, 1983.

24. Ibid.

25. D. Senior, Son of Man. In D. N. Freedman, A. C. Myers, & A. B. Beck (Eds.), *Eerdmans Dictionary of the Bible* (Grand Rapids, MI: W.B. Eerdmans, 2000), 1242.

26. Philip W. Comfort, *Encountering the Manuscripts: An Introduction to New Testament Paleography & Textual Criticism* (Nashville, TN: Broadman & Holman, 2005), 245.

27. Douglas J. Moo, *NT305 New Testament Theology* (Bellingham, WA: Lexham Press, 2015), Segment 30.

28. E. A. Blum, John. In J. F. Walvoord & R. B. Zuck (Eds.), *The Bible Knowledge Commentary: An Exposition of the Scriptures* (Wheaton, IL: Victor Books, 1985), Volume 2, 319.

29. Merrill Chapin Tenney, *John: The Gospel of Belief* (Grand Rapids, MI; Cambridge, U.K.: Wm. B. Eerdmans Publishing Co, 1976), 196.

30. Colin G. Kruse, *John: An Introduction and Commentary* (Downers Grove, IL: InterVarsity Press, 2003), Vol. 4, 272–273.

31. William Hendriksen, & S. J. Kistemaker, *Exposition of the Gospel According to Matthew* (Vol. 9) (Grand Rapids: Baker Book House, 1953–2001), 776.

32. Ibid., 786.

33. Ibid., 786.

34. Charles Price, *Matthew: Can Anything Good Come Out of Nazareth?*. (Fearn, Great Britain: Christian Focus Publications, 1998), 267.

35. "We Are Made in the Image of God," Ravi Zacharias remarks at No Compromise: 2013 National Conference, http://www.ligonier. org/blog/we-are-made-image-god/

36. Craig S. Keener, *Matthew* (Vol. 1) (Downers Grove, IL: InterVarsity Press, 1997).

37. Thomas Hale, *The Applied New Testament Commentary* (Colorado Springs, CO; Ontario, Canada; East Sussex, England: David C. Cook. 1996), 263.

38. Earl D. Radmacher, Ronald Barclay Allen, & H. Wayne House, *The Nelson Study Bible: New King James Version* (Nashville: T. Nelson Publishers, 1997).

39. D. W. Pao & E. J. Schnabel, Luke. In *Commentary on the New Testament Use of the Old Testament* (Grand Rapids, MI; Nottingham, UK: Baker Academic; Apollos, 2007), 370.

40. M. Eugene Boring, *Mark: A Commentary*. (C. C. Black, J. T. Carroll, & M. E. Boring, Eds.) (Louisville, KY: Westminster John Knox Press, 2012), 345.

41. J. D. Grassmick, Mark. In J. F. Walvoord & R. B. Zuck (Eds.), *The Bible Knowledge Commentary: An Exposition of the Scriptures* (Wheaton, IL: Victor Books, 1985), Volume 2, 164–165.

42. William Hendriksen & S. J. Kistemaker, *Exposition of the Gospel According to Mark* (Vol. 10) (Grand Rapids: Baker Book House, 1953–2001), 499.

43. Earl D. Radmacher, Ronald Barclay Allen, & H. Wayne House, *The Nelson Study Bible: New King James Version* (Nashville: T. Nelson Publishers, 1997).

44. Walter A. Elwell & Philip W. Comfort, In *Tyndale Bible Dictionary* (Wheaton, IL: Tyndale House Publishers, 2001), 1307.

45. Crossway Bibles, *The ESV Study Bible* (Wheaton, IL: Crossway Bibles, 2008), 1871.

46. L. A. Barbieri, Jr. Matthew, In J. F. Walvoord & R. B. Zuck (Eds.), *The Bible Knowledge Commentary: An Exposition of the Scriptures* (Wheaton, IL: Victor Books, 1985), Volume 2, 74.

47. Charles Price, *Matthew: Can Anything Good Come Out of Nazareth?* (Fearn, Great Britain: Christian Focus Publications, 1998), 286–287.

48. L. A. Barbieri, Jr. Matthew, In J. F. Walvoord & R. B. Zuck (Eds.), *The Bible Knowledge Commentary: An Exposition of the Scriptures* (Wheaton, IL: Victor Books, 1985), Volume 2, 75.

49. James R. Edwards, *The Gospel According to Mark* (Grand Rapids, MI; Leicester, England: Eerdmans; Apollos, 2002), 381.

50. Flavius Josephus & William Whiston, *The Works of Josephus: Complete and Unabridged* (Peabody: Hendrickson, 1987), Wars of the Jews 5.177.

51. Robert Picirilli, *The Gospel of Mark*. (R. E. Picirilli, Ed.) (First Edition) (Nashville, TN: Randall House Publications, 2003), 348.

52. Flavius Josephus & William Whiston, *The Works of Josephus: Complete and Unabridged* (Peabody: Hendrickson, 1987), Wars of the Jews 7.1.

53. William L. Lane, *The Gospel of Mark* (Grand Rapids, MI: Wm. B. Eerdmans Publishing Co, 1974), 453.

54. Robert Picirilli, *The Gospel of Mark*. (R. E. Picirilli, Ed.) (First Edition) (Nashville, TN: Randall House Publications, 2003), 349.

55. William L. Lane, *The Gospel of Mark* (Grand Rapids, MI: Wm. B. Eerdmans Publishing Co, 1974), 453.

56. L. A. Barbieri, Jr. Matthew, In J. F. Walvoord & R. B. Zuck (Eds.), *The Bible Knowledge Commentary: An Exposition of the Scriptures* (Wheaton, IL: Victor Books, 1985), Volume 2, 76.

57. John F. MacArthur, Jr., *The MacArthur Study Bible: New American Standard Bible* (Nashville, TN: Thomas Nelson Publishers, 2006).

58. Ibid.

59. Craig Blomberg, *Matthew* (Vol. 22) (Nashville: Broadman & Holman Publishers, 1992), 356.

60. John F. MacArthur, Jr., *The MacArthur Study Bible: New American Standard Bible* (Nashville, TN: Thomas Nelson Publishers, 2006).

61. Walter W. Wessel, Mark. In F. E. Gaebelein (Ed.), *The Expositor's Bible Commentary: Matthew, Mark, Luke* (Vol. 8) (Grand Rapids, MI: Zondervan Publishing House, 1984), 748.

62. Charles Caldwell Ryrie, *Ryrie Study Bible: New International Version* (Expanded ed.) (Chicago: Moody Publishers, 1994), 1506.

63. Crossway Bibles, *The ESV Study Bible* (Wheaton, IL: Crossway Bibles, 2008), 1876.

64. William Hendriksen & S. J. Kristemaker, *Exposition of the Gospel According to Matthew* (Vol. 9) (Grand Rapids: Baker Book House, 1953–2001).

65. D. A. Carson, Matthew. In F. E. Gaebelein (Ed.), *The Expositor's Bible Commentary: Matthew, Mark, Luke* (Vol. 8) (Grand Rapids, MI: Zondervan Publishing House, 1984), 519.

66. Ibid., 522.

67. John F. MacArthur, Jr., *The MacArthur Study Bible: New American Standard Bible* (Nashville, TN: Thomas Nelson Publishers, 2006).

68. Craig Blomberg, *Matthew* (Vol. 22) (Nashville: Broadman & Holman Publishers, 1992), 382–383.

69. Ibid.

70. Leadership Ministries Worldwide, *Matthew: Chapters 16:13–28:20* (Vol. II) (Chattanooga, TN: Leadership Ministries Worldwide, 1996), Volume 2, 235.

71. This was the first day of the seven-day Feast of Unleavened Bread. On the first day the Passover lambs were sacrificed (Mark 14:12). This feast followed immediately after the Passover and the eight-day event was called the Passover Week. L. A. Barbieri, Jr. Matthew, In J. F. Walvoord & R. B. Zuck (Eds.), *The Bible Knowledge Commentary: An Exposition of the Scriptures* (Wheaton, IL: Victor Books, 1985), Volume 2, 82.

72. Jim Dixon & Lee Strobel, *What Would Jesus Ask? 10 Questions That Will Transform Your Life* (Ventura, CA: Gospel Light, 2013).

73. D. A. Carson, *The Gospel According to John* (Leicester, England; Grand Rapids, MI: Inter-Varsity Press; W.B. Eerdmans, 1991), 462.

74. E. A. Blum, John. In J. F. Walvoord & R. B. Zuck (Eds.), *The Bible Knowledge Commentary: An Exposition of the Scriptures* (Wheaton, IL: Victor Books, 1985), Volume 2, 320.

75. Frederick Dale Bruner, *The Gospel of John: A Commentary* (Grand Rapids, MI;Cambridge, U.K.: Eerdmans, 2012), 765.

76. When Peter draws his sword and cuts off the right ear of the high priest's servant who has come to arrest Jesus (John 18:10).

77. Norman L. Geisler, *Systematic Theology, Volume Four: Church, Last Things* (Minneapolis, MN: Bethany House Publishers, 2005), Volume Four, 151.

78. Ronald F. Youngblood, F. F. Bruce, & R. K. Harrison, Thomas Nelson Publishers (Eds.), In *Nelson's New illustrated Bible Dictionary* (Nashville, TN: Thomas Nelson, Inc., 1995).

79. Craig Blomberg, *Matthew* (Vol. 22) (Nashville: Broadman & Holman Publishers, 1992), 390.

80. Norman L. Geisler, *Systematic Theology, Volume Four: Church, Last Things* (Minneapolis, MN: Bethany House Publishers, 2005), Volume Four, 157.

81. Ronald F. Youngblood, F. F. Bruce, & R. K. Harrison, Thomas Nelson Publishers (Eds.), In *Nelson's New illustrated Bible Dictionary* (Nashville, TN: Thomas Nelson, Inc., 1995).

82. Norman L. Geisler, *Systematic Theology, Volume Four: Church, Last Things* (Minneapolis, MN: Bethany House Publishers, 2005), Volume Four, 173; Paul P. Enns, *The Moody Handbook of Theology* (Chicago, IL: Moody Press, 1989), 361–362.

83. Ronald F. Youngblood, F. F. Bruce, & R. K. Harrison, Thomas Nelson Publishers (Eds.), In *Nelson's New illustrated Bible Dictionary* (Nashville, TN: Thomas Nelson, Inc., 1995).

84. Paul P. Enns, *The Moody Handbook of Theology* (Chicago, IL: Moody Press, 1989), 362.

85. Leon Morris, *The Gospel According to John* (Grand Rapids, MI: Wm. B. Eerdmans Publishing Co., 1995), 560.

86. Bruce B. Barton, *John* (Wheaton, IL: Tyndale House, 1993), 281.

CHAPTER 11: FROM JESUS' REASSURANCE TO PILATE'S JUDGMENT

1. A. W. Tozer, *Of God and Men* (Camp Hill, PA: WingSpread, 1995), 5.

2. D. A. Carson, *The Gospel According to John* (Leicester, England; Grand Rapids, MI: Inter-Varsity Press; W.B. Eerdmans, 1991), 491.

3. Crossway Bibles, *The ESV Study Bible* (Wheaton, IL: Crossway Bibles, 2008), 2056.

4. David K. Clark & John S. Feinberg, *To Know and Love God: Method for Theology* (Wheaton, IL: Crossway, 2003).

5. John Piper, "The Holy Spirit: He is God!" *Sermons from John Piper* (Minneapolis, MN: Desiring God, 1980–1989).

6. J. I. Packer, *Knowing God* (Downers Grove, Ill.: InterVarsity Press, 1973), 60.

7. James Montgomery Boice, *The Gospel of John: An Expositional Commentary* (Grand Rapids, MI: Baker Books, 2005), 1120.

8. Norman L. Geisler & Ron Rhodes, *When Cultists Ask: A Popular Handbook on Cultic Misinterpretations* (Grand Rapids, MI: Baker Books, 1997), 184.

9. Crossway Bibles, *The ESV Study Bible* (Wheaton, IL: Crossway Bibles, 2008), 2054.

10. Bruce Milne, *The Message of John: Here is Your King!: with study guide* (Leicester, England; Downers Grove, IL: InterVarsity Press, 1993), 221.

11. D. A. Carson, *The Gospel According to John* (Leicester, England; Grand Rapids, MI: Inter-Varsity Press; W.B. Eerdmans, 1991), 521.

12. John Brown, *Discourses and Sayings of Our Lord Jesus Christ, Illustrated in a Series of Expositions* (Vol. I & II) (New York: Robert Carter & Brothers, 1854), Volume 2, 393.

13. William Hendriksen, & S. J. Kistemaker, *Exposition of the Gospel According to John* (Vol. 1–2) (Grand Rapids: Baker Book House, 1953–2001), Volume 2, 310.

14. Gerald L. Borchert, *John 12–21* (Vol. 25B) (Nashville: Broadman & Holman Publishers, 2002), 154.

15. R. Kent Hughes, *John: That You May Believe* (Wheaton, IL: Crossway Books, 1999), 369.

16. Crossway Bibles, *The ESV Study Bible* (Wheaton, IL: Crossway Bibles, 2008), 2056.

17. Ibid.

18. E. A. Blum, E. A. John. In J. F. Walvoord & R. B. Zuck (Eds.), *The Bible Knowledge Commentary: An Exposition of the Scriptures* (Wheaton, IL: Victor Books 1985), Volume 2, 329.

19. Merrill Chapin Tenney, *John: The Gospel of Belief* (Grand Rapids, MI; Cambridge, U.K.: Wm. B. Eerdmans Publishing Co., 1976), 240.

20. John Calvin, *John* (Wheaton, IL: Crossway Books, 1994), John 16:23.

21. Leon Morris, *The Gospel According to John* (Grand Rapids, MI: Wm. B. Eerdmans Publishing Co., 1995), 628.

22. Crossway Bibles, *The ESV Study Bible* (Wheaton, IL: Crossway Bibles, 2008), 2053.

23. Warren W. Wiersbe, *Prayer: Basic Training* (Wheaton, IL: Tyndale, 1988), 9.

24. Ibid., 12.

25. Ibid., 13.

26. Timothy J. Keller, "Glory in Your Life," November 3, 2002, *The Timothy Keller Sermon Archive* New York City: Redeemer Presbyterian Church, 2013).

27. Rolland McCune, *A Systematic Theology of Biblical Christianity: The Doctrines of Man, Sin, Christ, and the Holy Spirit* (Vol. 2) (Allen Park, MI: Detroit Baptist Theological Seminary, 2009), 137.

28. Crossway Bibles, *The ESV Study Bible* (Wheaton, IL: Crossway Bibles, 2008), 2008.

29. Bruce B. Barton, *Matthew* (Wheaton, IL: Tyndale House Publishers, 1996), 532–533.

30. Bruce B. Barton, *Mark* (Wheaton, IL: Tyndale House Publishers, 1994), 447–448.

31. Mark E. Moore, *The Chronological Life of Christ* (Joplin, MO: College Press Publishing Company, 2011), 625, and E. A. Blum, in J. F. Walvoord and R. B. Zuck (eds.), *The Bible Knowledge Commentary: An Exposition of the Scriptures* (Wheaton, Il: Victor Books, 1985), Vol 2, 237.

32. D. A. Carson, Matthew. In F. E. Gaebelein (Ed.), *The Expositor's Bible Commentary: Matthew, Mark, Luke* (Vol. 8) (Grand Rapids, MI: Zondervan Publishing House, 1984), 563.

33. Robert H. Stein, *Luke* (Vol. 24) (Nashville: Broadman & Holman Publishers, 1992), 578–579.

34. Ravi Zacharias, *Deliver Us From Evil* (Nashville: Thomas Nelson Company, 2000).

35. Bruce B. Barton, *Matthew* (Wheaton, IL: Tyndale House Publishers, 1996), 549.

36. Gerald L. Borchert, *John 12–21* (Vol. 25B) (Nashville: Broadman & Holman Publishers, 2002), 252; Bruce B. Barton, *John* (Wheaton, IL: Tyndale House, 1993), 370.

CHAPTER 12: FROM THE FLOGGING OF JESUS TO HIS ASCENSION

1. John Blanchard, In *The Complete Gathered Gold: A Treasury of Quotations for Christians* (Webster, New York; Darlington, England: Evangelical Press, 2006), 537.
2. Ibid., 538.
3. Bruce B. Barton, *John* (Wheaton, IL: Tyndale House, 1993), 375.
4. Craig A. Evans, *The Bible Knowledge Background Commentary: Matthew–Luke.* (C. A. Evans & C. A. Bubeck, Eds.) (First Edition) (Colorado Springs, CO: David C Cook, 2003), 510.
5. Robert H. Stein, *Luke* (Vol. 24) (Nashville: Broadman & Holman Publishers, 1992), 586.
6. Ibid.
7. James A. Brooks, *Mark* (Vol. 23) (Nashville: Broadman & Holman Publishers, 1991), 258.
8. J. D. Grassmick, Mark. In J. F. Walvoord & R. B. Zuck (Eds.), *The Bible Knowledge Commentary: An Exposition of the Scriptures* (Wheaton, IL: Victor Books, 1985), Volume 2, 190; L. A. Barbieri, Jr. Matthew. In J. F. Walvoord & R. B. Zuck (Eds.), *The Bible Knowledge Commentary: An Exposition of the Scriptures* (Wheaton, IL: Victor Books, 1985), Volume 2, 90.
9. Crossway Bibles. *The ESV Study Bible* (Wheaton, IL: Crossway Bibles, 2008), 2010.
10. Charles H. Spurgeon, God's Tender Mercy. In *The Metropolitan Tabernacle Pulpit Sermons* (Vol. 53, pp. 109–120) (London: Passmore & Alabaster, 1907).
11. J. C. Ryle, *Holiness: Its Nature, Hindrances, Difficulties and Roots* (London: William Hunt and Company, 1889), 260–261.
12. Gerald L. Borchert, *John 12–21* (Vol. 25B) (Nashville: Broadman & Holman Publishers, 2002), 269.

13. William Hendriksen & S. J. Kistemaker, *Exposition of the Gospel According to John* (Vol. 1–2) (Grand Rapids: Baker Book House, 1953–2001), Volume 2, 428.

14. William Hendriksen & S. J. Kistemaker, *Exposition of the Gospel According to Matthew* (Vol. 9) (Grand Rapids: Baker Book House, 1953–2001), 966.

15. Charles Caldwell Ryrie, *Basic Theology: A Popular Systematic Guide to Understanding Biblical Truth* (Chicago, IL: Moody Press, 1999), 301.

16. J. D. Grassmick, "Mark," in J. F. Walvoord and R. B. Zuck, eds., *The Bible Knowledge Commentary: An Exposition of the Scriptures*, vol. 2 (Wheaton, IL: Victor Books, 1985), 189.

17. See the poignant description of Jesus' passion in Norman L. Geisler & Frank Turek, *I Don't Have Enough Faith To Be An Atheist* (Wheaton, IL: Crossway Books, 2004), 381–383.

18. Crossway Bibles. *The ESV Study Bible* (Wheaton, IL: Crossway Bibles, 2008), 2068.

19. Ibid., 1887.

20. E. A. Blum, John. In J. F. Walvoord & R. B. Zuck (Eds.), *The Bible Knowledge Commentary: An Exposition of the Scriptures* (Wheaton, IL: Victor Books, 1985), Volume 2, 340.

21. Harvey J. S. Blaney, The Gospel According to St. John, In *Matthew-Acts* (Vol. 4) (Grand Rapids, MI: William B. Eerdmans Publishing Company, 1966), 467.

22. James A. Brooks, *Mark* (Vol. 23) (Nashville: Broadman & Holman Publishers, 1991), 266.

23. Ibid.

24. Bruce B. Barton, *Matthew* (Wheaton, IL: Tyndale House Publishers, 1996) 566.

25. Norman L. Geisler & Frank Turek, *I Don't Have Enough Faith To Be An Atheist* (Wheaton, IL: Crossway Books, 2004), 301–314.

26. Ibid., 313.

27. Ibid., 314.

28. Norman L. Geisler and Thomas A. Howe, *When Critics Ask: A Popular Handbook on Biblical Difficulties* (Wheaton, IL: Victor Books, 1992), 365.

29. Luke only mentions Peter as going to the tomb and finding it is empty.

30. Mark E. Moore, *The Chronological Life of Christ* (Joplin, MO: College Press Publishing Company, 2011), 663.

31. Bruce B. Barton, *John* (Wheaton IL: Tyndale House, 1993), 389; Crossway Bibles. *The ESV Study Bible* (Wheaton, IL: Crossway Bibles, 2008), 2070.

32. Matthew Henry, *Matthew Henry's Commentary on the Whole Bible: Complete and Unabridged in One volume* (Peabody: Hendrickson, 1994), 2052.

33. It's not specified in the Gospels whether Mary Magdalene is part of this group and exactly who else is present. It's also not indicated whether Peter and John were among the group of disciples mentioned here, though they may well not have been.

34. L. A. Barbieri, Jr. Matthew. In J. F. Walvoord & R. B. Zuck (Eds.), *The Bible Knowledge Commentary: An Exposition of the Scriptures* (Wheaton, IL: Victor Books, 1985), Volume 2, 93.

35. For more on this see Norman L. Geisler & Frank Turek, *I Don't Have Enough Faith To Be An Atheist* (Wheaton, IL: Crossway Books, 2004).

36. Ted Cabal et al *The Apologetics Study Bible: Real Questions, Straight Answers, Stronger Faith* (Nashville, TN: Holman Bible Publishers, 2007), 1564.

37. Charles H. Spurgeon, The Alarum No. 996, *Spurgeon's Sermons* (electronic ed., Vol. 17). (Albany, OR: Ages Software, 1998).

38. Charles H. Spurgeon, Lessons from the Malta Fire, No. 3136, *Spurgeon's Sermons* (electronic ed., Vol. 55). (Albany, OR: Ages Software, 1998).

39. Luke says that "the eleven" were present at this meeting, but John reports that Thomas was not there, and Jesus appeared to him soon thereafter. At this point Judas was no longer one of the apostles so "eleven" would seem to suggest they were all present, including Thomas. Brooke Westcott contends that the accounts can be reconciled because though Thomas was absent, the apostles as a body ("the eleven") were assembled. Brooke Foss Westcott, *The Gospel According to St. John, Introduction and Notes on the Authorized Version*

(London: J. Murray, 1908), 294. Other commentators tend to agree with this. John MacEvilly says that the Apostolic College went by the name of "the eleven" after Jesus died so they might be called "the eleven" even if any of them were absent on any particular occasion. John MacEvilly, *An Exposition of the Gospel of St. John* (Dublin; New York: M. H. Gill & Son; Benziger Brothers, 1902) 363.

40. Beauford H. Bryant & Mark H. Krause, *John* (Joplin, MO: College Press Pub. Co., 1998).

41. Ibid.

42. Gerald L. Borchert, *John 12–21* (Vol. 25B) (Nashville: Broadman & Holman Publishers, 2002), 314.

43. Leon Morris, *The Gospel According to John* (Grand Rapids, MI: Wm. B. Eerdmans Publishing Co, 1995), 753.

44. Gerald L. Borchert, *John 12–21* (Vol. 25B) (Nashville: Broadman & Holman Publishers, 2002), 326.

45. Crossway Bibles. *The ESV Study Bible* (Wheaton, IL: Crossway Bibles, 2008), 2072.

46. Mark's Gospel adds some other details but I have not included it because there is great disagreement among scholars about whether Mark 16:9–20 was in Mark's original writing. Some Bibles omit the sections altogether, some include them in the margin, and some include them with a note of explanation. In any event, it is beyond the scope of this book to explore such questions in depth.

47. Earl D. Radmacher, Ronald Barclay Allen, & H. Wayne House, *The Nelson Study Bible: New King James Version* (Nashville: T. Nelson Publishers, 1997).

48. L. A. Barbieri, Jr. Matthew. In J. F. Walvoord & R. B. Zuck (Eds.), *The Bible Knowledge Commentary: An Exposition of the Scriptures* (Wheaton, IL: Victor Books, 1985), Volume 2, 93.

49. R. T. France, *The Gospel of Matthew* (Grand Rapids, MI: Wm. B. Eerdmans Publication Co., 2007), 1107–1108.

50. John F. MacArthur, Jr. *The MacArthur Study Bible: New American Standard Bible* (Nashville, TN: Thomas Nelson Publishers, 2006); Earl D. Radmacher, Ronald Barclay Allen, & H. Wayne House, *The Nelson Study Bible: New King James Version* (Nashville: T. Nelson Publishers, 1997).

51. Craig L. Blomberg, *Matthew* (Vol. 22) (Nashville: Broadman & Holman Publishers, 1992), 431.

52. Crossway Bibles. *The ESV Study Bible* (Wheaton, IL: Crossway Bibles, 2008), 1888.

53. The reference to Jesus sitting down at the right hand of God is in Mark 16:19, which, as I've noted, is a disputed passage, though the book of Acts confirms it (Acts 7:56).

54. Norval Geldenhuys, *Commentary on the Gospel of Luke: The English Text with Introduction, Exposition and Notes* (Grand Rapids, MI: Wm. B. Eerdmans Publishing Co., 1952), 646.

CONCLUSION

1. John Piper, *Seeing and Savoring Jesus Christ* (Wheaton, IL: Crossway Books, 2004), 119–20.

2. Lynn H. Cohick, *NT101 Introducing New Testament: Its Structure and Story* (Bellingham, WA: Lexham Press, 2013), segment 12.

3. John Blanchard, *Meet the Real Jesus* (Darlington, England; Carlisle, USA: Evangelical Press, 2001), 187–88.

4. Piper, *Seeing and Savoring Jesus Christ*, 121.

5. Jonathan Edwards, *The Works of Jonathan Edwards* (Banner of Truth Trust, 1974), vol. 1, 680.

6. Piper, *Seeing and Savoring Jesus Christ*, 29–30.

7. Ibid., 30.

8. Paul Barnett, *Jesus and the Rise of Early Christianity: A History of New Testament Times* (Downers Grove, IL: IVP Academic, 1999), 14.

9. G. K. Beale, *1–2 Thessalonians* (Downers Grove, IL: InterVarsity Press, 2003), 141.

10. R. A. Torrey, *Revival Addresses* (Chicago; New York: Fleming H. Revell Company, 1903), 215.

11. G. C. Jones, *1000 Illustrations for Preaching and Teaching* (Nashville, TN: Broadman & Holman Publishers, 1986), 199–200.

INDEX